Stories by Gardner Fox
Art by Joe Kubert

HAWKMAN

Originally published in magazine form as
THE BRAVE AND THE BOLD #34-36 and #42-44.

Published by DC Comics Inc.
Copyright 1989 DC Comics Inc.
All rights reserved.

The stories, characters, and incidents featured in this publication are entirely fictional. Hawkman and all related characters, the distinctive likenesses thereof, and all related indicia are trademarks of DC Comics Inc.

DC Comics Inc., 666 Fifth Ave., New York, NY 10103

A Warner Bros. Inc. Company
Printed in Canada. First Printing.

Cover illustration by Joe Kubert
Interior coloring by Tom Ziuko
Publication design by Janice Walker

DC COMICS INC.

JENETTE KAHN
President & Editor-In-Chief

PAUL LEVITZ
Executive V.P. & Publisher

DICK GIORDANO
V.P.–Editorial

JOE ORLANDO
V.P.–Creative Director

MARK WAID
RICHARD BRUNING
Editors, collected edition

BRUCE BRISTOW
V.P.–Sales & Marketing

JULIUS SCHWARTZ
Editor, original series

MATT RAGONE
Circulation Director

TERRI CUNNINGHAM
Managing Editor

TOM BALLOU
Advertising Director

BOB ROZAKIS
Production Director

PAT CALDON
V.P.–Controller

4
INTRODUCTION BY JULIUS SCHWARTZ

7
"CREATURE OF A THOUSAND SHAPES"
(The Brave and the Bold #34, Feb.-Mar. 1961)

32
"MENACE OF THE MATTER MASTER"
(The Brave and the Bold #35, Apr.-May 1961)

44
"VALLEY OF VANISHING MEN"
(The Brave and the Bold #35, Apr.-May 1961)

57
"STRANGE SPELLS OF THE SORCERER"
(The Brave and the Bold #36, June-July 1961)

70
"SHADOW-THIEF OF MIDWAY CITY"
(The Brave and the Bold #36, June-July 1961)

82
"THE MENACE OF THE DRAGONFLY RAIDERS"
(The Brave and the Bold #42, June-July 1962)

107
"THE MASKED MARAUDERS OF EARTH"
(The Brave and the Bold #43, Aug.-Sept. 1962)

132
"EARTH'S IMPOSSIBLE DAY"
(The Brave and the Bold #44, Oct.-Nov. 1962)

144
"THE MEN WHO MOVED THE WORLD"
(The Brave and the Bold #44, Oct.-Nov. 1962)

158
COVER GALLERY

A Little Bird Told Me

The thing I remember best about bringing back Hawkman in the early 1960s was the people who made up the creative team. Gardner Fox, the writer, always picked up the tab at lunch, and Joe Kubert, the artist, spent lunchtime driving my wife around the park.

Gardner Fox was a lawyer. I don't recall whether he ever actually practiced law, but he had a lawyer's mentality about him. He was organized, meticulous; he never walked into a room without knowing what he was going to say there, and he never sat down to write a story without knowing every twist and turn it would take. Gardner was always prepared. He might have been more Boy Scout than lawyer.

Gardner had written the original Hawkman strip back in the 1940s, so naturally I asked him to write the revival. Whereas the original Hawkman was Carter Hall, the reincarnation of an Egyptian prince named Khufu, the recreated Hawkman would be Carter Hall, née Katar Hol, a lawman from the planet Thanagar. I don't know which of us came up with the name "Thanagar," but I think it's one of the best place names around. If ever I discover a planet, I'll call it Thanagar.

Gardner came in like clockwork at 9:30 in the morning, first of the week. We plotted stories in great detail. At 11:45 I would look at my watch and declare that since every element of the plot was done except for bailing the hero out of the last plot trap, it was time for lunch. Actually, I had usually solved the story, but I was pulling a con job on Gardner. I wanted to get Gardner to lunch because he always paid. Over lunch, Gardner and I would talk about the news or the weather or the Cuban Missile Crisis, and we wouldn't think about the story. As soon as we got back in the office, I made a great show of snapping my fingers and saying, "Got it!" and the whole plot was locked up tight. And like clockwork, Gardner was there at 9:30 the next week, ready to plot the next story.

Joe Kubert was another matter. He was wholly unlike Gardner in character, but every bit as meticulous. Very often you got the impression that whatever you saw on the page was burned into Joe's brain before he drew it and he was just transcribing it, tension and all. Joe was the best war story artist anywhere, and his background in super-hero type stuff was thin. But with Hawkman's new origin, Joe's style worked just right.

Carter Hall the Thanagarian was a classicist, a museum curator, an expert on earlier historical periods. Especially classical weaponry. So here we had this futuristic crimefighter wearing wings and feathers and going after bad guys of the present with maces and lances and weapons of the past. So who was better at drawing fantasy weaponry in action than Joe Kubert?

That's a rhetorical question. The answer is "nobody."

But I guess the most important element we added to the new Hawkman series was Hawkgirl's sunset-colored hair. Of course we call her "Hawkwoman" now, but we didn't then. Sometime in the mid-Forties, there was this gorgeous gal named Jean Ordwein who came and worked at DC, with whom everyone wanted to go out. We used to say "gal" then, too; we really did. Jean had hair the color of sunset, just like Hawkgirl's, and Joe was apparently impressed with it. Joe was practically a teenager at the time, but he had this little red sports car and he sweet-talked Jean into going for a ride with him in Central Park. I guess that made me decide to ask her out myself. The happy ending was that Jean and I got married not long afterward.

Hawkgirl has Jean's hair. I guess it's a present from both Joe and me.

Julius Schwartz

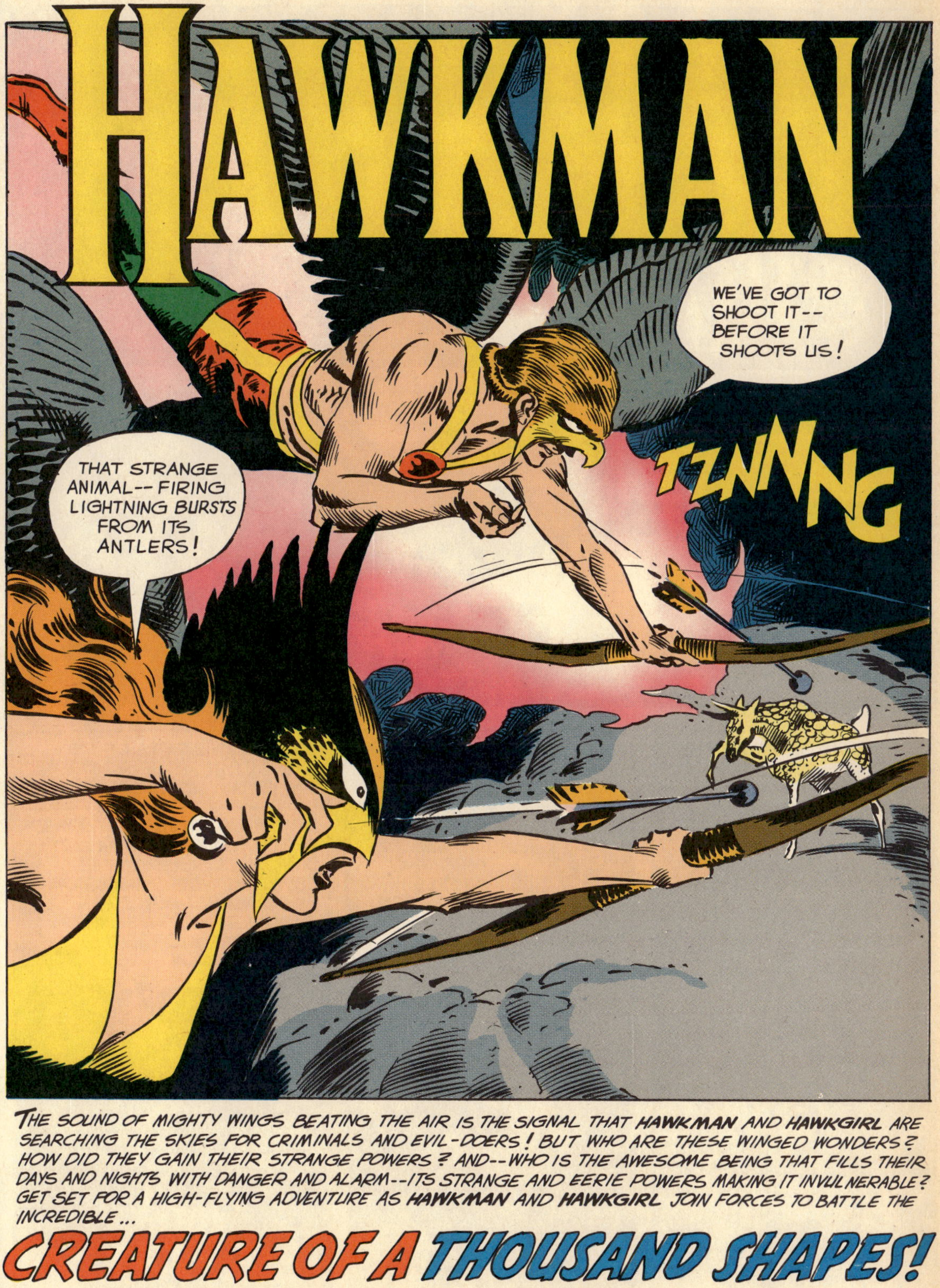
HAWKMAN
WE'VE GOT TO SHOOT IT-- BEFORE IT SHOOTS US!
THAT STRANGE ANIMAL--FIRING LIGHTNING BURSTS FROM ITS ANTLERS!
TZNNNG
THE SOUND OF MIGHTY WINGS BEATING THE AIR IS THE SIGNAL THAT HAWKMAN AND HAWKGIRL ARE SEARCHING THE SKIES FOR CRIMINALS AND EVIL-DOERS! BUT WHO ARE THESE WINGED WONDERS? HOW DID THEY GAIN THEIR STRANGE POWERS? AND--WHO IS THE AWESOME BEING THAT FILLS THEIR DAYS AND NIGHTS WITH DANGER AND ALARM--ITS STRANGE AND EERIE POWERS MAKING IT INVULNERABLE? GET SET FOR A HIGH-FLYING ADVENTURE AS HAWKMAN AND HAWKGIRL JOIN FORCES TO BATTLE THE INCREDIBLE...
CREATURE OF A THOUSAND SHAPES!

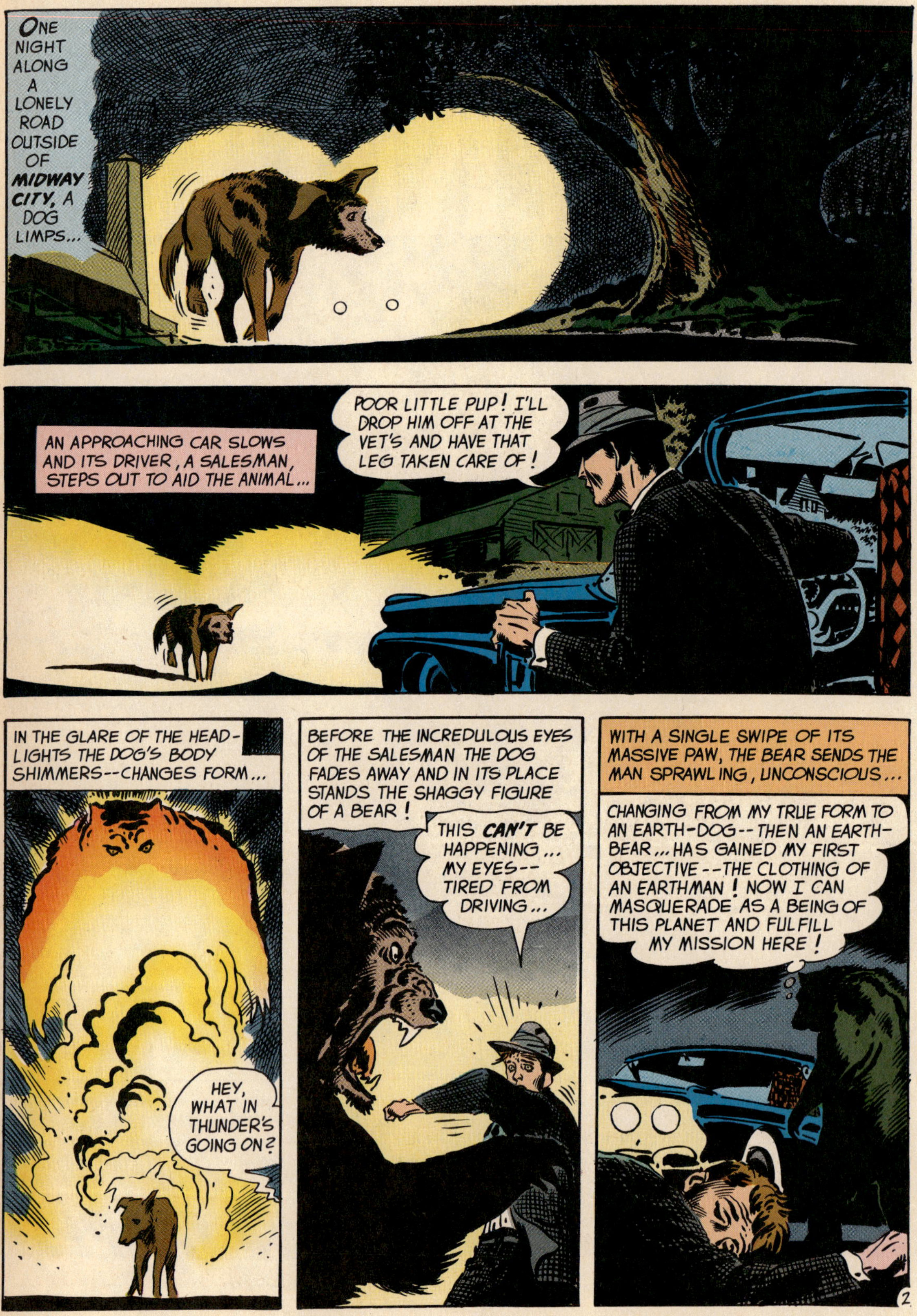
ONE NIGHT ALONG A LONELY ROAD OUTSIDE OF MIDWAY CITY, A DOG LIMPS...
AN APPROACHING CAR SLOWS AND ITS DRIVER, A SALESMAN, STEPS OUT TO AID THE ANIMAL...
POOR LITTLE PUP! I'LL DROP HIM OFF AT THE VET'S AND HAVE THAT LEG TAKEN CARE OF!
IN THE GLARE OF THE HEAD-LIGHTS THE DOG'S BODY SHIMMERS--CHANGES FORM...
HEY, WHAT IN THUNDER'S GOING ON?
BEFORE THE INCREDULOUS EYES OF THE SALESMAN THE DOG FADES AWAY AND IN ITS PLACE STANDS THE SHAGGY FIGURE OF A BEAR!
THIS CAN'T BE HAPPENING... MY EYES--TIRED FROM DRIVING...
WITH A SINGLE SWIPE OF ITS MASSIVE PAW, THE BEAR SENDS THE MAN SPRAWLING, UNCONSCIOUS...
CHANGING FROM MY TRUE FORM TO AN EARTH-DOG--THEN AN EARTH-BEAR... HAS GAINED MY FIRST OBJECTIVE--THE CLOTHING OF AN EARTHMAN! NOW I CAN MASQUERADE AS A BEING OF THIS PLANET AND FULFILL MY MISSION HERE!
2

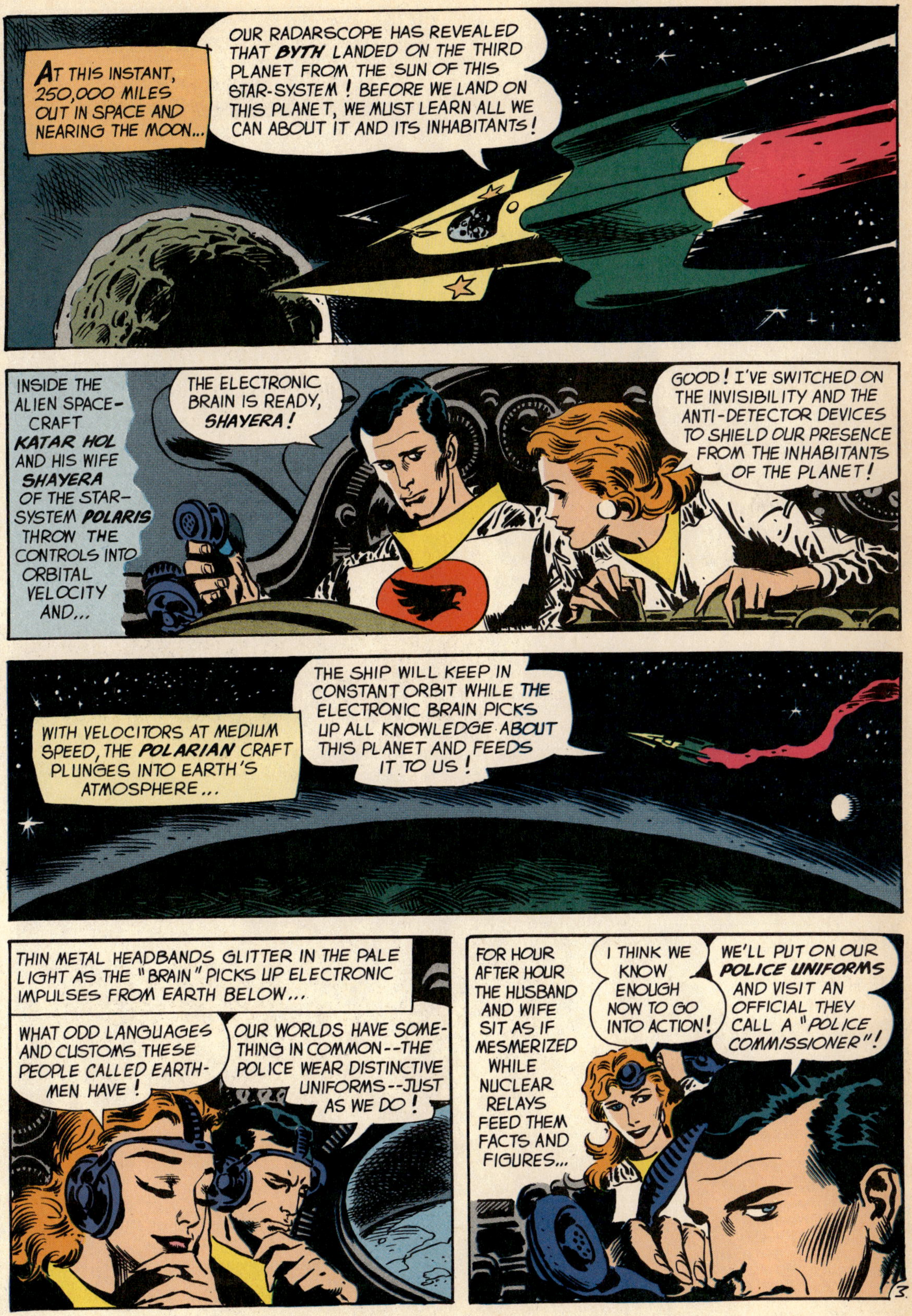
AT THIS INSTANT, 250,000 MILES OUT IN SPACE AND NEARING THE MOON...
OUR RADARSCOPE HAS REVEALED THAT BYTH LANDED ON THE THIRD PLANET FROM THE SUN OF THIS STAR-SYSTEM! BEFORE WE LAND ON THIS PLANET, WE MUST LEARN ALL WE CAN ABOUT IT AND ITS INHABITANTS!
INSIDE THE ALIEN SPACE-CRAFT KATAR HOL AND HIS WIFE SHAYERA OF THE STAR-SYSTEM POLARIS THROW THE CONTROLS INTO ORBITAL VELOCITY AND...
THE ELECTRONIC BRAIN IS READY, SHAYERA!
GOOD! I'VE SWITCHED ON THE INVISIBILITY AND THE ANTI-DETECTOR DEVICES TO SHIELD OUR PRESENCE FROM THE INHABITANTS OF THE PLANET!
WITH VELOCITORS AT MEDIUM SPEED, THE POLARIAN CRAFT PLUNGES INTO EARTH'S ATMOSPHERE...
THE SHIP WILL KEEP IN CONSTANT ORBIT WHILE THE ELECTRONIC BRAIN PICKS UP ALL KNOWLEDGE ABOUT THIS PLANET AND FEEDS IT TO US!
THIN METAL HEADBANDS GLITTER IN THE PALE LIGHT AS THE "BRAIN" PICKS UP ELECTRONIC IMPULSES FROM EARTH BELOW...
WHAT ODD LANGUAGES AND CUSTOMS THESE PEOPLE CALLED EARTH-MEN HAVE!
OUR WORLDS HAVE SOME-THING IN COMMON--THE POLICE WEAR DISTINCTIVE UNIFORMS--JUST AS WE DO!
FOR HOUR AFTER HOUR THE HUSBAND AND WIFE SIT AS IF MESMERIZED WHILE NUCLEAR RELAYS FEED THEM FACTS AND FIGURES...
I THINK WE KNOW ENOUGH NOW TO GO INTO ACTION!
WE'LL PUT ON OUR POLICE UNIFORMS AND VISIT AN OFFICIAL THEY CALL A "POLICE COMMISSIONER"!
3

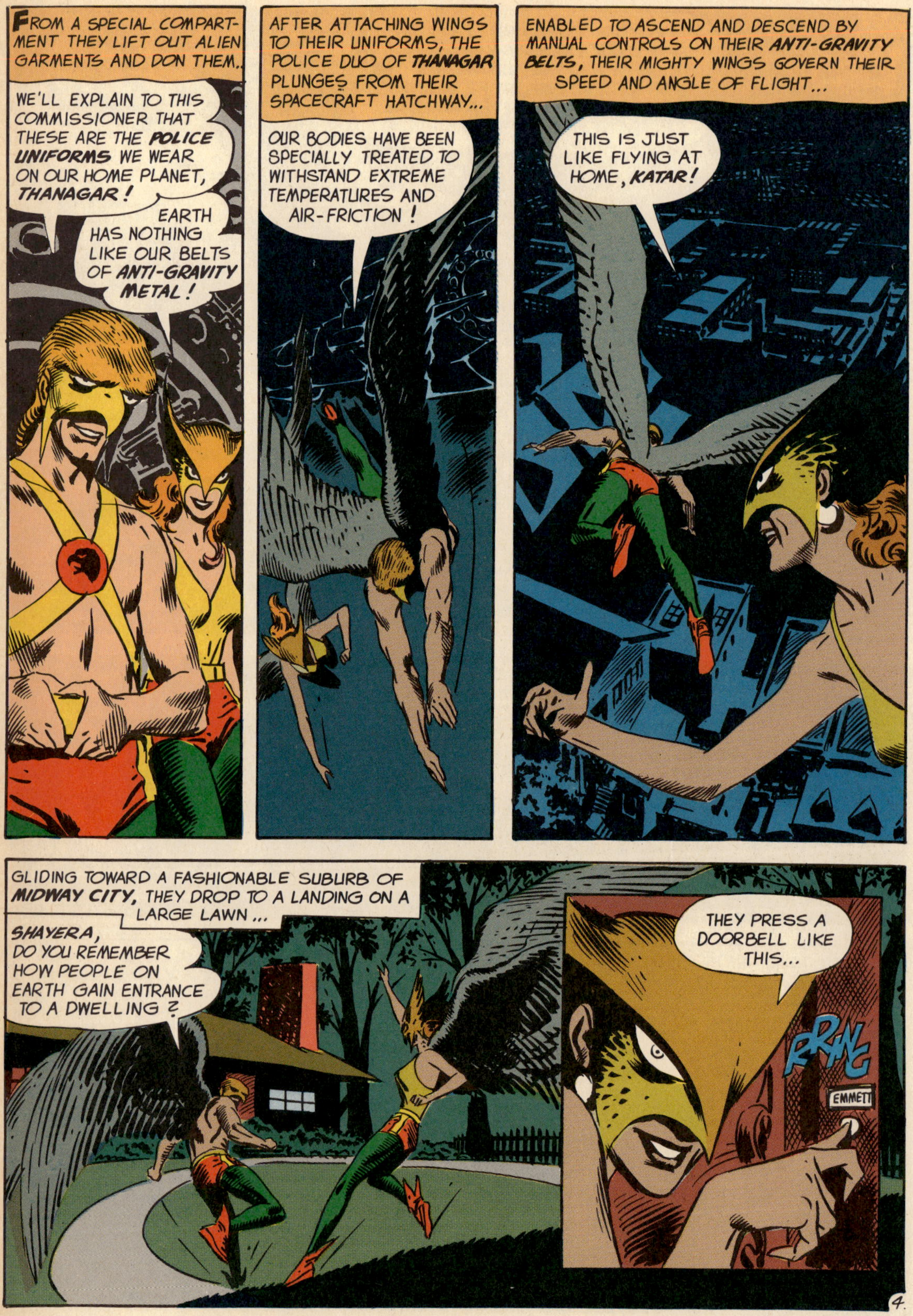
FROM A SPECIAL COMPARTMENT THEY LIFT OUT ALIEN GARMENTS AND DON THEM...
WE'LL EXPLAIN TO THIS COMMISSIONER THAT THESE ARE THE POLICE UNIFORMS WE WEAR ON OUR HOME PLANET, THANAGAR!
EARTH HAS NOTHING LIKE OUR BELTS OF ANTI-GRAVITY METAL!
AFTER ATTACHING WINGS TO THEIR UNIFORMS, THE POLICE DUO OF THANAGAR PLUNGES FROM THEIR SPACECRAFT HATCHWAY...
OUR BODIES HAVE BEEN SPECIALLY TREATED TO WITHSTAND EXTREME TEMPERATURES AND AIR-FRICTION!
ENABLED TO ASCEND AND DESCEND BY MANUAL CONTROLS ON THEIR ANTI-GRAVITY BELTS, THEIR MIGHTY WINGS GOVERN THEIR SPEED AND ANGLE OF FLIGHT...
THIS IS JUST LIKE FLYING AT HOME, KATAR!
GLIDING TOWARD A FASHIONABLE SUBURB OF MIDWAY CITY, THEY DROP TO A LANDING ON A LARGE LAWN...
SHAYERA, DO YOU REMEMBER HOW PEOPLE ON EARTH GAIN ENTRANCE TO A DWELLING?
THEY PRESS A DOORBELL LIKE THIS...
RRING
EMMETT
4.

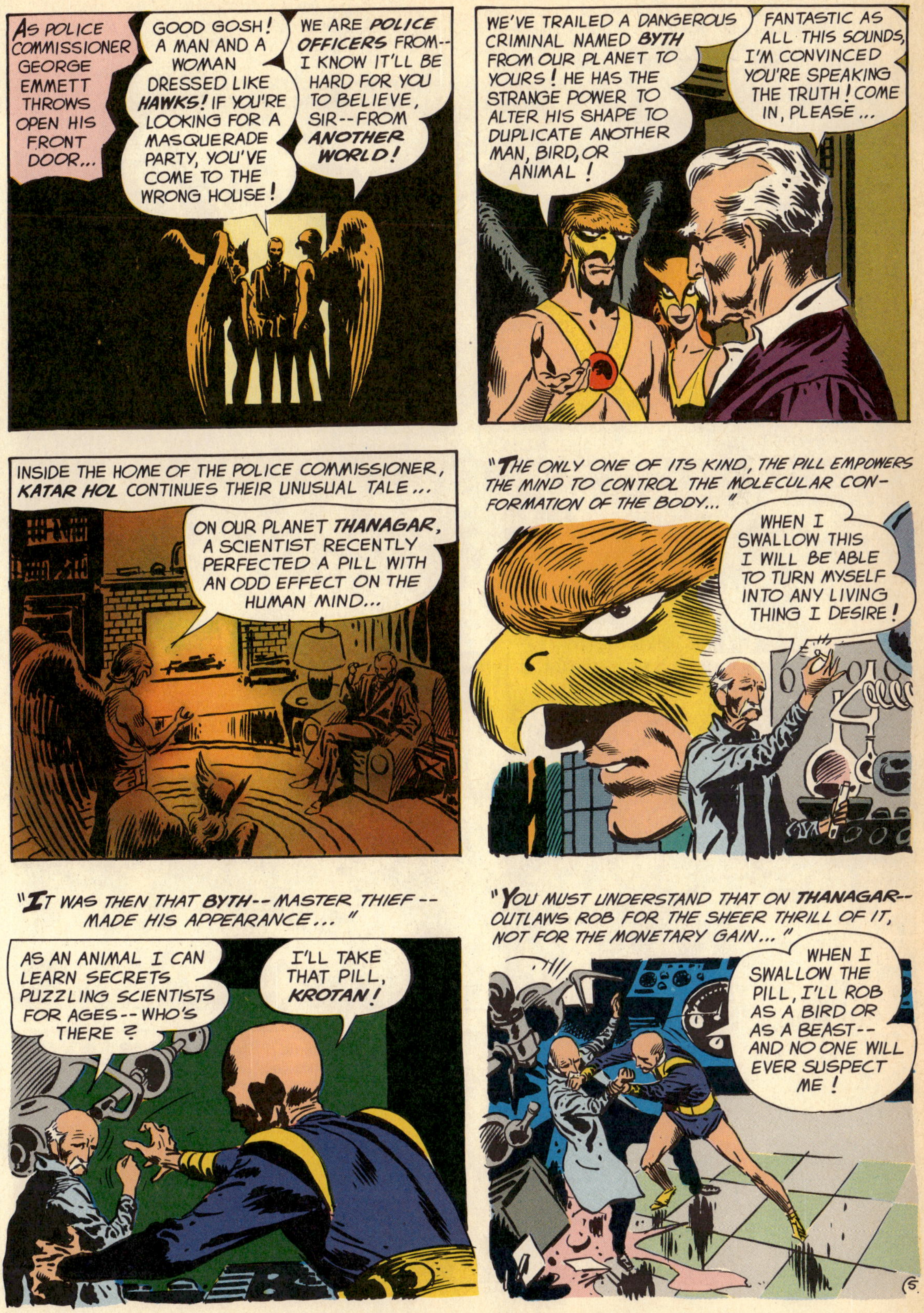
AS POLICE COMMISSIONER GEORGE EMMETT THROWS OPEN HIS FRONT DOOR...
GOOD GOSH! A MAN AND A WOMAN DRESSED LIKE HAWKS! IF YOU'RE LOOKING FOR A MASQUERADE PARTY, YOU'VE COME TO THE WRONG HOUSE!
WE ARE POLICE OFFICERS FROM-- I KNOW IT'LL BE HARD FOR YOU TO BELIEVE, SIR--FROM ANOTHER WORLD!
WE'VE TRAILED A DANGEROUS CRIMINAL NAMED BYTH FROM OUR PLANET TO YOURS! HE HAS THE STRANGE POWER TO ALTER HIS SHAPE TO DUPLICATE ANOTHER MAN, BIRD, OR ANIMAL!
FANTASTIC AS ALL THIS SOUNDS, I'M CONVINCED YOU'RE SPEAKING THE TRUTH! COME IN, PLEASE...
INSIDE THE HOME OF THE POLICE COMMISSIONER, KATAR HOL CONTINUES THEIR UNUSUAL TALE...
ON OUR PLANET THANAGAR, A SCIENTIST RECENTLY PERFECTED A PILL WITH AN ODD EFFECT ON THE HUMAN MIND...
"THE ONLY ONE OF ITS KIND, THE PILL EMPOWERS THE MIND TO CONTROL THE MOLECULAR CON-FORMATION OF THE BODY..."
WHEN I SWALLOW THIS I WILL BE ABLE TO TURN MYSELF INTO ANY LIVING THING I DESIRE!
"IT WAS THEN THAT BYTH--MASTER THIEF--MADE HIS APPEARANCE..."
AS AN ANIMAL I CAN LEARN SECRETS PUZZLING SCIENTISTS FOR AGES--WHO'S THERE?
I'LL TAKE THAT PILL, KROTAN!
"YOU MUST UNDERSTAND THAT ON THANAGAR--OUTLAWS ROB FOR THE SHEER THRILL OF IT, NOT FOR THE MONETARY GAIN..."
WHEN I SWALLOW THE PILL, I'LL ROB AS A BIRD OR AS A BEAST--AND NO ONE WILL EVER SUSPECT ME!
5

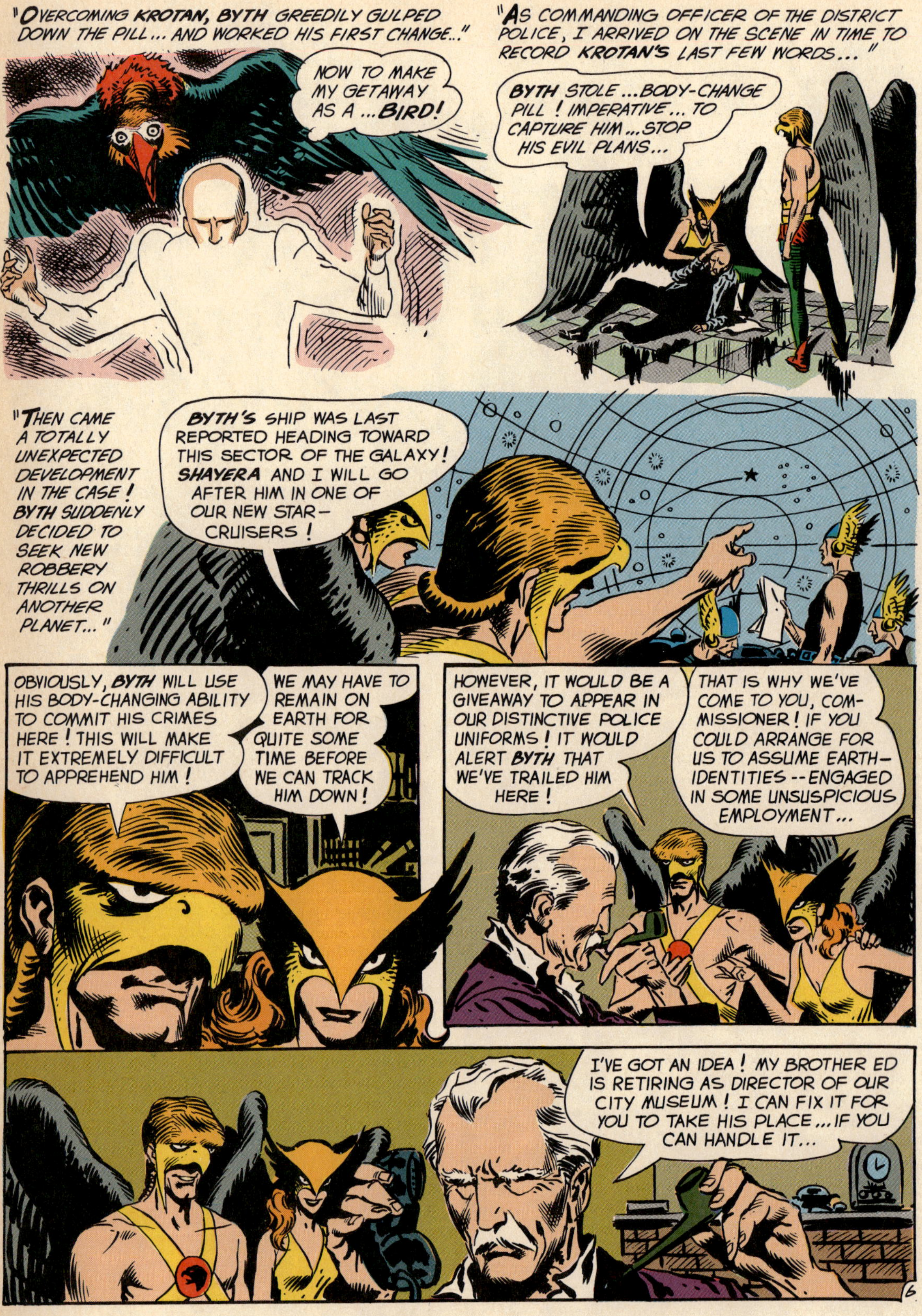
"OVERCOMING KROTAN, BYTH GREEDILY GULPED DOWN THE PILL... AND WORKED HIS FIRST CHANGE..."
NOW TO MAKE MY GETAWAY AS A ...BIRD!
"AS COMMANDING OFFICER OF THE DISTRICT POLICE, I ARRIVED ON THE SCENE IN TIME TO RECORD KROTAN'S LAST FEW WORDS..."
BYTH STOLE ...BODY-CHANGE PILL! IMPERATIVE... TO CAPTURE HIM...STOP HIS EVIL PLANS...
"THEN CAME A TOTALLY UNEXPECTED DEVELOPMENT IN THE CASE! BYTH SUDDENLY DECIDED TO SEEK NEW ROBBERY THRILLS ON ANOTHER PLANET..."
BYTH'S SHIP WAS LAST REPORTED HEADING TOWARD THIS SECTOR OF THE GALAXY! SHAYERA AND I WILL GO AFTER HIM IN ONE OF OUR NEW STAR-CRUISERS!
OBVIOUSLY, BYTH WILL USE HIS BODY-CHANGING ABILITY TO COMMIT HIS CRIMES HERE! THIS WILL MAKE IT EXTREMELY DIFFICULT TO APPREHEND HIM!
WE MAY HAVE TO REMAIN ON EARTH FOR QUITE SOME TIME BEFORE WE CAN TRACK HIM DOWN!
HOWEVER, IT WOULD BE A GIVEAWAY TO APPEAR IN OUR DISTINCTIVE POLICE UNIFORMS! IT WOULD ALERT BYTH THAT WE'VE TRAILED HIM HERE!
THAT IS WHY WE'VE COME TO YOU, COMMISSIONER! IF YOU COULD ARRANGE FOR US TO ASSUME EARTH-IDENTITIES --ENGAGED IN SOME UNSUSPICIOUS EMPLOYMENT...
I'VE GOT AN IDEA! MY BROTHER ED IS RETIRING AS DIRECTOR OF OUR CITY MUSEUM! I CAN FIX IT FOR YOU TO TAKE HIS PLACE... IF YOU CAN HANDLE IT...
6

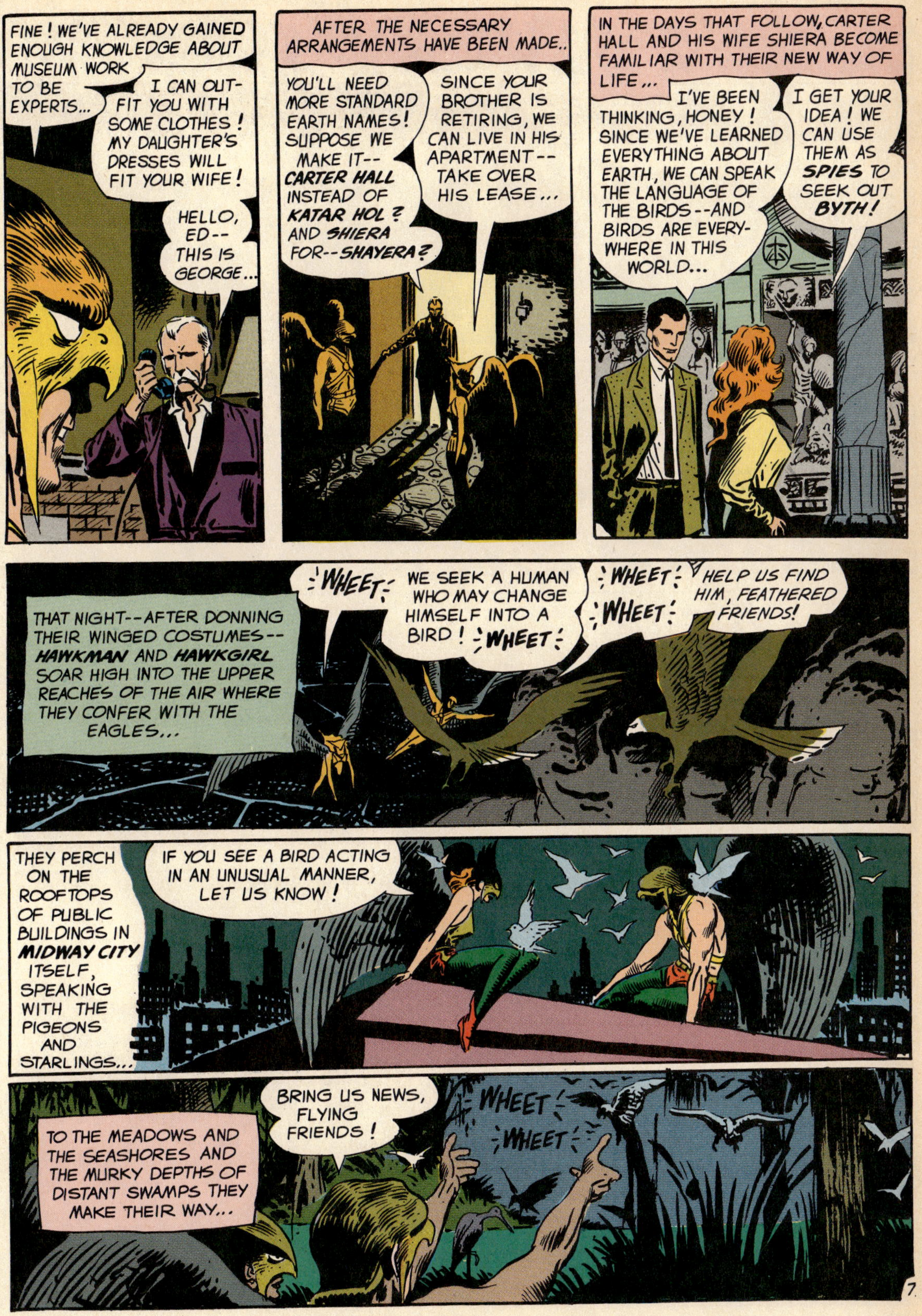
FINE! WE'VE ALREADY GAINED ENOUGH KNOWLEDGE ABOUT MUSEUM WORK TO BE EXPERTS...
I CAN OUTFIT YOU WITH SOME CLOTHES! MY DAUGHTER'S DRESSES WILL FIT YOUR WIFE!
HELLO, ED-- THIS IS GEORGE...
AFTER THE NECESSARY ARRANGEMENTS HAVE BEEN MADE..
YOU'LL NEED MORE STANDARD EARTH NAMES! SUPPOSE WE MAKE IT-- CARTER HALL INSTEAD OF KATAR HOL? AND SHIERA FOR--SHAYERA?
SINCE YOUR BROTHER IS RETIRING, WE CAN LIVE IN HIS APARTMENT-- TAKE OVER HIS LEASE...
IN THE DAYS THAT FOLLOW, CARTER HALL AND HIS WIFE SHIERA BECOME FAMILIAR WITH THEIR NEW WAY OF LIFE...
I'VE BEEN THINKING, HONEY! SINCE WE'VE LEARNED EVERYTHING ABOUT EARTH, WE CAN SPEAK THE LANGUAGE OF THE BIRDS--AND BIRDS ARE EVERYWHERE IN THIS WORLD...
I GET YOUR IDEA! WE CAN USE THEM AS SPIES TO SEEK OUT BYTH!
THAT NIGHT--AFTER DONNING THEIR WINGED COSTUMES-- HAWKMAN AND HAWKGIRL SOAR HIGH INTO THE UPPER REACHES OF THE AIR WHERE THEY CONFER WITH THE EAGLES...
WHEET
WE SEEK A HUMAN WHO MAY CHANGE HIMSELF INTO A BIRD! WHEET
WHEET WHEET
HELP US FIND HIM, FEATHERED FRIENDS!
THEY PERCH ON THE ROOFTOPS OF PUBLIC BUILDINGS IN MIDWAY CITY ITSELF, SPEAKING WITH THE PIGEONS AND STARLINGS...
IF YOU SEE A BIRD ACTING IN AN UNUSUAL MANNER, LET US KNOW!
TO THE MEADOWS AND THE SEASHORES AND THE MURKY DEPTHS OF DISTANT SWAMPS THEY MAKE THEIR WAY...
BRING US NEWS, FLYING FRIENDS!
WHEET
WHEET
7

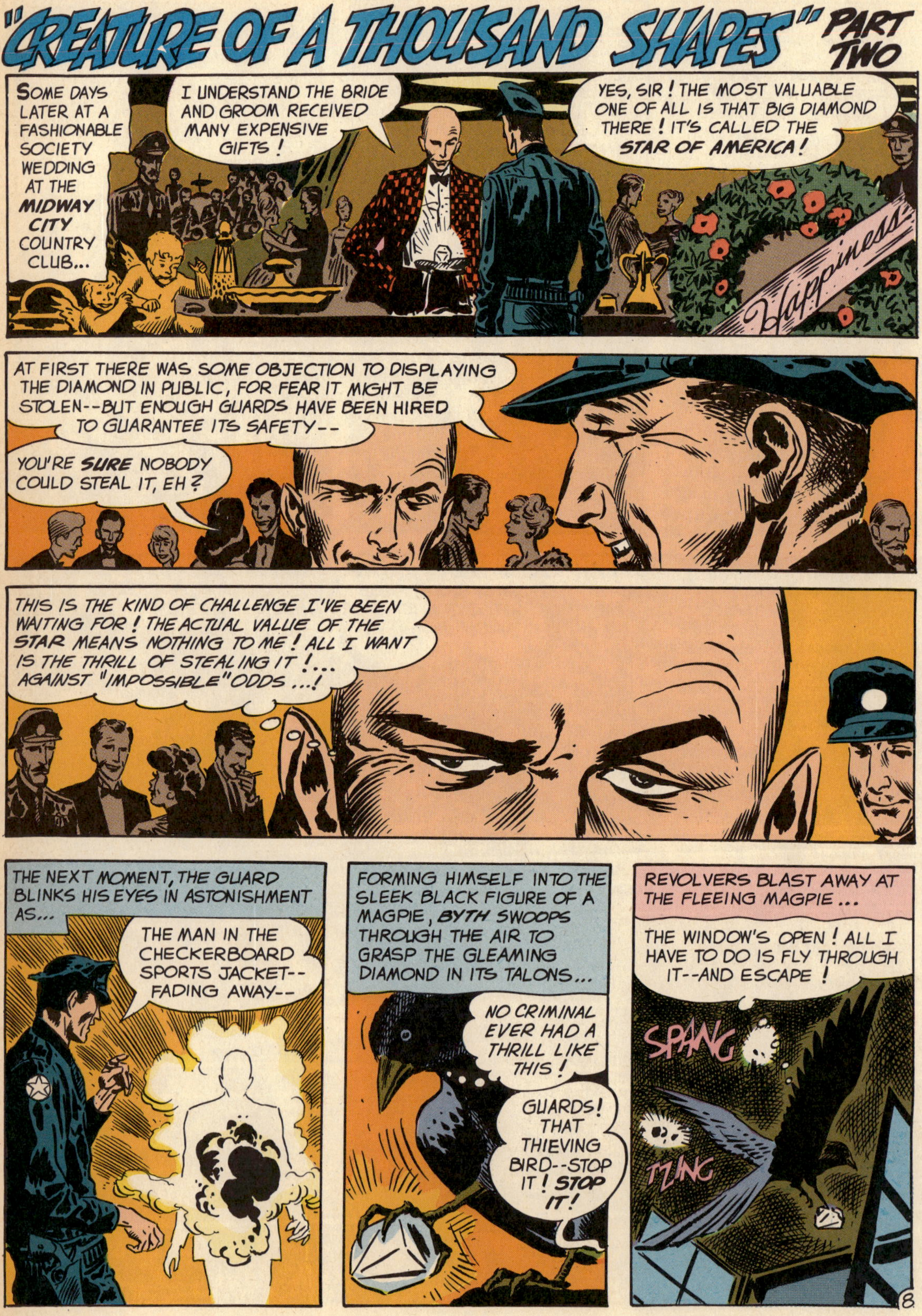
"CREATURE OF A THOUSAND SHAPES" PART TWO
SOME DAYS LATER AT A FASHIONABLE SOCIETY WEDDING AT THE MIDWAY CITY COUNTRY CLUB...
I UNDERSTAND THE BRIDE AND GROOM RECEIVED MANY EXPENSIVE GIFTS!
YES, SIR! THE MOST VALUABLE ONE OF ALL IS THAT BIG DIAMOND THERE! IT'S CALLED THE STAR OF AMERICA!
Happiness
AT FIRST THERE WAS SOME OBJECTION TO DISPLAYING THE DIAMOND IN PUBLIC, FOR FEAR IT MIGHT BE STOLEN--BUT ENOUGH GUARDS HAVE BEEN HIRED TO GUARANTEE ITS SAFETY--
YOU'RE SURE NOBODY COULD STEAL IT, EH?
THIS IS THE KIND OF CHALLENGE I'VE BEEN WAITING FOR! THE ACTUAL VALUE OF THE STAR MEANS NOTHING TO ME! ALL I WANT IS THE THRILL OF STEALING IT!... AGAINST "IMPOSSIBLE" ODDS...!
THE NEXT MOMENT, THE GUARD BLINKS HIS EYES IN ASTONISHMENT AS...
THE MAN IN THE CHECKERBOARD SPORTS JACKET--FADING AWAY--
FORMING HIMSELF INTO THE SLEEK BLACK FIGURE OF A MAGPIE, BYTH SWOOPS THROUGH THE AIR TO GRASP THE GLEAMING DIAMOND IN ITS TALONS...
NO CRIMINAL EVER HAD A THRILL LIKE THIS!
GUARDS! THAT THIEVING BIRD--STOP IT! STOP IT!
REVOLVERS BLAST AWAY AT THE FLEEING MAGPIE...
THE WINDOW'S OPEN! ALL I HAVE TO DO IS FLY THROUGH IT--AND ESCAPE!
SPANG
TZING
8

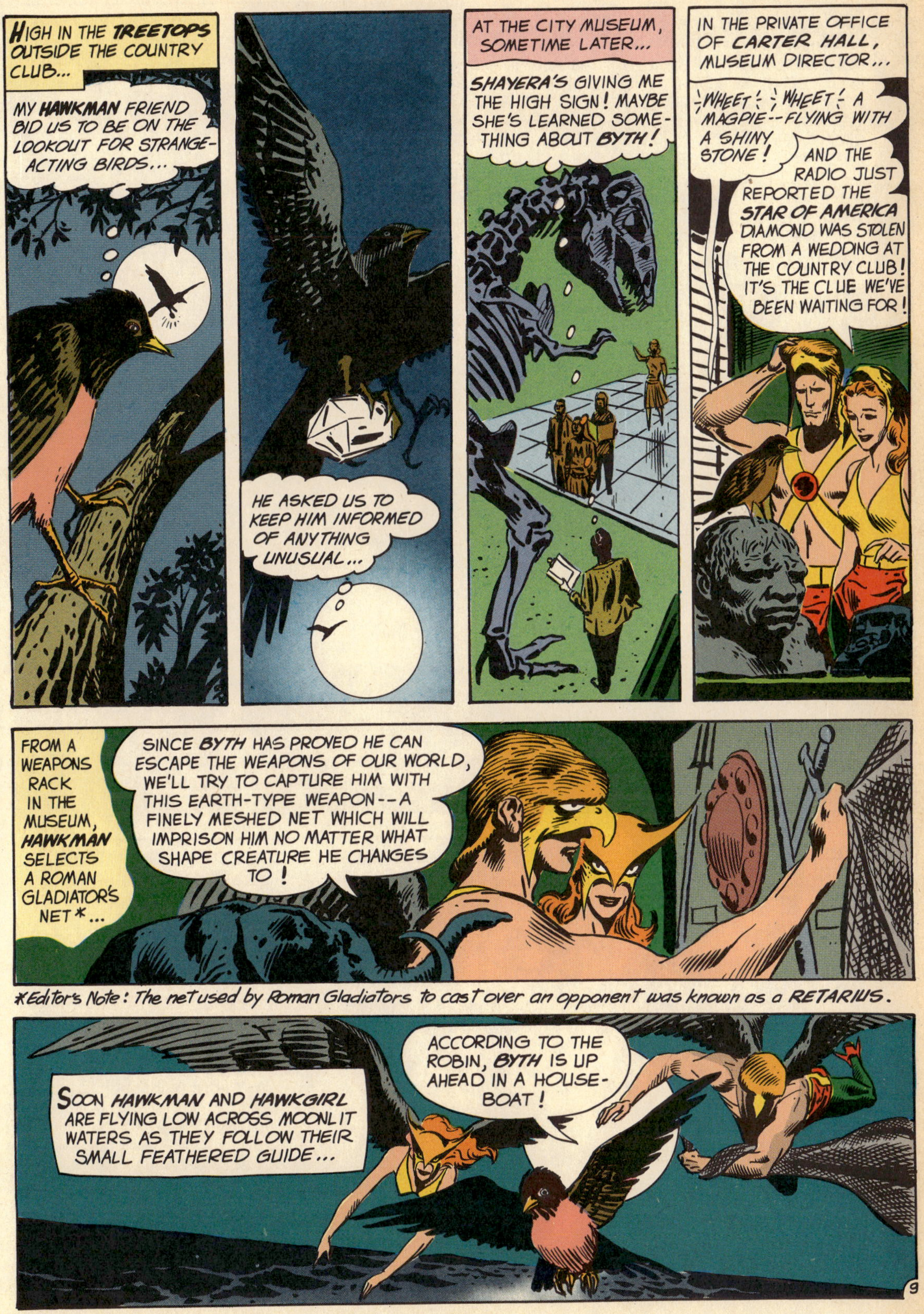
HIGH IN THE TREETOPS OUTSIDE THE COUNTRY CLUB...
MY HAWKMAN FRIEND BID US TO BE ON THE LOOKOUT FOR STRANGE-ACTING BIRDS...
HE ASKED US TO KEEP HIM INFORMED OF ANYTHING UNUSUAL...
AT THE CITY MUSEUM, SOMETIME LATER...
SHAYERA'S GIVING ME THE HIGH SIGN! MAYBE SHE'S LEARNED SOMETHING ABOUT BYTH!
IN THE PRIVATE OFFICE OF CARTER HALL, MUSEUM DIRECTOR...
-WHEET!- -WHEET!- A MAGPIE--FLYING WITH A SHINY STONE!
AND THE RADIO JUST REPORTED THE STAR OF AMERICA DIAMOND WAS STOLEN FROM A WEDDING AT THE COUNTRY CLUB! IT'S THE CLUE WE'VE BEEN WAITING FOR!
FROM A WEAPONS RACK IN THE MUSEUM, HAWKMAN SELECTS A ROMAN GLADIATOR'S NET*...
SINCE BYTH HAS PROVED HE CAN ESCAPE THE WEAPONS OF OUR WORLD, WE'LL TRY TO CAPTURE HIM WITH THIS EARTH-TYPE WEAPON--A FINELY MESHED NET WHICH WILL IMPRISON HIM NO MATTER WHAT SHAPE CREATURE HE CHANGES TO!
*Editor's Note: The net used by Roman Gladiators to cast over an opponent was known as a RETARIUS.
SOON HAWKMAN AND HAWKGIRL ARE FLYING LOW ACROSS MOONLIT WATERS AS THEY FOLLOW THEIR SMALL FEATHERED GUIDE...
ACCORDING TO THE ROBIN, BYTH IS UP AHEAD IN A HOUSE-BOAT!
9

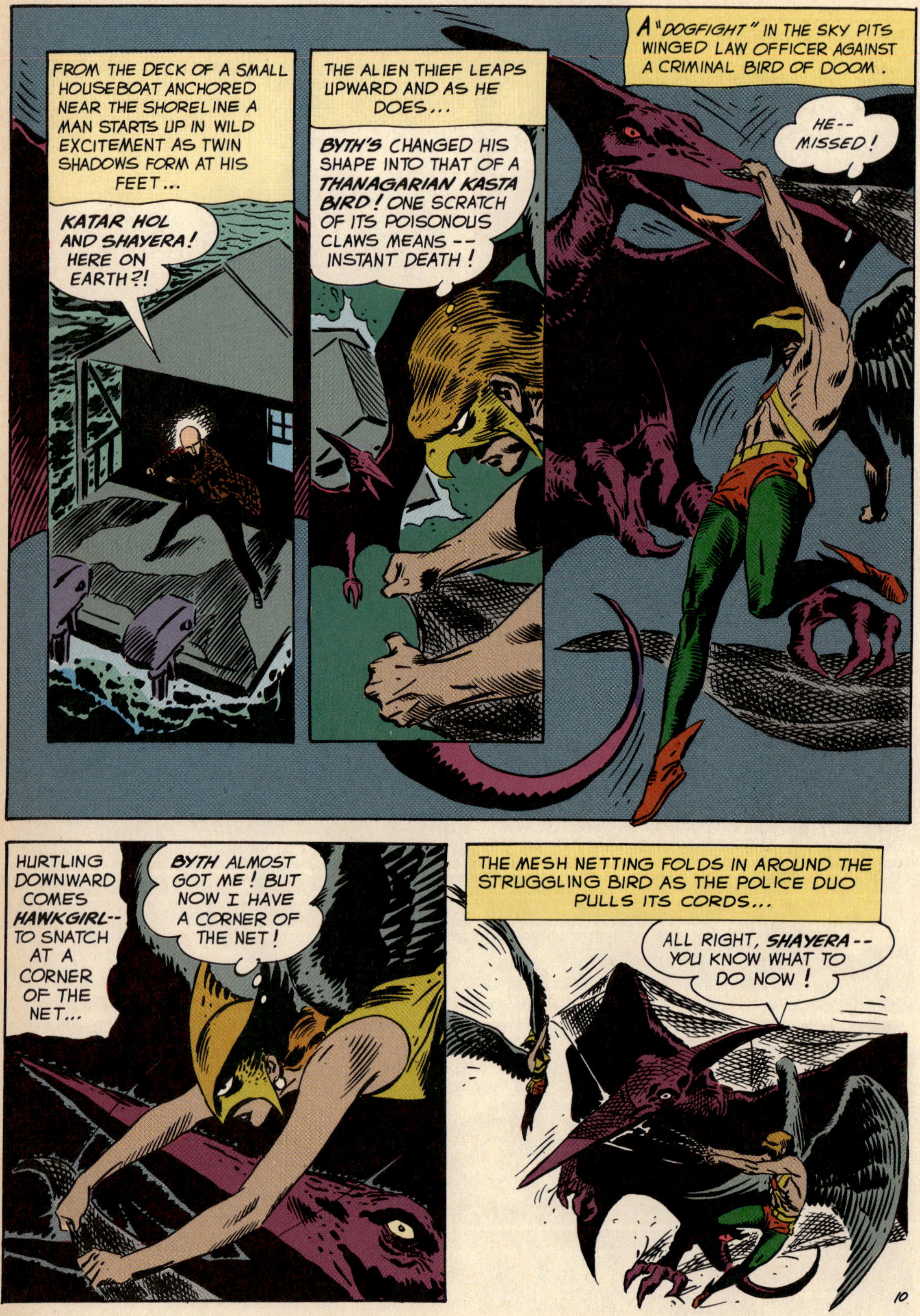
FROM THE DECK OF A SMALL HOUSEBOAT ANCHORED NEAR THE SHORELINE A MAN STARTS UP IN WILD EXCITEMENT AS TWIN SHADOWS FORM AT HIS FEET...
KATAR HOL AND SHAYERA! HERE ON EARTH?!
THE ALIEN THIEF LEAPS UPWARD AND AS HE DOES...
BYTH'S CHANGED HIS SHAPE INTO THAT OF A THANAGARIAN KASTA BIRD! ONE SCRATCH OF ITS POISONOUS CLAWS MEANS -- INSTANT DEATH!
A "DOGFIGHT" IN THE SKY PITS WINGED LAW OFFICER AGAINST A CRIMINAL BIRD OF DOOM.
HE-- MISSED!
HURTLING DOWNWARD COMES HAWKGIRL-- TO SNATCH AT A CORNER OF THE NET...
BYTH ALMOST GOT ME! BUT NOW I HAVE A CORNER OF THE NET!
THE MESH NETTING FOLDS IN AROUND THE STRUGGLING BIRD AS THE POLICE DUO PULLS ITS CORDS...
ALL RIGHT, SHAYERA-- YOU KNOW WHAT TO DO NOW!
10

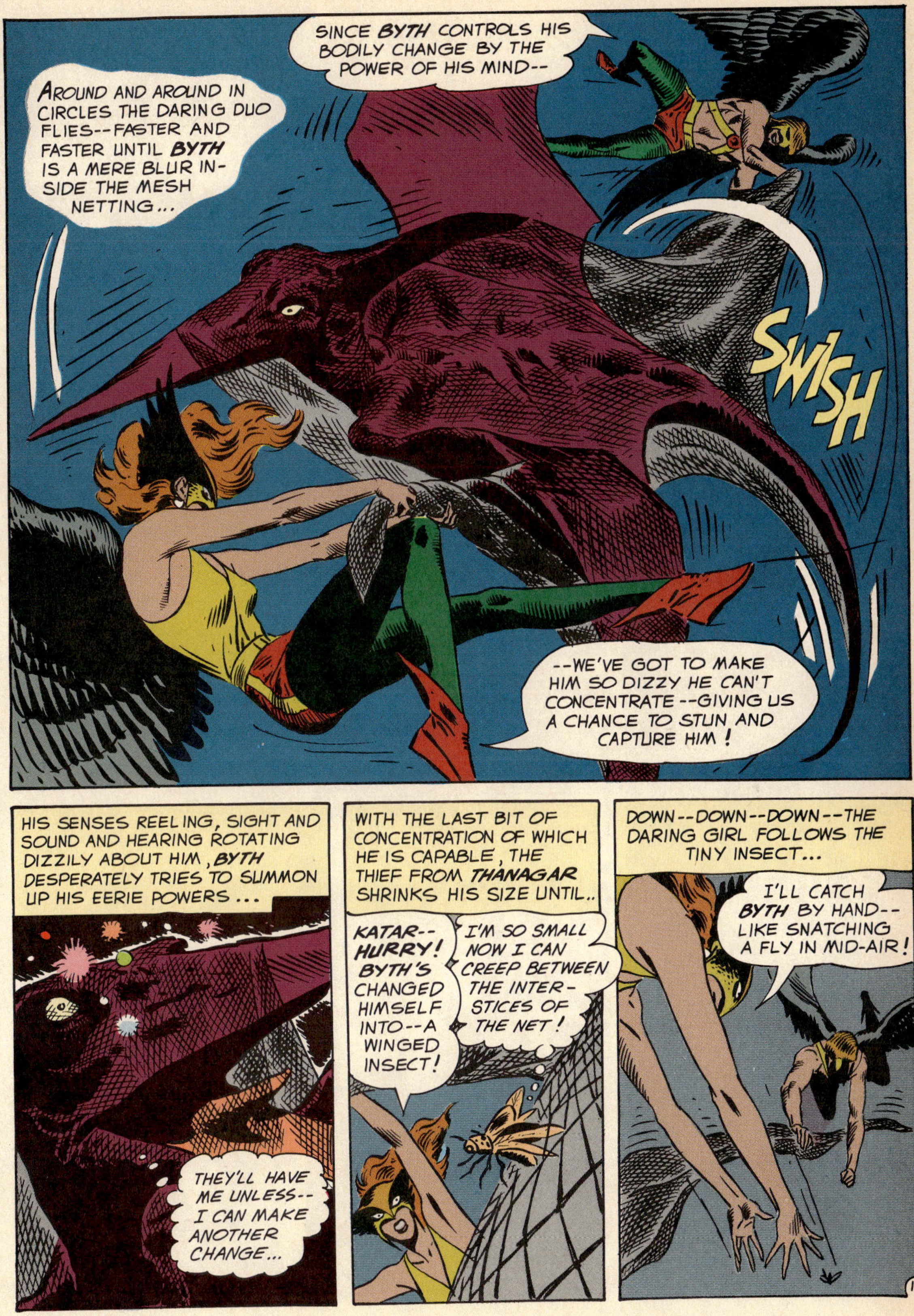

AROUND AND AROUND IN CIRCLES THE DARING DUO FLIES--FASTER AND FASTER UNTIL BYTH IS A MERE BLUR INSIDE THE MESH NETTING...
SINCE BYTH CONTROLS HIS BODILY CHANGE BY THE POWER OF HIS MIND--
SWISH
--WE'VE GOT TO MAKE HIM SO DIZZY HE CAN'T CONCENTRATE--GIVING US A CHANCE TO STUN AND CAPTURE HIM!
HIS SENSES REELING, SIGHT AND SOUND AND HEARING ROTATING DIZZILY ABOUT HIM, BYTH DESPERATELY TRIES TO SUMMON UP HIS EERIE POWERS...
THEY'LL HAVE ME UNLESS-- I CAN MAKE ANOTHER CHANGE...
WITH THE LAST BIT OF CONCENTRATION OF WHICH HE IS CAPABLE, THE THIEF FROM THANAGAR SHRINKS HIS SIZE UNTIL..
KATAR--HURRY! BYTH'S CHANGED HIMSELF INTO--A WINGED INSECT!
I'M SO SMALL NOW I CAN CREEP BETWEEN THE INTERSTICES OF THE NET!
DOWN--DOWN--DOWN--THE DARING GIRL FOLLOWS THE TINY INSECT...
I'LL CATCH BYTH BY HAND--LIKE SNATCHING A FLY IN MID-AIR!
11

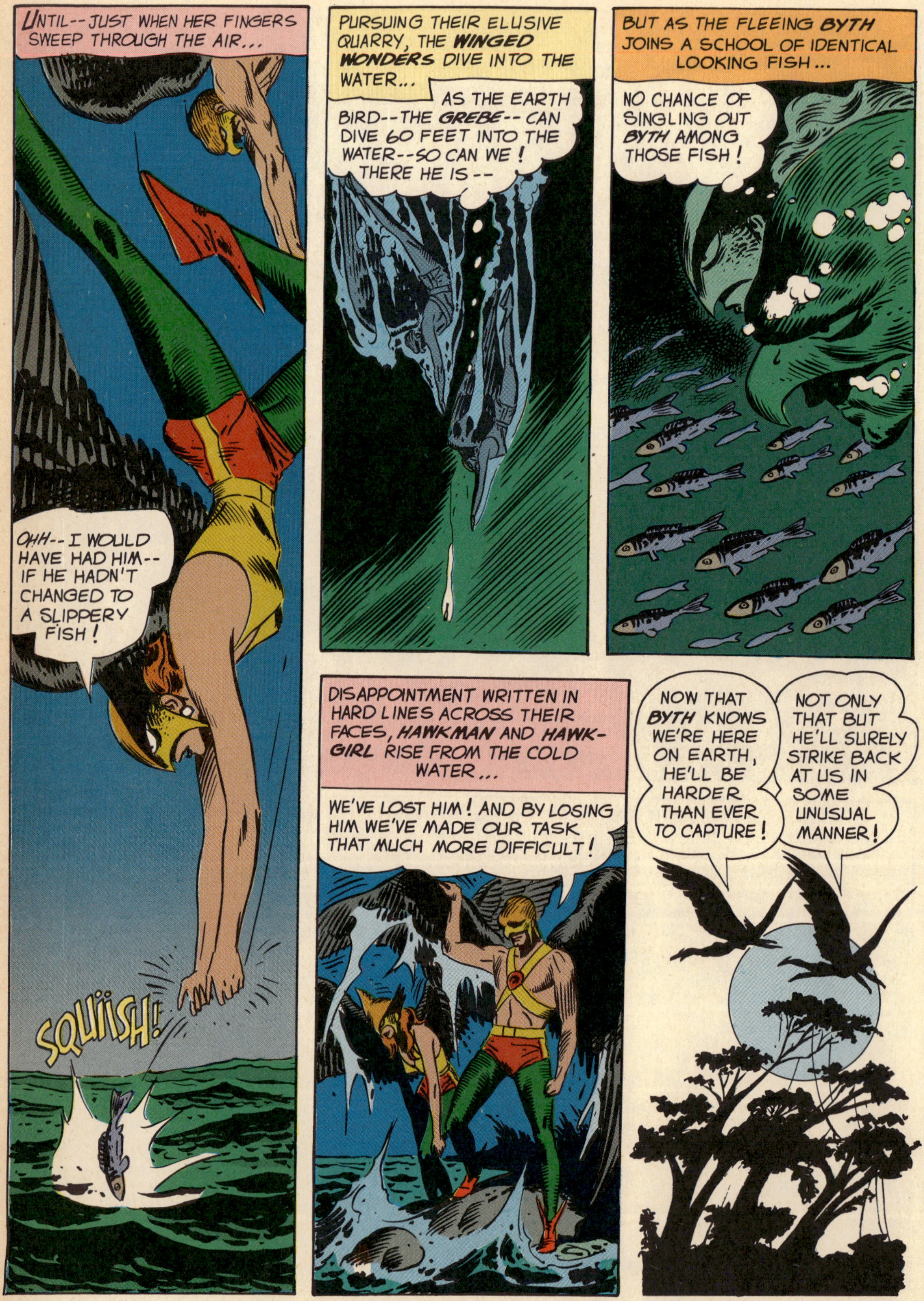
UNTIL-- JUST WHEN HER FINGERS SWEEP THROUGH THE AIR...
OHH-- I WOULD HAVE HAD HIM-- IF HE HADN'T CHANGED TO A SLIPPERY FISH!
SQUIISH!
PURSUING THEIR ELUSIVE QUARRY, THE WINGED WONDERS DIVE INTO THE WATER...
AS THE EARTH BIRD--THE GREBE-- CAN DIVE 60 FEET INTO THE WATER--SO CAN WE! THERE HE IS--
BUT AS THE FLEEING BYTH JOINS A SCHOOL OF IDENTICAL LOOKING FISH...
NO CHANCE OF SINGLING OUT BYTH AMONG THOSE FISH!
DISAPPOINTMENT WRITTEN IN HARD LINES ACROSS THEIR FACES, HAWKMAN AND HAWK-GIRL RISE FROM THE COLD WATER...
WE'VE LOST HIM! AND BY LOSING HIM WE'VE MADE OUR TASK THAT MUCH MORE DIFFICULT!
NOW THAT BYTH KNOWS WE'RE HERE ON EARTH, HE'LL BE HARDER THAN EVER TO CAPTURE!
NOT ONLY THAT BUT HE'LL SURELY STRIKE BACK AT US IN SOME UNUSUAL MANNER!

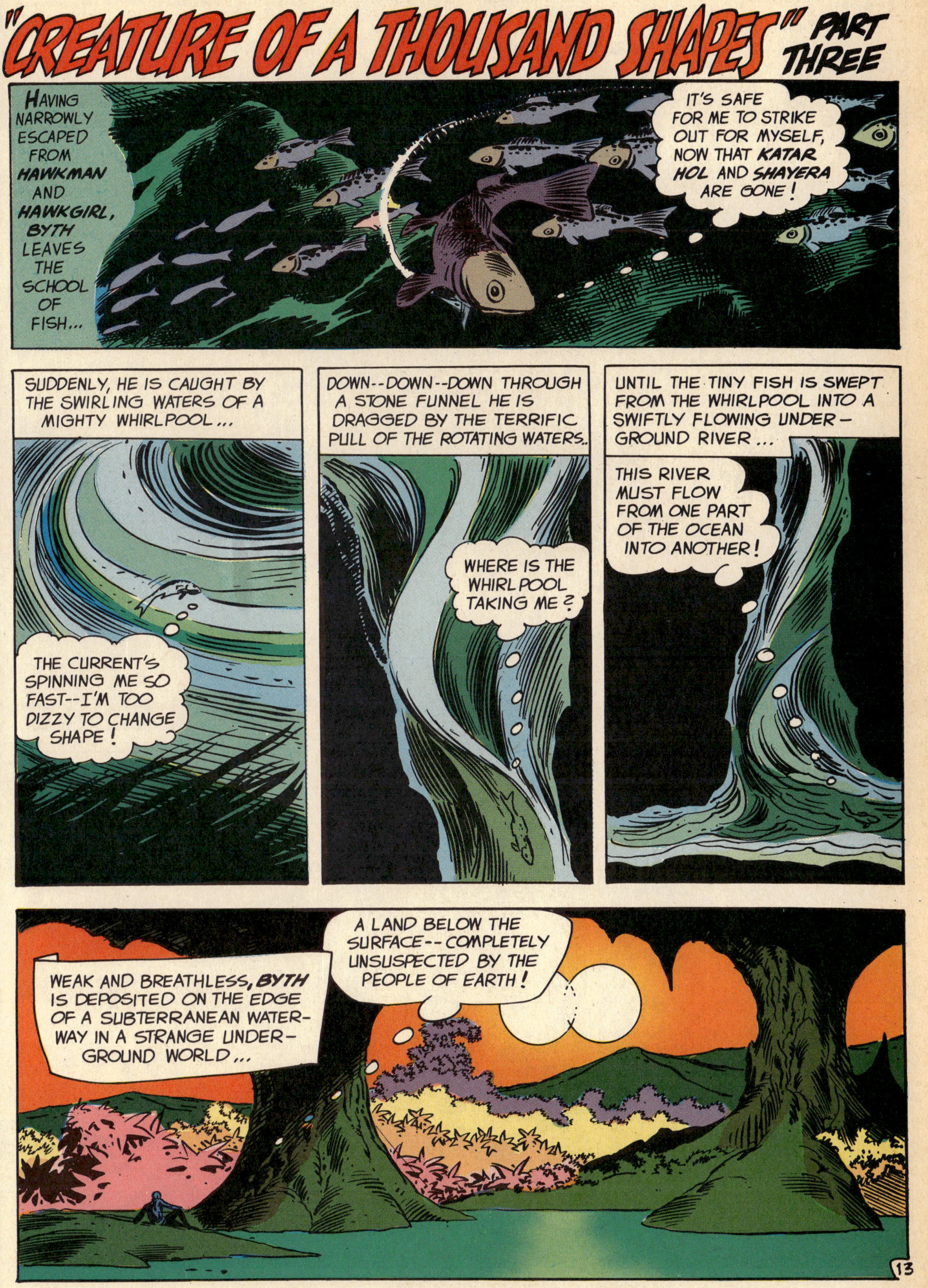
"CREATURE OF A THOUSAND SHAPES" PART THREE
HAVING NARROWLY ESCAPED FROM HAWKMAN AND HAWKGIRL, BYTH LEAVES THE SCHOOL OF FISH...
IT'S SAFE FOR ME TO STRIKE OUT FOR MYSELF, NOW THAT KATAR HOL AND SHAYERA ARE GONE!
SUDDENLY, HE IS CAUGHT BY THE SWIRLING WATERS OF A MIGHTY WHIRLPOOL...
THE CURRENT'S SPINNING ME SO FAST--I'M TOO DIZZY TO CHANGE SHAPE!
DOWN--DOWN--DOWN THROUGH A STONE FUNNEL HE IS DRAGGED BY THE TERRIFIC PULL OF THE ROTATING WATERS.
WHERE IS THE WHIRLPOOL TAKING ME?
UNTIL THE TINY FISH IS SWEPT FROM THE WHIRLPOOL INTO A SWIFTLY FLOWING UNDER-GROUND RIVER...
THIS RIVER MUST FLOW FROM ONE PART OF THE OCEAN INTO ANOTHER!
WEAK AND BREATHLESS, BYTH IS DEPOSITED ON THE EDGE OF A SUBTERRANEAN WATER-WAY IN A STRANGE UNDER-GROUND WORLD...
A LAND BELOW THE SURFACE--COMPLETELY UNSUSPECTED BY THE PEOPLE OF EARTH!
13

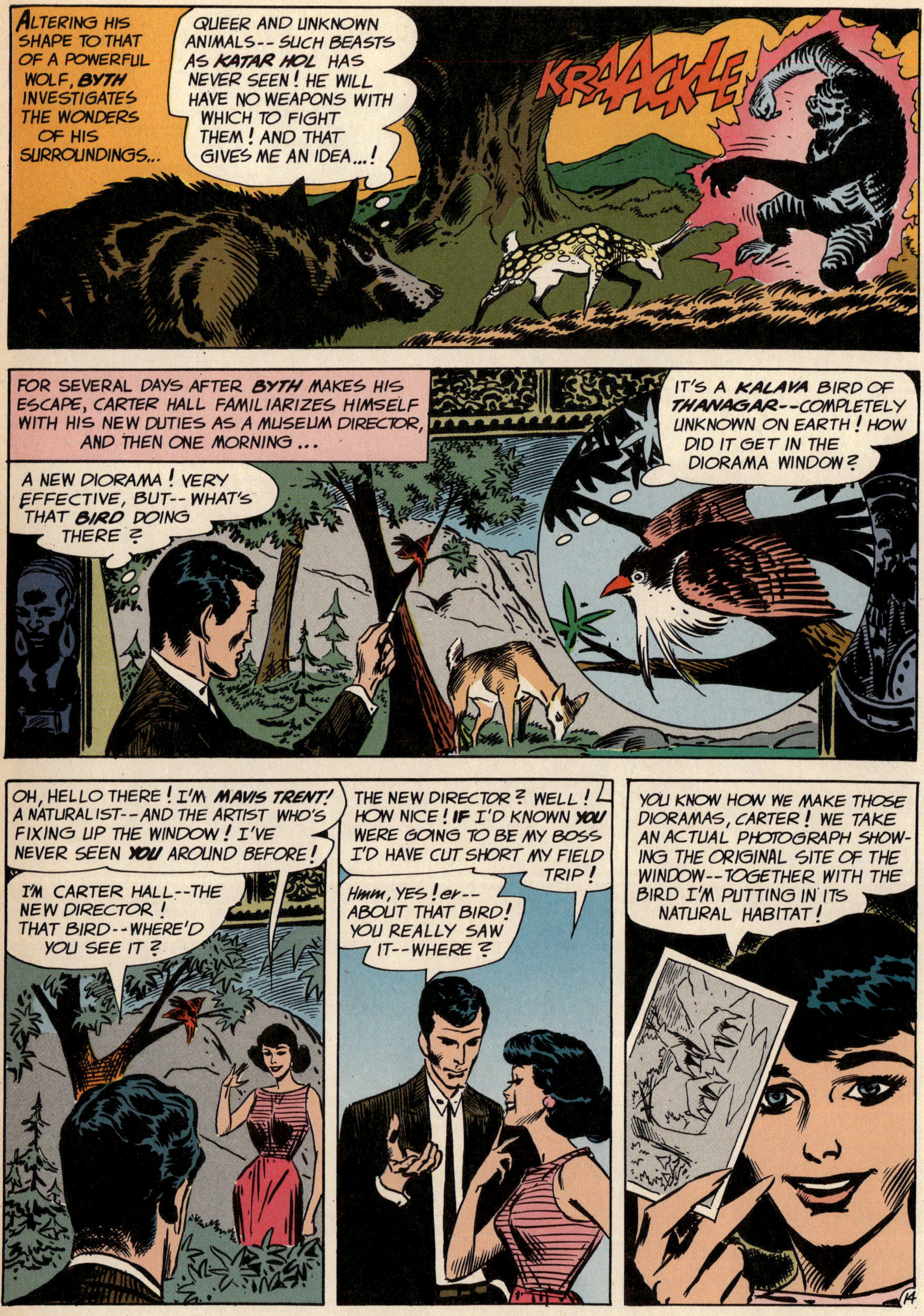
ALTERING HIS SHAPE TO THAT OF A POWERFUL WOLF, BYTH INVESTIGATES THE WONDERS OF HIS SURROUNDINGS...
QUEER AND UNKNOWN ANIMALS-- SUCH BEASTS AS KATAR HOL HAS NEVER SEEN! HE WILL HAVE NO WEAPONS WITH WHICH TO FIGHT THEM! AND THAT GIVES ME AN IDEA...!
KRAACKLE
FOR SEVERAL DAYS AFTER BYTH MAKES HIS ESCAPE, CARTER HALL FAMILIARIZES HIMSELF WITH HIS NEW DUTIES AS A MUSEUM DIRECTOR, AND THEN ONE MORNING...
A NEW DIORAMA! VERY EFFECTIVE, BUT-- WHAT'S THAT BIRD DOING THERE?
IT'S A KALAVA BIRD OF THANAGAR--COMPLETELY UNKNOWN ON EARTH! HOW DID IT GET IN THE DIORAMA WINDOW?
OH, HELLO THERE! I'M MAVIS TRENT! A NATURALIST--AND THE ARTIST WHO'S FIXING UP THE WINDOW! I'VE NEVER SEEN YOU AROUND BEFORE!
I'M CARTER HALL--THE NEW DIRECTOR! THAT BIRD--WHERE'D YOU SEE IT?
THE NEW DIRECTOR? WELL! HOW NICE! IF I'D KNOWN YOU WERE GOING TO BE MY BOSS I'D HAVE CUT SHORT MY FIELD TRIP!
Hmm, YES! er-- ABOUT THAT BIRD! YOU REALLY SAW IT--WHERE?
YOU KNOW HOW WE MAKE THOSE DIORAMAS, CARTER! WE TAKE AN ACTUAL PHOTOGRAPH SHOWING THE ORIGINAL SITE OF THE WINDOW--TOGETHER WITH THE BIRD I'M PUTTING IN ITS NATURAL HABITAT!
14

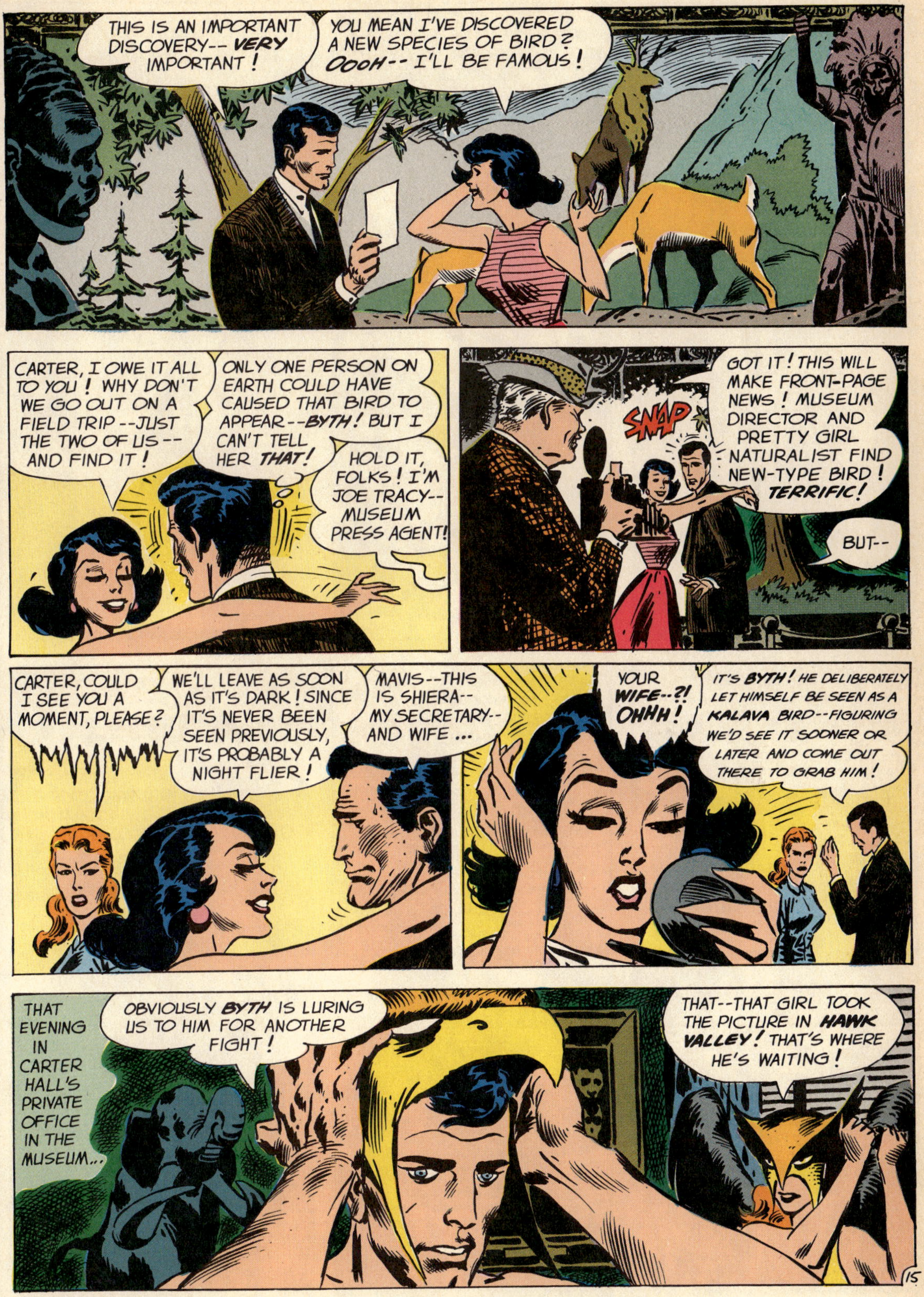
THIS IS AN IMPORTANT DISCOVERY-- VERY IMPORTANT!
YOU MEAN I'VE DISCOVERED A NEW SPECIES OF BIRD? OOOH-- I'LL BE FAMOUS!
CARTER, I OWE IT ALL TO YOU! WHY DON'T WE GO OUT ON A FIELD TRIP--JUST THE TWO OF US-- AND FIND IT!
ONLY ONE PERSON ON EARTH COULD HAVE CAUSED THAT BIRD TO APPEAR--BYTH! BUT I CAN'T TELL HER THAT!
HOLD IT, FOLKS! I'M JOE TRACY-- MUSEUM PRESS AGENT!
SNAP
GOT IT! THIS WILL MAKE FRONT-PAGE NEWS! MUSEUM DIRECTOR AND PRETTY GIRL NATURALIST FIND NEW-TYPE BIRD! TERRIFIC!
BUT--
CARTER, COULD I SEE YOU A MOMENT, PLEASE?
WE'LL LEAVE AS SOON AS IT'S DARK! SINCE IT'S NEVER BEEN SEEN PREVIOUSLY, IT'S PROBABLY A NIGHT FLIER!
MAVIS--THIS IS SHIERA-- MY SECRETARY-- AND WIFE...
YOUR WIFE--?! OHHH!
IT'S BYTH! HE DELIBERATELY LET HIMSELF BE SEEN AS A KALAVA BIRD--FIGURING WE'D SEE IT SOONER OR LATER AND COME OUT THERE TO GRAB HIM!
THAT EVENING IN CARTER HALL'S PRIVATE OFFICE IN THE MUSEUM...
OBVIOUSLY BYTH IS LURING US TO HIM FOR ANOTHER FIGHT!
THAT--THAT GIRL TOOK THE PICTURE IN HAWK VALLEY! THAT'S WHERE HE'S WAITING!
15

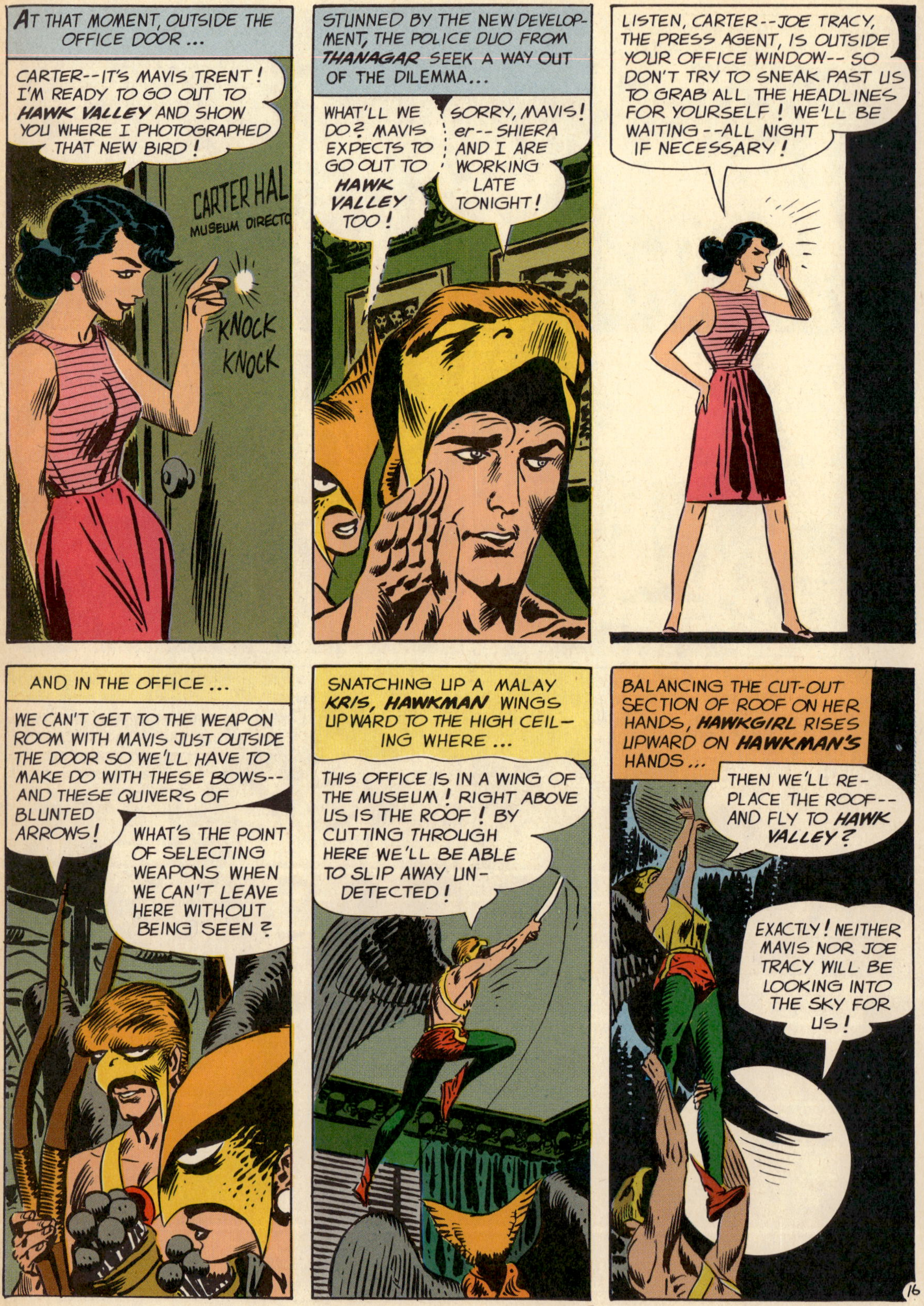
AT THAT MOMENT, OUTSIDE THE OFFICE DOOR ...
CARTER--IT'S MAVIS TRENT! I'M READY TO GO OUT TO HAWK VALLEY AND SHOW YOU WHERE I PHOTOGRAPHED THAT NEW BIRD!
CARTER HAL
MUSEUM DIRECTO
KNOCK KNOCK
STUNNED BY THE NEW DEVELOPMENT, THE POLICE DUO FROM THANAGAR SEEK A WAY OUT OF THE DILEMMA...
WHAT'LL WE DO? MAVIS EXPECTS TO GO OUT TO HAWK VALLEY TOO!
SORRY, MAVIS! er--SHIERA AND I ARE WORKING LATE TONIGHT!
LISTEN, CARTER--JOE TRACY, THE PRESS AGENT, IS OUTSIDE YOUR OFFICE WINDOW-- SO DON'T TRY TO SNEAK PAST US TO GRAB ALL THE HEADLINES FOR YOURSELF! WE'LL BE WAITING--ALL NIGHT IF NECESSARY!
AND IN THE OFFICE ...
WE CAN'T GET TO THE WEAPON ROOM WITH MAVIS JUST OUTSIDE THE DOOR SO WE'LL HAVE TO MAKE DO WITH THESE BOWS--AND THESE QUIVERS OF BLUNTED ARROWS!
WHAT'S THE POINT OF SELECTING WEAPONS WHEN WE CAN'T LEAVE HERE WITHOUT BEING SEEN?
SNATCHING UP A MALAY KRIS, HAWKMAN WINGS UPWARD TO THE HIGH CEILING WHERE ...
THIS OFFICE IS IN A WING OF THE MUSEUM! RIGHT ABOVE US IS THE ROOF! BY CUTTING THROUGH HERE WE'LL BE ABLE TO SLIP AWAY UNDETECTED!
BALANCING THE CUT-OUT SECTION OF ROOF ON HER HANDS, HAWKGIRL RISES UPWARD ON HAWKMAN'S HANDS...
THEN WE'LL REPLACE THE ROOF--AND FLY TO HAWK VALLEY?
EXACTLY! NEITHER MAVIS NOR JOE TRACY WILL BE LOOKING INTO THE SKY FOR US!
16

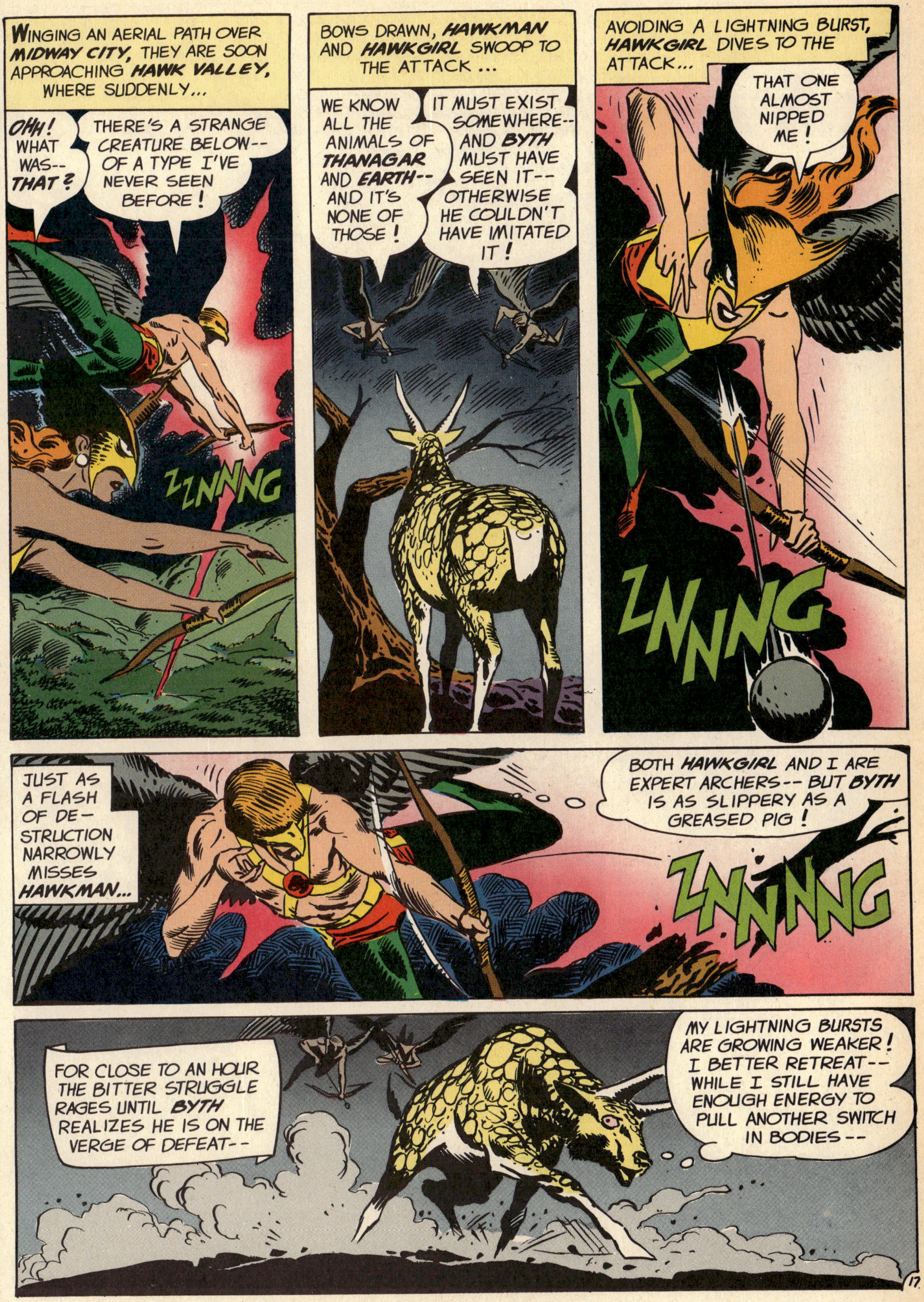
WINGING AN AERIAL PATH OVER MIDWAY CITY, THEY ARE SOON APPROACHING HAWK VALLEY, WHERE SUDDENLY...
OHH! WHAT WAS-- THAT?
THERE'S A STRANGE CREATURE BELOW-- OF A TYPE I'VE NEVER SEEN BEFORE!
ZNNNG
BOWS DRAWN, HAWKMAN AND HAWKGIRL SWOOP TO THE ATTACK...
WE KNOW ALL THE ANIMALS OF THANAGAR AND EARTH-- AND IT'S NONE OF THOSE!
IT MUST EXIST SOMEWHERE-- AND BYTH MUST HAVE SEEN IT-- OTHERWISE HE COULDN'T HAVE IMITATED IT!
AVOIDING A LIGHTNING BURST, HAWKGIRL DIVES TO THE ATTACK...
THAT ONE ALMOST NIPPED ME!
ZNNNG
JUST AS A FLASH OF DE-STRUCTION NARROWLY MISSES HAWKMAN...
BOTH HAWKGIRL AND I ARE EXPERT ARCHERS-- BUT BYTH IS AS SLIPPERY AS A GREASED PIG!
ZNNNNG
FOR CLOSE TO AN HOUR THE BITTER STRUGGLE RAGES UNTIL BYTH REALIZES HE IS ON THE VERGE OF DEFEAT--
MY LIGHTNING BURSTS ARE GROWING WEAKER! I BETTER RETREAT-- WHILE I STILL HAVE ENOUGH ENERGY TO PULL ANOTHER SWITCH IN BODIES--
17

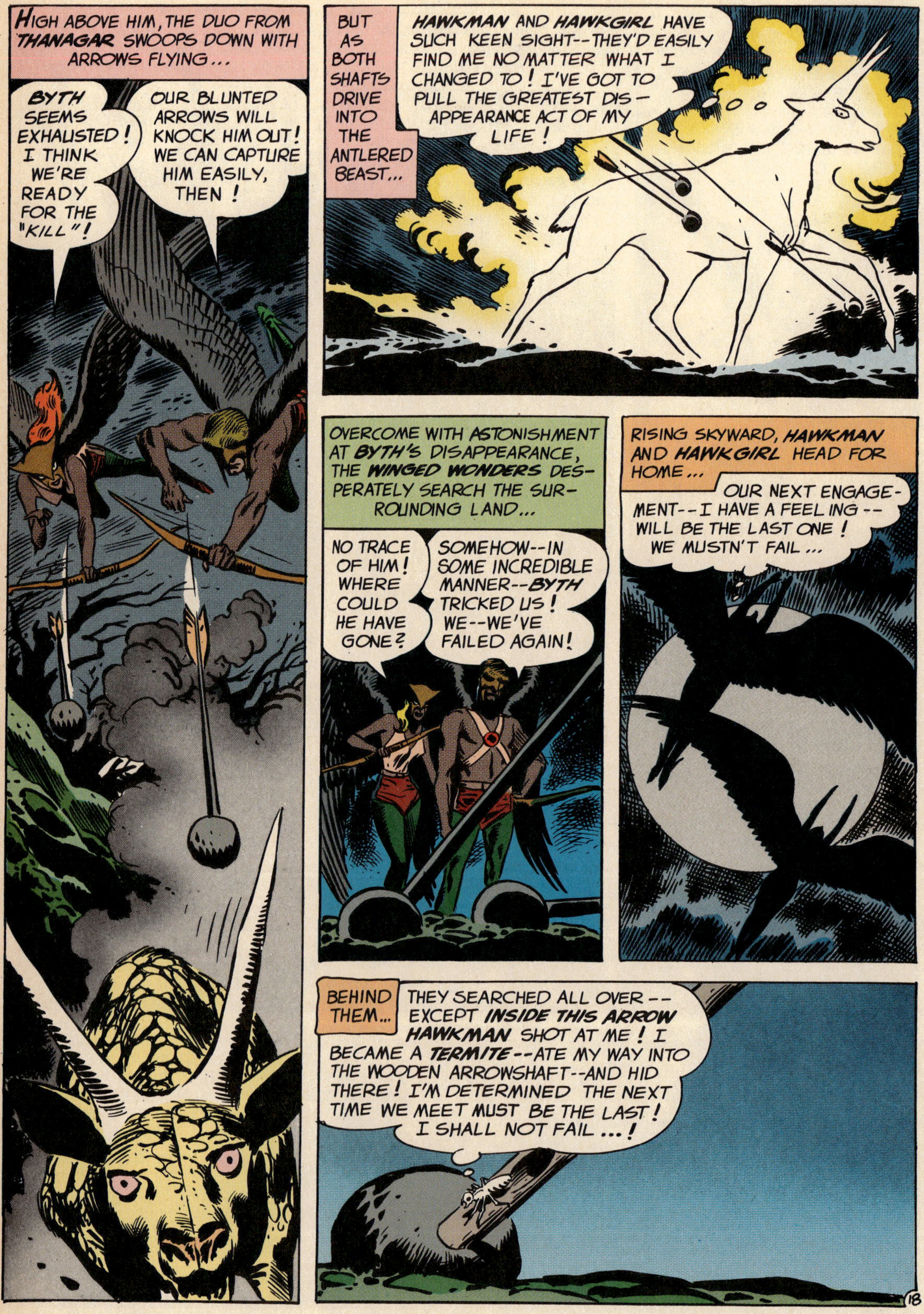

HIGH ABOVE HIM, THE DUO FROM THANAGAR SWOOPS DOWN WITH ARROWS FLYING...
BYTH SEEMS EXHAUSTED! I THINK WE'RE READY FOR THE "KILL"!
OUR BLUNTED ARROWS WILL KNOCK HIM OUT! WE CAN CAPTURE HIM EASILY, THEN!
BUT AS BOTH SHAFTS DRIVE INTO THE ANTLERED BEAST...
HAWKMAN AND HAWKGIRL HAVE SUCH KEEN SIGHT--THEY'D EASILY FIND ME NO MATTER WHAT I CHANGED TO! I'VE GOT TO PULL THE GREATEST DIS-APPEARANCE ACT OF MY LIFE!
OVERCOME WITH ASTONISHMENT AT BYTH'S DISAPPEARANCE, THE WINGED WONDERS DES-PERATELY SEARCH THE SUR-ROUNDING LAND...
NO TRACE OF HIM! WHERE COULD HE HAVE GONE?
SOMEHOW--IN SOME INCREDIBLE MANNER--BYTH TRICKED US! WE--WE'VE FAILED AGAIN!
RISING SKYWARD, HAWKMAN AND HAWKGIRL HEAD FOR HOME...
OUR NEXT ENGAGE-MENT--I HAVE A FEELING--WILL BE THE LAST ONE! WE MUSTN'T FAIL...
BEHIND THEM...
THEY SEARCHED ALL OVER--EXCEPT INSIDE THIS ARROW HAWKMAN SHOT AT ME! I BECAME A TERMITE--ATE MY WAY INTO THE WOODEN ARROWSHAFT--AND HID THERE! I'M DETERMINED THE NEXT TIME WE MEET MUST BE THE LAST! I SHALL NOT FAIL...!
18

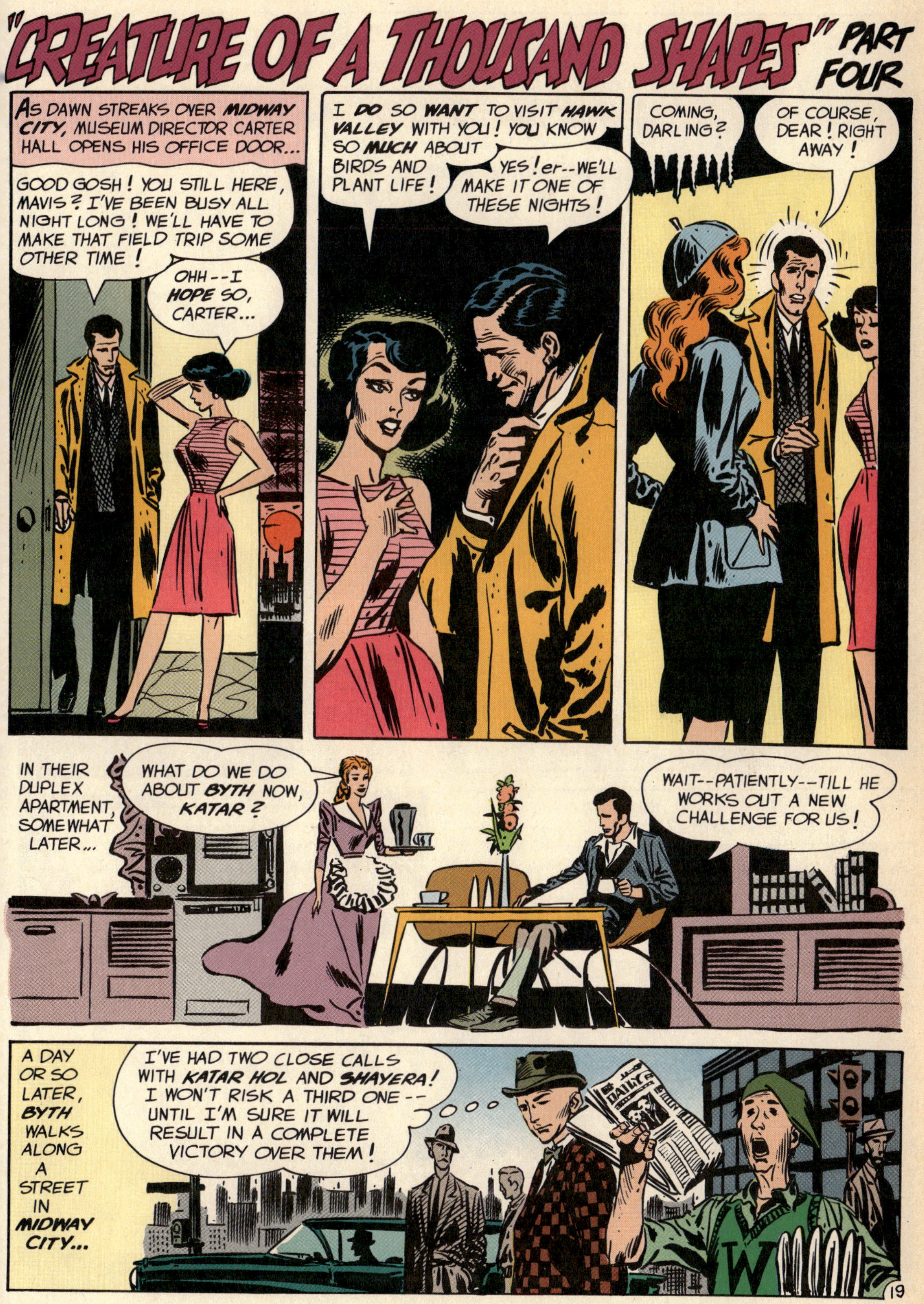

"CREATURE OF A THOUSAND SHAPES" PART FOUR
AS DAWN STREAKS OVER MIDWAY CITY, MUSEUM DIRECTOR CARTER HALL OPENS HIS OFFICE DOOR...
GOOD GOSH! YOU STILL HERE, MAVIS? I'VE BEEN BUSY ALL NIGHT LONG! WE'LL HAVE TO MAKE THAT FIELD TRIP SOME OTHER TIME!
OHH--I HOPE SO, CARTER...
I DO SO WANT TO VISIT HAWK VALLEY WITH YOU! YOU KNOW SO MUCH ABOUT BIRDS AND PLANT LIFE!
YES! er--WE'LL MAKE IT ONE OF THESE NIGHTS!
COMING, DARLING?
OF COURSE, DEAR! RIGHT AWAY!
IN THEIR DUPLEX APARTMENT, SOMEWHAT LATER...
WHAT DO WE DO ABOUT BYTH NOW, KATAR?
WAIT--PATIENTLY--TILL HE WORKS OUT A NEW CHALLENGE FOR US!
A DAY OR SO LATER, BYTH WALKS ALONG A STREET IN MIDWAY CITY...
I'VE HAD TWO CLOSE CALLS WITH KATAR HOL AND SHAYERA! I WON'T RISK A THIRD ONE--UNTIL I'M SURE IT WILL RESULT IN A COMPLETE VICTORY OVER THEM!
19

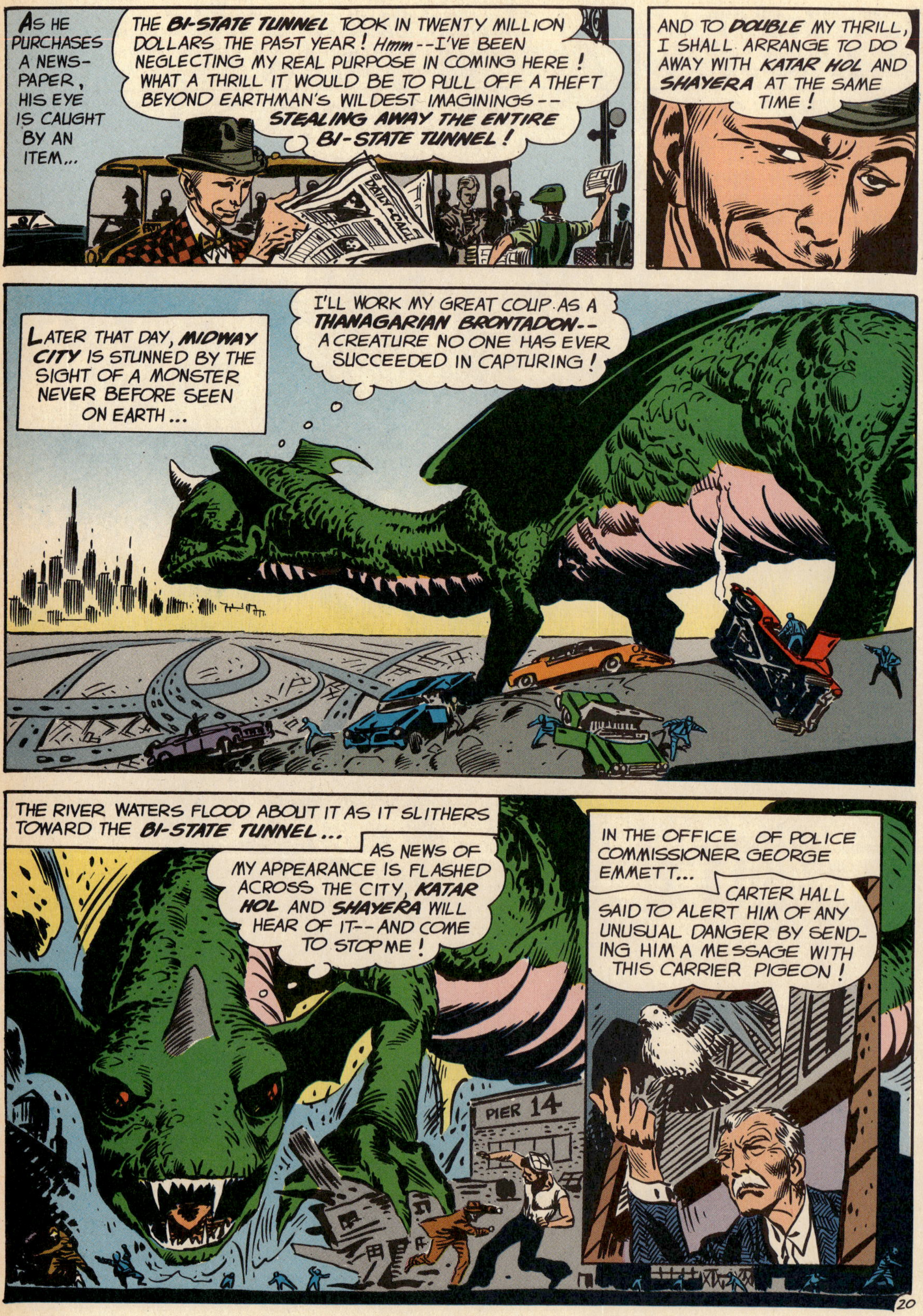
AS HE PURCHASES A NEWSPAPER, HIS EYE IS CAUGHT BY AN ITEM...
THE BI-STATE TUNNEL TOOK IN TWENTY MILLION DOLLARS THE PAST YEAR! Hmm--I'VE BEEN NEGLECTING MY REAL PURPOSE IN COMING HERE! WHAT A THRILL IT WOULD BE TO PULL OFF A THEFT BEYOND EARTHMAN'S WILDEST IMAGININGS--STEALING AWAY THE ENTIRE BI-STATE TUNNEL!
DAILY CALL
AND TO DOUBLE MY THRILL, I SHALL ARRANGE TO DO AWAY WITH KATAR HOL AND SHAYERA AT THE SAME TIME!
LATER THAT DAY, MIDWAY CITY IS STUNNED BY THE SIGHT OF A MONSTER NEVER BEFORE SEEN ON EARTH...
I'LL WORK MY GREAT COUP AS A THANAGARIAN BRONTADON--A CREATURE NO ONE HAS EVER SUCCEEDED IN CAPTURING!
THE RIVER WATERS FLOOD ABOUT IT AS IT SLITHERS TOWARD THE BI-STATE TUNNEL...
AS NEWS OF MY APPEARANCE IS FLASHED ACROSS THE CITY, KATAR HOL AND SHAYERA WILL HEAR OF IT--AND COME TO STOP ME!
PIER 14
IN THE OFFICE OF POLICE COMMISSIONER GEORGE EMMETT...
CARTER HALL SAID TO ALERT HIM OF ANY UNUSUAL DANGER BY SENDING HIM A MESSAGE WITH THIS CARRIER PIGEON!
20

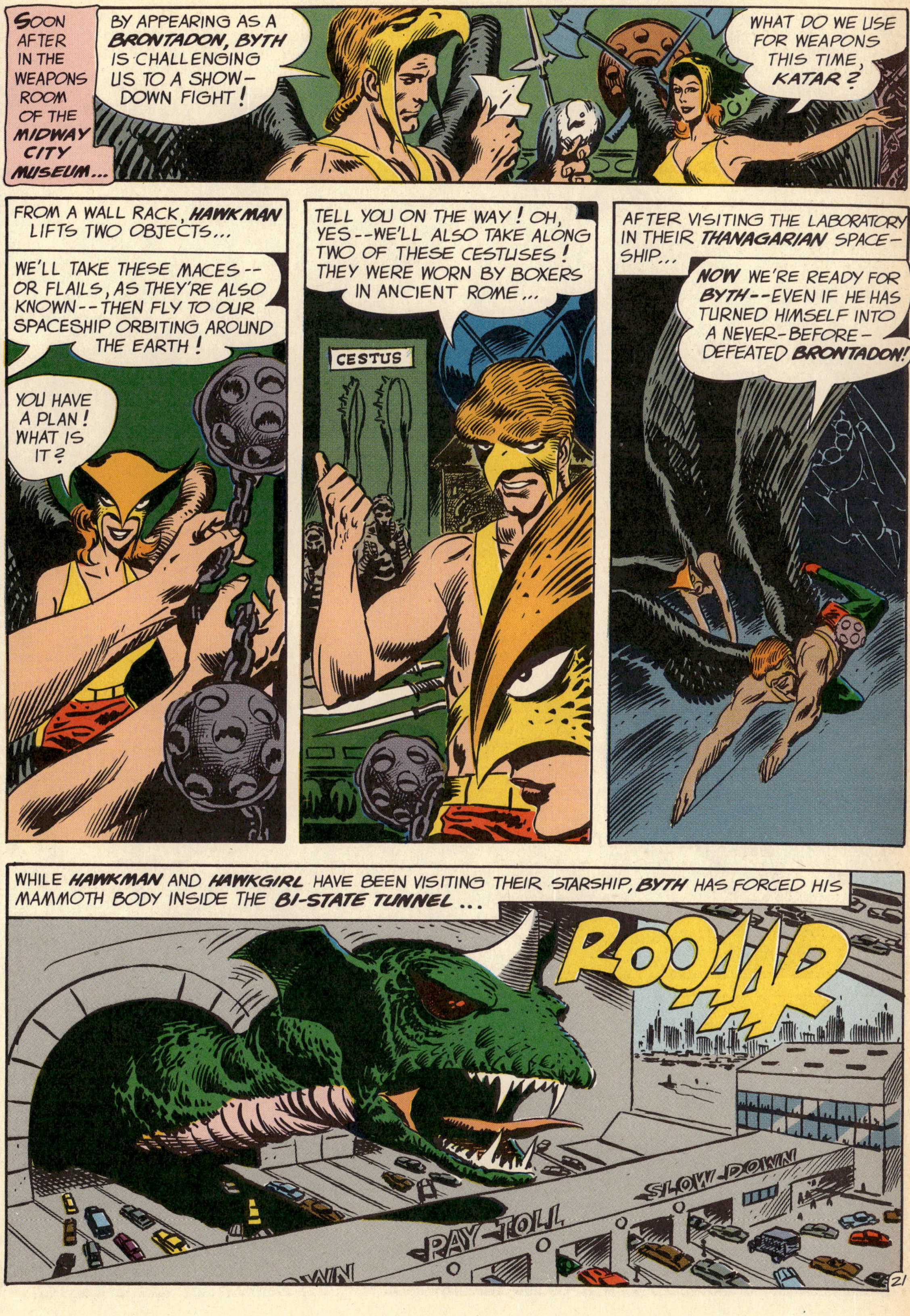
SOON AFTER IN THE WEAPONS ROOM OF THE MIDWAY CITY MUSEUM...
BY APPEARING AS A BRONTADON, BYTH IS CHALLENGING US TO A SHOW-DOWN FIGHT!
WHAT DO WE USE FOR WEAPONS THIS TIME, KATAR?
FROM A WALL RACK, HAWKMAN LIFTS TWO OBJECTS...
WE'LL TAKE THESE MACES--OR FLAILS, AS THEY'RE ALSO KNOWN--THEN FLY TO OUR SPACESHIP ORBITING AROUND THE EARTH!
YOU HAVE A PLAN! WHAT IS IT?
TELL YOU ON THE WAY! OH, YES--WE'LL ALSO TAKE ALONG TWO OF THESE CESTUSES! THEY WERE WORN BY BOXERS IN ANCIENT ROME...
CESTUS
AFTER VISITING THE LABORATORY IN THEIR THANAGARIAN SPACE-SHIP...
NOW WE'RE READY FOR BYTH--EVEN IF HE HAS TURNED HIMSELF INTO A NEVER-BEFORE-DEFEATED BRONTADON!
WHILE HAWKMAN AND HAWKGIRL HAVE BEEN VISITING THEIR STARSHIP, BYTH HAS FORCED HIS MAMMOTH BODY INSIDE THE BI-STATE TUNNEL...
ROOAAR
SLOW DOWN
PAY TOLL
21

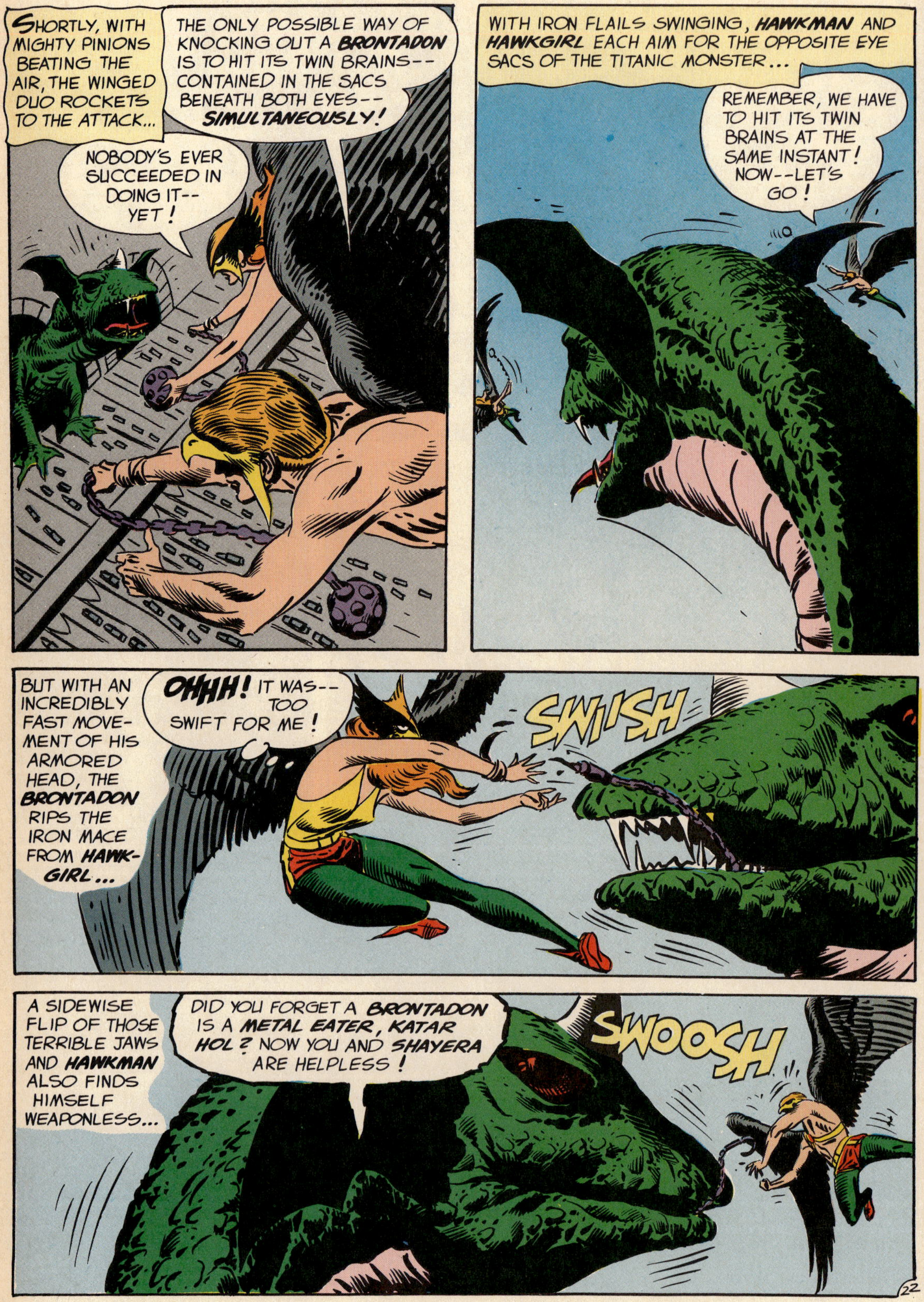
SHORTLY, WITH MIGHTY PINIONS BEATING THE AIR, THE WINGED DUO ROCKETS TO THE ATTACK...
THE ONLY POSSIBLE WAY OF KNOCKING OUT A BRONTADON IS TO HIT ITS TWIN BRAINS-- CONTAINED IN THE SACS BENEATH BOTH EYES-- SIMULTANEOUSLY!
NOBODY'S EVER SUCCEEDED IN DOING IT-- YET!
WITH IRON FLAILS SWINGING, HAWKMAN AND HAWKGIRL EACH AIM FOR THE OPPOSITE EYE SACS OF THE TITANIC MONSTER...
REMEMBER, WE HAVE TO HIT ITS TWIN BRAINS AT THE SAME INSTANT! NOW--LET'S GO!
BUT WITH AN INCREDIBLY FAST MOVEMENT OF HIS ARMORED HEAD, THE BRONTADON RIPS THE IRON MACE FROM HAWKGIRL...
OHHH! IT WAS-- TOO SWIFT FOR ME!
SWISH
A SIDEWISE FLIP OF THOSE TERRIBLE JAWS AND HAWKMAN ALSO FINDS HIMSELF WEAPONLESS...
DID YOU FORGET A BRONTADON IS A METAL EATER, KATAR HOL? NOW YOU AND SHAYERA ARE HELPLESS!
SWOOSH
22

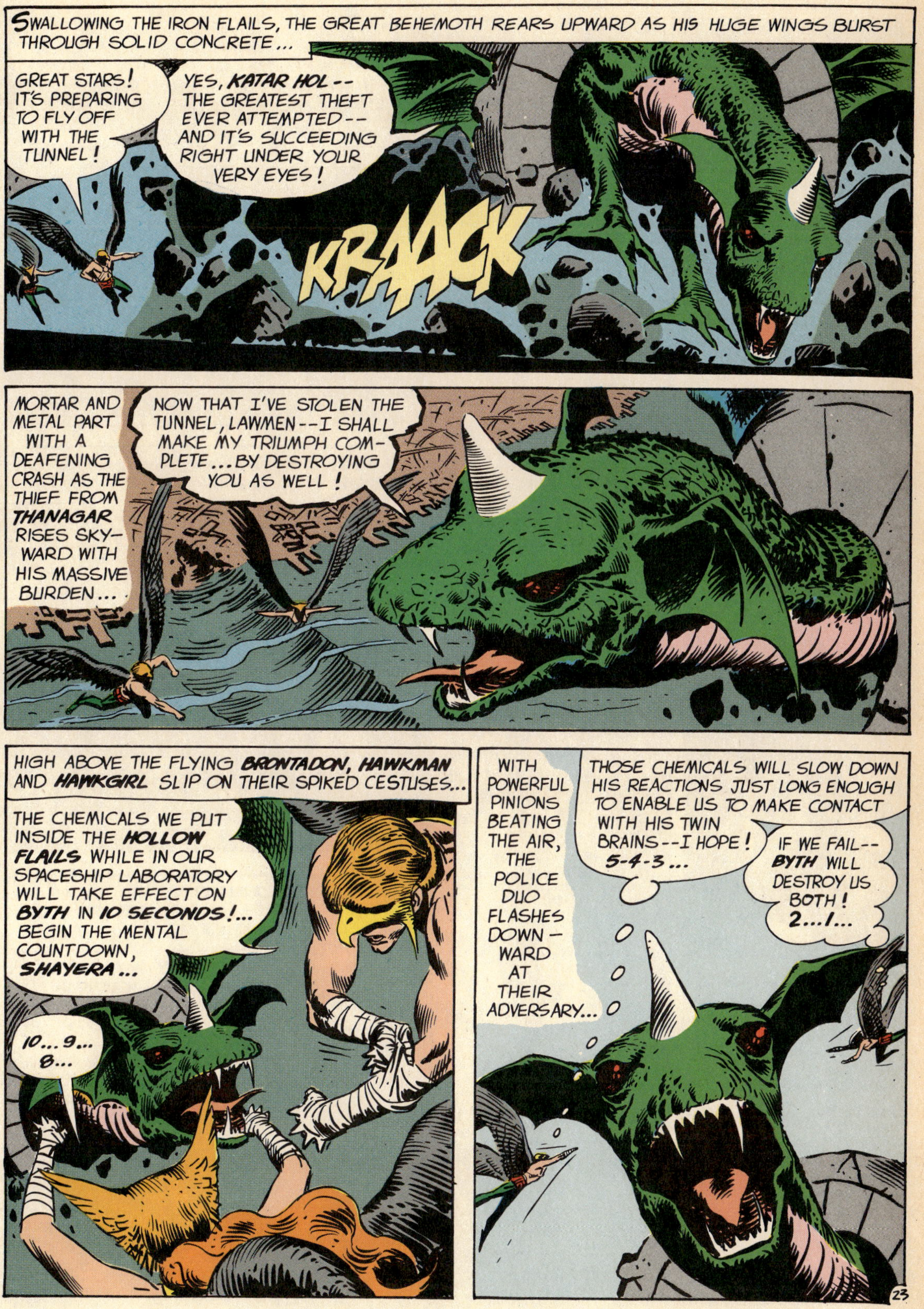
SWALLOWING THE IRON FLAILS, THE GREAT BEHEMOTH REARS UPWARD AS HIS HUGE WINGS BURST THROUGH SOLID CONCRETE...
GREAT STARS! IT'S PREPARING TO FLY OFF WITH THE TUNNEL!
YES, KATAR HOL -- THE GREATEST THEFT EVER ATTEMPTED -- AND IT'S SUCCEEDING RIGHT UNDER YOUR VERY EYES!
KRAAACK
MORTAR AND METAL PART WITH A DEAFENING CRASH AS THE THIEF FROM THANAGAR RISES SKYWARD WITH HIS MASSIVE BURDEN...
NOW THAT I'VE STOLEN THE TUNNEL, LAWMEN -- I SHALL MAKE MY TRIUMPH COMPLETE... BY DESTROYING YOU AS WELL!
HIGH ABOVE THE FLYING BRONTADON, HAWKMAN AND HAWKGIRL SLIP ON THEIR SPIKED CESTUSES...
THE CHEMICALS WE PUT INSIDE THE HOLLOW FLAILS WHILE IN OUR SPACESHIP LABORATORY WILL TAKE EFFECT ON BYTH IN 10 SECONDS!... BEGIN THE MENTAL COUNTDOWN, SHAYERA...
10... 9... 8...
WITH POWERFUL PINIONS BEATING THE AIR, THE POLICE DUO FLASHES DOWNWARD AT THEIR ADVERSARY...
THOSE CHEMICALS WILL SLOW DOWN HIS REACTIONS JUST LONG ENOUGH TO ENABLE US TO MAKE CONTACT WITH HIS TWIN BRAINS -- I HOPE! 5-4-3...
IF WE FAIL -- BYTH WILL DESTROY US BOTH! 2...1...
23

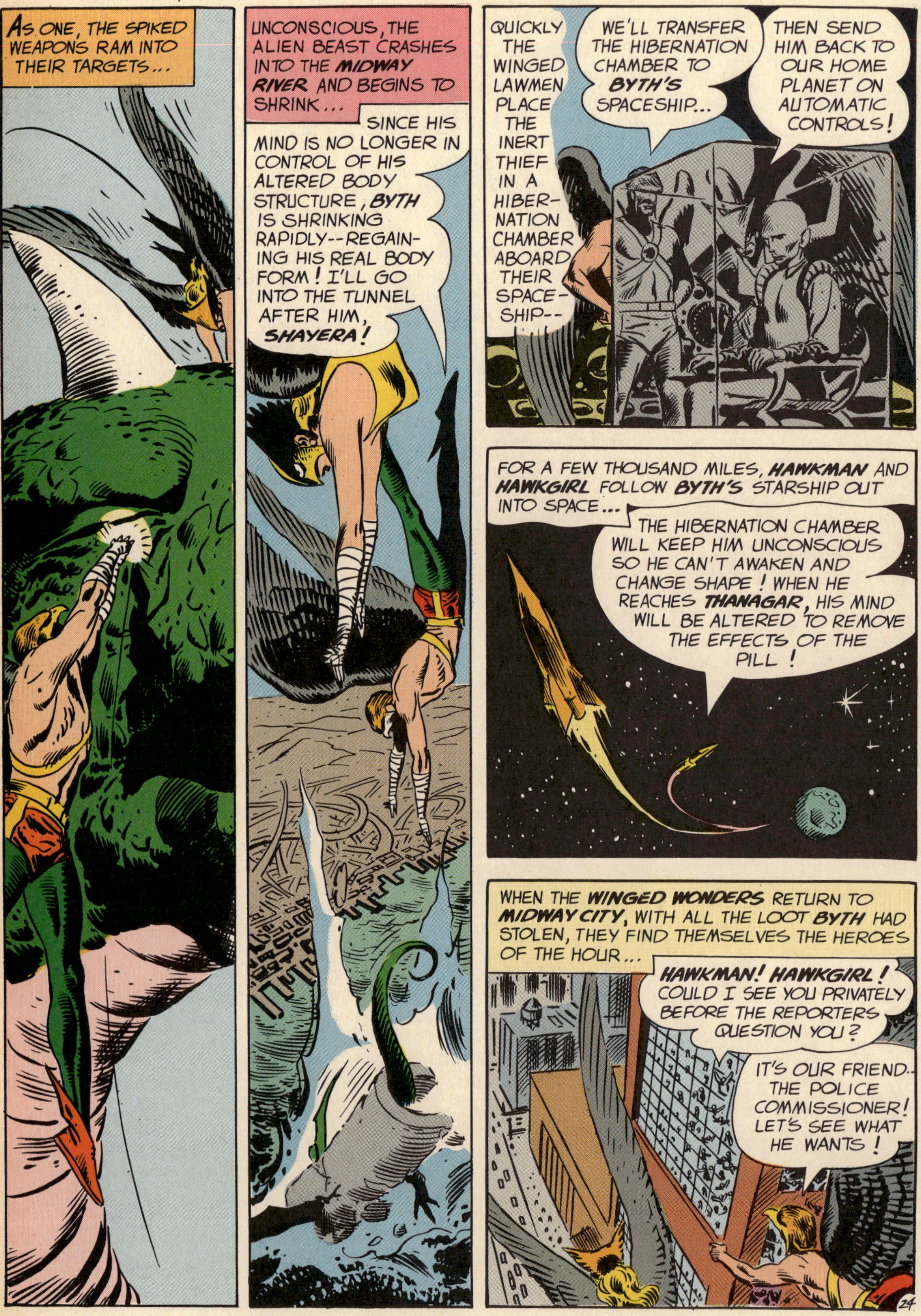
AS ONE, THE SPIKED WEAPONS RAM INTO THEIR TARGETS...
UNCONSCIOUS, THE ALIEN BEAST CRASHES INTO THE MIDWAY RIVER AND BEGINS TO SHRINK...
SINCE HIS MIND IS NO LONGER IN CONTROL OF HIS ALTERED BODY STRUCTURE, BYTH IS SHRINKING RAPIDLY--REGAINING HIS REAL BODY FORM! I'LL GO INTO THE TUNNEL AFTER HIM, SHAYERA!
QUICKLY THE WINGED LAWMEN PLACE THE INERT THIEF IN A HIBERNATION CHAMBER ABOARD THEIR SPACESHIP--
WE'LL TRANSFER THE HIBERNATION CHAMBER TO BYTH'S SPACESHIP...
THEN SEND HIM BACK TO OUR HOME PLANET ON AUTOMATIC CONTROLS!
FOR A FEW THOUSAND MILES, HAWKMAN AND HAWKGIRL FOLLOW BYTH'S STARSHIP OUT INTO SPACE...
THE HIBERNATION CHAMBER WILL KEEP HIM UNCONSCIOUS SO HE CAN'T AWAKEN AND CHANGE SHAPE! WHEN HE REACHES THANAGAR, HIS MIND WILL BE ALTERED TO REMOVE THE EFFECTS OF THE PILL!
WHEN THE WINGED WONDERS RETURN TO MIDWAY CITY, WITH ALL THE LOOT BYTH HAD STOLEN, THEY FIND THEMSELVES THE HEROES OF THE HOUR...
HAWKMAN! HAWKGIRL! COULD I SEE YOU PRIVATELY BEFORE THE REPORTERS QUESTION YOU?
IT'S OUR FRIEND--THE POLICE COMMISSIONER! LET'S SEE WHAT HE WANTS!
24

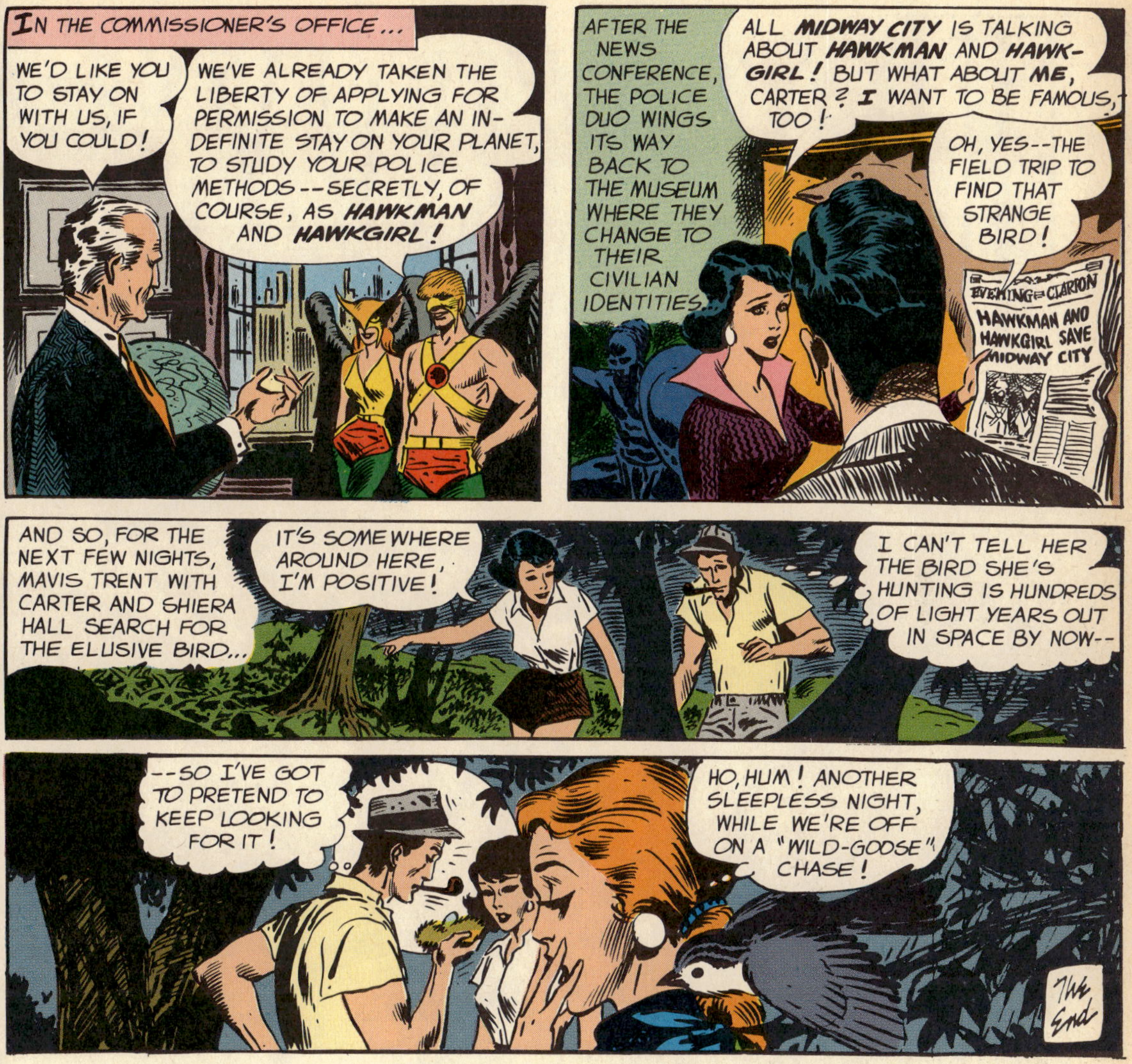
IN THE COMMISSIONER'S OFFICE...
WE'D LIKE YOU TO STAY ON WITH US, IF YOU COULD!
WE'VE ALREADY TAKEN THE LIBERTY OF APPLYING FOR PERMISSION TO MAKE AN IN-DEFINITE STAY ON YOUR PLANET, TO STUDY YOUR POLICE METHODS--SECRETLY, OF COURSE, AS HAWKMAN AND HAWKGIRL!
AFTER THE NEWS CONFERENCE, THE POLICE DUO WINGS ITS WAY BACK TO THE MUSEUM WHERE THEY CHANGE TO THEIR CIVILIAN IDENTITIES.
ALL MIDWAY CITY IS TALKING ABOUT HAWKMAN AND HAWK-GIRL! BUT WHAT ABOUT ME, CARTER? I WANT TO BE FAMOUS, TOO!
OH, YES--THE FIELD TRIP TO FIND THAT STRANGE BIRD!
EVENING CLARION
HAWKMAN AND HAWKGIRL SAVE MIDWAY CITY
AND SO, FOR THE NEXT FEW NIGHTS, MAVIS TRENT WITH CARTER AND SHIERA HALL SEARCH FOR THE ELUSIVE BIRD...
IT'S SOMEWHERE AROUND HERE, I'M POSITIVE!
I CAN'T TELL HER THE BIRD SHE'S HUNTING IS HUNDREDS OF LIGHT YEARS OUT IN SPACE BY NOW--
--SO I'VE GOT TO PRETEND TO KEEP LOOKING FOR IT!
HO, HUM! ANOTHER SLEEPLESS NIGHT, WHILE WE'RE OFF ON A "WILD-GOOSE" CHASE!
The End

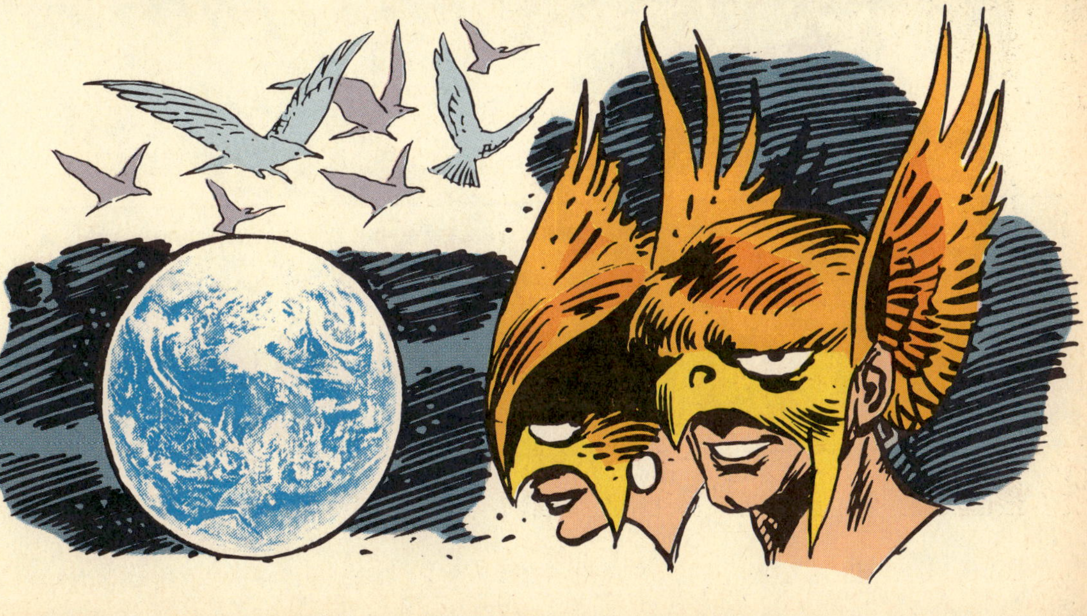

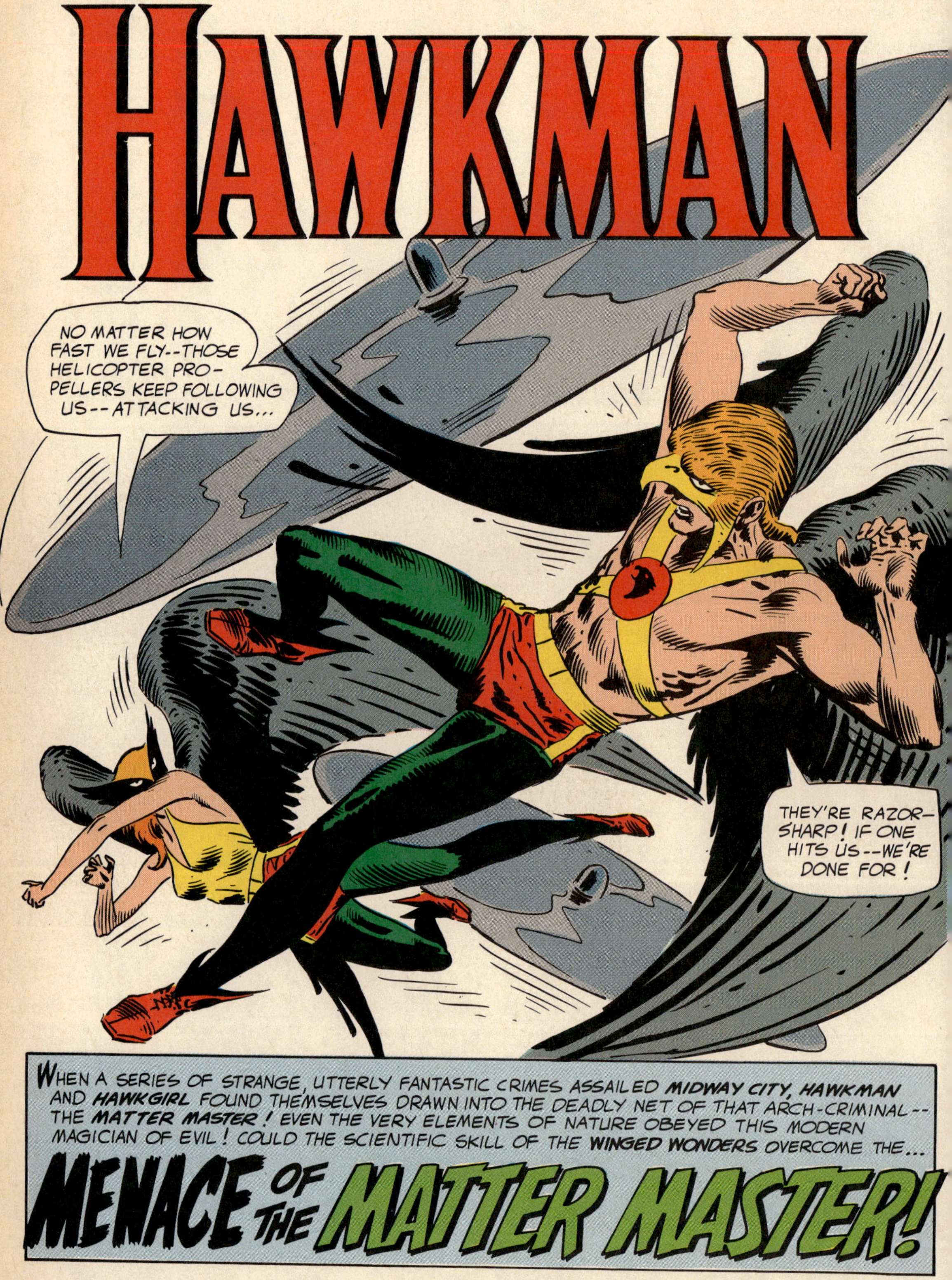
HAWKMAN
NO MATTER HOW FAST WE FLY--THOSE HELICOPTER PROPELLERS KEEP FOLLOWING US--ATTACKING US...
THEY'RE RAZOR-SHARP! IF ONE HITS US--WE'RE DONE FOR!
WHEN A SERIES OF STRANGE, UTTERLY FANTASTIC CRIMES ASSAILED MIDWAY CITY, HAWKMAN AND HAWKGIRL FOUND THEMSELVES DRAWN INTO THE DEADLY NET OF THAT ARCH-CRIMINAL--THE MATTER MASTER! EVEN THE VERY ELEMENTS OF NATURE OBEYED THIS MODERN MAGICIAN OF EVIL! COULD THE SCIENTIFIC SKILL OF THE WINGED WONDERS OVERCOME THE...
MENACE OF THE MATTER MASTER!

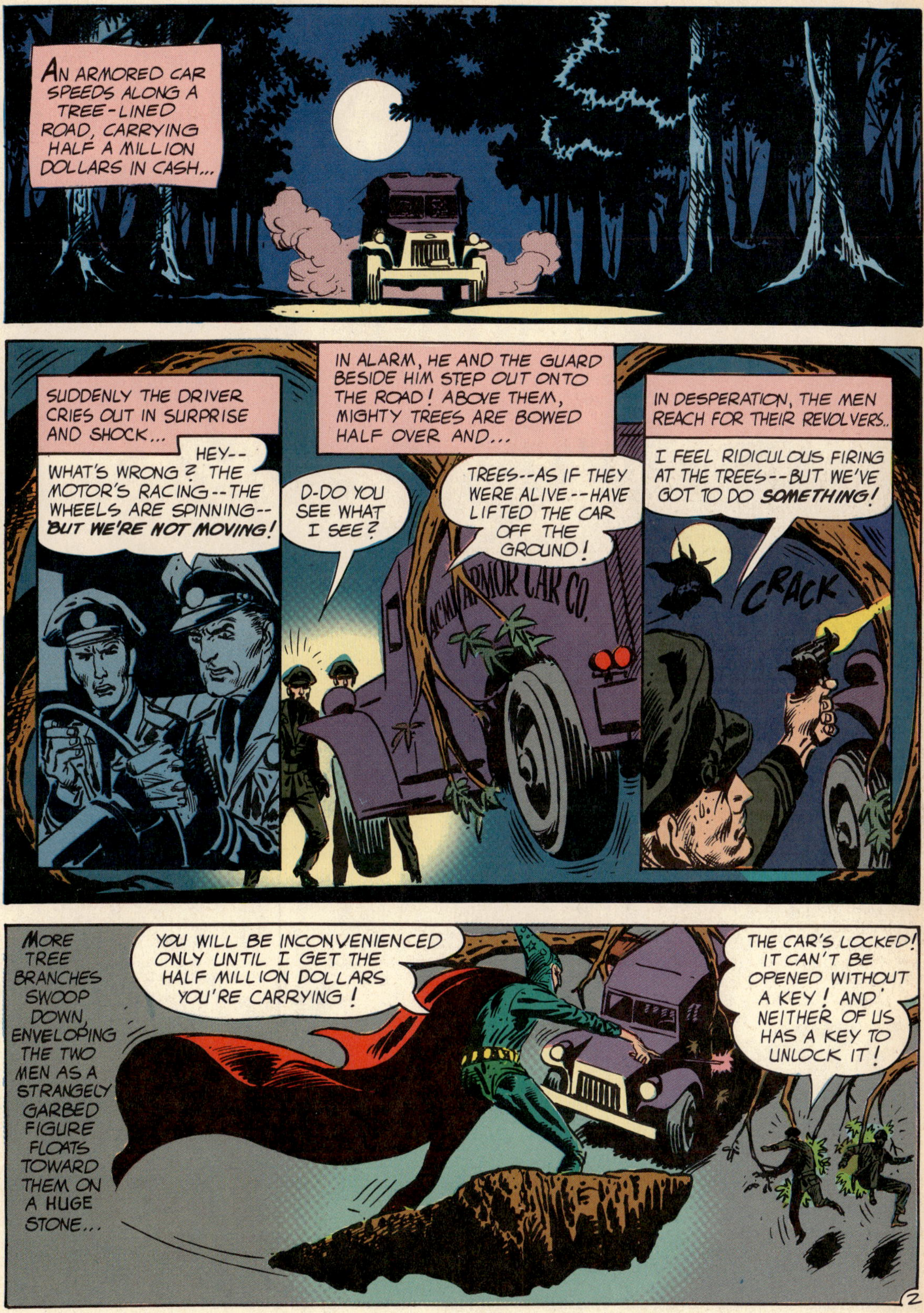
AN ARMORED CAR SPEEDS ALONG A TREE-LINED ROAD, CARRYING HALF A MILLION DOLLARS IN CASH...
SUDDENLY THE DRIVER CRIES OUT IN SURPRISE AND SHOCK...
HEY--
WHAT'S WRONG? THE MOTOR'S RACING--THE WHEELS ARE SPINNING--BUT WE'RE NOT MOVING!
IN ALARM, HE AND THE GUARD BESIDE HIM STEP OUT ONTO THE ROAD! ABOVE THEM, MIGHTY TREES ARE BOWED HALF OVER AND...
D-DO YOU SEE WHAT I SEE?
TREES--AS IF THEY WERE ALIVE--HAVE LIFTED THE CAR OFF THE GROUND!
ACME ARMOR CAR CO.
IN DESPERATION, THE MEN REACH FOR THEIR REVOLVERS..
I FEEL RIDICULOUS FIRING AT THE TREES--BUT WE'VE GOT TO DO SOMETHING!
CRACK
MORE TREE BRANCHES SWOOP DOWN, ENVELOPING THE TWO MEN AS A STRANGELY GARBED FIGURE FLOATS TOWARD THEM ON A HUGE STONE...
YOU WILL BE INCONVENIENCED ONLY UNTIL I GET THE HALF MILLION DOLLARS YOU'RE CARRYING!
THE CAR'S LOCKED! IT CAN'T BE OPENED WITHOUT A KEY! AND NEITHER OF US HAS A KEY TO UNLOCK IT!
2

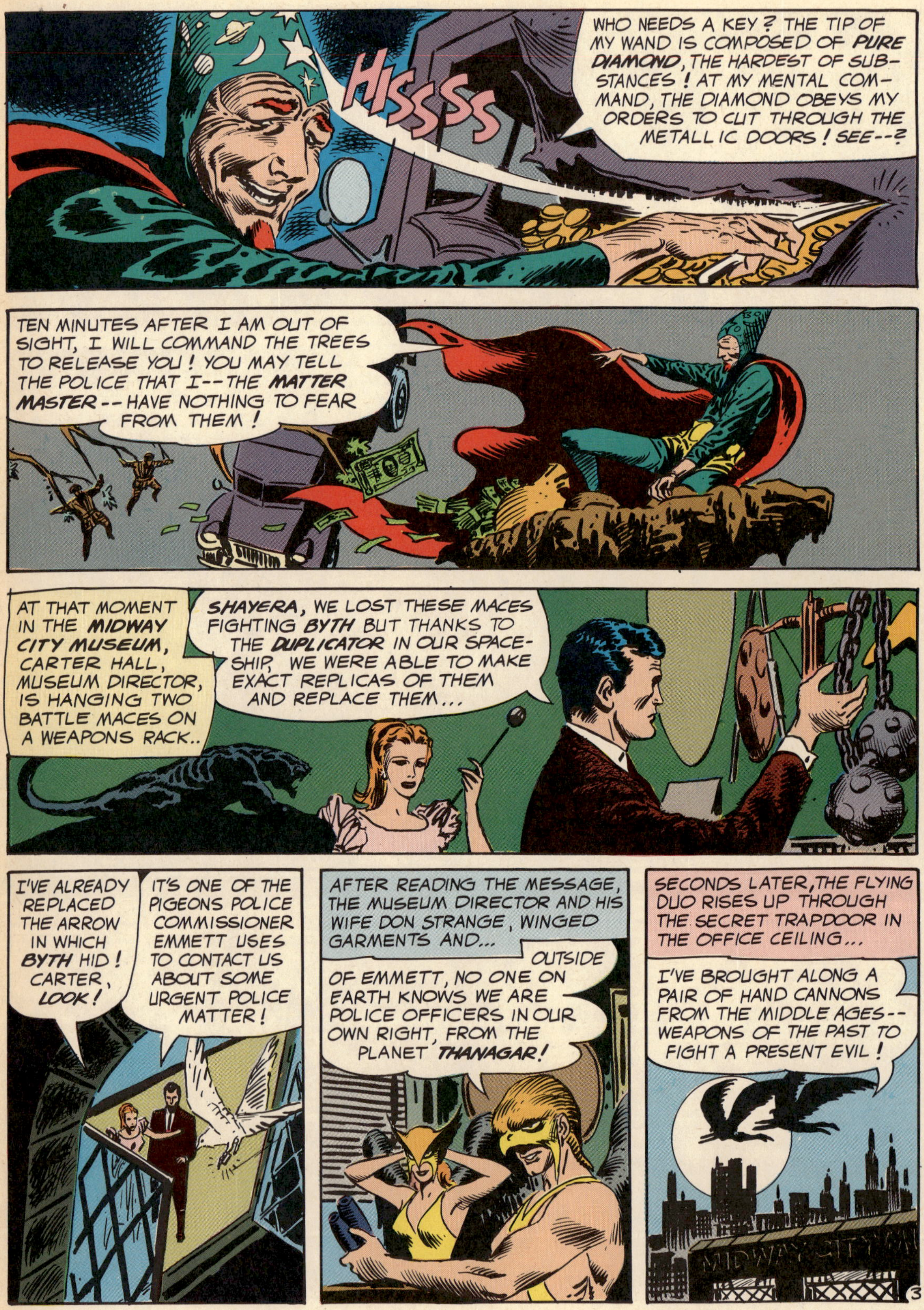
HISSSS
WHO NEEDS A KEY? THE TIP OF MY WAND IS COMPOSED OF PURE DIAMOND, THE HARDEST OF SUBSTANCES! AT MY MENTAL COMMAND, THE DIAMOND OBEYS MY ORDERS TO CUT THROUGH THE METALLIC DOORS! SEE--?
TEN MINUTES AFTER I AM OUT OF SIGHT, I WILL COMMAND THE TREES TO RELEASE YOU! YOU MAY TELL THE POLICE THAT I--THE MATTER MASTER--HAVE NOTHING TO FEAR FROM THEM!
AT THAT MOMENT IN THE MIDWAY CITY MUSEUM, CARTER HALL, MUSEUM DIRECTOR, IS HANGING TWO BATTLE MACES ON A WEAPONS RACK..
SHAYERA, WE LOST THESE MACES FIGHTING BYTH BUT THANKS TO THE DUPLICATOR IN OUR SPACESHIP, WE WERE ABLE TO MAKE EXACT REPLICAS OF THEM AND REPLACE THEM...
I'VE ALREADY REPLACED THE ARROW IN WHICH BYTH HID! CARTER, LOOK!
IT'S ONE OF THE PIGEONS POLICE COMMISSIONER EMMETT USES TO CONTACT US ABOUT SOME URGENT POLICE MATTER!
AFTER READING THE MESSAGE, THE MUSEUM DIRECTOR AND HIS WIFE DON STRANGE, WINGED GARMENTS AND...
OUTSIDE OF EMMETT, NO ONE ON EARTH KNOWS WE ARE POLICE OFFICERS IN OUR OWN RIGHT, FROM THE PLANET THANAGAR!
SECONDS LATER, THE FLYING DUO RISES UP THROUGH THE SECRET TRAPDOOR IN THE OFFICE CEILING...
I'VE BROUGHT ALONG A PAIR OF HAND CANNONS FROM THE MIDDLE AGES--WEAPONS OF THE PAST TO FIGHT A PRESENT EVIL!
3

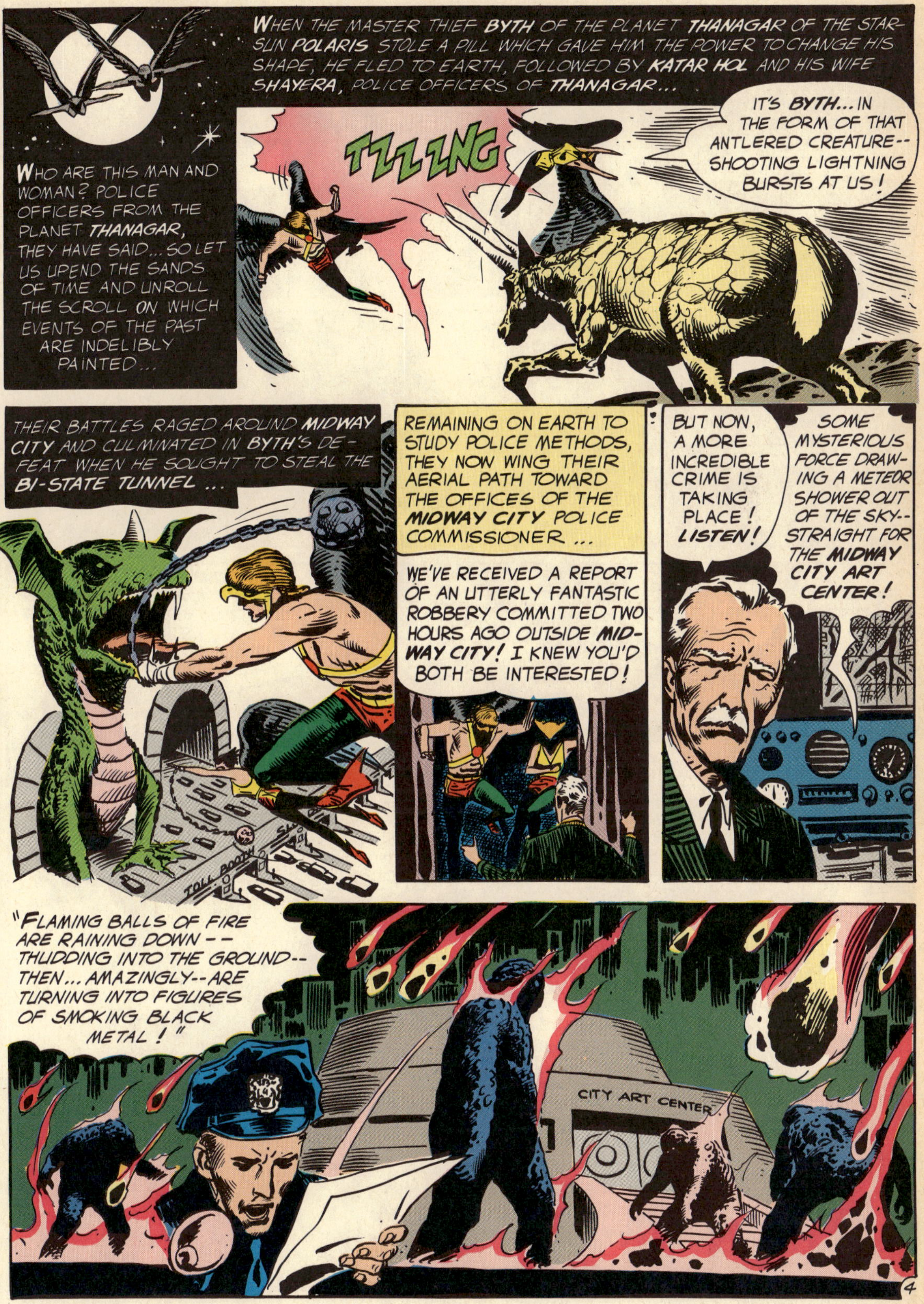
WHEN THE MASTER THIEF BYTH OF THE PLANET THANAGAR OF THE STAR-SUN POLARIS STOLE A PILL WHICH GAVE HIM THE POWER TO CHANGE HIS SHAPE, HE FLED TO EARTH, FOLLOWED BY KATAR HOL AND HIS WIFE SHAYERA, POLICE OFFICERS OF THANAGAR...
WHO ARE THIS MAN AND WOMAN? POLICE OFFICERS FROM THE PLANET THANAGAR, THEY HAVE SAID... SO LET US UPEND THE SANDS OF TIME AND UNROLL THE SCROLL ON WHICH EVENTS OF THE PAST ARE INDELIBLY PAINTED...
TZZZNG
IT'S BYTH... IN THE FORM OF THAT ANTLERED CREATURE-- SHOOTING LIGHTNING BURSTS AT US!
THEIR BATTLES RAGED AROUND MIDWAY CITY AND CULMINATED IN BYTH'S DEFEAT WHEN HE SOUGHT TO STEAL THE BI-STATE TUNNEL...
TOLL BOOTH
REMAINING ON EARTH TO STUDY POLICE METHODS, THEY NOW WING THEIR AERIAL PATH TOWARD THE OFFICES OF THE MIDWAY CITY POLICE COMMISSIONER...
WE'VE RECEIVED A REPORT OF AN UTTERLY FANTASTIC ROBBERY COMMITTED TWO HOURS AGO OUTSIDE MIDWAY CITY! I KNEW YOU'D BOTH BE INTERESTED!
BUT NOW, A MORE INCREDIBLE CRIME IS TAKING PLACE! LISTEN!
SOME MYSTERIOUS FORCE DRAWING A METEOR SHOWER OUT OF THE SKY-- STRAIGHT FOR THE MIDWAY CITY ART CENTER!
"FLAMING BALLS OF FIRE ARE RAINING DOWN-- THUDDING INTO THE GROUND-- THEN... AMAZINGLY-- ARE TURNING INTO FIGURES OF SMOKING BLACK METAL!"
CITY ART CENTER
4

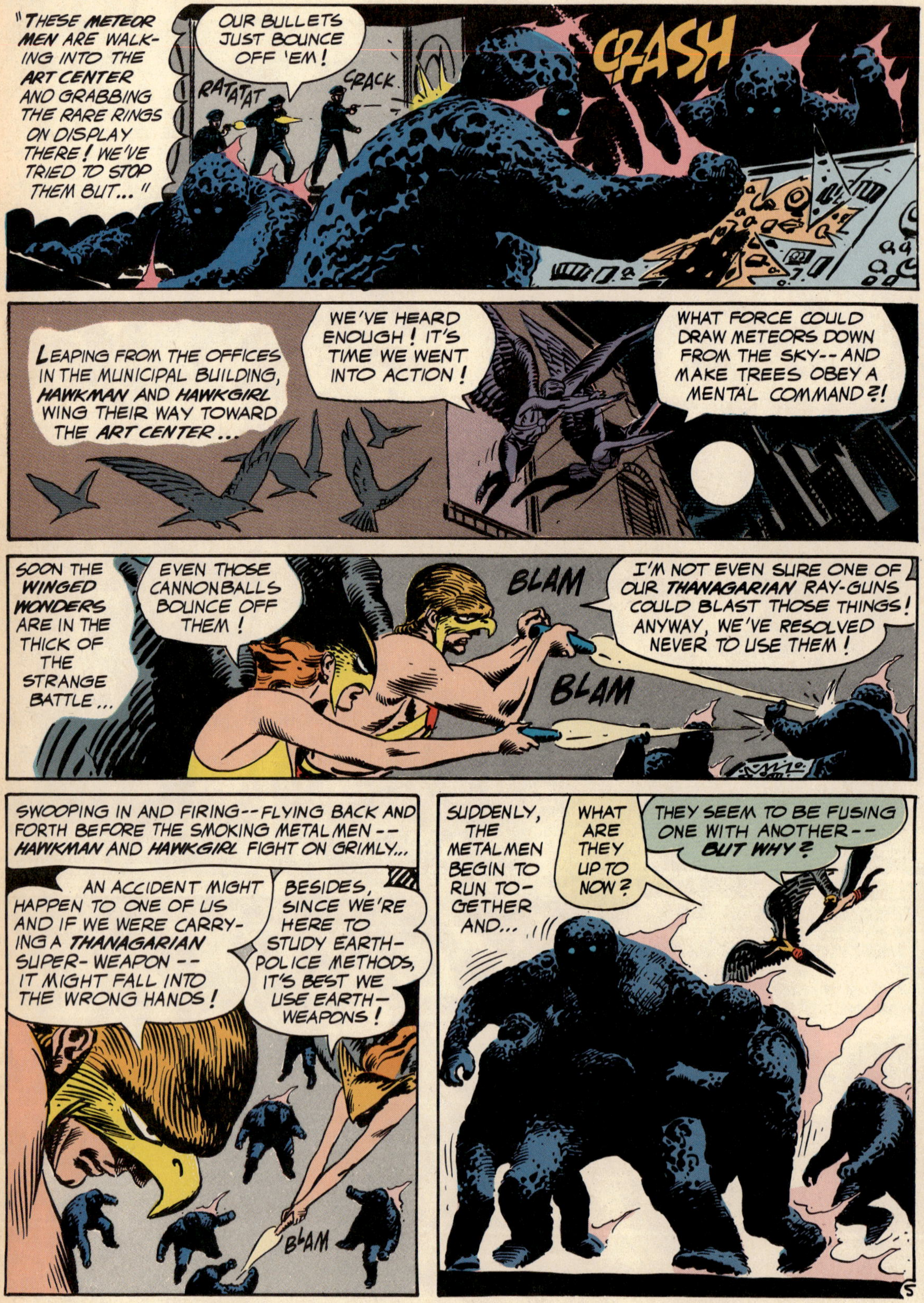

"THESE METEOR MEN ARE WALKING INTO THE ART CENTER AND GRABBING THE RARE RINGS ON DISPLAY THERE! WE'VE TRIED TO STOP THEM BUT..."
OUR BULLETS JUST BOUNCE OFF 'EM!
RATATAT
CRACK
CRASH
LEAPING FROM THE OFFICES IN THE MUNICIPAL BUILDING, HAWKMAN AND HAWKGIRL WING THEIR WAY TOWARD THE ART CENTER...
WE'VE HEARD ENOUGH! IT'S TIME WE WENT INTO ACTION!
WHAT FORCE COULD DRAW METEORS DOWN FROM THE SKY--AND MAKE TREES OBEY A MENTAL COMMAND?!
SOON THE WINGED WONDERS ARE IN THE THICK OF THE STRANGE BATTLE...
EVEN THOSE CANNONBALLS BOUNCE OFF THEM!
BLAM
I'M NOT EVEN SURE ONE OF OUR THANAGARIAN RAY-GUNS COULD BLAST THOSE THINGS! ANYWAY, WE'VE RESOLVED NEVER TO USE THEM!
BLAM
SWOOPING IN AND FIRING--FLYING BACK AND FORTH BEFORE THE SMOKING METAL MEN--HAWKMAN AND HAWKGIRL FIGHT ON GRIMLY...
AN ACCIDENT MIGHT HAPPEN TO ONE OF US AND IF WE WERE CARRYING A THANAGARIAN SUPER-WEAPON--IT MIGHT FALL INTO THE WRONG HANDS!
BESIDES, SINCE WE'RE HERE TO STUDY EARTH-POLICE METHODS, IT'S BEST WE USE EARTH-WEAPONS!
BLAM
SUDDENLY, THE METAL MEN BEGIN TO RUN TOGETHER AND...
WHAT ARE THEY UP TO NOW?
THEY SEEM TO BE FUSING ONE WITH ANOTHER--BUT WHY?
5

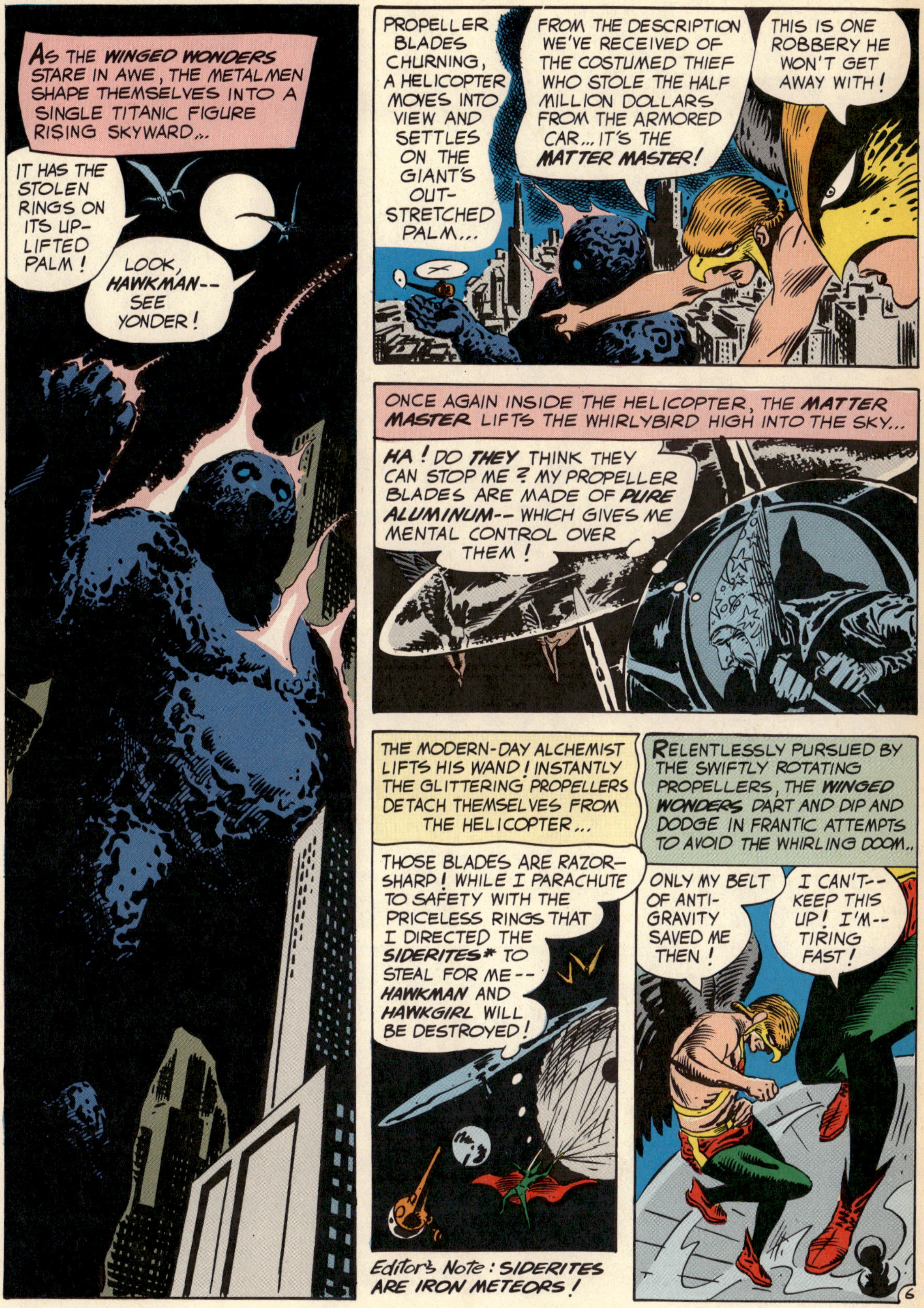
AS THE WINGED WONDERS STARE IN AWE, THE METALMEN SHAPE THEMSELVES INTO A SINGLE TITANIC FIGURE RISING SKYWARD...
IT HAS THE STOLEN RINGS ON ITS UP-LIFTED PALM!
LOOK, HAWKMAN-- SEE YONDER!
PROPELLER BLADES CHURNING, A HELICOPTER MOVES INTO VIEW AND SETTLES ON THE GIANT'S OUT-STRETCHED PALM...
FROM THE DESCRIPTION WE'VE RECEIVED OF THE COSTUMED THIEF WHO STOLE THE HALF MILLION DOLLARS FROM THE ARMORED CAR... IT'S THE MATTER MASTER!
THIS IS ONE ROBBERY HE WON'T GET AWAY WITH!
ONCE AGAIN INSIDE THE HELICOPTER, THE MATTER MASTER LIFTS THE WHIRLYBIRD HIGH INTO THE SKY...
HA! DO THEY THINK THEY CAN STOP ME? MY PROPELLER BLADES ARE MADE OF PURE ALUMINUM-- WHICH GIVES ME MENTAL CONTROL OVER THEM!
THE MODERN-DAY ALCHEMIST LIFTS HIS WAND! INSTANTLY THE GLITTERING PROPELLERS DETACH THEMSELVES FROM THE HELICOPTER...
THOSE BLADES ARE RAZOR-SHARP! WHILE I PARACHUTE TO SAFETY WITH THE PRICELESS RINGS THAT I DIRECTED THE SIDERITES* TO STEAL FOR ME-- HAWKMAN AND HAWKGIRL WILL BE DESTROYED!
Editor's Note: SIDERITES ARE IRON METEORS!
RELENTLESSLY PURSUED BY THE SWIFTLY ROTATING PROPELLERS, THE WINGED WONDERS DART AND DIP AND DODGE IN FRANTIC ATTEMPTS TO AVOID THE WHIRLING DOOM...
ONLY MY BELT OF ANTI-GRAVITY SAVED ME THEN!
I CAN'T-- KEEP THIS UP! I'M-- TIRING FAST!
6

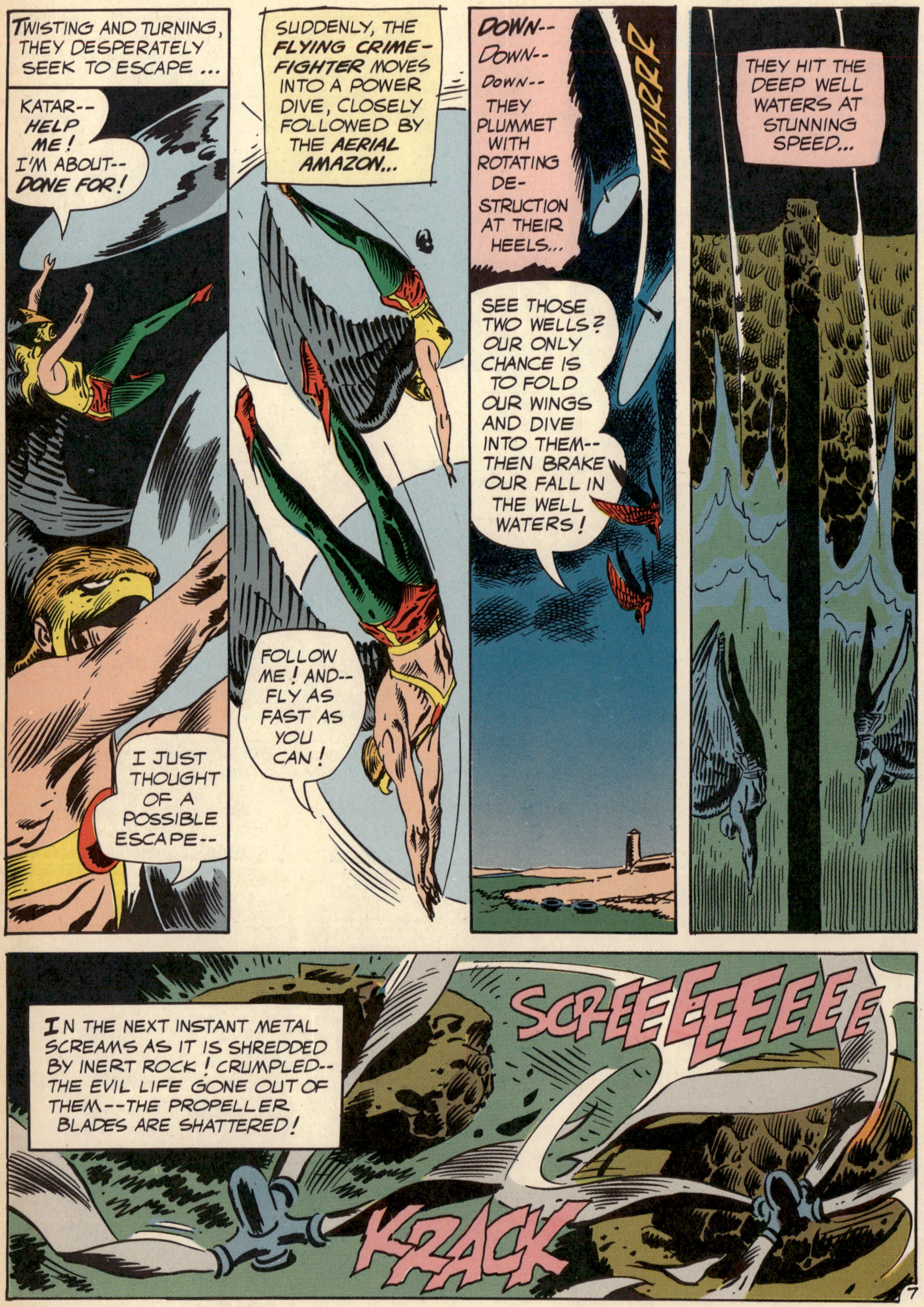
TWISTING AND TURNING, THEY DESPERATELY SEEK TO ESCAPE ...
KATAR-- HELP ME! I'M ABOUT-- DONE FOR!
I JUST THOUGHT OF A POSSIBLE ESCAPE--
SUDDENLY, THE FLYING CRIME-FIGHTER MOVES INTO A POWER DIVE, CLOSELY FOLLOWED BY THE AERIAL AMAZON...
FOLLOW ME! AND-- FLY AS FAST AS YOU CAN!
DOWN-- DOWN-- DOWN-- THEY PLUMMET WITH ROTATING DE-STRUCTION AT THEIR HEELS...
WHIRRR
SEE THOSE TWO WELLS? OUR ONLY CHANCE IS TO FOLD OUR WINGS AND DIVE INTO THEM-- THEN BRAKE OUR FALL IN THE WELL WATERS!
THEY HIT THE DEEP WELL WATERS AT STUNNING SPEED...
IN THE NEXT INSTANT METAL SCREAMS AS IT IS SHREDDED BY INERT ROCK! CRUMPLED-- THE EVIL LIFE GONE OUT OF THEM--THE PROPELLER BLADES ARE SHATTERED!
SCREEEEEEEE
KRACK
7

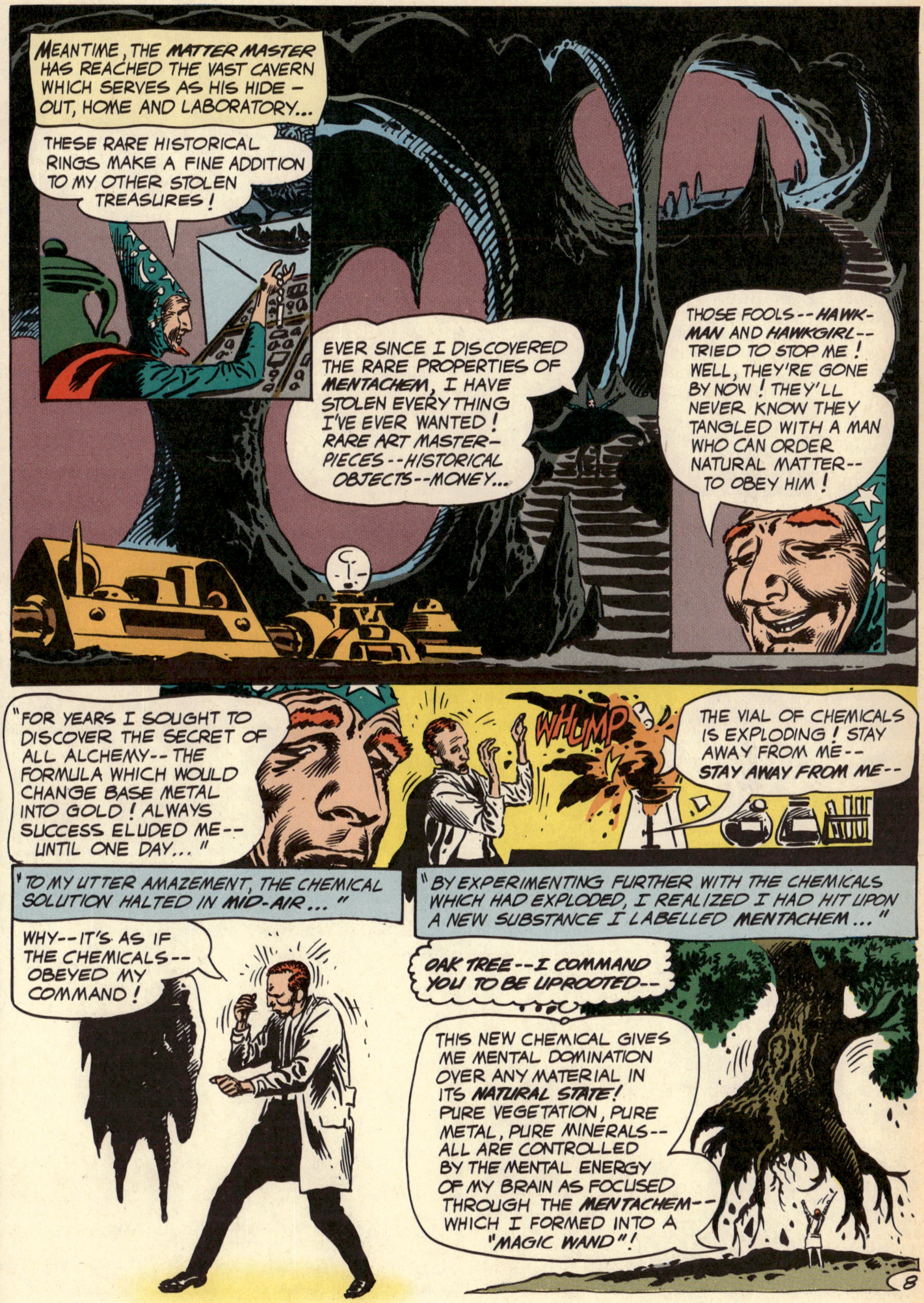
MEANTIME, THE MATTER MASTER HAS REACHED THE VAST CAVERN WHICH SERVES AS HIS HIDE-OUT, HOME AND LABORATORY...
THESE RARE HISTORICAL RINGS MAKE A FINE ADDITION TO MY OTHER STOLEN TREASURES!
EVER SINCE I DISCOVERED THE RARE PROPERTIES OF MENTACHEM, I HAVE STOLEN EVERYTHING I'VE EVER WANTED! RARE ART MASTER-PIECES--HISTORICAL OBJECTS--MONEY...
THOSE FOOLS--HAWK-MAN AND HAWKGIRL--TRIED TO STOP ME! WELL, THEY'RE GONE BY NOW! THEY'LL NEVER KNOW THEY TANGLED WITH A MAN WHO CAN ORDER NATURAL MATTER--TO OBEY HIM!
"FOR YEARS I SOUGHT TO DISCOVER THE SECRET OF ALL ALCHEMY--THE FORMULA WHICH WOULD CHANGE BASE METAL INTO GOLD! ALWAYS SUCCESS ELUDED ME--UNTIL ONE DAY..."
WHUMP
THE VIAL OF CHEMICALS IS EXPLODING! STAY AWAY FROM ME--STAY AWAY FROM ME--
"TO MY UTTER AMAZEMENT, THE CHEMICAL SOLUTION HALTED IN MID-AIR..."
WHY--IT'S AS IF THE CHEMICALS--OBEYED MY COMMAND!
"BY EXPERIMENTING FURTHER WITH THE CHEMICALS WHICH HAD EXPLODED, I REALIZED I HAD HIT UPON A NEW SUBSTANCE I LABELLED MENTACHEM..."
OAK TREE--I COMMAND YOU TO BE UPROOTED--
THIS NEW CHEMICAL GIVES ME MENTAL DOMINATION OVER ANY MATERIAL IN ITS NATURAL STATE! PURE VEGETATION, PURE METAL, PURE MINERALS--ALL ARE CONTROLLED BY THE MENTAL ENERGY OF MY BRAIN AS FOCUSED THROUGH THE MENTACHEM--WHICH I FORMED INTO A "MAGIC WAND"!
8

OF COURSE, I COULD HAVE ORDERED THE JEWELS IN THE ART CENTER TO FLY TO ME--BUT THE "IMPURE" SETTINGS ARE OF HISTORICAL IMPORTANCE, SO I HAD TO DIRECT THE METEORS TO STEAL THEM!
DONNING STREET CLOTHES, HE VISITS A NEWSPAPER STAND IN MIDWAY CITY WHERE...
WHAT'S THIS? HAWKMAN AND HAWKGIRL ARE ALIVE? I'D COUNTED ON ADDING THE NEWSPAPER ACCOUNTS OF THEIR DEATH TO MY PUBLICITY SCRAPBOOK--BUT NO MATTER!
IF EVER THEY INTERFERE WITH MY THEFTS AGAIN--IN ANY MANNER WHATSOEVER--I'LL HAVE A FOOL-PROOF WAY OF ELIMINATING THEM!
NEXT DAY IN THE MIDWAY CITY MUSEUM, ARTIST-NATURALIST MAVIS TRENT THROWS HER ARMS AROUND HER BOSS...
OOOOOOH, CARTER--I JUST ADORE FRESH FLOWERS! YOU KNEW I WAS WORKING LATE LAST NIGHT--SO YOU SENT THEM TO ME! HOW THOUGHTFUL!
I DIDN'T SEND ANY FLOWERS--BUT WILL SHE BELIEVE ME IF I TELL HER SO?
CARTER HALL MAY NOT BE SURE WHAT TO DO, BUT HIS WIFE SHIERA HAS NO SUCH DOUBTS, SO A LITTLE LATER...
YOU MARCH RIGHT BACK AND TELL THAT MINX THAT IF YOU SEND FLOWERS TO ANYBODY, IT'LL BE ME!
NOW, NOW, DARLING--DON'T BE JEALOUS! I WONDER WHO DID SEND HER THE FLOWERS--
AS CARTER PREPARES TO CONFRONT MAVIS...
CARTER! THOSE LOVELY FLOWERS YOU SENT ME--HAVE DISAPPEARED!
I HAVE WORSE NEWS THAN THAT! A RARE EGYPTIAN PARCHMENT HAS VANISHED!
9

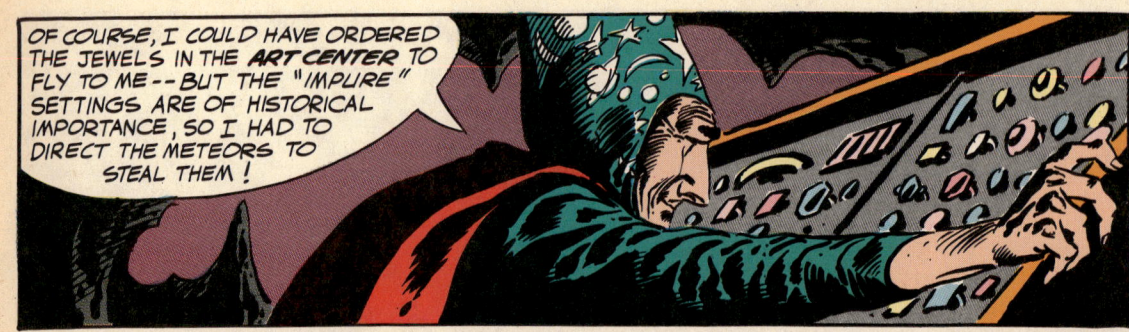

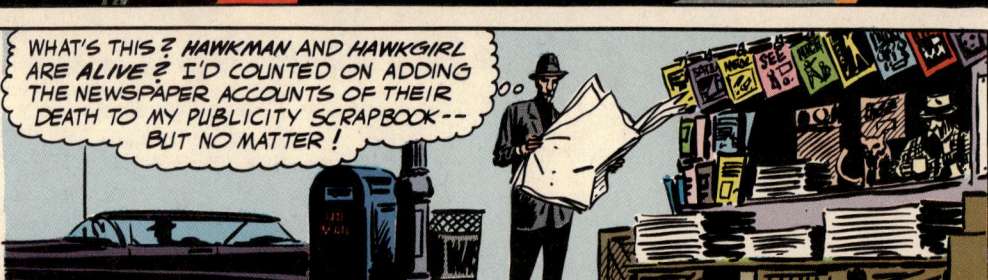

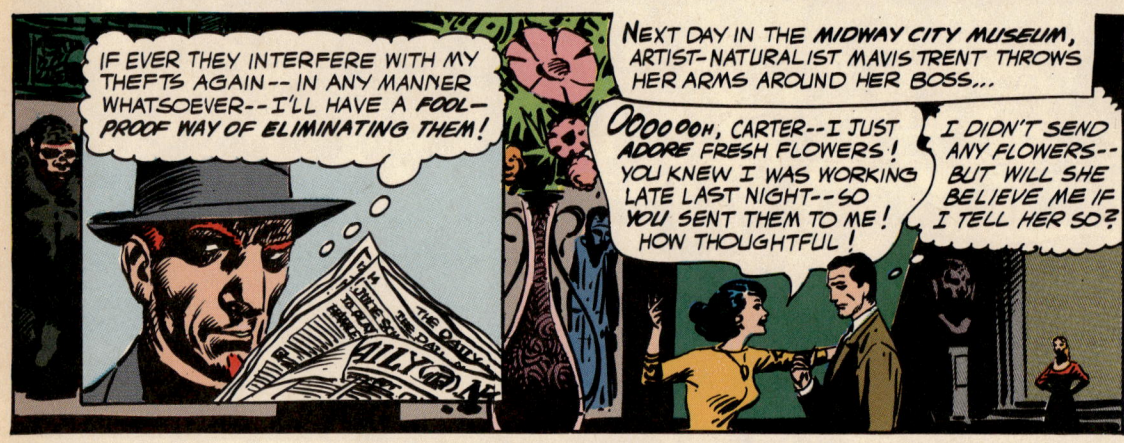

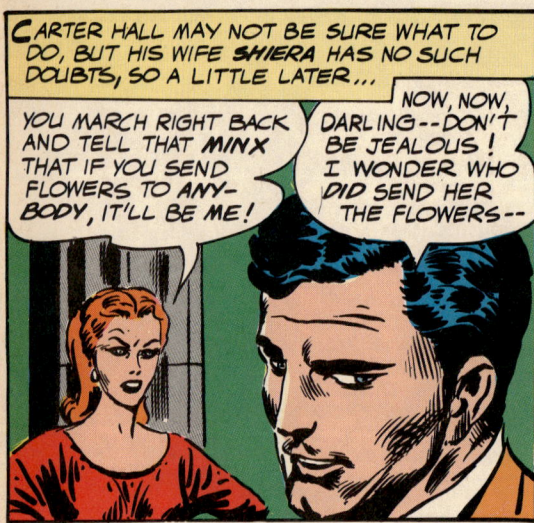

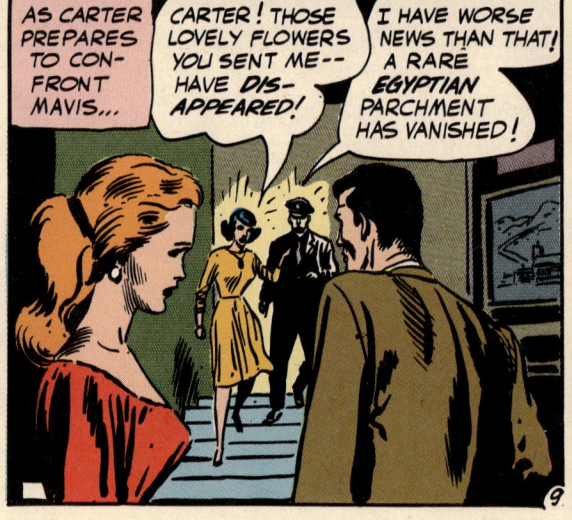

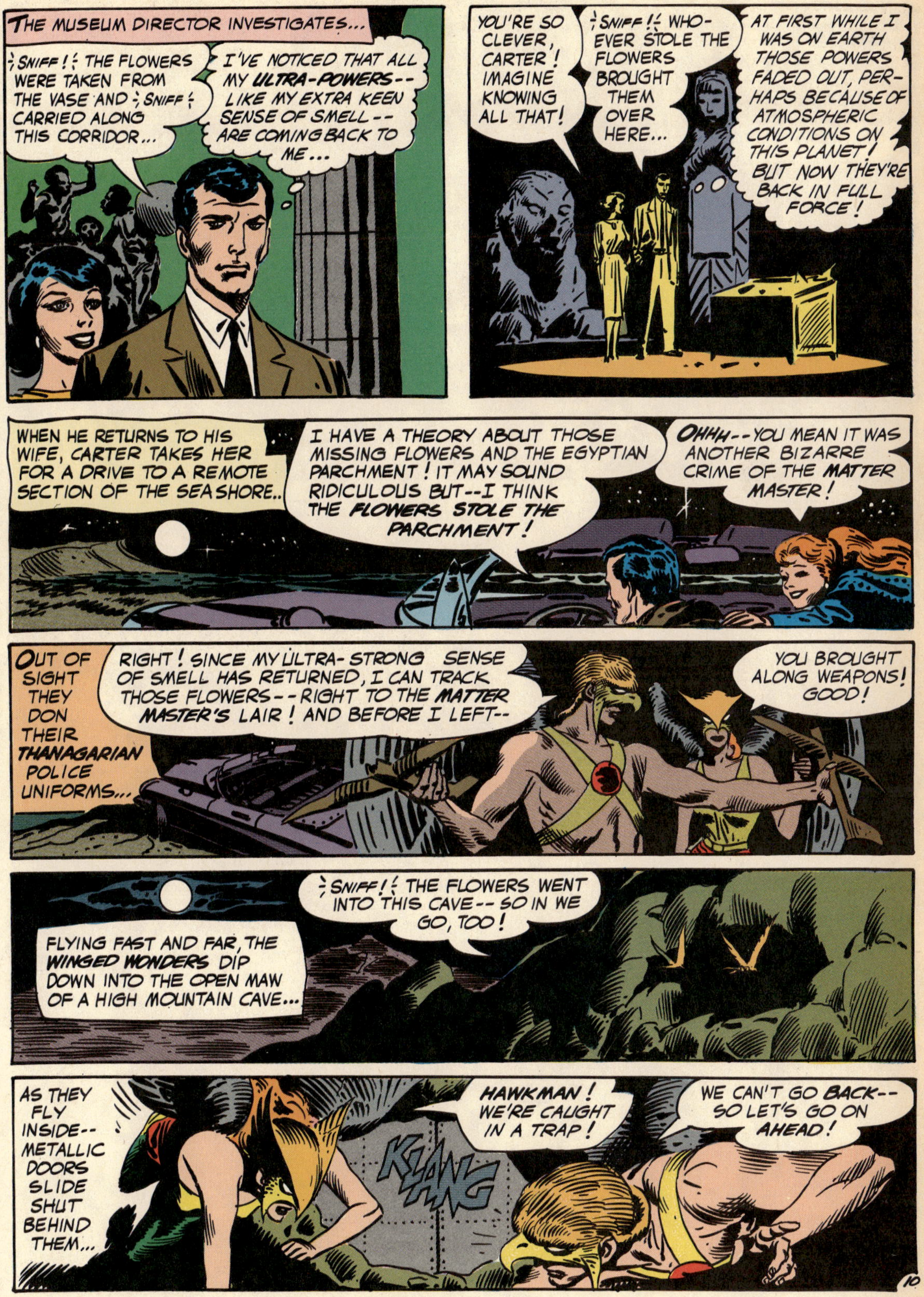
THE MUSEUM DIRECTOR INVESTIGATES...
-SNIFF!- THE FLOWERS WERE TAKEN FROM THE VASE AND -SNIFF- CARRIED ALONG THIS CORRIDOR...
I'VE NOTICED THAT ALL MY ULTRA-POWERS--LIKE MY EXTRA KEEN SENSE OF SMELL--ARE COMING BACK TO ME...
YOU'RE SO CLEVER, CARTER! IMAGINE KNOWING ALL THAT!
-SNIFF!- WHO-EVER STOLE THE FLOWERS BROUGHT THEM OVER HERE...
AT FIRST WHILE I WAS ON EARTH THOSE POWERS FADED OUT, PERHAPS BECAUSE OF ATMOSPHERIC CONDITIONS ON THIS PLANET! BUT NOW THEY'RE BACK IN FULL FORCE!
WHEN HE RETURNS TO HIS WIFE, CARTER TAKES HER FOR A DRIVE TO A REMOTE SECTION OF THE SEASHORE..
I HAVE A THEORY ABOUT THOSE MISSING FLOWERS AND THE EGYPTIAN PARCHMENT! IT MAY SOUND RIDICULOUS BUT--I THINK THE FLOWERS STOLE THE PARCHMENT!
OHHH--YOU MEAN IT WAS ANOTHER BIZARRE CRIME OF THE MATTER MASTER!
OUT OF SIGHT THEY DON THEIR THANAGARIAN POLICE UNIFORMS...
RIGHT! SINCE MY ULTRA-STRONG SENSE OF SMELL HAS RETURNED, I CAN TRACK THOSE FLOWERS--RIGHT TO THE MATTER MASTER'S LAIR! AND BEFORE I LEFT--
YOU BROUGHT ALONG WEAPONS! GOOD!
FLYING FAST AND FAR, THE WINGED WONDERS DIP DOWN INTO THE OPEN MAW OF A HIGH MOUNTAIN CAVE...
-SNIFF!- THE FLOWERS WENT INTO THIS CAVE--SO IN WE GO, TOO!
AS THEY FLY INSIDE--METALLIC DOORS SLIDE SHUT BEHIND THEM...
KLANG
HAWKMAN! WE'RE CAUGHT IN A TRAP!
WE CAN'T GO BACK--SO LET'S GO ON AHEAD!
10

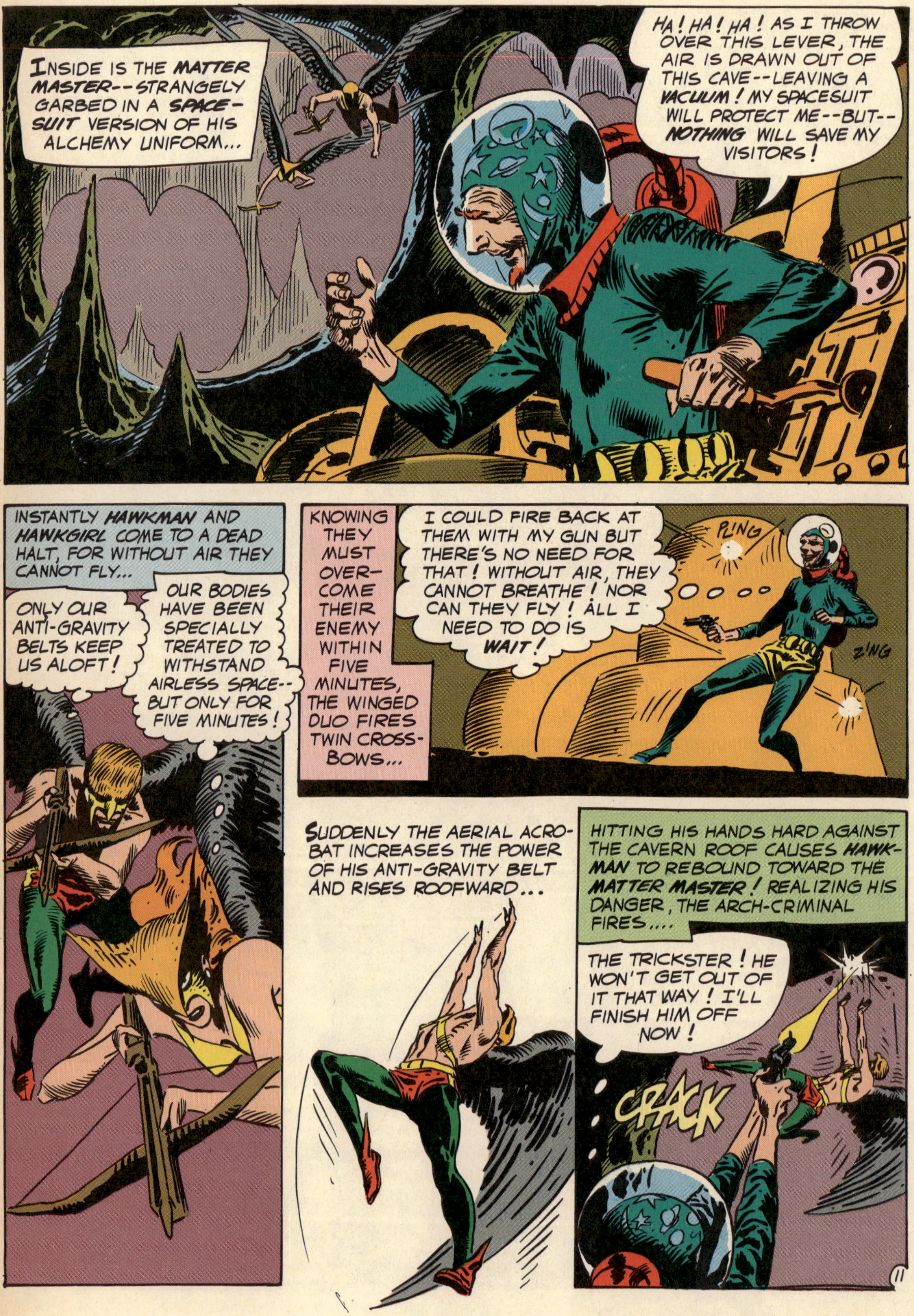
INSIDE IS THE MATTER MASTER--STRANGELY GARBED IN A SPACE-SUIT VERSION OF HIS ALCHEMY UNIFORM...
HA! HA! HA! AS I THROW OVER THIS LEVER, THE AIR IS DRAWN OUT OF THIS CAVE--LEAVING A VACUUM! MY SPACESUIT WILL PROTECT ME--BUT--NOTHING WILL SAVE MY VISITORS!
INSTANTLY HAWKMAN AND HAWKGIRL COME TO A DEAD HALT, FOR WITHOUT AIR THEY CANNOT FLY...
ONLY OUR ANTI-GRAVITY BELTS KEEP US ALOFT!
OUR BODIES HAVE BEEN SPECIALLY TREATED TO WITHSTAND AIRLESS SPACE--BUT ONLY FOR FIVE MINUTES!
KNOWING THEY MUST OVER-COME THEIR ENEMY WITHIN FIVE MINUTES, THE WINGED DUO FIRES TWIN CROSS-BOWS...
I COULD FIRE BACK AT THEM WITH MY GUN BUT THERE'S NO NEED FOR THAT! WITHOUT AIR, THEY CANNOT BREATHE! NOR CAN THEY FLY! ALL I NEED TO DO IS WAIT!
PLING
Z'ING
SUDDENLY THE AERIAL ACRO-BAT INCREASES THE POWER OF HIS ANTI-GRAVITY BELT AND RISES ROOFWARD...
HITTING HIS HANDS HARD AGAINST THE CAVERN ROOF CAUSES HAWK-MAN TO REBOUND TOWARD THE MATTER MASTER! REALIZING HIS DANGER, THE ARCH-CRIMINAL FIRES....
THE TRICKSTER! HE WON'T GET OUT OF IT THAT WAY! I'LL FINISH HIM OFF NOW!
CRACK
11

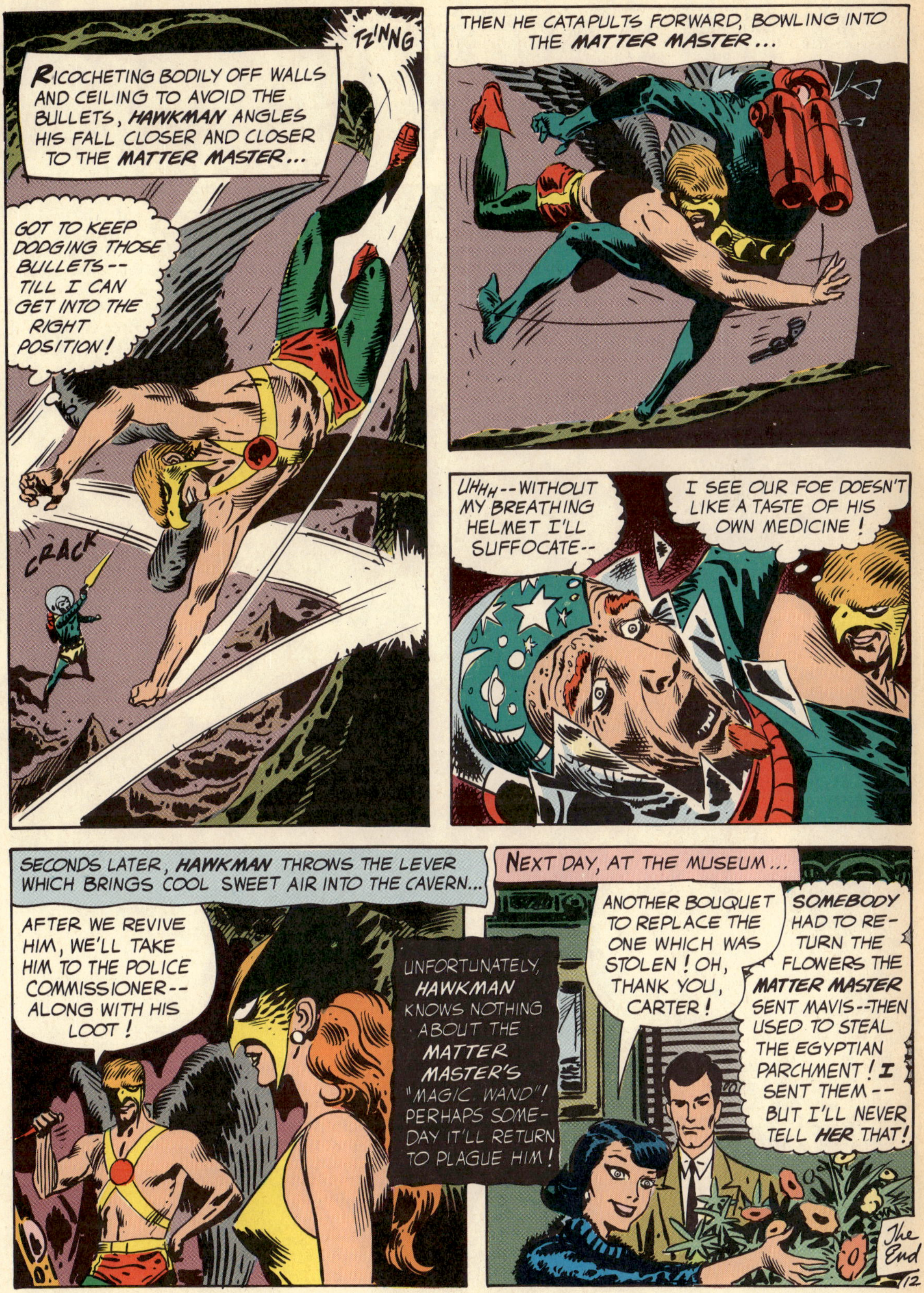

TZ'NNG
RICOCHETING BODILY OFF WALLS AND CEILING TO AVOID THE BULLETS, HAWKMAN ANGLES HIS FALL CLOSER AND CLOSER TO THE MATTER MASTER...
GOT TO KEEP DODGING THOSE BULLETS-- TILL I CAN GET INTO THE RIGHT POSITION!
CRACK
THEN HE CATAPULTS FORWARD, BOWLING INTO THE MATTER MASTER...
UHHH--WITHOUT MY BREATHING HELMET I'LL SUFFOCATE--
I SEE OUR FOE DOESN'T LIKE A TASTE OF HIS OWN MEDICINE!
SECONDS LATER, HAWKMAN THROWS THE LEVER WHICH BRINGS COOL SWEET AIR INTO THE CAVERN...
AFTER WE REVIVE HIM, WE'LL TAKE HIM TO THE POLICE COMMISSIONER-- ALONG WITH HIS LOOT!
UNFORTUNATELY, HAWKMAN KNOWS NOTHING ABOUT THE MATTER MASTER'S "MAGIC WAND"! PERHAPS SOME-DAY IT'LL RETURN TO PLAGUE HIM!
NEXT DAY, AT THE MUSEUM...
ANOTHER BOUQUET TO REPLACE THE ONE WHICH WAS STOLEN! OH, THANK YOU, CARTER!
SOMEBODY HAD TO RE-TURN THE FLOWERS THE MATTER MASTER SENT MAVIS--THEN USED TO STEAL THE EGYPTIAN PARCHMENT! I SENT THEM-- BUT I'LL NEVER TELL HER THAT!
The End
12

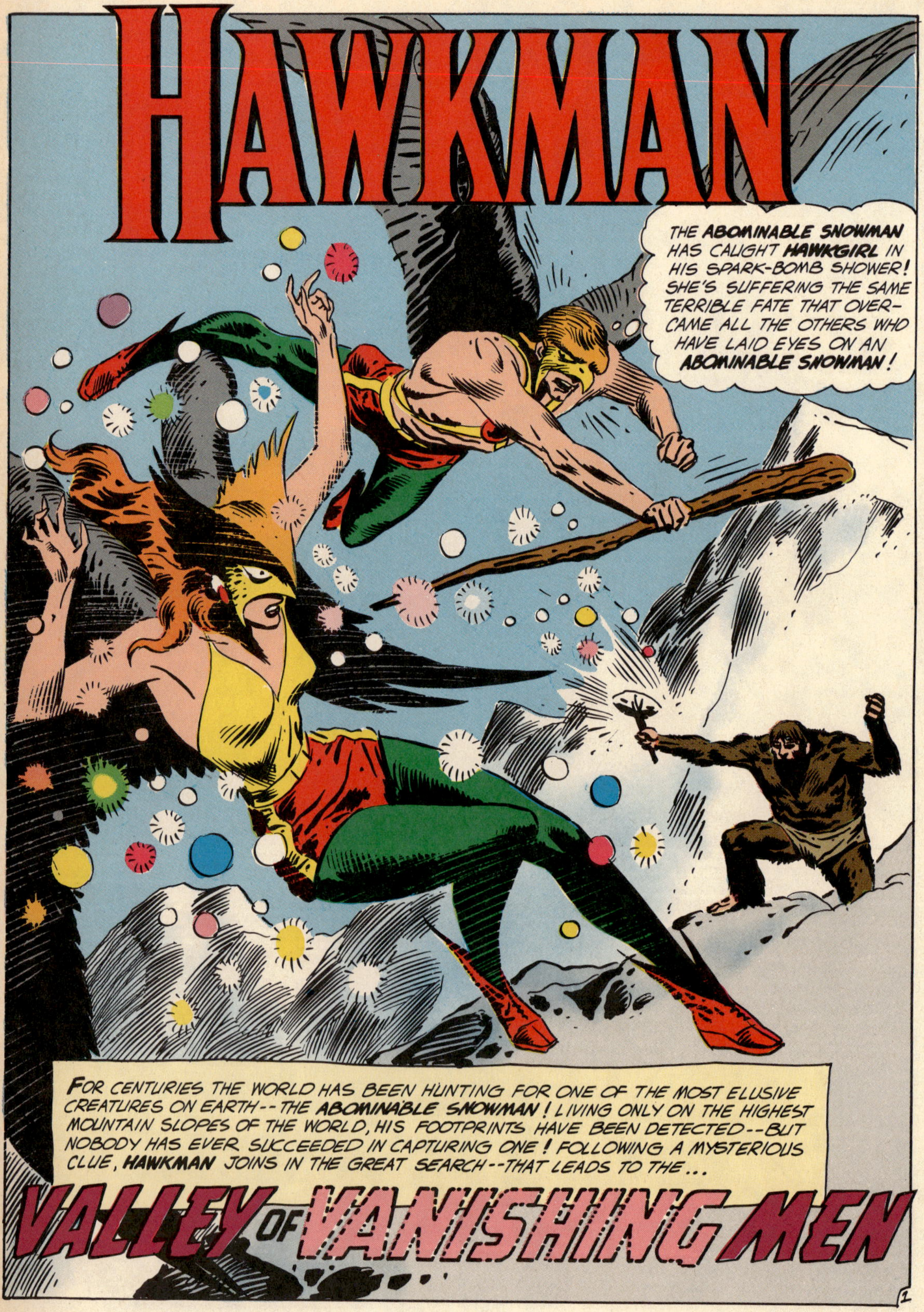
HAWKMAN
THE ABOMINABLE SNOWMAN HAS CAUGHT HAWKGIRL IN HIS SPARK-BOMB SHOWER! SHE'S SUFFERING THE SAME TERRIBLE FATE THAT OVER-CAME ALL THE OTHERS WHO HAVE LAID EYES ON AN ABOMINABLE SNOWMAN!
FOR CENTURIES THE WORLD HAS BEEN HUNTING FOR ONE OF THE MOST ELUSIVE CREATURES ON EARTH--THE ABOMINABLE SNOWMAN! LIVING ONLY ON THE HIGHEST MOUNTAIN SLOPES OF THE WORLD, HIS FOOTPRINTS HAVE BEEN DETECTED--BUT NOBODY HAS EVER SUCCEEDED IN CAPTURING ONE! FOLLOWING A MYSTERIOUS CLUE, HAWKMAN JOINS IN THE GREAT SEARCH--THAT LEADS TO THE...
VALLEY OF VANISHING MEN
1

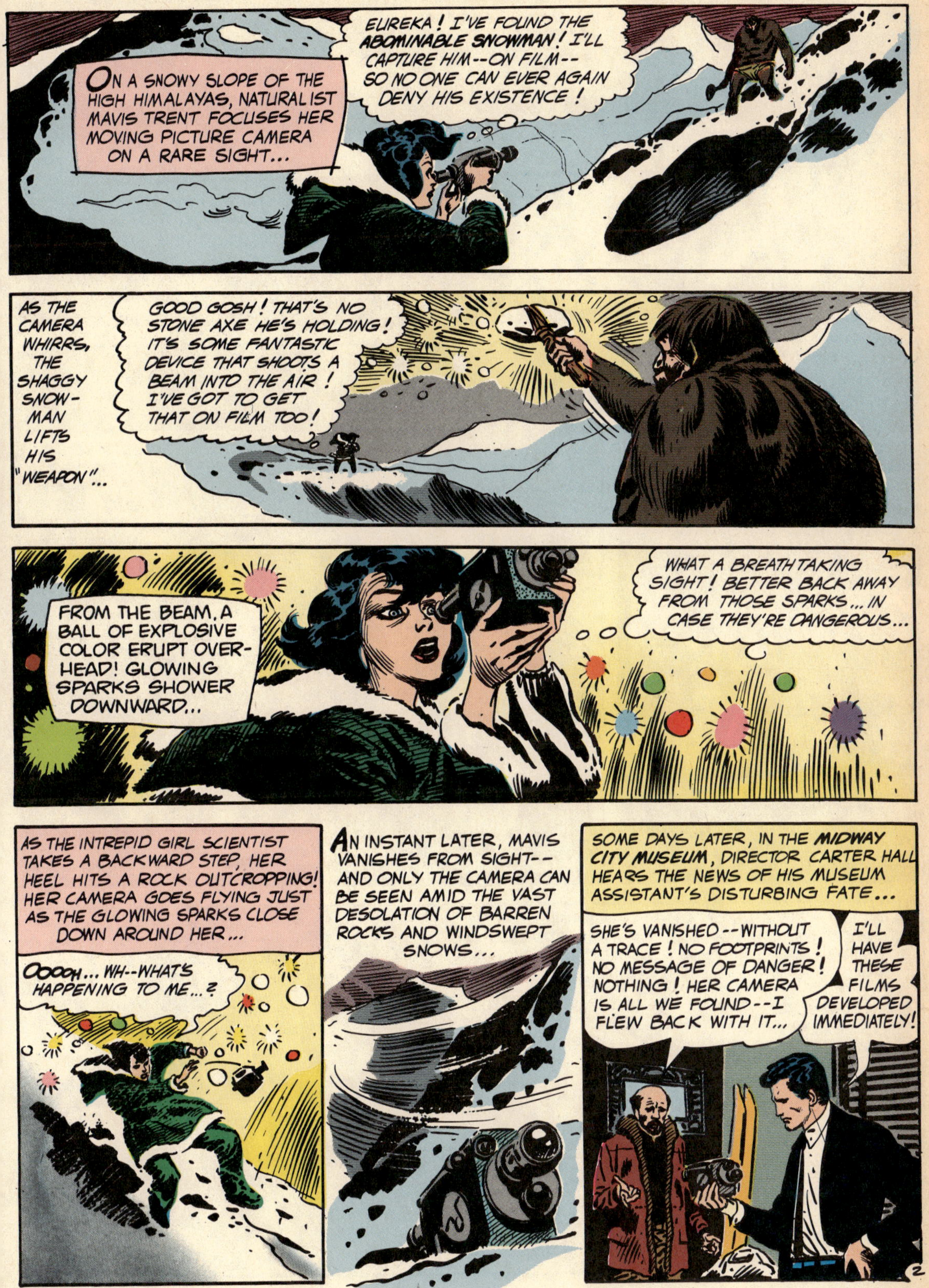
ON A SNOWY SLOPE OF THE HIGH HIMALAYAS, NATURALIST MAVIS TRENT FOCUSES HER MOVING PICTURE CAMERA ON A RARE SIGHT...
EUREKA! I'VE FOUND THE ABOMINABLE SNOWMAN! I'LL CAPTURE HIM--ON FILM--SO NO ONE CAN EVER AGAIN DENY HIS EXISTENCE!
AS THE CAMERA WHIRRS, THE SHAGGY SNOW-MAN LIFTS HIS "WEAPON"...
GOOD GOSH! THAT'S NO STONE AXE HE'S HOLDING! IT'S SOME FANTASTIC DEVICE THAT SHOOTS A BEAM INTO THE AIR! I'VE GOT TO GET THAT ON FILM TOO!
FROM THE BEAM, A BALL OF EXPLOSIVE COLOR ERUPT OVER-HEAD! GLOWING SPARKS SHOWER DOWNWARD...
WHAT A BREATHTAKING SIGHT! BETTER BACK AWAY FROM THOSE SPARKS... IN CASE THEY'RE DANGEROUS...
AS THE INTREPID GIRL SCIENTIST TAKES A BACKWARD STEP, HER HEEL HITS A ROCK OUTCROPPING! HER CAMERA GOES FLYING JUST AS THE GLOWING SPARKS CLOSE DOWN AROUND HER...
OOOOH... WH--WHAT'S HAPPENING TO ME...?
AN INSTANT LATER, MAVIS VANISHES FROM SIGHT--AND ONLY THE CAMERA CAN BE SEEN AMID THE VAST DESOLATION OF BARREN ROCKS AND WINDSWEPT SNOWS...
SOME DAYS LATER, IN THE MIDWAY CITY MUSEUM, DIRECTOR CARTER HALL HEARS THE NEWS OF HIS MUSEUM ASSISTANT'S DISTURBING FATE...
SHE'S VANISHED--WITHOUT A TRACE! NO FOOTPRINTS! NO MESSAGE OF DANGER! NOTHING! HER CAMERA IS ALL WE FOUND--I FLEW BACK WITH IT...
I'LL HAVE THESE FILMS DEVELOPED IMMEDIATELY!
2

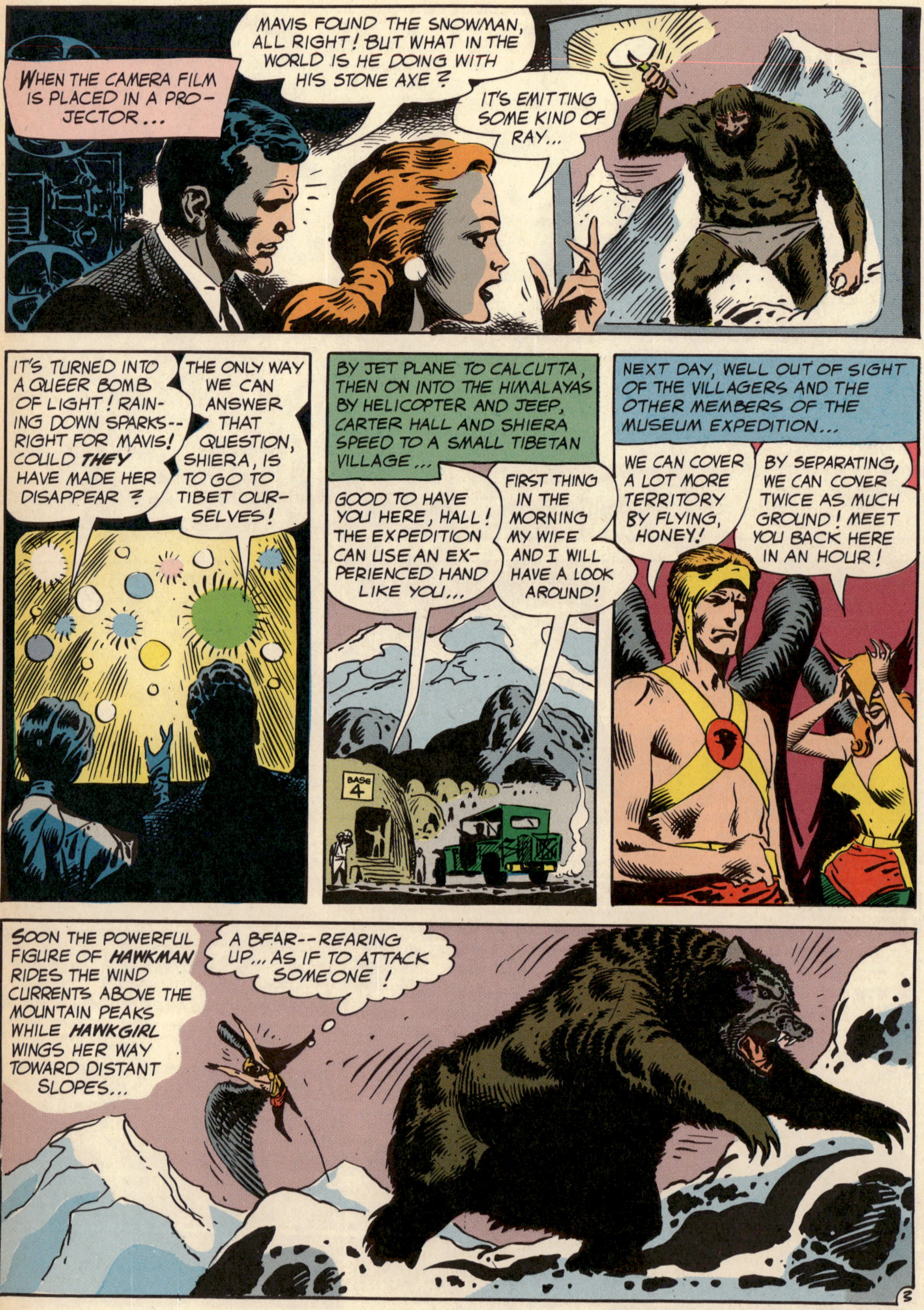
WHEN THE CAMERA FILM IS PLACED IN A PROJECTOR...
MAVIS FOUND THE SNOWMAN, ALL RIGHT! BUT WHAT IN THE WORLD IS HE DOING WITH HIS STONE AXE?
IT'S EMITTING SOME KIND OF RAY...
IT'S TURNED INTO A QUEER BOMB OF LIGHT! RAINING DOWN SPARKS-- RIGHT FOR MAVIS! COULD THEY HAVE MADE HER DISAPPEAR?
THE ONLY WAY WE CAN ANSWER THAT QUESTION, SHIERA, IS TO GO TO TIBET OURSELVES!
BY JET PLANE TO CALCUTTA, THEN ON INTO THE HIMALAYAS BY HELICOPTER AND JEEP, CARTER HALL AND SHIERA SPEED TO A SMALL TIBETAN VILLAGE...
GOOD TO HAVE YOU HERE, HALL! THE EXPEDITION CAN USE AN EXPERIENCED HAND LIKE YOU...
FIRST THING IN THE MORNING MY WIFE AND I WILL HAVE A LOOK AROUND!
BASE 4
NEXT DAY, WELL OUT OF SIGHT OF THE VILLAGERS AND THE OTHER MEMBERS OF THE MUSEUM EXPEDITION...
WE CAN COVER A LOT MORE TERRITORY BY FLYING, HONEY!
BY SEPARATING, WE CAN COVER TWICE AS MUCH GROUND! MEET YOU BACK HERE IN AN HOUR!
SOON THE POWERFUL FIGURE OF HAWKMAN RIDES THE WIND CURRENTS ABOVE THE MOUNTAIN PEAKS WHILE HAWKGIRL WINGS HER WAY TOWARD DISTANT SLOPES...
A BEAR--REARING UP... AS IF TO ATTACK SOMEONE!
3

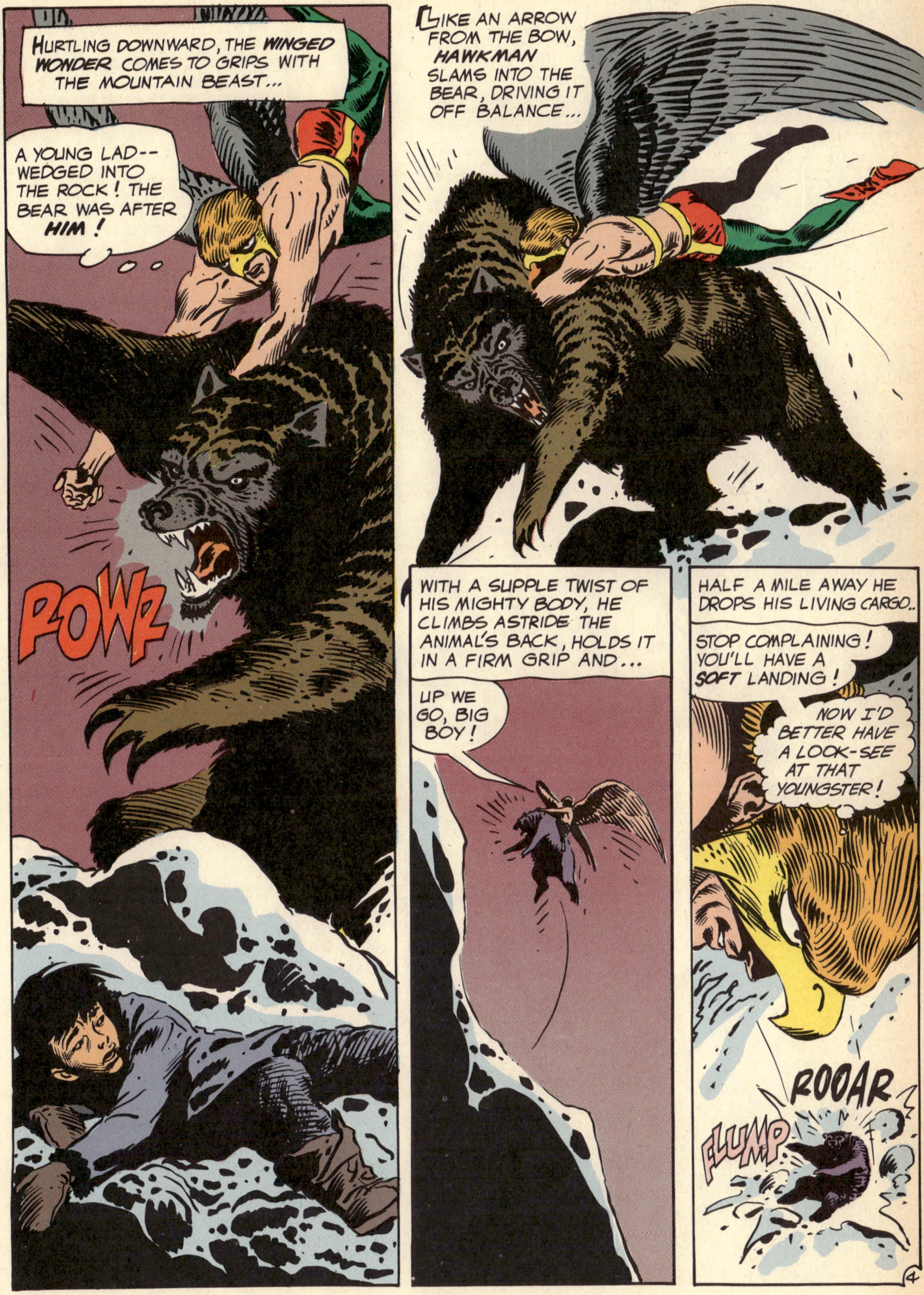
HURTLING DOWNWARD, THE WINGED WONDER COMES TO GRIPS WITH THE MOUNTAIN BEAST...
A YOUNG LAD-- WEDGED INTO THE ROCK! THE BEAR WAS AFTER HIM!
POWR
LIKE AN ARROW FROM THE BOW, HAWKMAN SLAMS INTO THE BEAR, DRIVING IT OFF BALANCE...
WITH A SUPPLE TWIST OF HIS MIGHTY BODY, HE CLIMBS ASTRIDE THE ANIMAL'S BACK, HOLDS IT IN A FIRM GRIP AND...
UP WE GO, BIG BOY!
HALF A MILE AWAY HE DROPS HIS LIVING CARGO..
STOP COMPLAINING! YOU'LL HAVE A SOFT LANDING!
NOW I'D BETTER HAVE A LOOK-SEE AT THAT YOUNGSTER!
ROOAR
FLUMP
4

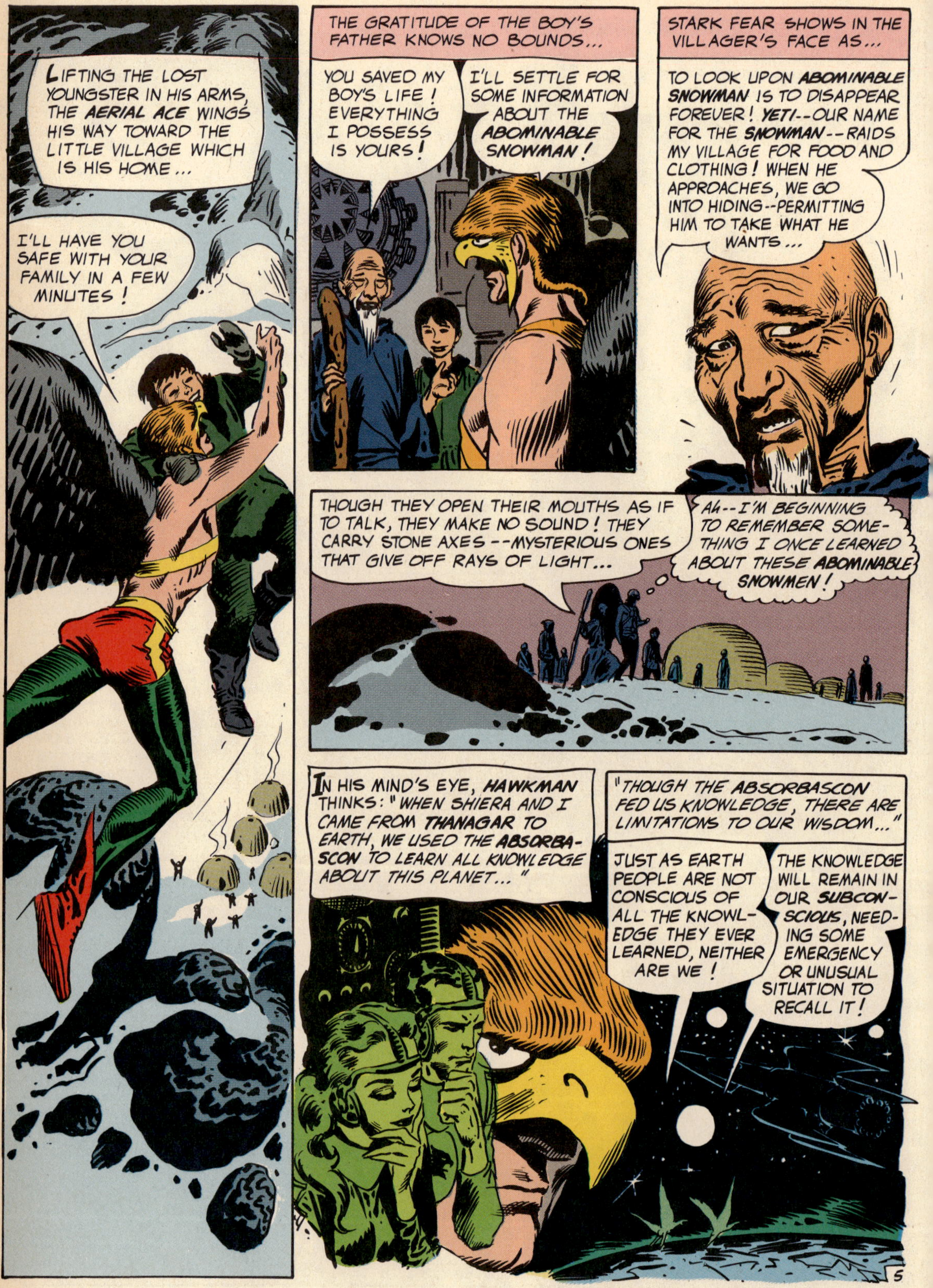
LIFTING THE LOST YOUNGSTER IN HIS ARMS, THE AERIAL ACE WINGS HIS WAY TOWARD THE LITTLE VILLAGE WHICH IS HIS HOME...
I'LL HAVE YOU SAFE WITH YOUR FAMILY IN A FEW MINUTES!
THE GRATITUDE OF THE BOY'S FATHER KNOWS NO BOUNDS...
YOU SAVED MY BOY'S LIFE! EVERYTHING I POSSESS IS YOURS!
I'LL SETTLE FOR SOME INFORMATION ABOUT THE ABOMINABLE SNOWMAN!
STARK FEAR SHOWS IN THE VILLAGER'S FACE AS...
TO LOOK UPON ABOMINABLE SNOWMAN IS TO DISAPPEAR FOREVER! YETI--OUR NAME FOR THE SNOWMAN--RAIDS MY VILLAGE FOR FOOD AND CLOTHING! WHEN HE APPROACHES, WE GO INTO HIDING--PERMITTING HIM TO TAKE WHAT HE WANTS...
THOUGH THEY OPEN THEIR MOUTHS AS IF TO TALK, THEY MAKE NO SOUND! THEY CARRY STONE AXES--MYSTERIOUS ONES THAT GIVE OFF RAYS OF LIGHT...
AH--I'M BEGINNING TO REMEMBER SOMETHING I ONCE LEARNED ABOUT THESE ABOMINABLE SNOWMEN!
IN HIS MIND'S EYE, HAWKMAN THINKS: "WHEN SHIERA AND I CAME FROM THANAGAR TO EARTH, WE USED THE ABSORBASCON TO LEARN ALL KNOWLEDGE ABOUT THIS PLANET..."
"THOUGH THE ABSORBASCON FED US KNOWLEDGE, THERE ARE LIMITATIONS TO OUR WISDOM..."
JUST AS EARTH PEOPLE ARE NOT CONSCIOUS OF ALL THE KNOWLEDGE THEY EVER LEARNED, NEITHER ARE WE!
THE KNOWLEDGE WILL REMAIN IN OUR SUBCONSCIOUS, NEEDING SOME EMERGENCY OR UNUSUAL SITUATION TO RECALL IT!
5

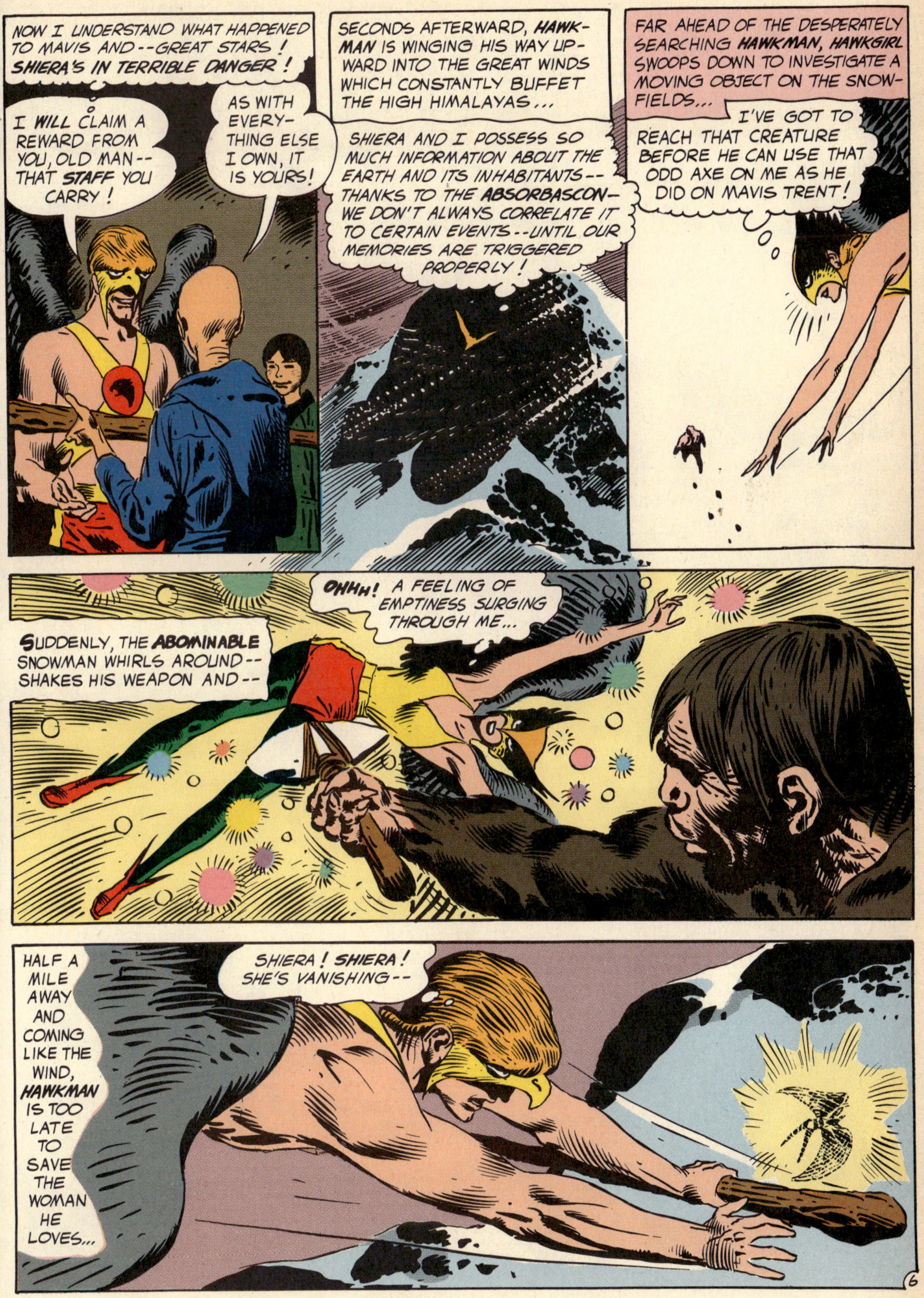
NOW I UNDERSTAND WHAT HAPPENED TO MAVIS AND--GREAT STARS! SHIERA'S IN TERRIBLE DANGER!
I WILL CLAIM A REWARD FROM YOU, OLD MAN--THAT STAFF YOU CARRY!
AS WITH EVERYTHING ELSE I OWN, IT IS YOURS!
SECONDS AFTERWARD, HAWKMAN IS WINGING HIS WAY UPWARD INTO THE GREAT WINDS WHICH CONSTANTLY BUFFET THE HIGH HIMALAYAS...
SHIERA AND I POSSESS SO MUCH INFORMATION ABOUT THE EARTH AND ITS INHABITANTS--THANKS TO THE ABSORBASCON--WE DON'T ALWAYS CORRELATE IT TO CERTAIN EVENTS--UNTIL OUR MEMORIES ARE TRIGGERED PROPERLY!
FAR AHEAD OF THE DESPERATELY SEARCHING HAWKMAN, HAWKGIRL SWOOPS DOWN TO INVESTIGATE A MOVING OBJECT ON THE SNOW-FIELDS...
I'VE GOT TO REACH THAT CREATURE BEFORE HE CAN USE THAT ODD AXE ON ME AS HE DID ON MAVIS TRENT!
SUDDENLY, THE ABOMINABLE SNOWMAN WHIRLS AROUND--SHAKES HIS WEAPON AND--
OHHH! A FEELING OF EMPTINESS SURGING THROUGH ME...
HALF A MILE AWAY AND COMING LIKE THE WIND, HAWKMAN IS TOO LATE TO SAVE THE WOMAN HE LOVES...
SHIERA! SHIERA! SHE'S VANISHING--
6

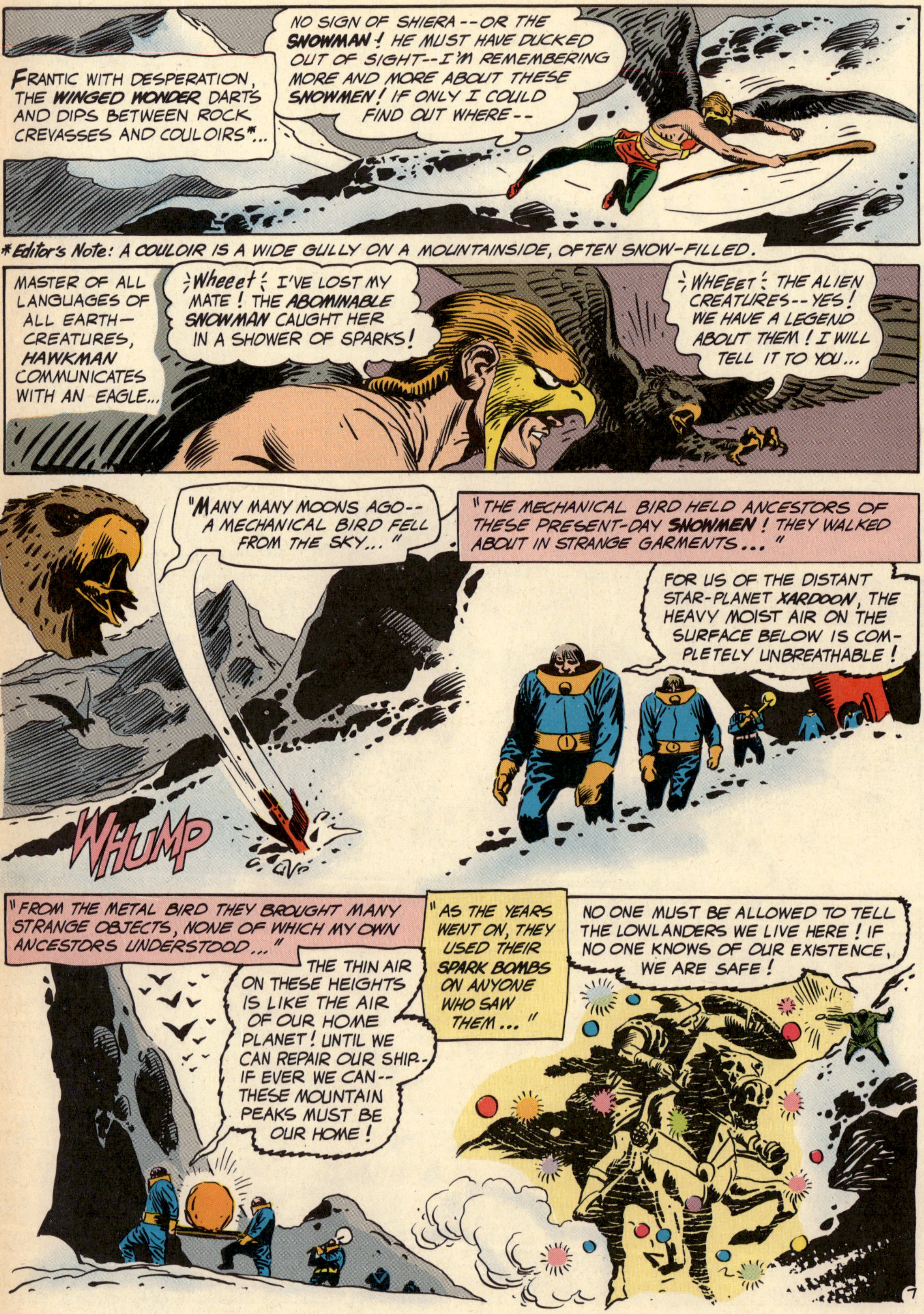
FRANTIC WITH DESPERATION, THE WINGED WONDER DARTS AND DIPS BETWEEN ROCK CREVASSES AND COULOIRS*...
NO SIGN OF SHIERA -- OR THE SNOWMAN! HE MUST HAVE DUCKED OUT OF SIGHT--I'M REMEMBERING MORE AND MORE ABOUT THESE SNOWMEN! IF ONLY I COULD FIND OUT WHERE --
*Editor's Note: A COULOIR IS A WIDE GULLY ON A MOUNTAINSIDE, OFTEN SNOW-FILLED.
MASTER OF ALL LANGUAGES OF ALL EARTH-CREATURES, HAWKMAN COMMUNICATES WITH AN EAGLE...
Wheeet I'VE LOST MY MATE! THE ABOMINABLE SNOWMAN CAUGHT HER IN A SHOWER OF SPARKS!
WHEEET THE ALIEN CREATURES--YES! WE HAVE A LEGEND ABOUT THEM! I WILL TELL IT TO YOU...
"MANY MANY MOONS AGO-- A MECHANICAL BIRD FELL FROM THE SKY..."
"THE MECHANICAL BIRD HELD ANCESTORS OF THESE PRESENT-DAY SNOWMEN! THEY WALKED ABOUT IN STRANGE GARMENTS..."
FOR US OF THE DISTANT STAR-PLANET XARDOON, THE HEAVY MOIST AIR ON THE SURFACE BELOW IS COMPLETELY UNBREATHABLE!
WHUMP
"FROM THE METAL BIRD THEY BROUGHT MANY STRANGE OBJECTS, NONE OF WHICH MY OWN ANCESTORS UNDERSTOOD..."
THE THIN AIR ON THESE HEIGHTS IS LIKE THE AIR OF OUR HOME PLANET! UNTIL WE CAN REPAIR OUR SHIP-- IF EVER WE CAN-- THESE MOUNTAIN PEAKS MUST BE OUR HOME!
"AS THE YEARS WENT ON, THEY USED THEIR SPARK BOMBS ON ANYONE WHO SAW THEM..."
NO ONE MUST BE ALLOWED TO TELL THE LOWLANDERS WE LIVE HERE! IF NO ONE KNOWS OF OUR EXISTENCE, WE ARE SAFE!
7

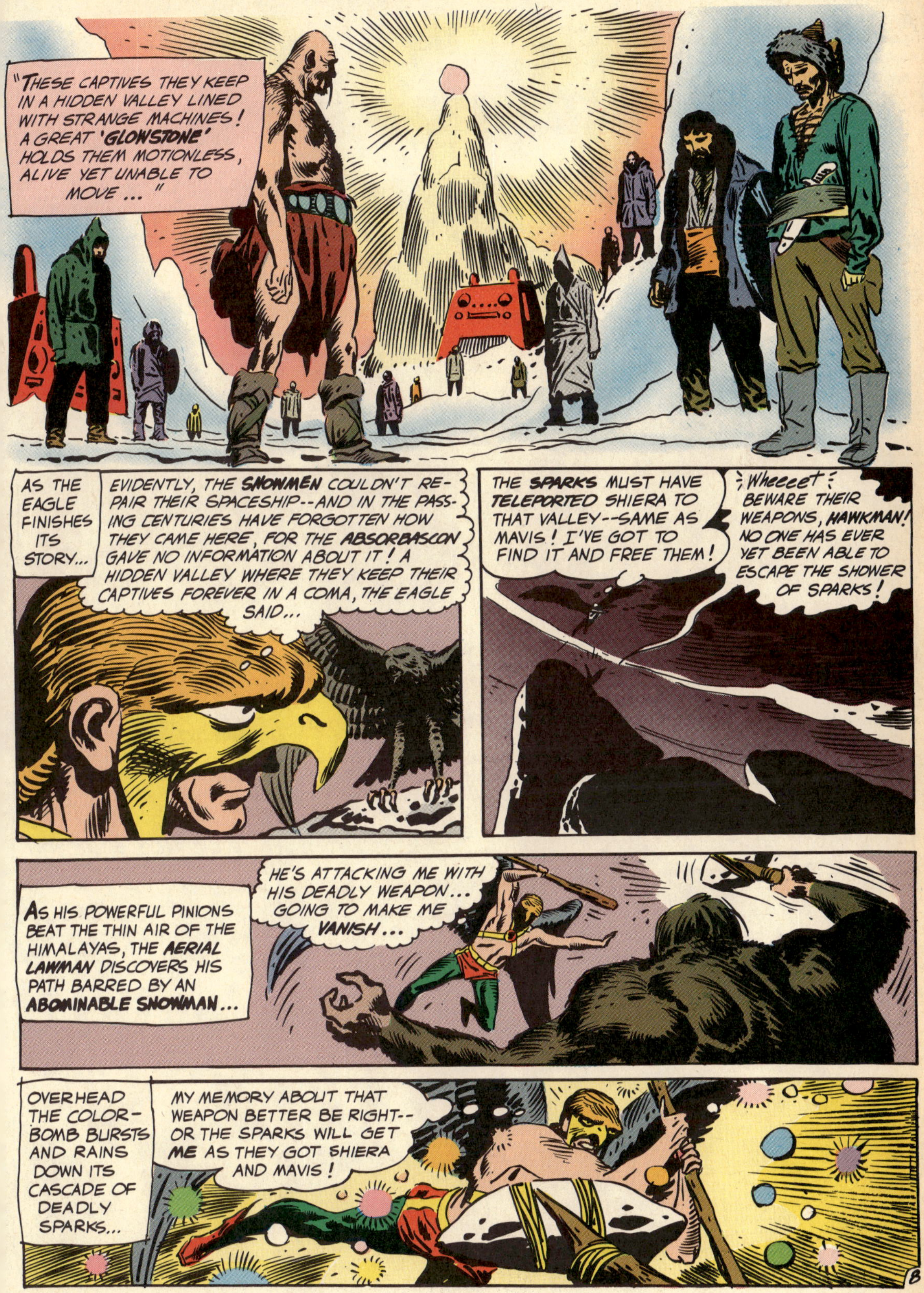
"THESE CAPTIVES THEY KEEP IN A HIDDEN VALLEY LINED WITH STRANGE MACHINES! A GREAT 'GLOWSTONE' HOLDS THEM MOTIONLESS, ALIVE YET UNABLE TO MOVE ..."
AS THE EAGLE FINISHES ITS STORY...
EVIDENTLY, THE SNOWMEN COULDN'T REPAIR THEIR SPACESHIP--AND IN THE PASSING CENTURIES HAVE FORGOTTEN HOW THEY CAME HERE, FOR THE ABSORBASCON GAVE NO INFORMATION ABOUT IT! A HIDDEN VALLEY WHERE THEY KEEP THEIR CAPTIVES FOREVER IN A COMA, THE EAGLE SAID...
THE SPARKS MUST HAVE TELEPORTED SHIERA TO THAT VALLEY--SAME AS MAVIS! I'VE GOT TO FIND IT AND FREE THEM!
Wheeeet! BEWARE THEIR WEAPONS, HAWKMAN! NO ONE HAS EVER YET BEEN ABLE TO ESCAPE THE SHOWER OF SPARKS!
AS HIS POWERFUL PINIONS BEAT THE THIN AIR OF THE HIMALAYAS, THE AERIAL LAWMAN DISCOVERS HIS PATH BARRED BY AN ABOMINABLE SNOWMAN...
HE'S ATTACKING ME WITH HIS DEADLY WEAPON... GOING TO MAKE ME VANISH...
OVERHEAD THE COLOR-BOMB BURSTS AND RAINS DOWN ITS CASCADE OF DEADLY SPARKS...
MY MEMORY ABOUT THAT WEAPON BETTER BE RIGHT--OR THE SPARKS WILL GET ME AS THEY GOT SHIERA AND MAVIS!
8

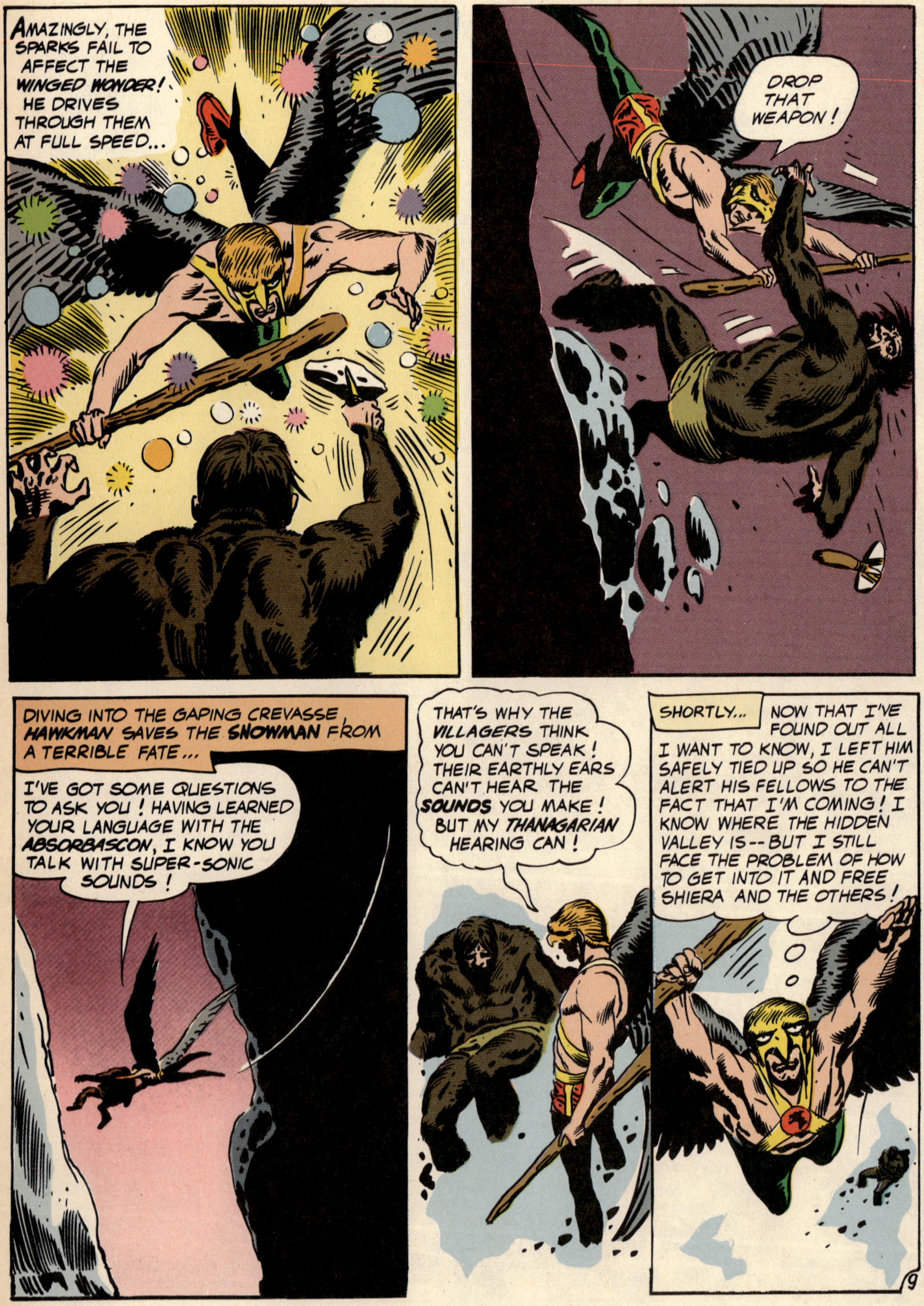
AMAZINGLY, THE SPARKS FAIL TO AFFECT THE WINGED WONDER! HE DRIVES THROUGH THEM AT FULL SPEED...
DROP THAT WEAPON!
DIVING INTO THE GAPING CREVASSE, HAWKMAN SAVES THE SNOWMAN FROM A TERRIBLE FATE...
I'VE GOT SOME QUESTIONS TO ASK YOU! HAVING LEARNED YOUR LANGUAGE WITH THE ABSORBASCON, I KNOW YOU TALK WITH SUPER-SONIC SOUNDS!
THAT'S WHY THE VILLAGERS THINK YOU CAN'T SPEAK! THEIR EARTHLY EARS CAN'T HEAR THE SOUNDS YOU MAKE! BUT MY THANAGARIAN HEARING CAN!
SHORTLY...
NOW THAT I'VE FOUND OUT ALL I WANT TO KNOW, I LEFT HIM SAFELY TIED UP SO HE CAN'T ALERT HIS FELLOWS TO THE FACT THAT I'M COMING! I KNOW WHERE THE HIDDEN VALLEY IS--BUT I STILL FACE THE PROBLEM OF HOW TO GET INTO IT AND FREE SHIERA AND THE OTHERS!
9

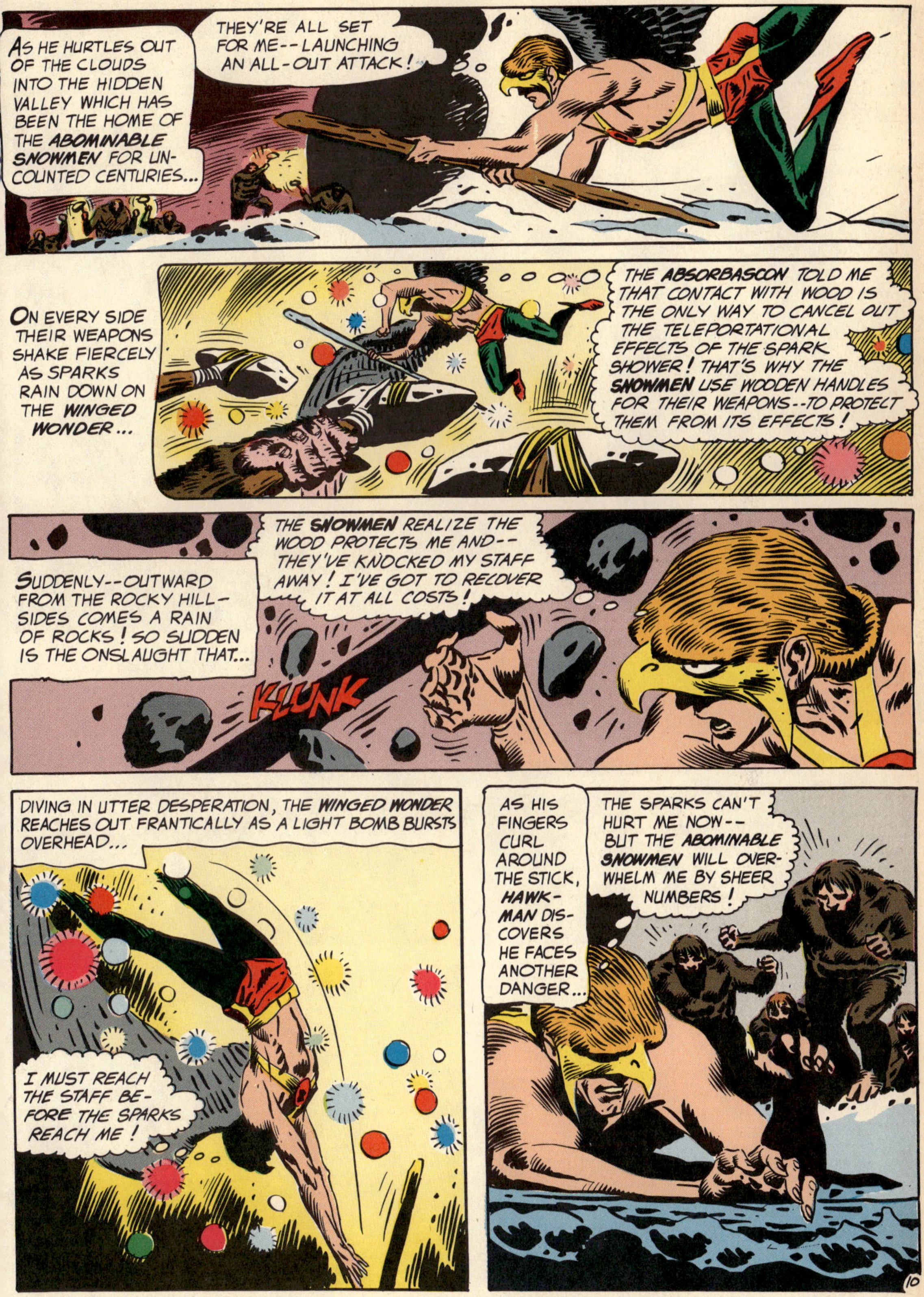
AS HE HURTLES OUT OF THE CLOUDS INTO THE HIDDEN VALLEY WHICH HAS BEEN THE HOME OF THE ABOMINABLE SNOWMEN FOR UN-COUNTED CENTURIES...
THEY'RE ALL SET FOR ME--LAUNCHING AN ALL-OUT ATTACK!
ON EVERY SIDE THEIR WEAPONS SHAKE FIERCELY AS SPARKS RAIN DOWN ON THE WINGED WONDER...
THE ABSORBASCON TOLD ME THAT CONTACT WITH WOOD IS THE ONLY WAY TO CANCEL OUT THE TELEPORTATIONAL EFFECTS OF THE SPARK SHOWER! THAT'S WHY THE SNOWMEN USE WOODEN HANDLES FOR THEIR WEAPONS--TO PROTECT THEM FROM ITS EFFECTS!
SUDDENLY--OUTWARD FROM THE ROCKY HILL-SIDES COMES A RAIN OF ROCKS! SO SUDDEN IS THE ONSLAUGHT THAT...
THE SNOWMEN REALIZE THE WOOD PROTECTS ME AND--THEY'VE KNOCKED MY STAFF AWAY! I'VE GOT TO RECOVER IT AT ALL COSTS!
KLUNK
DIVING IN UTTER DESPERATION, THE WINGED WONDER REACHES OUT FRANTICALLY AS A LIGHT BOMB BURSTS OVERHEAD...
I MUST REACH THE STAFF BE-FORE THE SPARKS REACH ME!
AS HIS FINGERS CURL AROUND THE STICK, HAWK-MAN DIS-COVERS HE FACES ANOTHER DANGER...
THE SPARKS CAN'T HURT ME NOW--BUT THE ABOMINABLE SNOWMEN WILL OVER-WHELM ME BY SHEER NUMBERS!
10

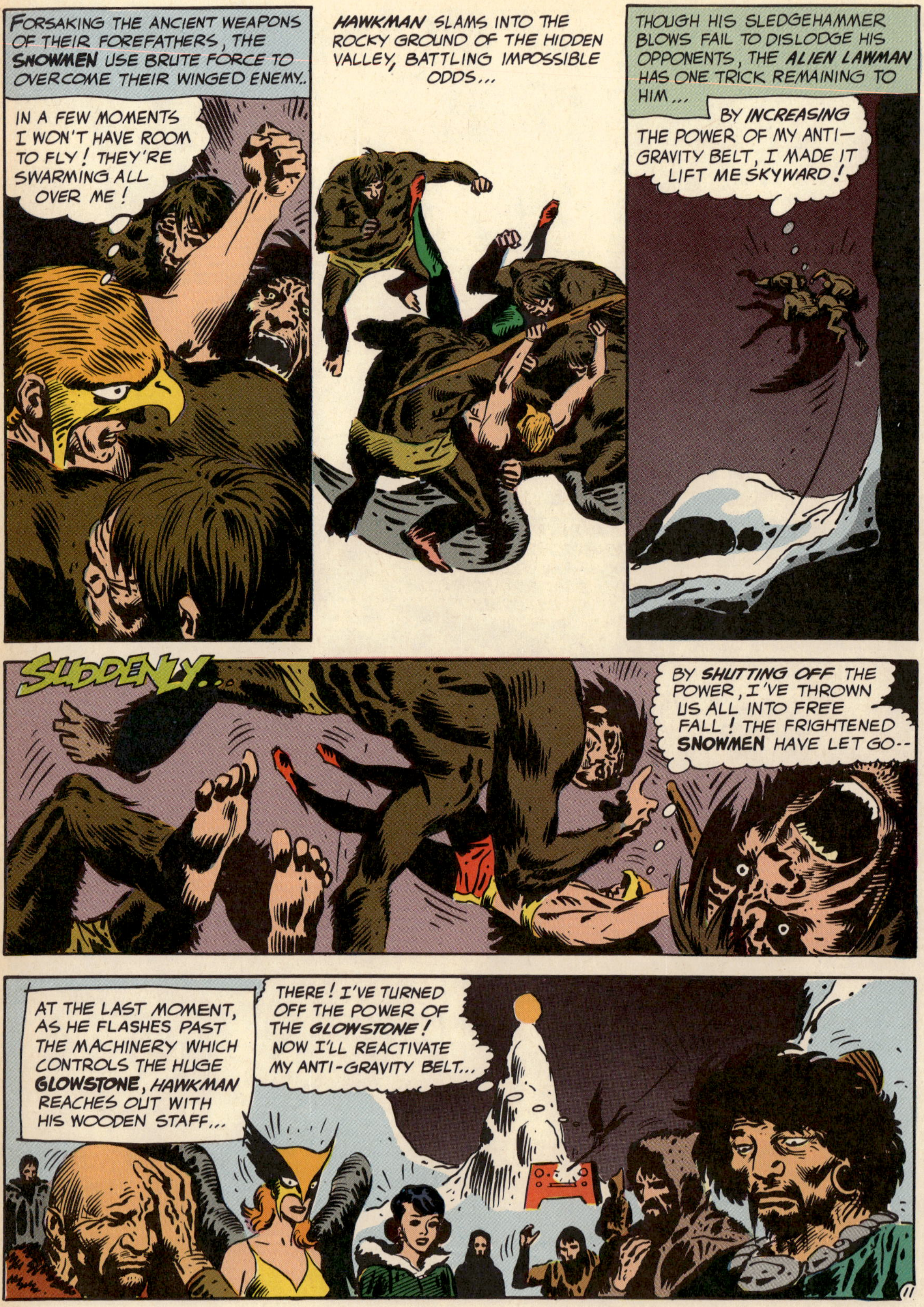
FORSAKING THE ANCIENT WEAPONS OF THEIR FOREFATHERS, THE SNOWMEN USE BRUTE FORCE TO OVERCOME THEIR WINGED ENEMY...
IN A FEW MOMENTS I WON'T HAVE ROOM TO FLY! THEY'RE SWARMING ALL OVER ME!
HAWKMAN SLAMS INTO THE ROCKY GROUND OF THE HIDDEN VALLEY, BATTLING IMPOSSIBLE ODDS...
THOUGH HIS SLEDGEHAMMER BLOWS FAIL TO DISLODGE HIS OPPONENTS, THE ALIEN LAWMAN HAS ONE TRICK REMAINING TO HIM...
BY INCREASING THE POWER OF MY ANTI-GRAVITY BELT, I MADE IT LIFT ME SKYWARD!
SUDDENLY...
BY SHUTTING OFF THE POWER, I'VE THROWN US ALL INTO FREE FALL! THE FRIGHTENED SNOWMEN HAVE LET GO--
AT THE LAST MOMENT, AS HE FLASHES PAST THE MACHINERY WHICH CONTROLS THE HUGE GLOWSTONE, HAWKMAN REACHES OUT WITH HIS WOODEN STAFF...
THERE! I'VE TURNED OFF THE POWER OF THE GLOWSTONE! NOW I'LL REACTIVATE MY ANTI-GRAVITY BELT...
11

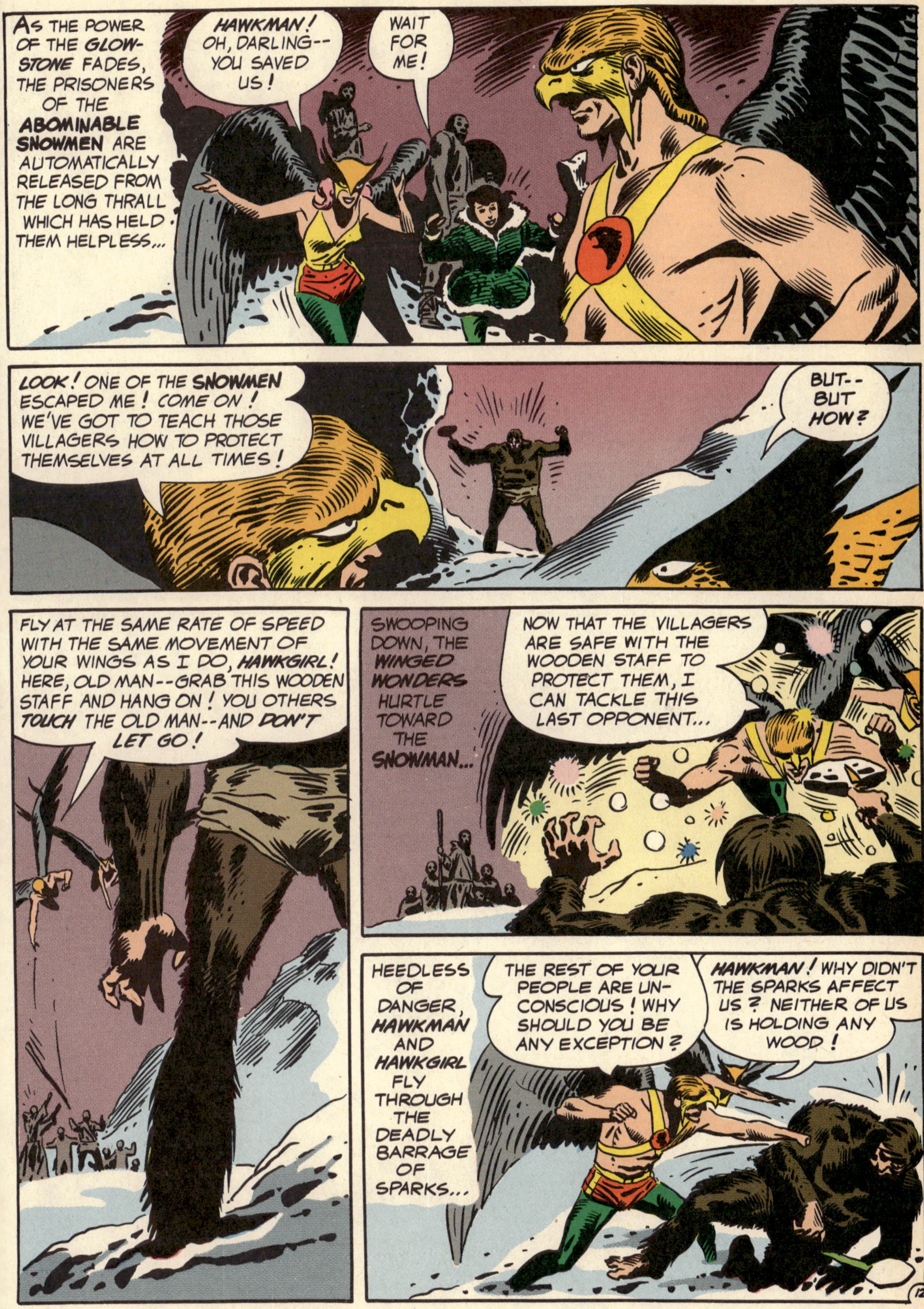
AS THE POWER OF THE GLOW-STONE FADES, THE PRISONERS OF THE ABOMINABLE SNOWMEN ARE AUTOMATICALLY RELEASED FROM THE LONG THRALL WHICH HAS HELD THEM HELPLESS...
HAWKMAN! OH, DARLING--YOU SAVED US!
WAIT FOR ME!
LOOK! ONE OF THE SNOWMEN ESCAPED ME! COME ON! WE'VE GOT TO TEACH THOSE VILLAGERS HOW TO PROTECT THEMSELVES AT ALL TIMES!
BUT--BUT HOW?
FLY AT THE SAME RATE OF SPEED WITH THE SAME MOVEMENT OF YOUR WINGS AS I DO, HAWKGIRL! HERE, OLD MAN--GRAB THIS WOODEN STAFF AND HANG ON! YOU OTHERS TOUCH THE OLD MAN--AND DON'T LET GO!
SWOOPING DOWN, THE WINGED WONDERS HURTLE TOWARD THE SNOWMAN...
NOW THAT THE VILLAGERS ARE SAFE WITH THE WOODEN STAFF TO PROTECT THEM, I CAN TACKLE THIS LAST OPPONENT...
HEEDLESS OF DANGER, HAWKMAN AND HAWKGIRL FLY THROUGH THE DEADLY BARRAGE OF SPARKS...
THE REST OF YOUR PEOPLE ARE UN-CONSCIOUS! WHY SHOULD YOU BE ANY EXCEPTION?
HAWKMAN! WHY DIDN'T THE SPARKS AFFECT US? NEITHER OF US IS HOLDING ANY WOOD!
12

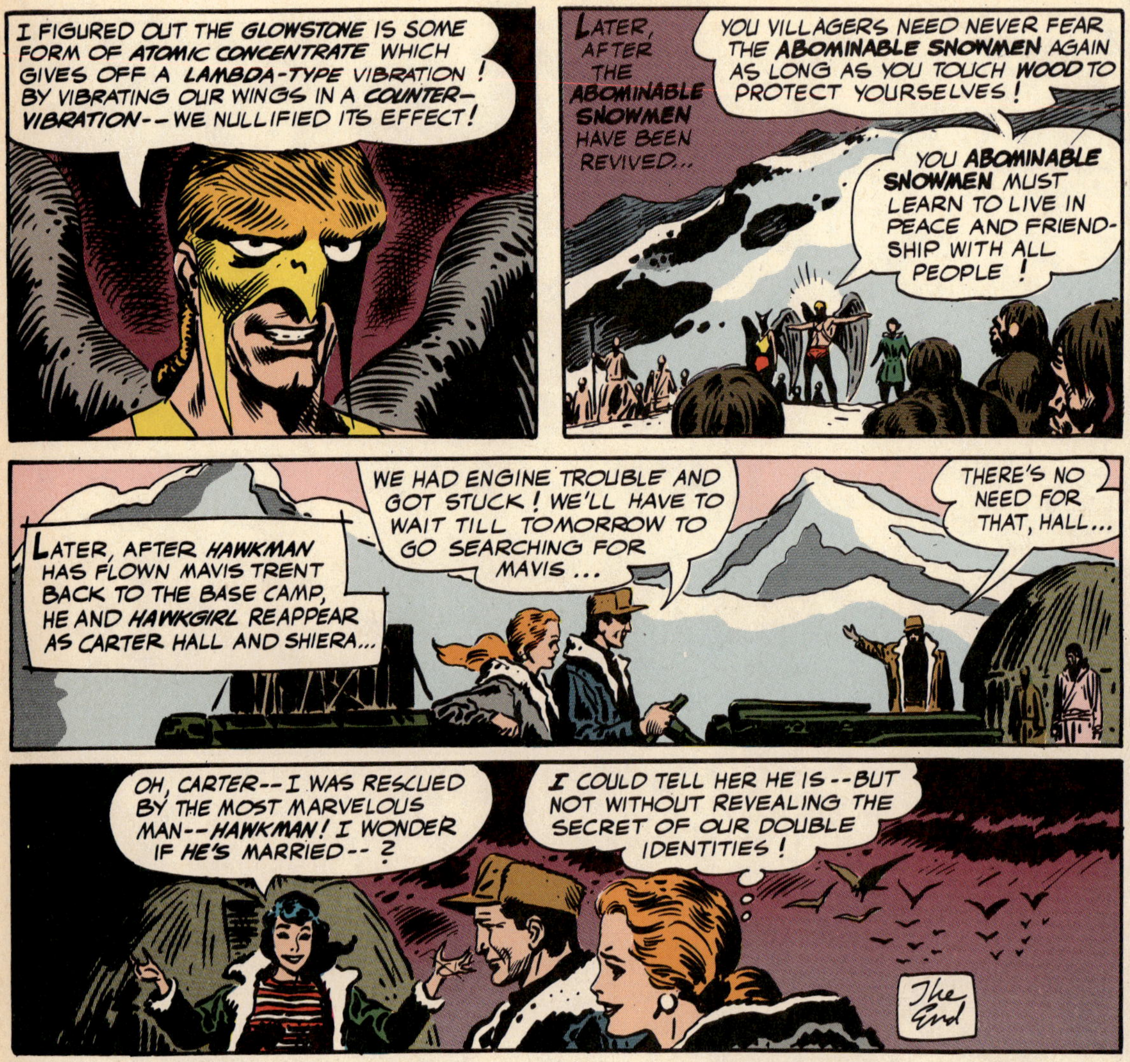

I FIGURED OUT THE GLOWSTONE IS SOME FORM OF ATOMIC CONCENTRATE WHICH GIVES OFF A LAMBDA-TYPE VIBRATION! BY VIBRATING OUR WINGS IN A COUNTER-VIBRATION--WE NULLIFIED ITS EFFECT!
LATER, AFTER THE ABOMINABLE SNOWMEN HAVE BEEN REVIVED...
YOU VILLAGERS NEED NEVER FEAR THE ABOMINABLE SNOWMEN AGAIN AS LONG AS YOU TOUCH WOOD TO PROTECT YOURSELVES!
YOU ABOMINABLE SNOWMEN MUST LEARN TO LIVE IN PEACE AND FRIENDSHIP WITH ALL PEOPLE!
LATER, AFTER HAWKMAN HAS FLOWN MAVIS TRENT BACK TO THE BASE CAMP, HE AND HAWKGIRL REAPPEAR AS CARTER HALL AND SHIERA...
WE HAD ENGINE TROUBLE AND GOT STUCK! WE'LL HAVE TO WAIT TILL TOMORROW TO GO SEARCHING FOR MAVIS...
THERE'S NO NEED FOR THAT, HALL...
OH, CARTER--I WAS RESCUED BY THE MOST MARVELOUS MAN--HAWKMAN! I WONDER IF HE'S MARRIED--?
I COULD TELL HER HE IS--BUT NOT WITHOUT REVEALING THE SECRET OF OUR DOUBLE IDENTITIES!
The End

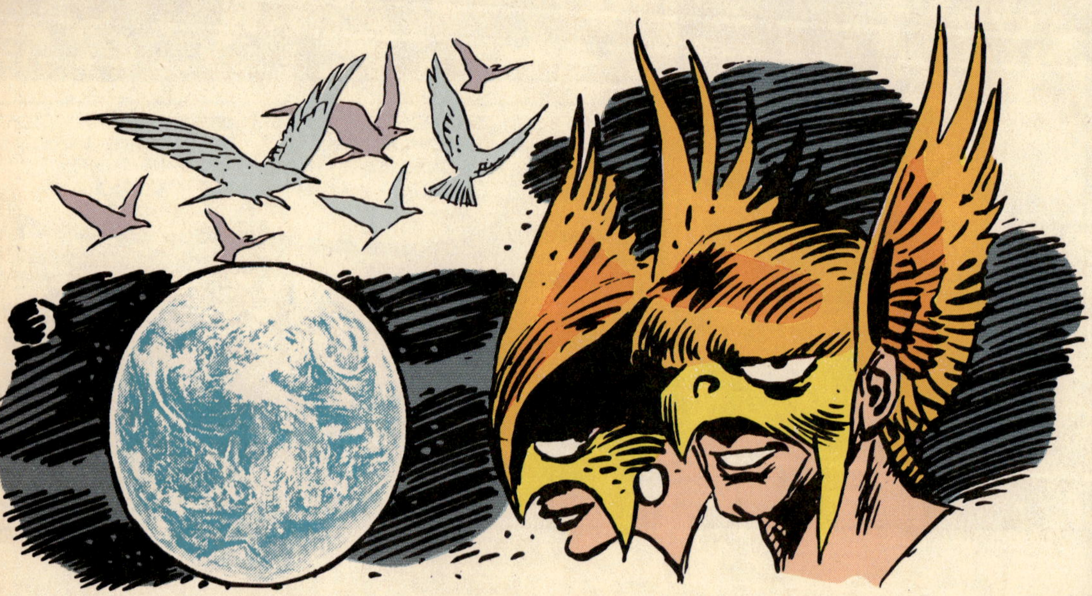

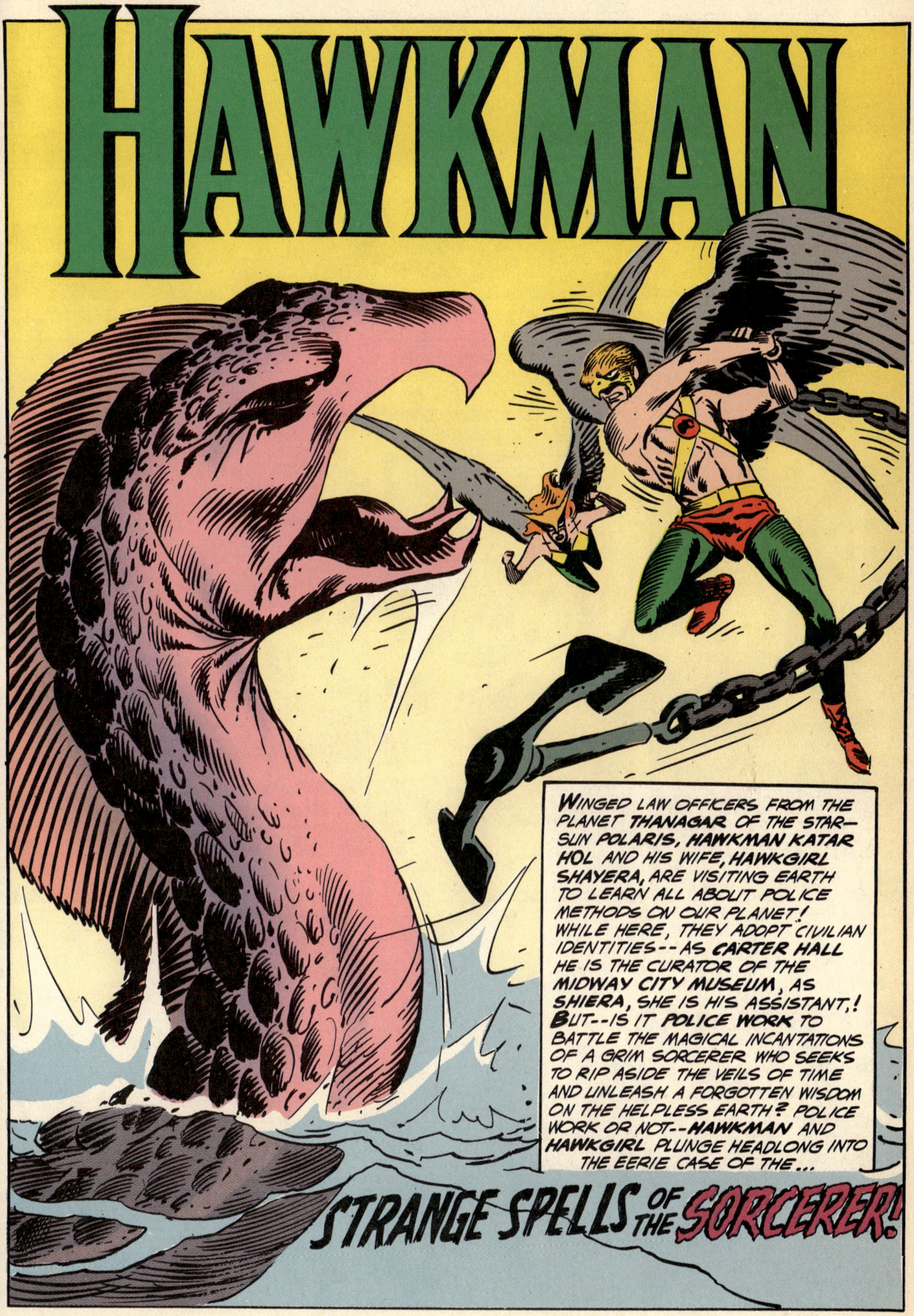
HAWKMAN
WINGED LAW OFFICERS FROM THE PLANET THANAGAR OF THE STAR-SUN POLARIS, HAWKMAN KATAR HOL AND HIS WIFE, HAWKGIRL SHAYERA, ARE VISITING EARTH TO LEARN ALL ABOUT POLICE METHODS ON OUR PLANET! WHILE HERE, THEY ADOPT CIVILIAN IDENTITIES--AS CARTER HALL HE IS THE CURATOR OF THE MIDWAY CITY MUSEUM, AS SHIERA, SHE IS HIS ASSISTANT,! BUT--IS IT POLICE WORK TO BATTLE THE MAGICAL INCANTATIONS OF A GRIM SORCERER WHO SEEKS TO RIP ASIDE THE VEILS OF TIME AND UNLEASH A FORGOTTEN WISDOM ON THE HELPLESS EARTH? POLICE WORK OR NOT--HAWKMAN AND HAWKGIRL PLUNGE HEADLONG INTO THE EERIE CASE OF THE...
STRANGE SPELLS OF THE SORCERER!

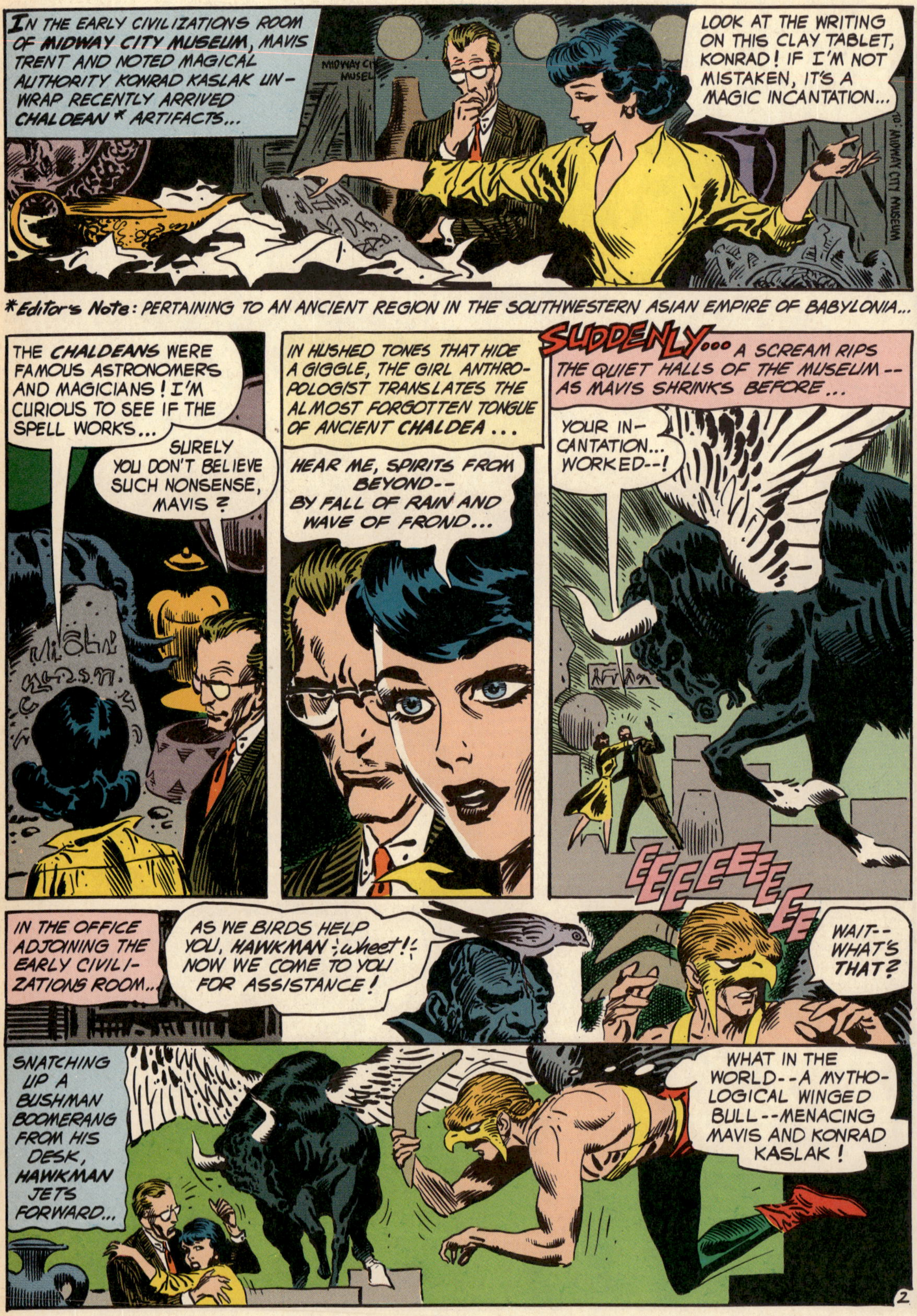
IN THE EARLY CIVILIZATIONS ROOM OF MIDWAY CITY MUSEUM, MAVIS TRENT AND NOTED MAGICAL AUTHORITY KONRAD KASLAK UNWRAP RECENTLY ARRIVED CHALDEAN * ARTIFACTS...
LOOK AT THE WRITING ON THIS CLAY TABLET, KONRAD! IF I'M NOT MISTAKEN, IT'S A MAGIC INCANTATION...
TO: MIDWAY CITY MUSEUM
*Editor's Note: PERTAINING TO AN ANCIENT REGION IN THE SOUTHWESTERN ASIAN EMPIRE OF BABYLONIA...
THE CHALDEANS WERE FAMOUS ASTRONOMERS AND MAGICIANS! I'M CURIOUS TO SEE IF THE SPELL WORKS...
SURELY YOU DON'T BELIEVE SUCH NONSENSE, MAVIS?
IN HUSHED TONES THAT HIDE A GIGGLE, THE GIRL ANTHROPOLOGIST TRANSLATES THE ALMOST FORGOTTEN TONGUE OF ANCIENT CHALDEA...
HEAR ME, SPIRITS FROM BEYOND-- BY FALL OF RAIN AND WAVE OF FROND...
SUDDENLY... A SCREAM RIPS THE QUIET HALLS OF THE MUSEUM -- AS MAVIS SHRINKS BEFORE...
YOUR INCANTATION... WORKED--!
EEEEEEEEE
IN THE OFFICE ADJOINING THE EARLY CIVILIZATIONS ROOM...
AS WE BIRDS HELP YOU, HAWKMAN -wheet!- NOW WE COME TO YOU FOR ASSISTANCE!
WAIT-- WHAT'S THAT?
SNATCHING UP A BUSHMAN BOOMERANG FROM HIS DESK, HAWKMAN JETS FORWARD...
WHAT IN THE WORLD--A MYTHOLOGICAL WINGED BULL--MENACING MAVIS AND KONRAD KASLAK!
2

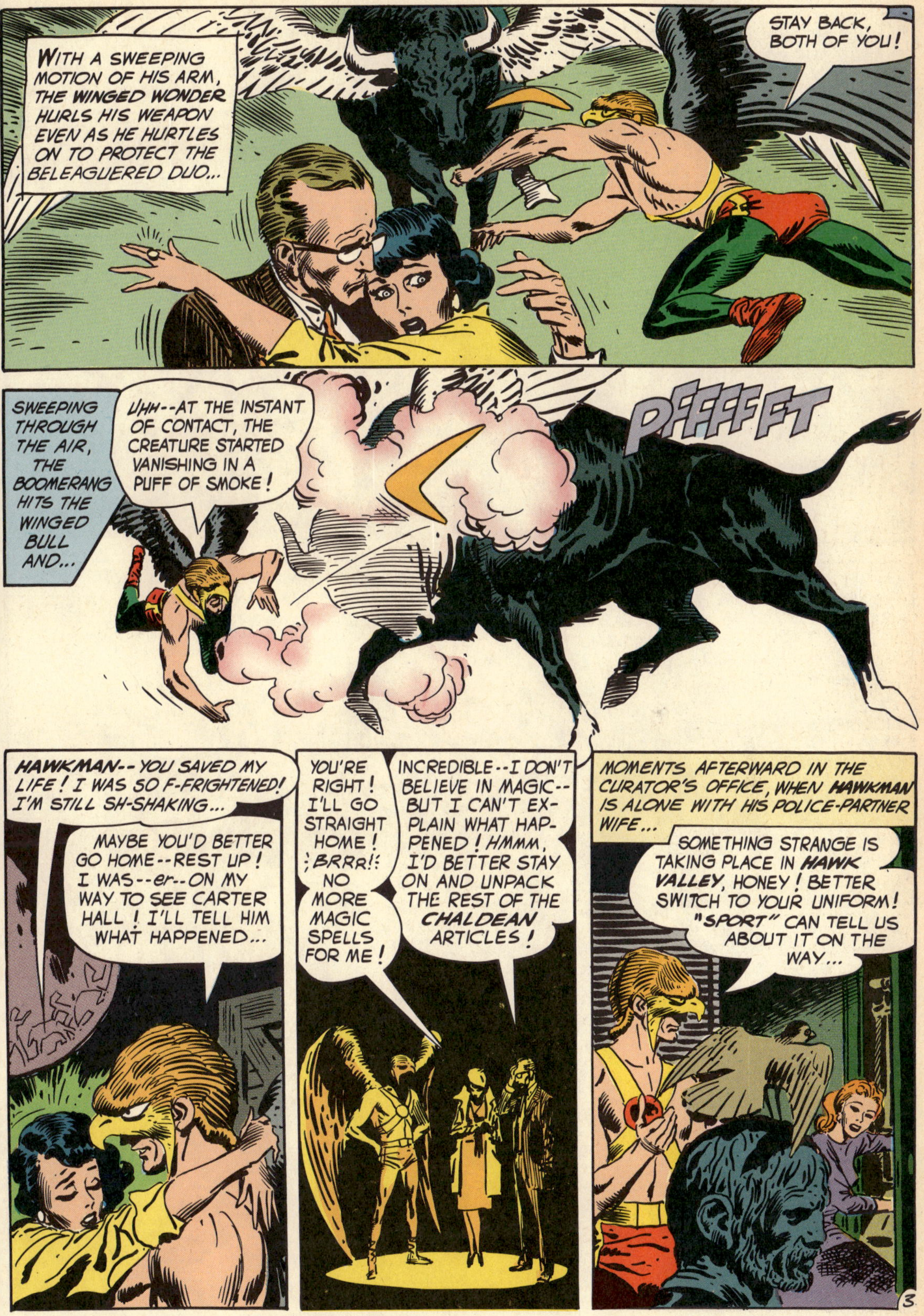
WITH A SWEEPING MOTION OF HIS ARM, THE WINGED WONDER HURLS HIS WEAPON EVEN AS HE HURTLES ON TO PROTECT THE BELEAGUERED DUO...
STAY BACK, BOTH OF YOU!
SWEEPING THROUGH THE AIR, THE BOOMERANG HITS THE WINGED BULL AND...
UHH--AT THE INSTANT OF CONTACT, THE CREATURE STARTED VANISHING IN A PUFF OF SMOKE!
PFFFFFT
HAWKMAN--YOU SAVED MY LIFE! I WAS SO F-FRIGHTENED! I'M STILL SH-SHAKING...
MAYBE YOU'D BETTER GO HOME--REST UP! I WAS--er--ON MY WAY TO SEE CARTER HALL! I'LL TELL HIM WHAT HAPPENED...
YOU'RE RIGHT! I'LL GO STRAIGHT HOME! BRRR! NO MORE MAGIC SPELLS FOR ME!
INCREDIBLE--I DON'T BELIEVE IN MAGIC--BUT I CAN'T EXPLAIN WHAT HAPPENED! HMMM, I'D BETTER STAY ON AND UNPACK THE REST OF THE CHALDEAN ARTICLES!
MOMENTS AFTERWARD IN THE CURATOR'S OFFICE, WHEN HAWKMAN IS ALONE WITH HIS POLICE-PARTNER WIFE...
SOMETHING STRANGE IS TAKING PLACE IN HAWK VALLEY, HONEY! BETTER SWITCH TO YOUR UNIFORM! "SPORT" CAN TELL US ABOUT IT ON THE WAY...
3

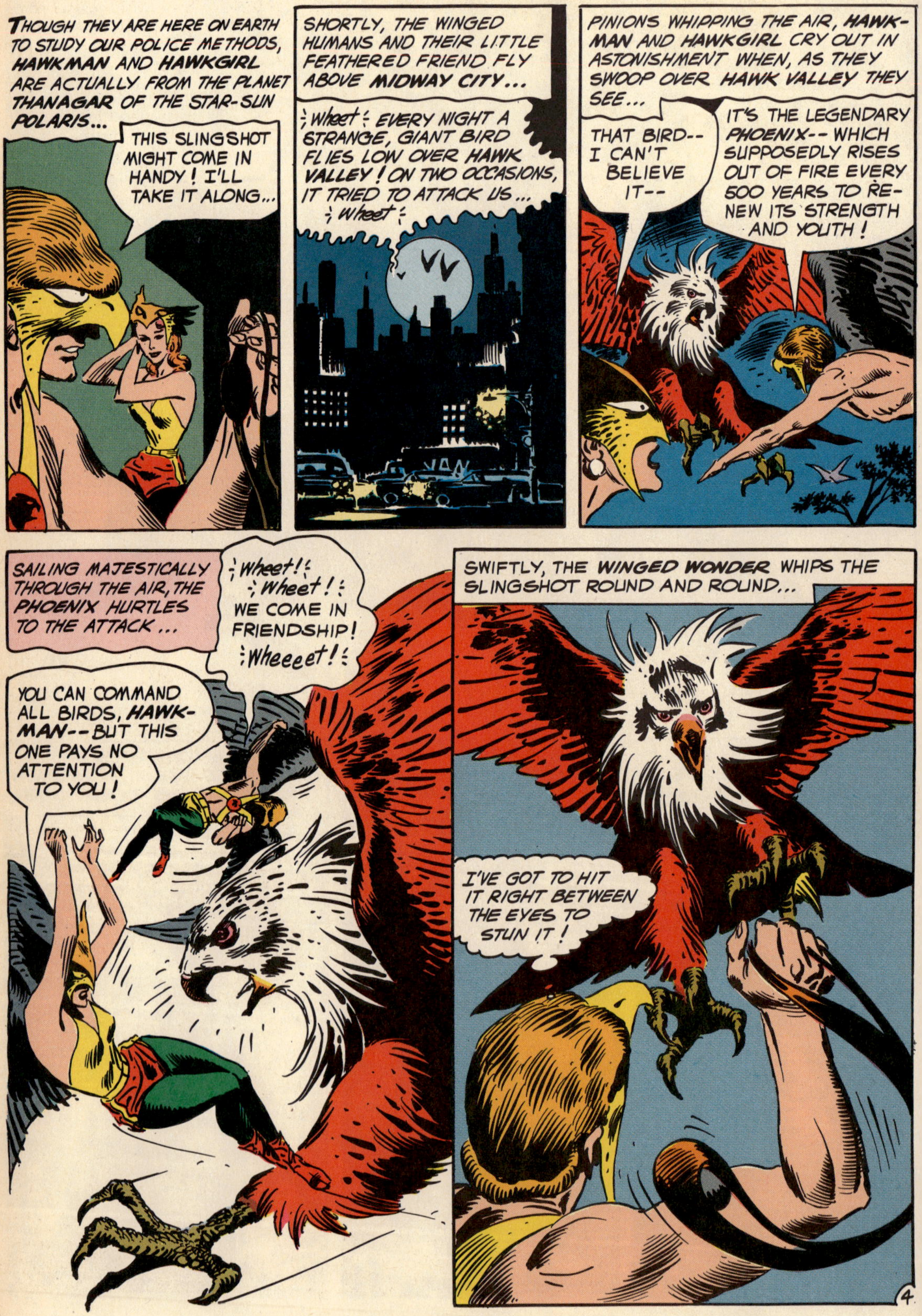
THOUGH THEY ARE HERE ON EARTH TO STUDY OUR POLICE METHODS, HAWKMAN AND HAWKGIRL ARE ACTUALLY FROM THE PLANET THANAGAR OF THE STAR-SUN POLARIS...
THIS SLINGSHOT MIGHT COME IN HANDY! I'LL TAKE IT ALONG...
SHORTLY, THE WINGED HUMANS AND THEIR LITTLE FEATHERED FRIEND FLY ABOVE MIDWAY CITY...
Wheet EVERY NIGHT A STRANGE, GIANT BIRD FLIES LOW OVER HAWK VALLEY! ON TWO OCCASIONS, IT TRIED TO ATTACK US... Wheet
PINIONS WHIPPING THE AIR, HAWKMAN AND HAWKGIRL CRY OUT IN ASTONISHMENT WHEN, AS THEY SWOOP OVER HAWK VALLEY THEY SEE...
THAT BIRD-- I CAN'T BELIEVE IT--
IT'S THE LEGENDARY PHOENIX-- WHICH SUPPOSEDLY RISES OUT OF FIRE EVERY 500 YEARS TO RENEW ITS STRENGTH AND YOUTH!
SAILING MAJESTICALLY THROUGH THE AIR, THE PHOENIX HURTLES TO THE ATTACK...
Wheet! Wheet! WE COME IN FRIENDSHIP! Wheeeet!
YOU CAN COMMAND ALL BIRDS, HAWKMAN-- BUT THIS ONE PAYS NO ATTENTION TO YOU!
SWIFTLY, THE WINGED WONDER WHIPS THE SLINGSHOT ROUND AND ROUND...
I'VE GOT TO HIT IT RIGHT BETWEEN THE EYES TO STUN IT!
4

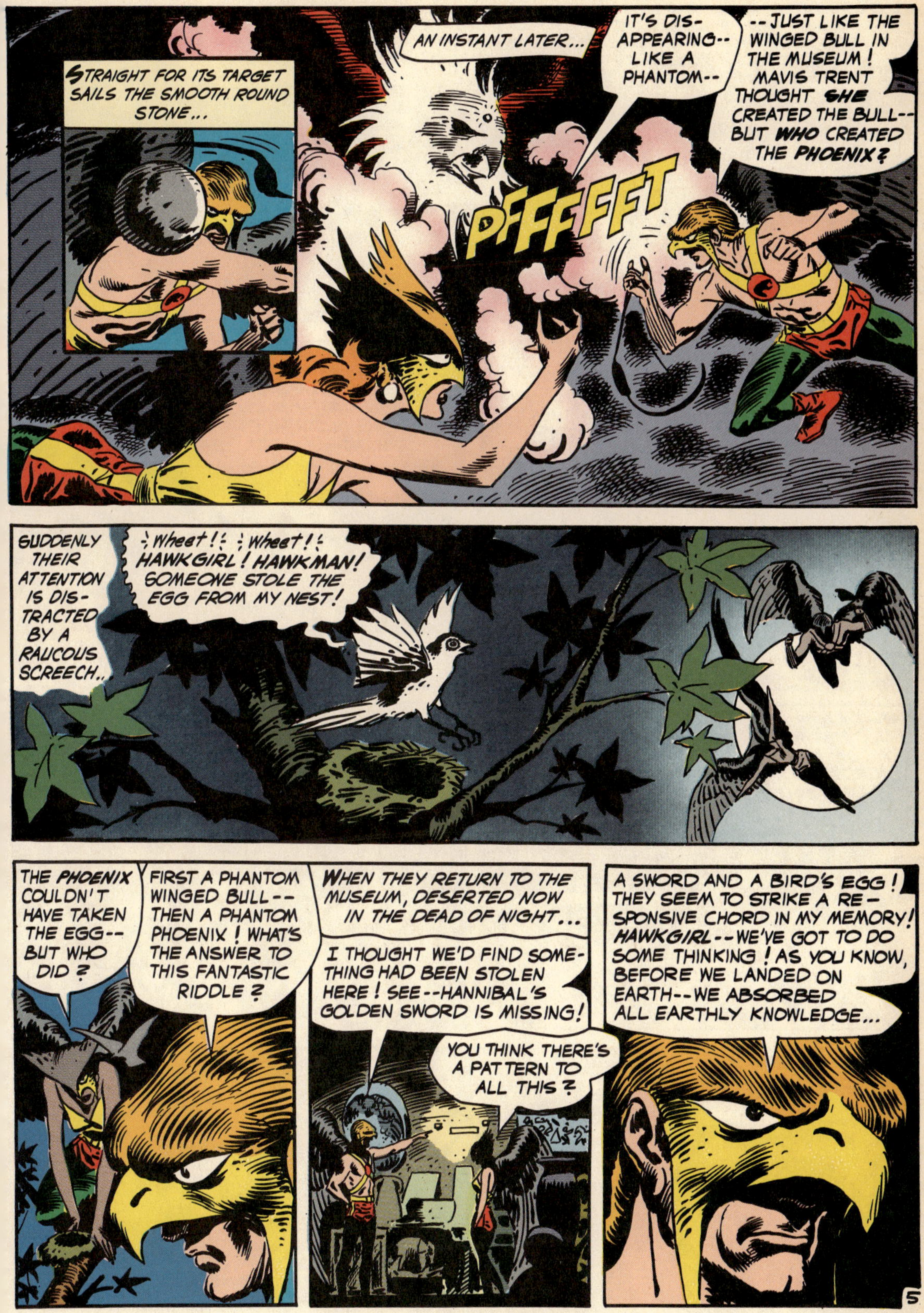
STRAIGHT FOR ITS TARGET SAILS THE SMOOTH ROUND STONE...
AN INSTANT LATER...
IT'S DIS-APPEARING-- LIKE A PHANTOM--
--JUST LIKE THE WINGED BULL IN THE MUSEUM! MAVIS TRENT THOUGHT SHE CREATED THE BULL-- BUT WHO CREATED THE PHOENIX?
PFFFFFT
SUDDENLY THEIR ATTENTION IS DIS-TRACTED BY A RAUCOUS SCREECH..
Wheet! Wheet! HAWKGIRL! HAWKMAN! SOMEONE STOLE THE EGG FROM MY NEST!
THE PHOENIX COULDN'T HAVE TAKEN THE EGG-- BUT WHO DID?
FIRST A PHANTOM WINGED BULL-- THEN A PHANTOM PHOENIX! WHAT'S THE ANSWER TO THIS FANTASTIC RIDDLE?
WHEN THEY RETURN TO THE MUSEUM, DESERTED NOW IN THE DEAD OF NIGHT...
I THOUGHT WE'D FIND SOME-THING HAD BEEN STOLEN HERE! SEE--HANNIBAL'S GOLDEN SWORD IS MISSING!
YOU THINK THERE'S A PATTERN TO ALL THIS?
A SWORD AND A BIRD'S EGG! THEY SEEM TO STRIKE A RE-SPONSIVE CHORD IN MY MEMORY! HAWKGIRL--WE'VE GOT TO DO SOME THINKING! AS YOU KNOW, BEFORE WE LANDED ON EARTH--WE ABSORBED ALL EARTHLY KNOWLEDGE...
5

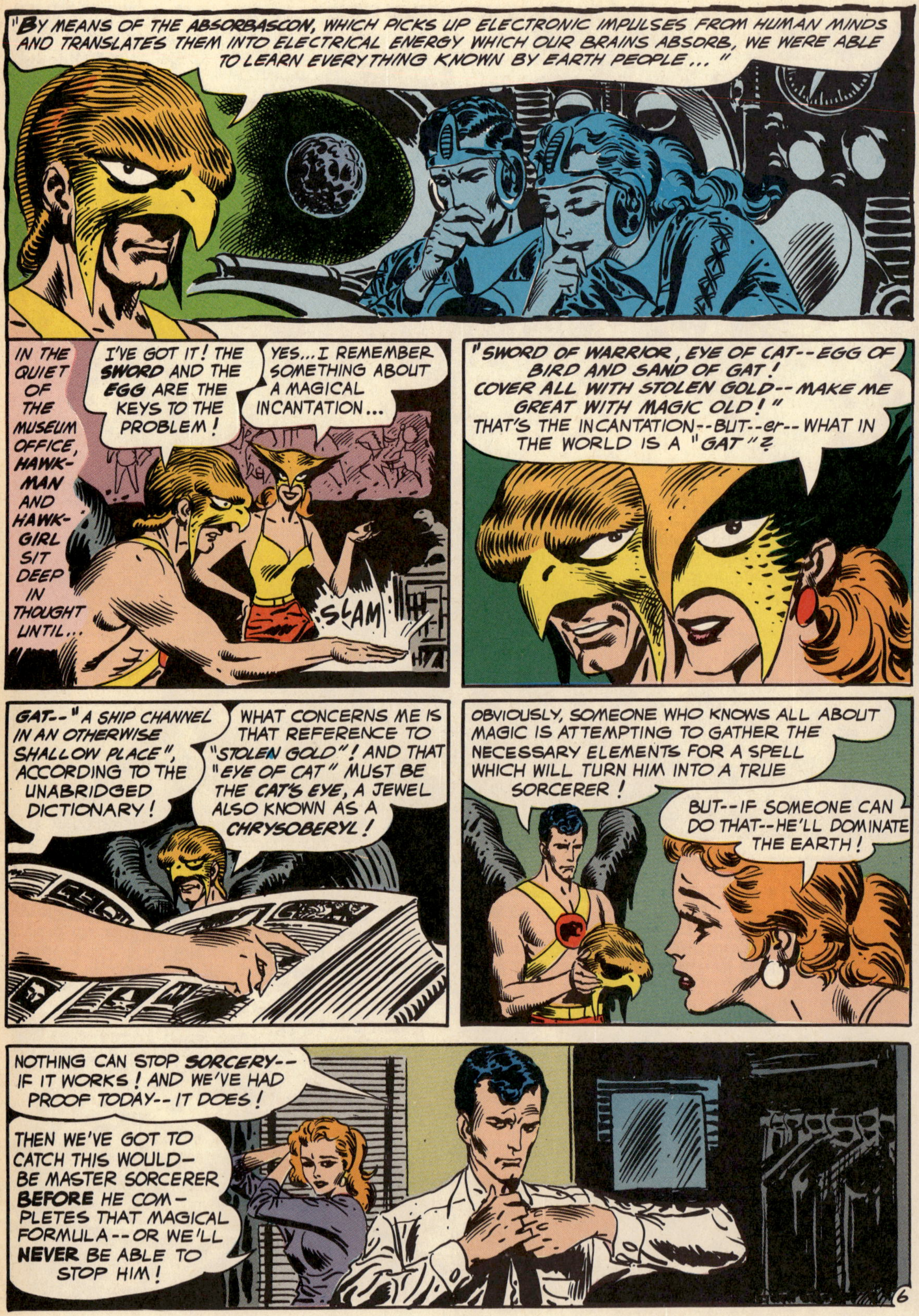
"BY MEANS OF THE ABSORBASCON, WHICH PICKS UP ELECTRONIC IMPULSES FROM HUMAN MINDS AND TRANSLATES THEM INTO ELECTRICAL ENERGY WHICH OUR BRAINS ABSORB, WE WERE ABLE TO LEARN EVERYTHING KNOWN BY EARTH PEOPLE ... "
IN THE QUIET OF THE MUSEUM OFFICE, HAWKMAN AND HAWKGIRL SIT DEEP IN THOUGHT UNTIL...
I'VE GOT IT! THE SWORD AND THE EGG ARE THE KEYS TO THE PROBLEM!
SLAM
YES...I REMEMBER SOMETHING ABOUT A MAGICAL INCANTATION...
"SWORD OF WARRIOR, EYE OF CAT--EGG OF BIRD AND SAND OF GAT! COVER ALL WITH STOLEN GOLD--MAKE ME GREAT WITH MAGIC OLD!" THAT'S THE INCANTATION--BUT--er--WHAT IN THE WORLD IS A "GAT"?
GAT--"A SHIP CHANNEL IN AN OTHERWISE SHALLOW PLACE", ACCORDING TO THE UNABRIDGED DICTIONARY!
WHAT CONCERNS ME IS THAT REFERENCE TO "STOLEN GOLD"! AND THAT "EYE OF CAT" MUST BE THE CAT'S EYE, A JEWEL ALSO KNOWN AS A CHRYSOBERYL!
OBVIOUSLY, SOMEONE WHO KNOWS ALL ABOUT MAGIC IS ATTEMPTING TO GATHER THE NECESSARY ELEMENTS FOR A SPELL WHICH WILL TURN HIM INTO A TRUE SORCERER!
BUT--IF SOMEONE CAN DO THAT--HE'LL DOMINATE THE EARTH!
NOTHING CAN STOP SORCERY--IF IT WORKS! AND WE'VE HAD PROOF TODAY--IT DOES!
THEN WE'VE GOT TO CATCH THIS WOULD-BE MASTER SORCERER BEFORE HE COMPLETES THAT MAGICAL FORMULA--OR WE'LL NEVER BE ABLE TO STOP HIM!
6

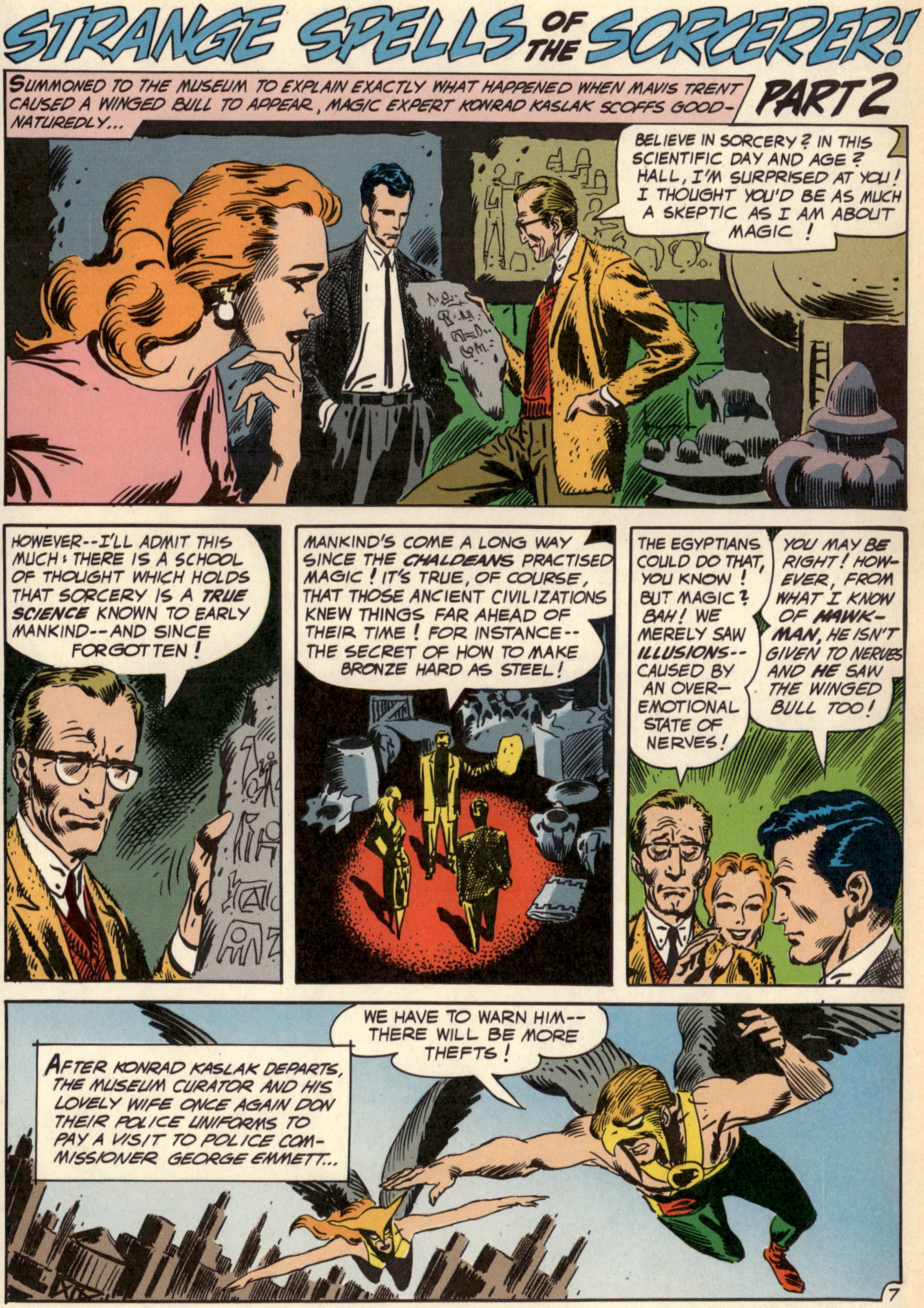
STRANGE SPELLS OF THE SORCERER!
SUMMONED TO THE MUSEUM TO EXPLAIN EXACTLY WHAT HAPPENED WHEN MAVIS TRENT CAUSED A WINGED BULL TO APPEAR, MAGIC EXPERT KONRAD KASLAK SCOFFS GOOD-NATUREDLY...
PART 2
BELIEVE IN SORCERY? IN THIS SCIENTIFIC DAY AND AGE? HALL, I'M SURPRISED AT YOU! I THOUGHT YOU'D BE AS MUCH A SKEPTIC AS I AM ABOUT MAGIC!
HOWEVER--I'LL ADMIT THIS MUCH: THERE IS A SCHOOL OF THOUGHT WHICH HOLDS THAT SORCERY IS A TRUE SCIENCE KNOWN TO EARLY MANKIND--AND SINCE FORGOTTEN!
MANKIND'S COME A LONG WAY SINCE THE CHALDEANS PRACTISED MAGIC! IT'S TRUE, OF COURSE, THAT THOSE ANCIENT CIVILIZATIONS KNEW THINGS FAR AHEAD OF THEIR TIME! FOR INSTANCE-- THE SECRET OF HOW TO MAKE BRONZE HARD AS STEEL!
THE EGYPTIANS COULD DO THAT, YOU KNOW! BUT MAGIC? BAH! WE MERELY SAW ILLUSIONS-- CAUSED BY AN OVER-EMOTIONAL STATE OF NERVES!
YOU MAY BE RIGHT! HOW-EVER, FROM WHAT I KNOW OF HAWK-MAN, HE ISN'T GIVEN TO NERVES AND HE SAW THE WINGED BULL TOO!
AFTER KONRAD KASLAK DEPARTS, THE MUSEUM CURATOR AND HIS LOVELY WIFE ONCE AGAIN DON THEIR POLICE UNIFORMS TO PAY A VISIT TO POLICE COM-MISSIONER GEORGE EMMETT...
WE HAVE TO WARN HIM-- THERE WILL BE MORE THEFTS!

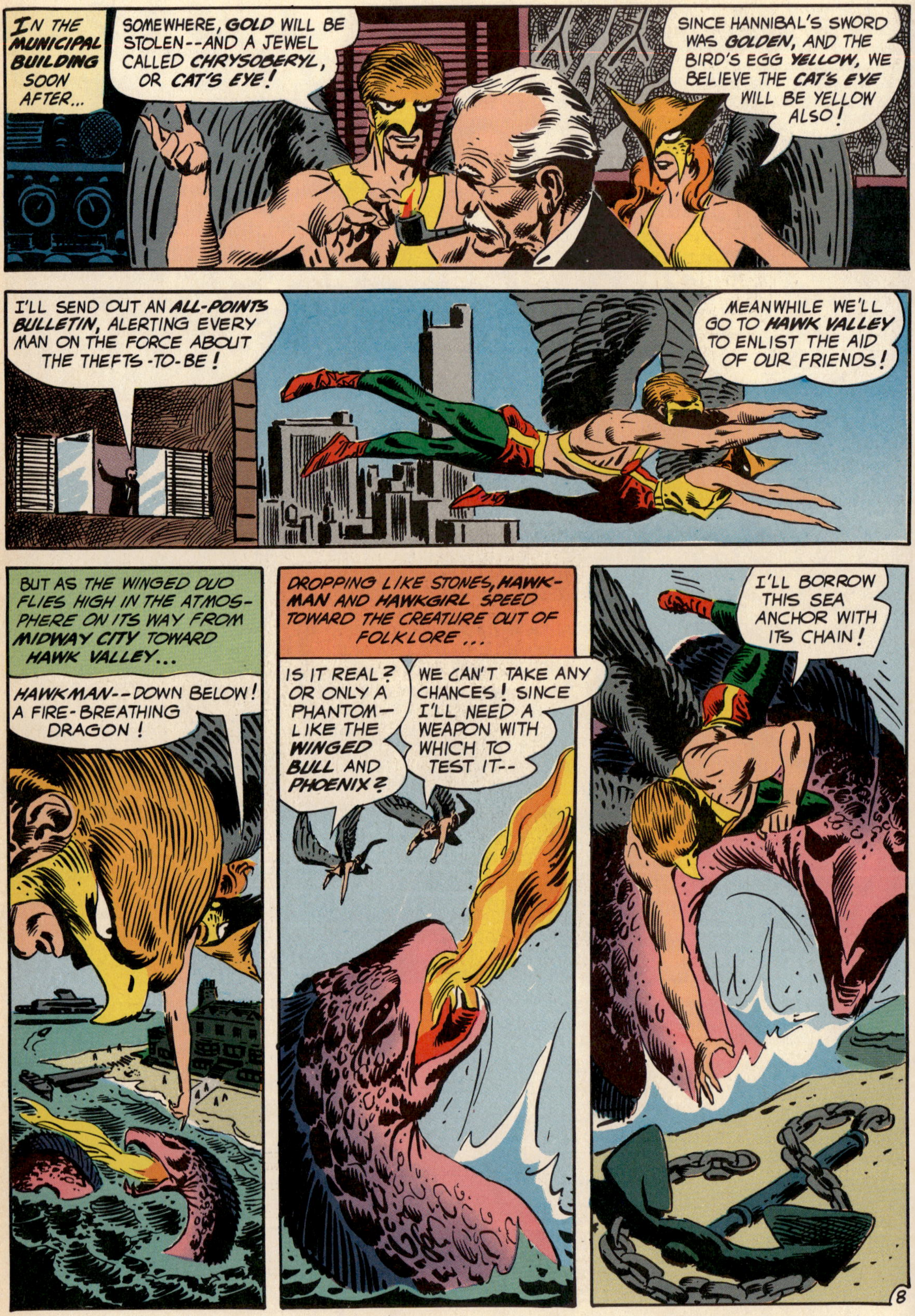
IN THE MUNICIPAL BUILDING SOON AFTER...
SOMEWHERE, GOLD WILL BE STOLEN--AND A JEWEL CALLED CHRYSOBERYL, OR CAT'S EYE!
SINCE HANNIBAL'S SWORD WAS GOLDEN, AND THE BIRD'S EGG YELLOW, WE BELIEVE THE CAT'S EYE WILL BE YELLOW ALSO!
I'LL SEND OUT AN ALL-POINTS BULLETIN, ALERTING EVERY MAN ON THE FORCE ABOUT THE THEFTS-TO-BE!
MEANWHILE WE'LL GO TO HAWK VALLEY TO ENLIST THE AID OF OUR FRIENDS!
BUT AS THE WINGED DUO FLIES HIGH IN THE ATMOSPHERE ON ITS WAY FROM MIDWAY CITY TOWARD HAWK VALLEY...
HAWKMAN--DOWN BELOW! A FIRE-BREATHING DRAGON!
DROPPING LIKE STONES, HAWKMAN AND HAWKGIRL SPEED TOWARD THE CREATURE OUT OF FOLKLORE...
IS IT REAL? OR ONLY A PHANTOM--LIKE THE WINGED BULL AND PHOENIX?
WE CAN'T TAKE ANY CHANCES! SINCE I'LL NEED A WEAPON WITH WHICH TO TEST IT--
I'LL BORROW THIS SEA ANCHOR WITH ITS CHAIN!
8

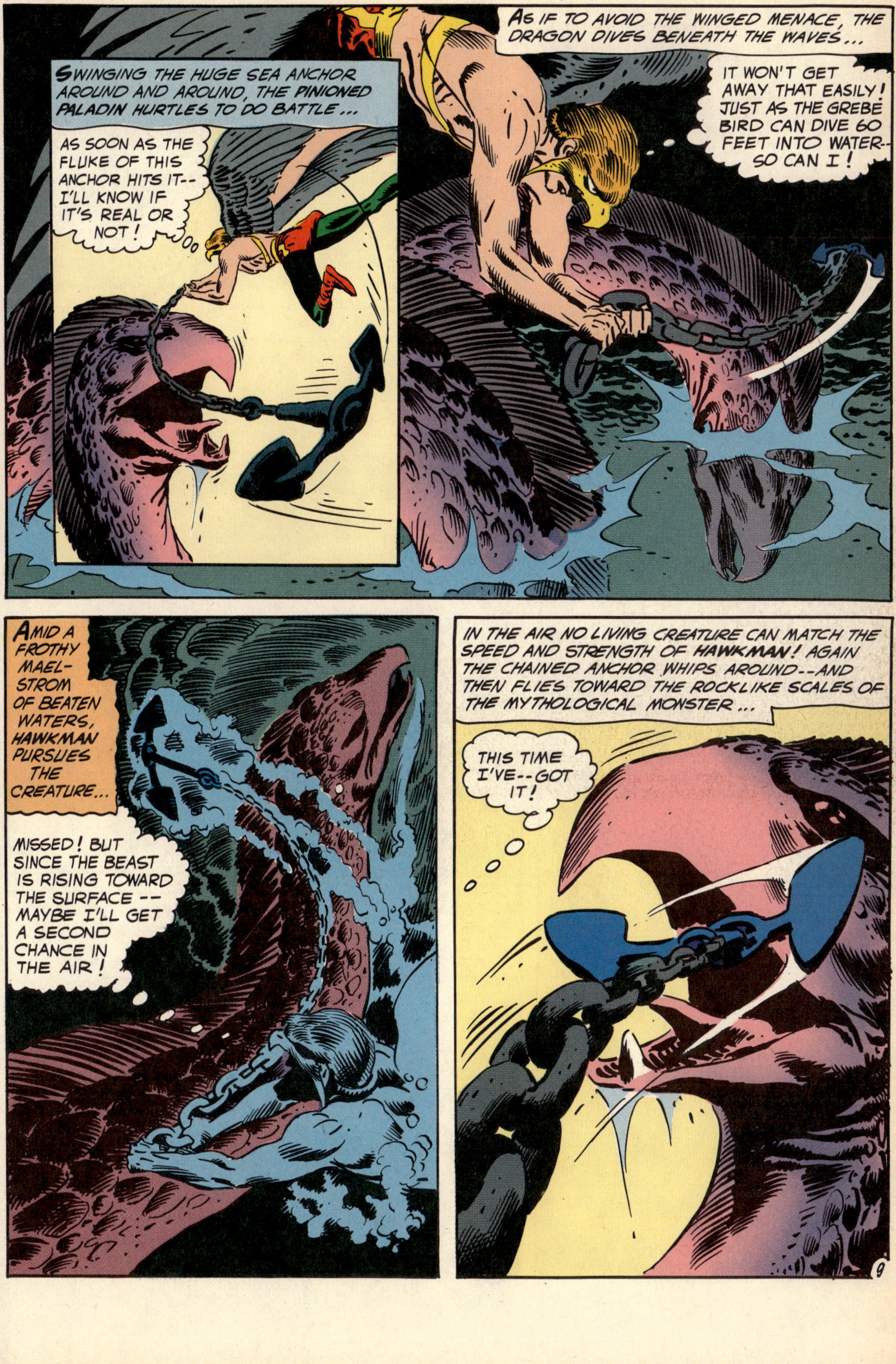
SWINGING THE HUGE SEA ANCHOR AROUND AND AROUND, THE PINIONED PALADIN HURTLES TO DO BATTLE...
AS SOON AS THE FLUKE OF THIS ANCHOR HITS IT-- I'LL KNOW IF IT'S REAL OR NOT!
AS IF TO AVOID THE WINGED MENACE, THE DRAGON DIVES BENEATH THE WAVES...
IT WON'T GET AWAY THAT EASILY! JUST AS THE GREBE BIRD CAN DIVE 60 FEET INTO WATER-- SO CAN I!
AMID A FROTHY MAEL-STROM OF BEATEN WATERS, HAWKMAN PURSUES THE CREATURE...
MISSED! BUT SINCE THE BEAST IS RISING TOWARD THE SURFACE -- MAYBE I'LL GET A SECOND CHANCE IN THE AIR!
IN THE AIR NO LIVING CREATURE CAN MATCH THE SPEED AND STRENGTH OF HAWKMAN! AGAIN THE CHAINED ANCHOR WHIPS AROUND--AND THEN FLIES TOWARD THE ROCKLIKE SCALES OF THE MYTHOLOGICAL MONSTER...
THIS TIME I'VE--GOT IT!
9

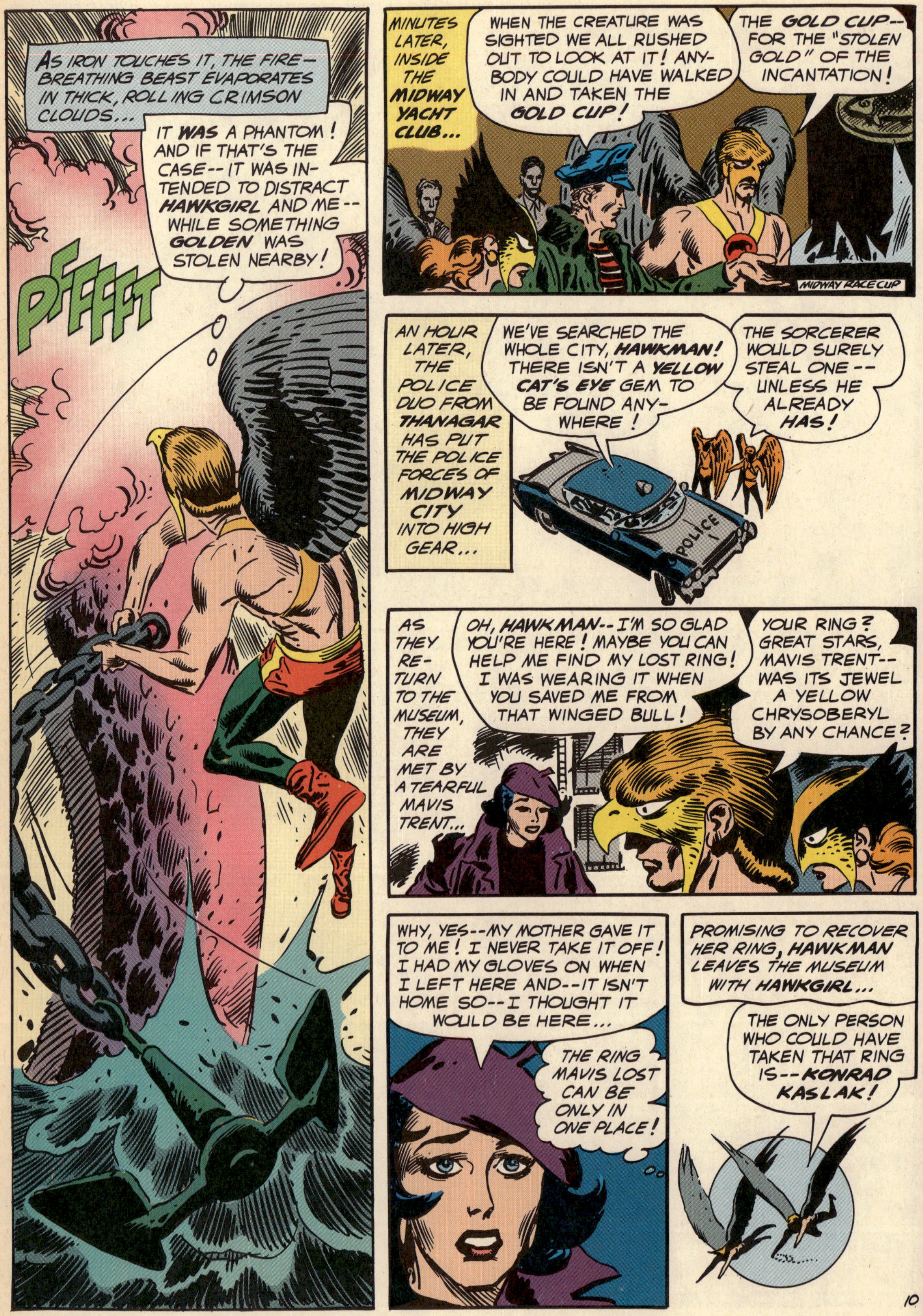
AS IRON TOUCHES IT, THE FIRE-BREATHING BEAST EVAPORATES IN THICK, ROLLING CRIMSON CLOUDS...
IT WAS A PHANTOM! AND IF THAT'S THE CASE--IT WAS INTENDED TO DISTRACT HAWKGIRL AND ME--WHILE SOMETHING GOLDEN WAS STOLEN NEARBY!
PFFFFT
MINUTES LATER, INSIDE THE MIDWAY YACHT CLUB...
WHEN THE CREATURE WAS SIGHTED WE ALL RUSHED OUT TO LOOK AT IT! ANYBODY COULD HAVE WALKED IN AND TAKEN THE GOLD CUP!
THE GOLD CUP--FOR THE "STOLEN GOLD" OF THE INCANTATION!
MIDWAY RACE CUP
AN HOUR LATER, THE POLICE DUO FROM THANAGAR HAS PUT THE POLICE FORCES OF MIDWAY CITY INTO HIGH GEAR...
WE'VE SEARCHED THE WHOLE CITY, HAWKMAN! THERE ISN'T A YELLOW CAT'S EYE GEM TO BE FOUND ANYWHERE!
THE SORCERER WOULD SURELY STEAL ONE--UNLESS HE ALREADY HAS!
POLICE
AS THEY RETURN TO THE MUSEUM, THEY ARE MET BY A TEARFUL MAVIS TRENT...
OH, HAWKMAN--I'M SO GLAD YOU'RE HERE! MAYBE YOU CAN HELP ME FIND MY LOST RING! I WAS WEARING IT WHEN YOU SAVED ME FROM THAT WINGED BULL!
YOUR RING? GREAT STARS, MAVIS TRENT--WAS ITS JEWEL A YELLOW CHRYSOBERYL BY ANY CHANCE?
WHY, YES--MY MOTHER GAVE IT TO ME! I NEVER TAKE IT OFF! I HAD MY GLOVES ON WHEN I LEFT HERE AND--IT ISN'T HOME SO--I THOUGHT IT WOULD BE HERE...
THE RING MAVIS LOST CAN BE ONLY IN ONE PLACE!
PROMISING TO RECOVER HER RING, HAWKMAN LEAVES THE MUSEUM WITH HAWKGIRL...
THE ONLY PERSON WHO COULD HAVE TAKEN THAT RING IS--KONRAD KASLAK!
10

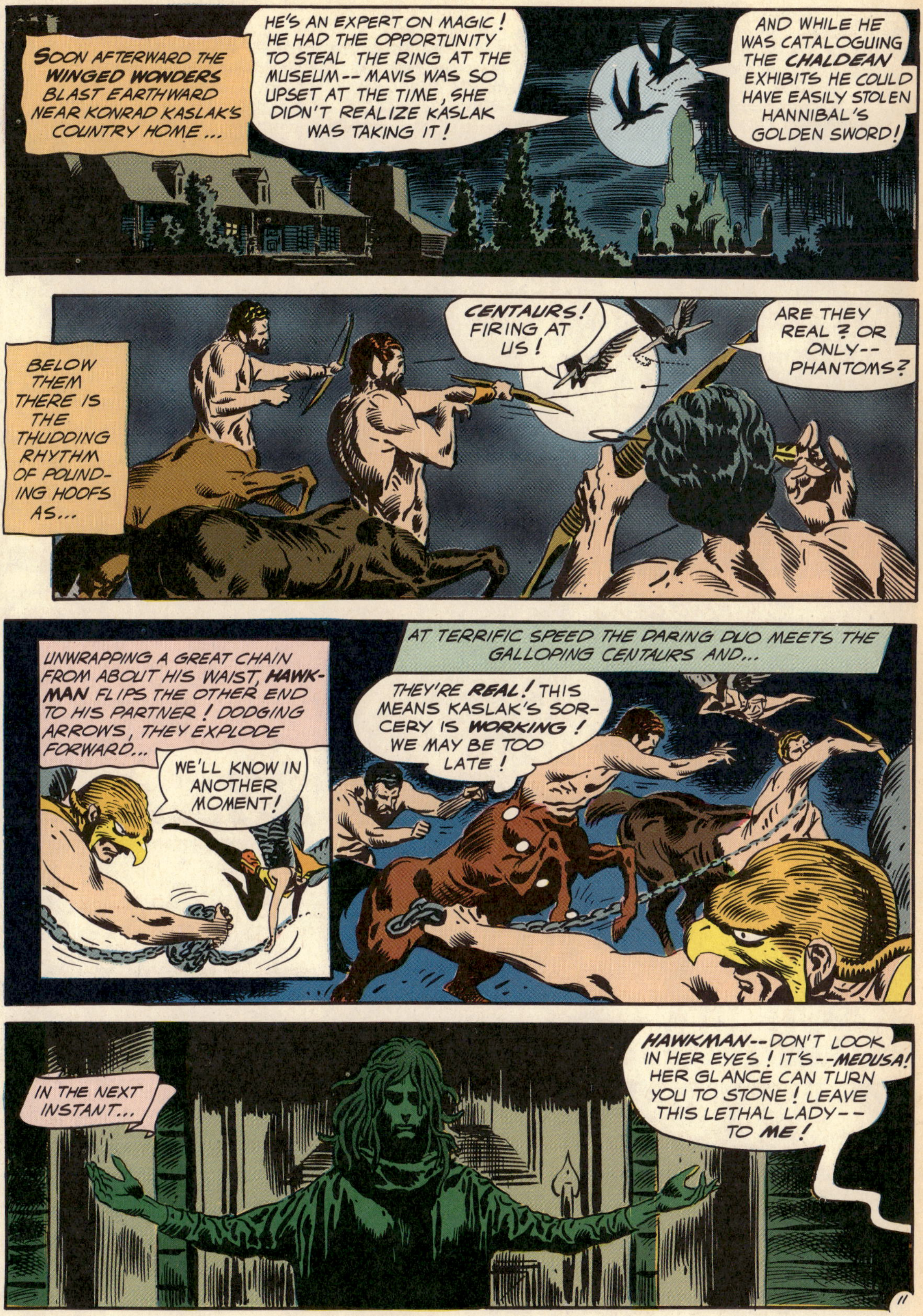
SOON AFTERWARD THE WINGED WONDERS BLAST EARTHWARD NEAR KONRAD KASLAK'S COUNTRY HOME...
HE'S AN EXPERT ON MAGIC! HE HAD THE OPPORTUNITY TO STEAL THE RING AT THE MUSEUM--MAVIS WAS SO UPSET AT THE TIME, SHE DIDN'T REALIZE KASLAK WAS TAKING IT!
AND WHILE HE WAS CATALOGUING THE CHALDEAN EXHIBITS HE COULD HAVE EASILY STOLEN HANNIBAL'S GOLDEN SWORD!
BELOW THEM THERE IS THE THUDDING RHYTHM OF POUNDING HOOFS AS...
CENTAURS! FIRING AT US!
ARE THEY REAL? OR ONLY--PHANTOMS?
UNWRAPPING A GREAT CHAIN FROM ABOUT HIS WAIST, HAWKMAN FLIPS THE OTHER END TO HIS PARTNER! DODGING ARROWS, THEY EXPLODE FORWARD...
WE'LL KNOW IN ANOTHER MOMENT!
AT TERRIFIC SPEED THE DARING DUO MEETS THE GALLOPING CENTAURS AND...
THEY'RE REAL! THIS MEANS KASLAK'S SORCERY IS WORKING! WE MAY BE TOO LATE!
IN THE NEXT INSTANT...
HAWKMAN--DON'T LOOK IN HER EYES! IT'S--MEDUSA! HER GLANCE CAN TURN YOU TO STONE! LEAVE THIS LETHAL LADY--TO ME!
11

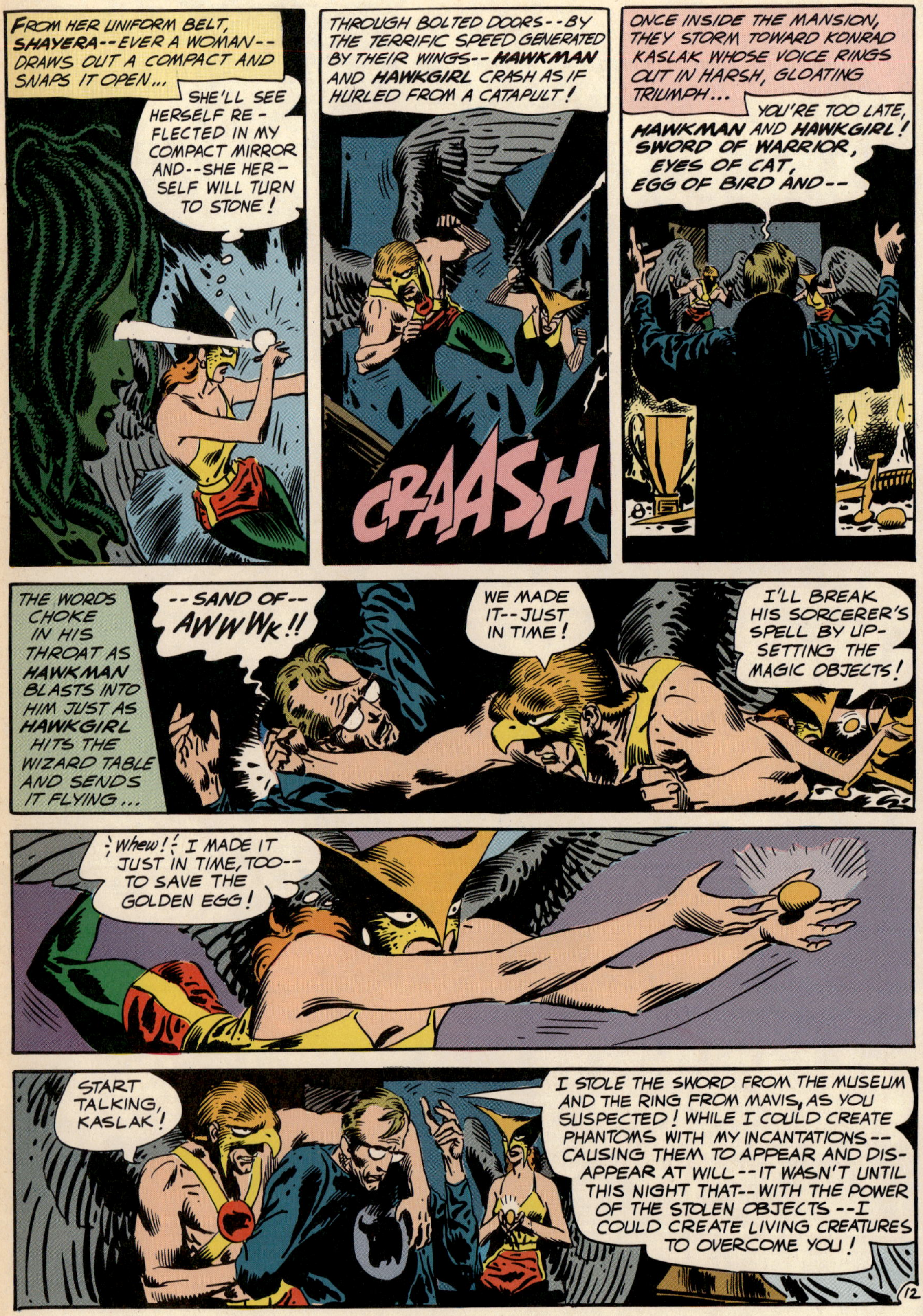
FROM HER UNIFORM BELT, SHAYERA--EVER A WOMAN--DRAWS OUT A COMPACT AND SNAPS IT OPEN...
SHE'LL SEE HERSELF RE-FLECTED IN MY COMPACT MIRROR AND--SHE HER-SELF WILL TURN TO STONE!
THROUGH BOLTED DOORS--BY THE TERRIFIC SPEED GENERATED BY THEIR WINGS--HAWKMAN AND HAWKGIRL CRASH AS IF HURLED FROM A CATAPULT!
CRAASH
ONCE INSIDE THE MANSION, THEY STORM TOWARD KONRAD KASLAK WHOSE VOICE RINGS OUT IN HARSH, GLOATING TRIUMPH...
YOU'RE TOO LATE, HAWKMAN AND HAWKGIRL! SWORD OF WARRIOR, EYES OF CAT, EGG OF BIRD AND--
THE WORDS CHOKE IN HIS THROAT AS HAWKMAN BLASTS INTO HIM JUST AS HAWKGIRL HITS THE WIZARD TABLE AND SENDS IT FLYING...
--SAND OF-- AWWWK!!
WE MADE IT--JUST IN TIME!
I'LL BREAK HIS SORCERER'S SPELL BY UP-SETTING THE MAGIC OBJECTS!
Whew!-I MADE IT JUST IN TIME, TOO--TO SAVE THE GOLDEN EGG!
START TALKING, KASLAK!
I STOLE THE SWORD FROM THE MUSEUM AND THE RING FROM MAVIS, AS YOU SUSPECTED! WHILE I COULD CREATE PHANTOMS WITH MY INCANTATIONS--CAUSING THEM TO APPEAR AND DIS-APPEAR AT WILL--IT WASN'T UNTIL THIS NIGHT THAT--WITH THE POWER OF THE STOLEN OBJECTS--I COULD CREATE LIVING CREATURES TO OVERCOME YOU!
12

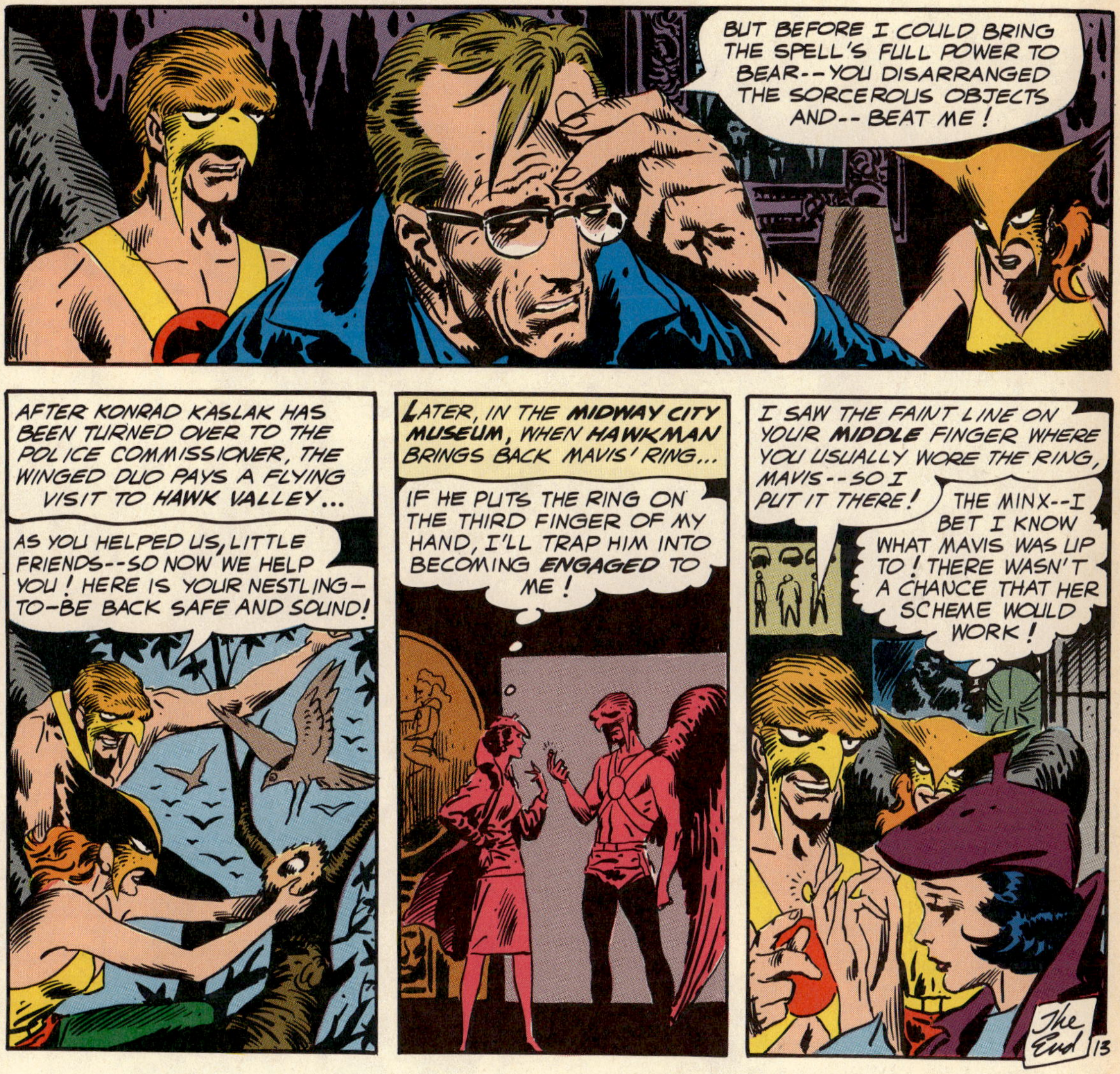
BUT BEFORE I COULD BRING THE SPELL'S FULL POWER TO BEAR--YOU DISARRANGED THE SORCEROUS OBJECTS AND--BEAT ME!
AFTER KONRAD KASLAK HAS BEEN TURNED OVER TO THE POLICE COMMISSIONER, THE WINGED DUO PAYS A FLYING VISIT TO HAWK VALLEY...
AS YOU HELPED US, LITTLE FRIENDS--SO NOW WE HELP YOU! HERE IS YOUR NESTLING-TO-BE BACK SAFE AND SOUND!
LATER, IN THE MIDWAY CITY MUSEUM, WHEN HAWKMAN BRINGS BACK MAVIS' RING...
IF HE PUTS THE RING ON THE THIRD FINGER OF MY HAND, I'LL TRAP HIM INTO BECOMING ENGAGED TO ME!
I SAW THE FAINT LINE ON YOUR MIDDLE FINGER WHERE YOU USUALLY WORE THE RING, MAVIS--SO I PUT IT THERE!
THE MINX--I BET I KNOW WHAT MAVIS WAS UP TO! THERE WASN'T A CHANCE THAT HER SCHEME WOULD WORK!
The End
13

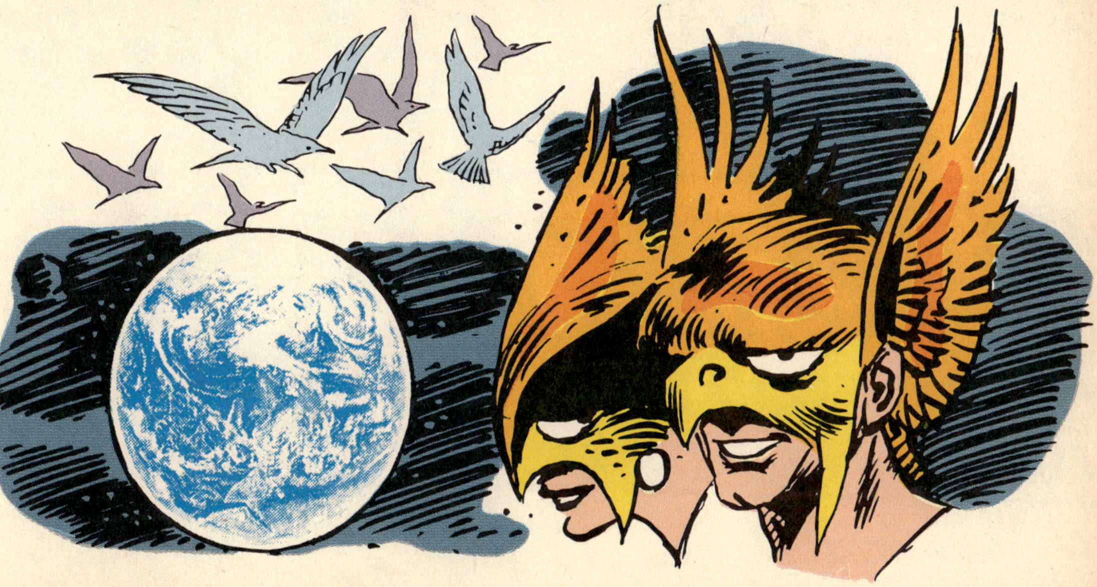

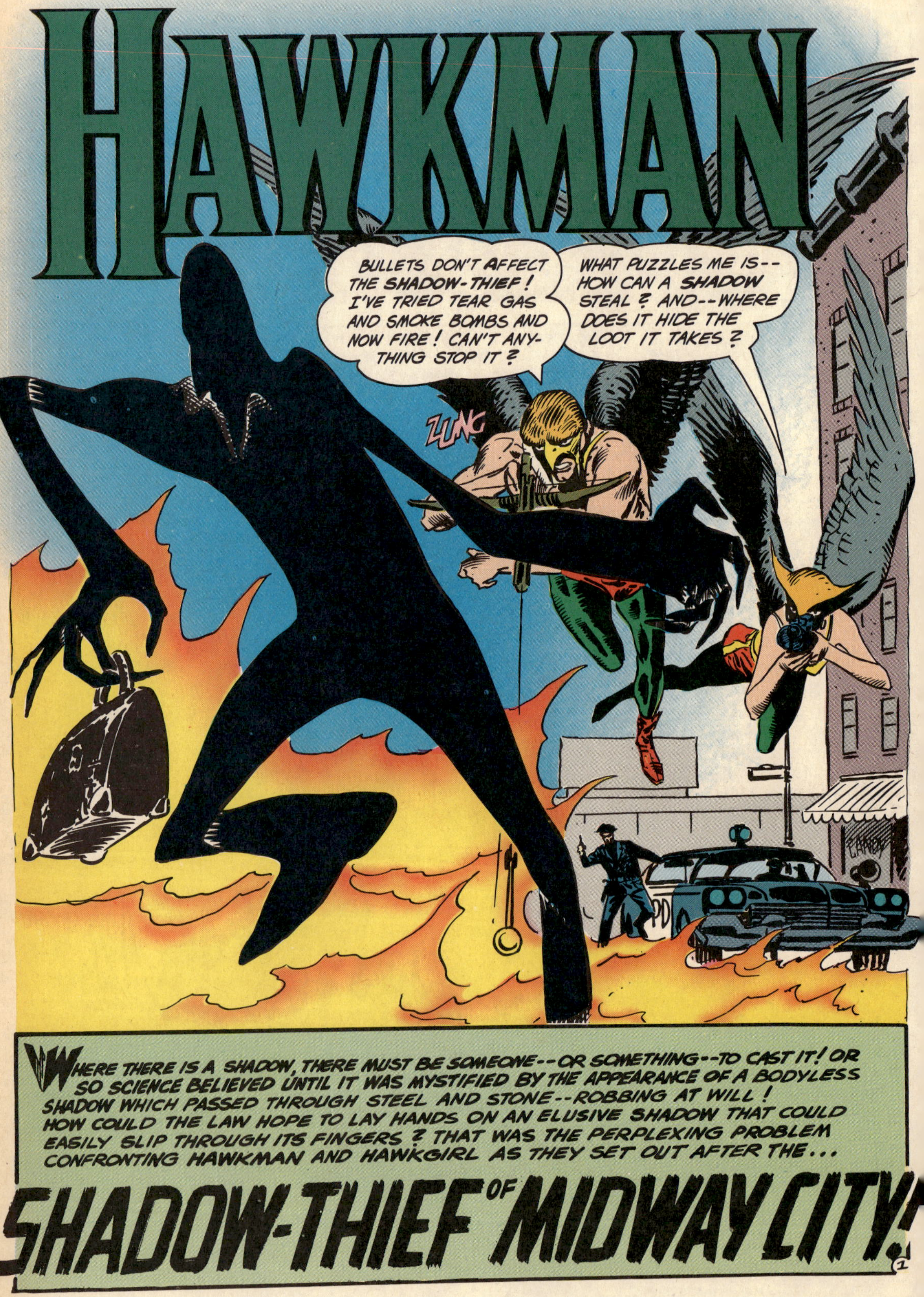
HAWKMAN
BULLETS DON'T AFFECT THE SHADOW-THIEF! I'VE TRIED TEAR GAS AND SMOKE BOMBS AND NOW FIRE! CAN'T ANYTHING STOP IT?
WHAT PUZZLES ME IS--HOW CAN A SHADOW STEAL? AND--WHERE DOES IT HIDE THE LOOT IT TAKES?
ZUNG
WHERE THERE IS A SHADOW, THERE MUST BE SOMEONE--OR SOMETHING--TO CAST IT! OR SO SCIENCE BELIEVED UNTIL IT WAS MYSTIFIED BY THE APPEARANCE OF A BODYLESS SHADOW WHICH PASSED THROUGH STEEL AND STONE--ROBBING AT WILL! HOW COULD THE LAW HOPE TO LAY HANDS ON AN ELUSIVE SHADOW THAT COULD EASILY SLIP THROUGH ITS FINGERS? THAT WAS THE PERPLEXING PROBLEM CONFRONTING HAWKMAN AND HAWKGIRL AS THEY SET OUT AFTER THE...
SHADOW-THIEF OF MIDWAY CITY!

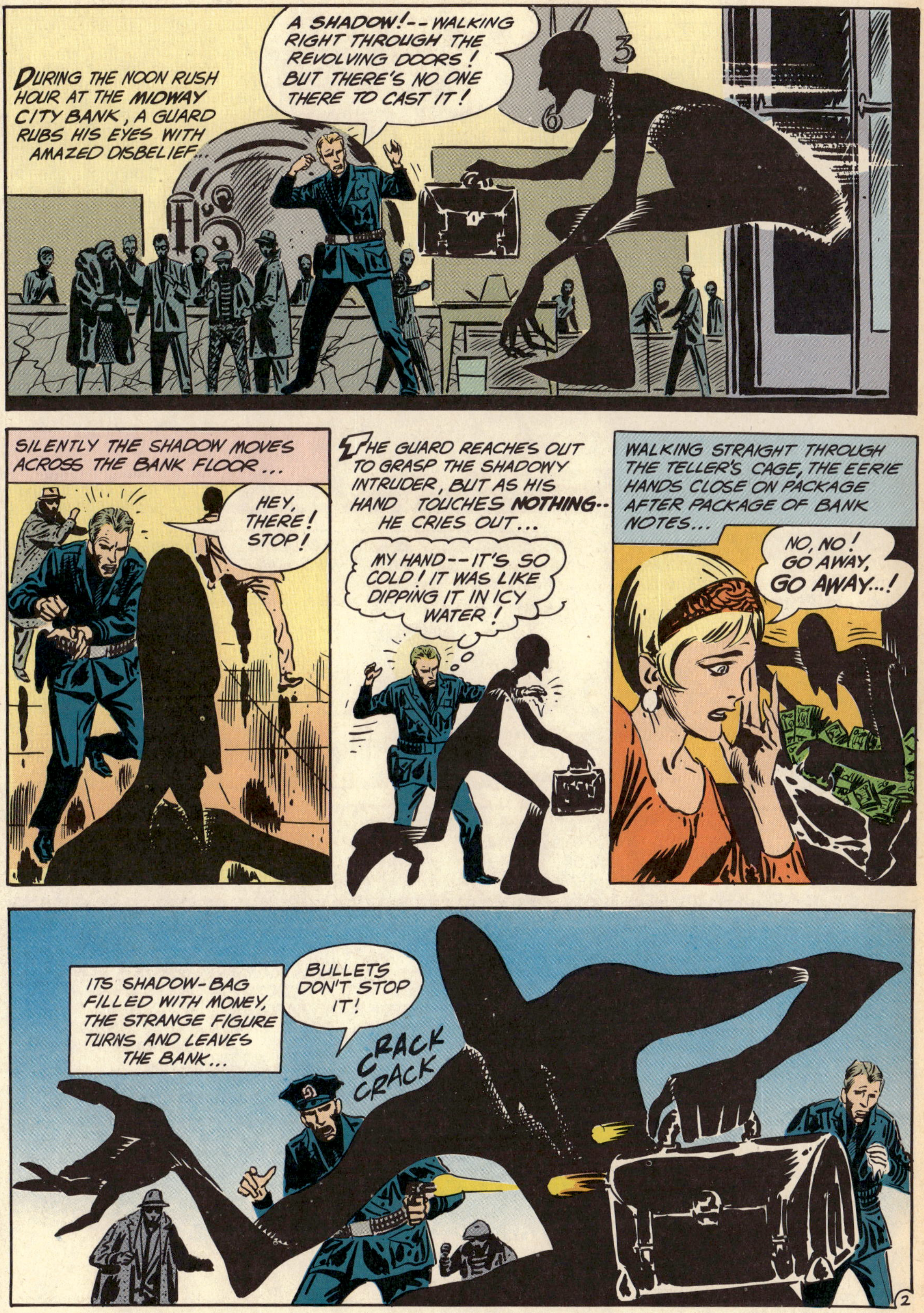
DURING THE NOON RUSH HOUR AT THE MIDWAY CITY BANK, A GUARD RUBS HIS EYES WITH AMAZED DISBELIEF...
A SHADOW!--WALKING RIGHT THROUGH THE REVOLVING DOORS! BUT THERE'S NO ONE THERE TO CAST IT!
SILENTLY THE SHADOW MOVES ACROSS THE BANK FLOOR...
HEY, THERE! STOP!
THE GUARD REACHES OUT TO GRASP THE SHADOWY INTRUDER, BUT AS HIS HAND TOUCHES NOTHING.. HE CRIES OUT...
MY HAND--IT'S SO COLD! IT WAS LIKE DIPPING IT IN ICY WATER!
WALKING STRAIGHT THROUGH THE TELLER'S CAGE, THE EERIE HANDS CLOSE ON PACKAGE AFTER PACKAGE OF BANK NOTES...
NO, NO! GO AWAY, GO AWAY...!
ITS SHADOW-BAG FILLED WITH MONEY, THE STRANGE FIGURE TURNS AND LEAVES THE BANK...
BULLETS DON'T STOP IT!
CRACK CRACK
2

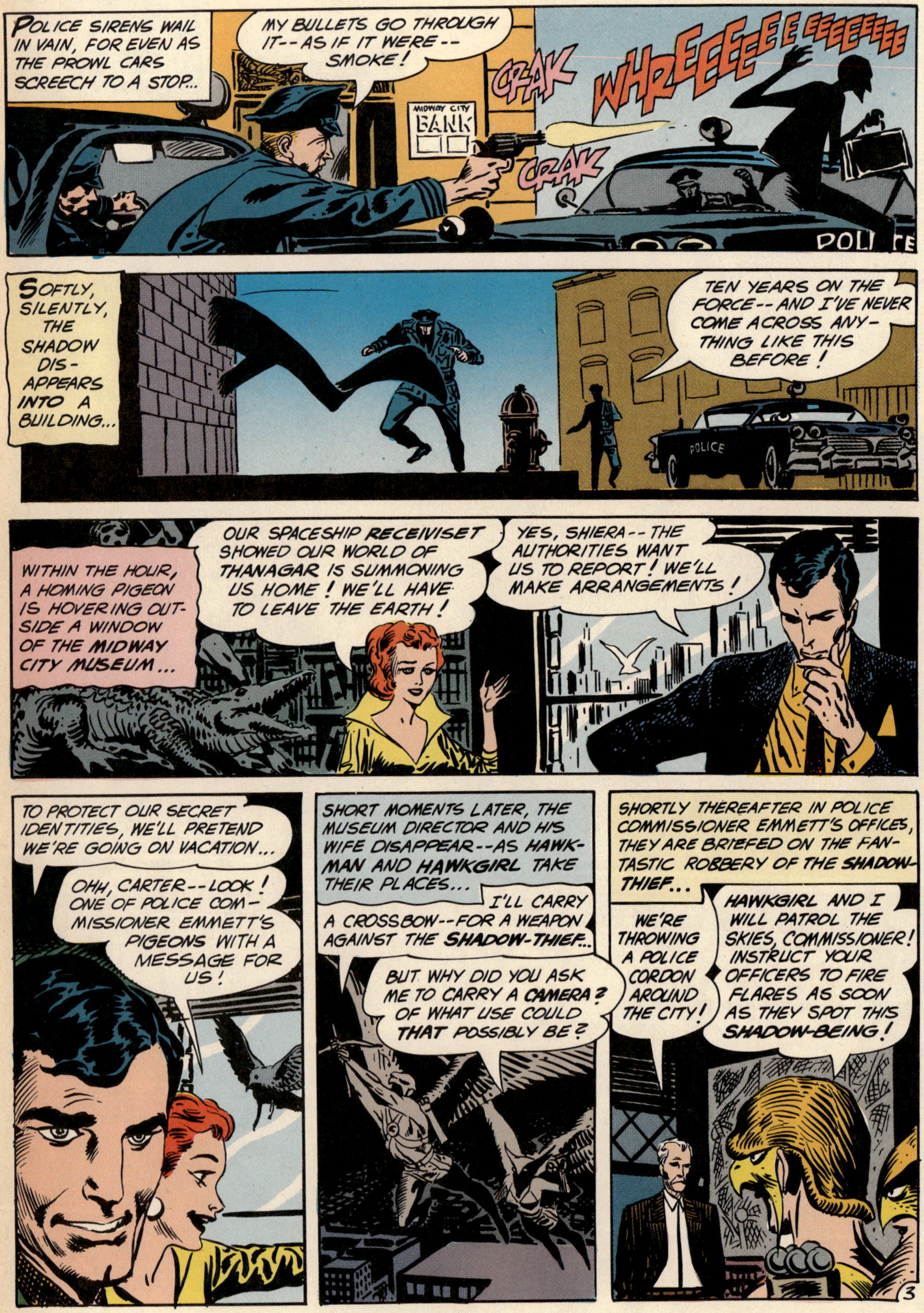
POLICE SIRENS WAIL IN VAIN, FOR EVEN AS THE PROWL CARS SCREECH TO A STOP...
MY BULLETS GO THROUGH IT-- AS IF IT WERE-- SMOKE!
MIDWAY CITY BANK
CRAK
WHREEEEEEEEEEEEE
CRAK
POLICE
SOFTLY, SILENTLY, THE SHADOW DIS-APPEARS INTO A BUILDING...
TEN YEARS ON THE FORCE-- AND I'VE NEVER COME ACROSS ANY-THING LIKE THIS BEFORE!
POLICE
WITHIN THE HOUR, A HOMING PIGEON IS HOVERING OUT-SIDE A WINDOW OF THE MIDWAY CITY MUSEUM...
OUR SPACESHIP RECEIVISET SHOWED OUR WORLD OF THANAGAR IS SUMMONING US HOME! WE'LL HAVE TO LEAVE THE EARTH!
YES, SHIERA-- THE AUTHORITIES WANT US TO REPORT! WE'LL MAKE ARRANGEMENTS!
TO PROTECT OUR SECRET IDENTITIES, WE'LL PRETEND WE'RE GOING ON VACATION...
OHH, CARTER-- LOOK! ONE OF POLICE COM-MISSIONER EMMETT'S PIGEONS WITH A MESSAGE FOR US!
SHORT MOMENTS LATER, THE MUSEUM DIRECTOR AND HIS WIFE DISAPPEAR-- AS HAWK-MAN AND HAWKGIRL TAKE THEIR PLACES...
I'LL CARRY A CROSSBOW-- FOR A WEAPON AGAINST THE SHADOW-THIEF...
BUT WHY DID YOU ASK ME TO CARRY A CAMERA? OF WHAT USE COULD THAT POSSIBLY BE?
SHORTLY THEREAFTER IN POLICE COMMISSIONER EMMETT'S OFFICES, THEY ARE BRIEFED ON THE FAN-TASTIC ROBBERY OF THE SHADOW-THIEF...
WE'RE THROWING A POLICE CORDON AROUND THE CITY!
HAWKGIRL AND I WILL PATROL THE SKIES, COMMISSIONER! INSTRUCT YOUR OFFICERS TO FIRE FLARES AS SOON AS THEY SPOT THIS SHADOW-BEING!
3

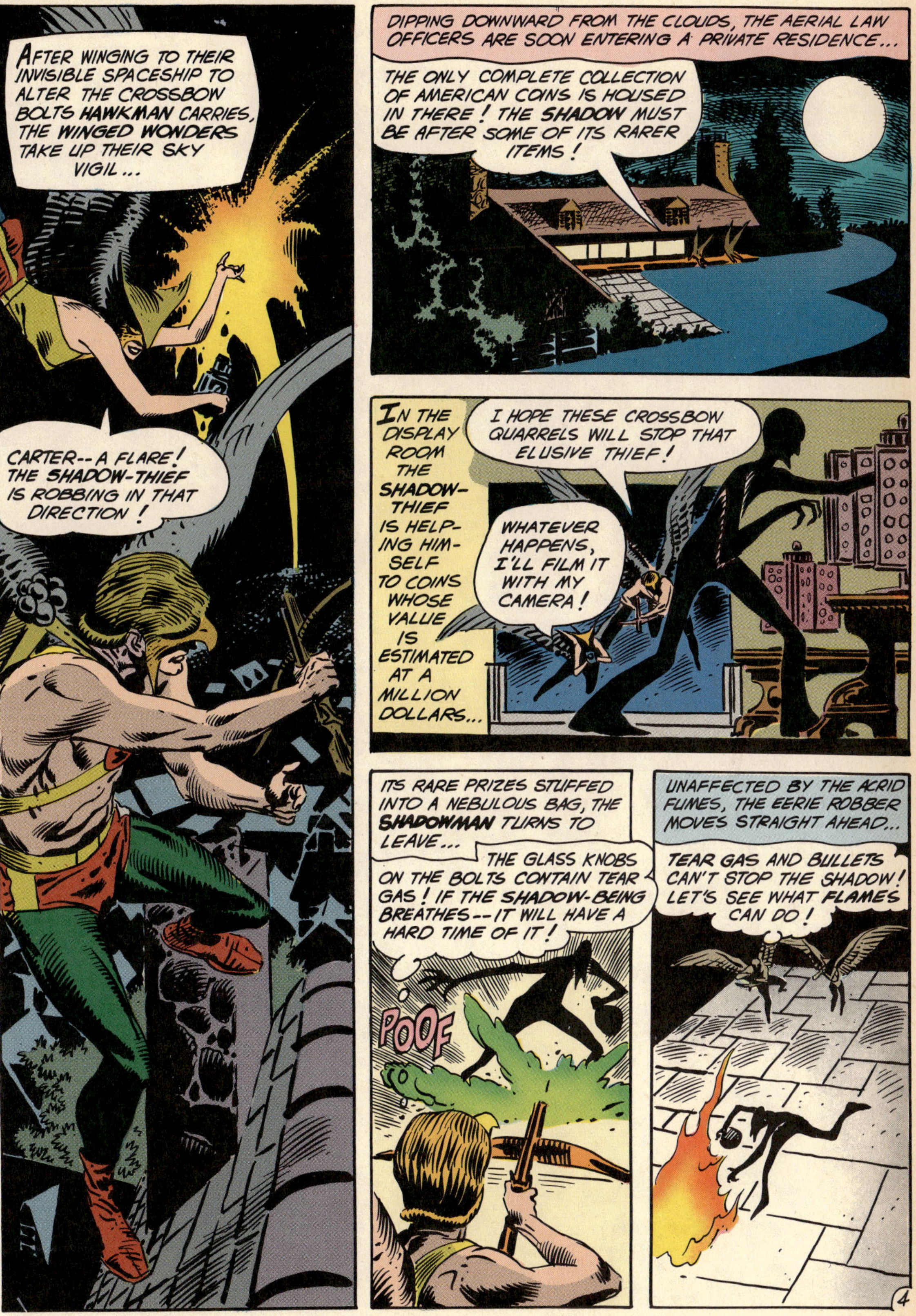
AFTER WINGING TO THEIR INVISIBLE SPACESHIP TO ALTER THE CROSSBOW BOLTS HAWKMAN CARRIES, THE WINGED WONDERS TAKE UP THEIR SKY VIGIL...
CARTER-- A FLARE! THE SHADOW-THIEF IS ROBBING IN THAT DIRECTION!
DIPPING DOWNWARD FROM THE CLOUDS, THE AERIAL LAW OFFICERS ARE SOON ENTERING A PRIVATE RESIDENCE...
THE ONLY COMPLETE COLLECTION OF AMERICAN COINS IS HOUSED IN THERE! THE SHADOW MUST BE AFTER SOME OF ITS RARER ITEMS!
IN THE DISPLAY ROOM THE SHADOW-THIEF IS HELPING HIMSELF TO COINS WHOSE VALUE IS ESTIMATED AT A MILLION DOLLARS...
I HOPE THESE CROSSBOW QUARRELS WILL STOP THAT ELUSIVE THIEF!
WHATEVER HAPPENS, I'LL FILM IT WITH MY CAMERA!
ITS RARE PRIZES STUFFED INTO A NEBULOUS BAG, THE SHADOWMAN TURNS TO LEAVE...
THE GLASS KNOBS ON THE BOLTS CONTAIN TEAR GAS! IF THE SHADOW-BEING BREATHES-- IT WILL HAVE A HARD TIME OF IT!
POOF
UNAFFECTED BY THE ACRID FUMES, THE EERIE ROBBER MOVES STRAIGHT AHEAD...
TEAR GAS AND BULLETS CAN'T STOP THE SHADOW! LET'S SEE WHAT FLAMES CAN DO!
4

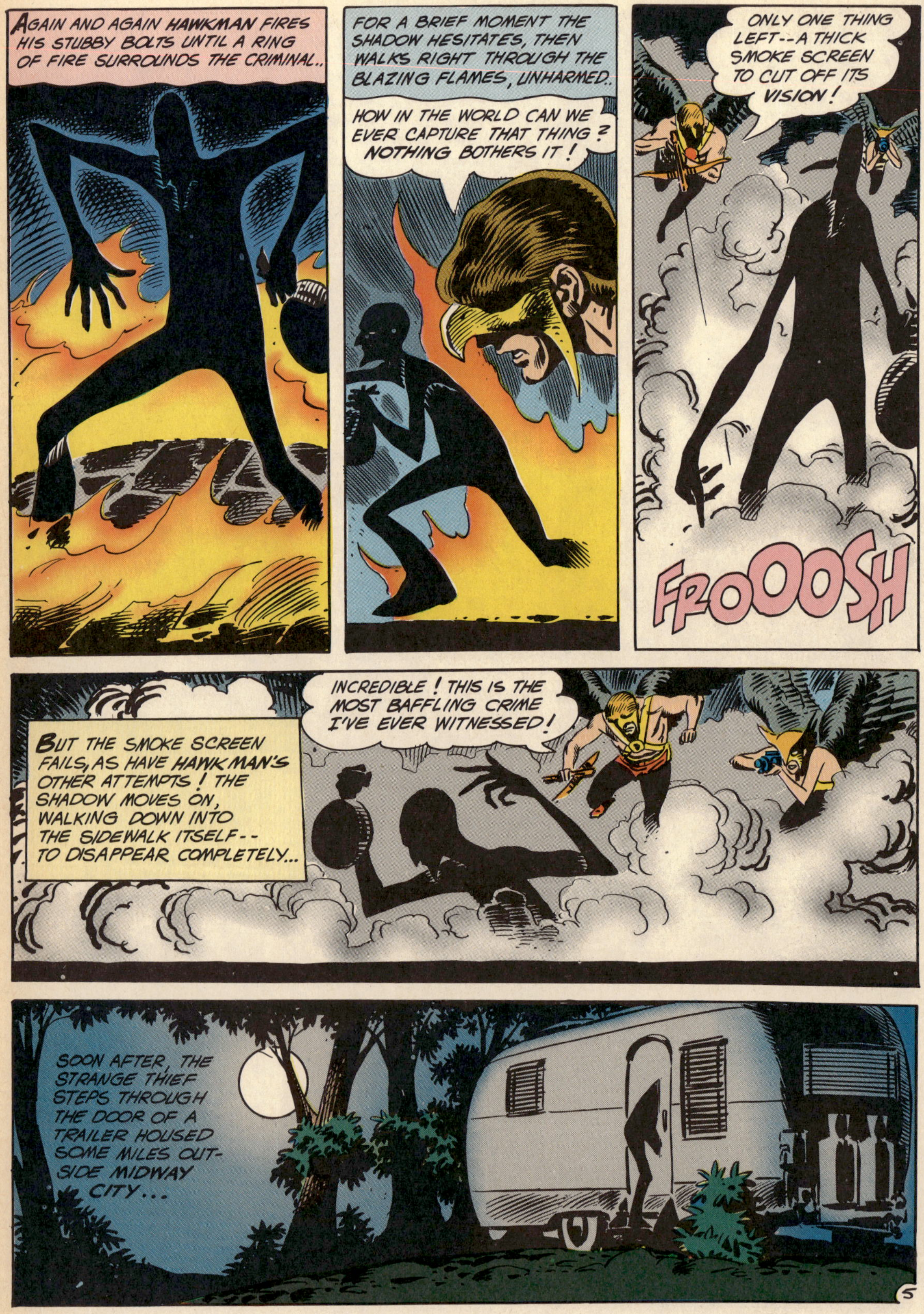
AGAIN AND AGAIN HAWKMAN FIRES HIS STUBBY BOLTS UNTIL A RING OF FIRE SURROUNDS THE CRIMINAL..
FOR A BRIEF MOMENT THE SHADOW HESITATES, THEN WALKS RIGHT THROUGH THE BLAZING FLAMES, UNHARMED.
HOW IN THE WORLD CAN WE EVER CAPTURE THAT THING? NOTHING BOTHERS IT!
ONLY ONE THING LEFT--A THICK SMOKE SCREEN TO CUT OFF ITS VISION!
FROOOOSH
BUT THE SMOKE SCREEN FAILS, AS HAVE HAWKMAN'S OTHER ATTEMPTS! THE SHADOW MOVES ON, WALKING DOWN INTO THE SIDEWALK ITSELF-- TO DISAPPEAR COMPLETELY...
INCREDIBLE! THIS IS THE MOST BAFFLING CRIME I'VE EVER WITNESSED!
SOON AFTER, THE STRANGE THIEF STEPS THROUGH THE DOOR OF A TRAILER HOUSED SOME MILES OUTSIDE MIDWAY CITY...
5

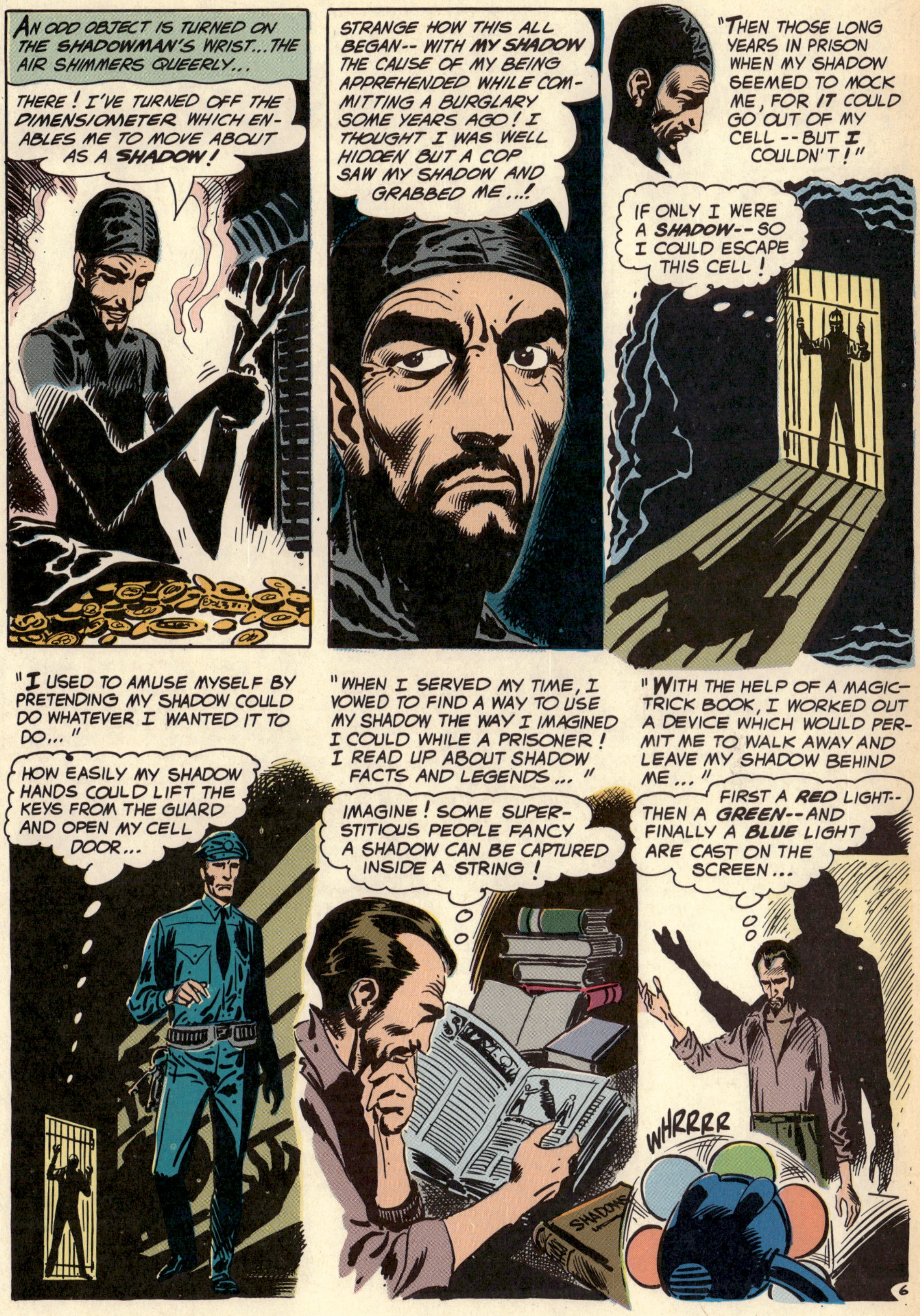
AN ODD OBJECT IS TURNED ON THE SHADOWMAN'S WRIST... THE AIR SHIMMERS QUEERLY...
THERE! I'VE TURNED OFF THE DIMENSIOMETER WHICH ENABLES ME TO MOVE ABOUT AS A SHADOW!
STRANGE HOW THIS ALL BEGAN-- WITH MY SHADOW THE CAUSE OF MY BEING APPREHENDED WHILE COMMITTING A BURGLARY SOME YEARS AGO! I THOUGHT I WAS WELL HIDDEN BUT A COP SAW MY SHADOW AND GRABBED ME...!
"THEN THOSE LONG YEARS IN PRISON WHEN MY SHADOW SEEMED TO MOCK ME, FOR IT COULD GO OUT OF MY CELL -- BUT I COULDN'T!"
IF ONLY I WERE A SHADOW-- SO I COULD ESCAPE THIS CELL!
"I USED TO AMUSE MYSELF BY PRETENDING MY SHADOW COULD DO WHATEVER I WANTED IT TO DO..."
HOW EASILY MY SHADOW HANDS COULD LIFT THE KEYS FROM THE GUARD AND OPEN MY CELL DOOR...
"WHEN I SERVED MY TIME, I VOWED TO FIND A WAY TO USE MY SHADOW THE WAY I IMAGINED I COULD WHILE A PRISONER! I READ UP ABOUT SHADOW FACTS AND LEGENDS..."
IMAGINE! SOME SUPERSTITIOUS PEOPLE FANCY A SHADOW CAN BE CAPTURED INSIDE A STRING!
SHADOWS
"WITH THE HELP OF A MAGIC-TRICK BOOK, I WORKED OUT A DEVICE WHICH WOULD PERMIT ME TO WALK AWAY AND LEAVE MY SHADOW BEHIND ME..."
FIRST A RED LIGHT-- THEN A GREEN--AND FINALLY A BLUE LIGHT ARE CAST ON THE SCREEN...
WHRRRR
6

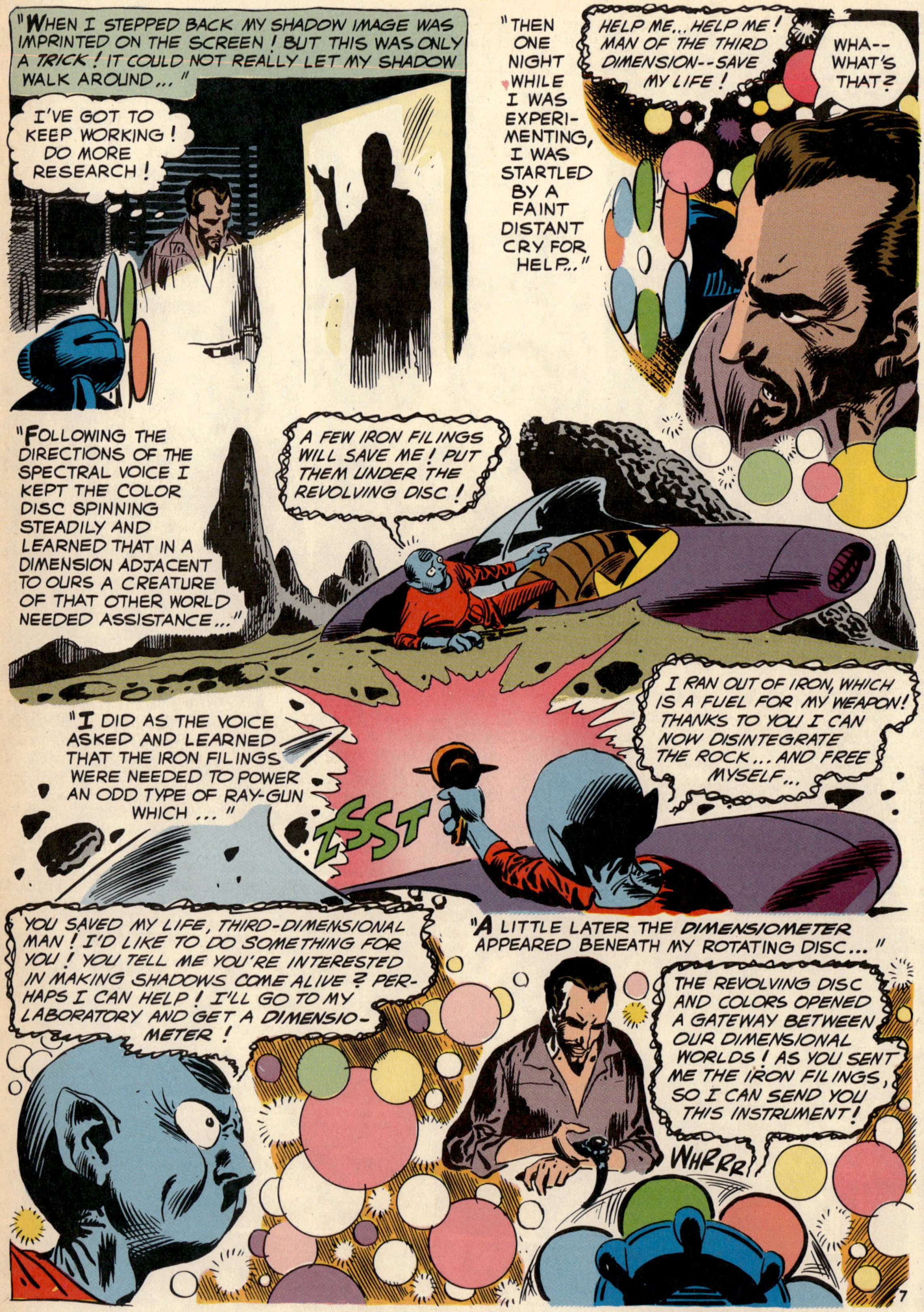
"WHEN I STEPPED BACK MY SHADOW IMAGE WAS IMPRINTED ON THE SCREEN! BUT THIS WAS ONLY A TRICK! IT COULD NOT REALLY LET MY SHADOW WALK AROUND..."
I'VE GOT TO KEEP WORKING! DO MORE RESEARCH!
"THEN ONE NIGHT WHILE I WAS EXPERIMENTING, I WAS STARTLED BY A FAINT DISTANT CRY FOR HELP..."
HELP ME... HELP ME! MAN OF THE THIRD DIMENSION--SAVE MY LIFE!
WHA-- WHAT'S THAT?
"FOLLOWING THE DIRECTIONS OF THE SPECTRAL VOICE I KEPT THE COLOR DISC SPINNING STEADILY AND LEARNED THAT IN A DIMENSION ADJACENT TO OURS A CREATURE OF THAT OTHER WORLD NEEDED ASSISTANCE..."
A FEW IRON FILINGS WILL SAVE ME! PUT THEM UNDER THE REVOLVING DISC!
"I DID AS THE VOICE ASKED AND LEARNED THAT THE IRON FILINGS WERE NEEDED TO POWER AN ODD TYPE OF RAY-GUN WHICH..."
I RAN OUT OF IRON, WHICH IS A FUEL FOR MY WEAPON! THANKS TO YOU I CAN NOW DISINTEGRATE THE ROCK... AND FREE MYSELF...
ZSST
YOU SAVED MY LIFE, THIRD-DIMENSIONAL MAN! I'D LIKE TO DO SOMETHING FOR YOU! YOU TELL ME YOU'RE INTERESTED IN MAKING SHADOWS COME ALIVE? PERHAPS I CAN HELP! I'LL GO TO MY LABORATORY AND GET A DIMENSIOMETER!
"A LITTLE LATER THE DIMENSIOMETER APPEARED BENEATH MY ROTATING DISC..."
THE REVOLVING DISC AND COLORS OPENED A GATEWAY BETWEEN OUR DIMENSIONAL WORLDS! AS YOU SENT ME THE IRON FILINGS, SO I CAN SEND YOU THIS INSTRUMENT!
WHRRR
7

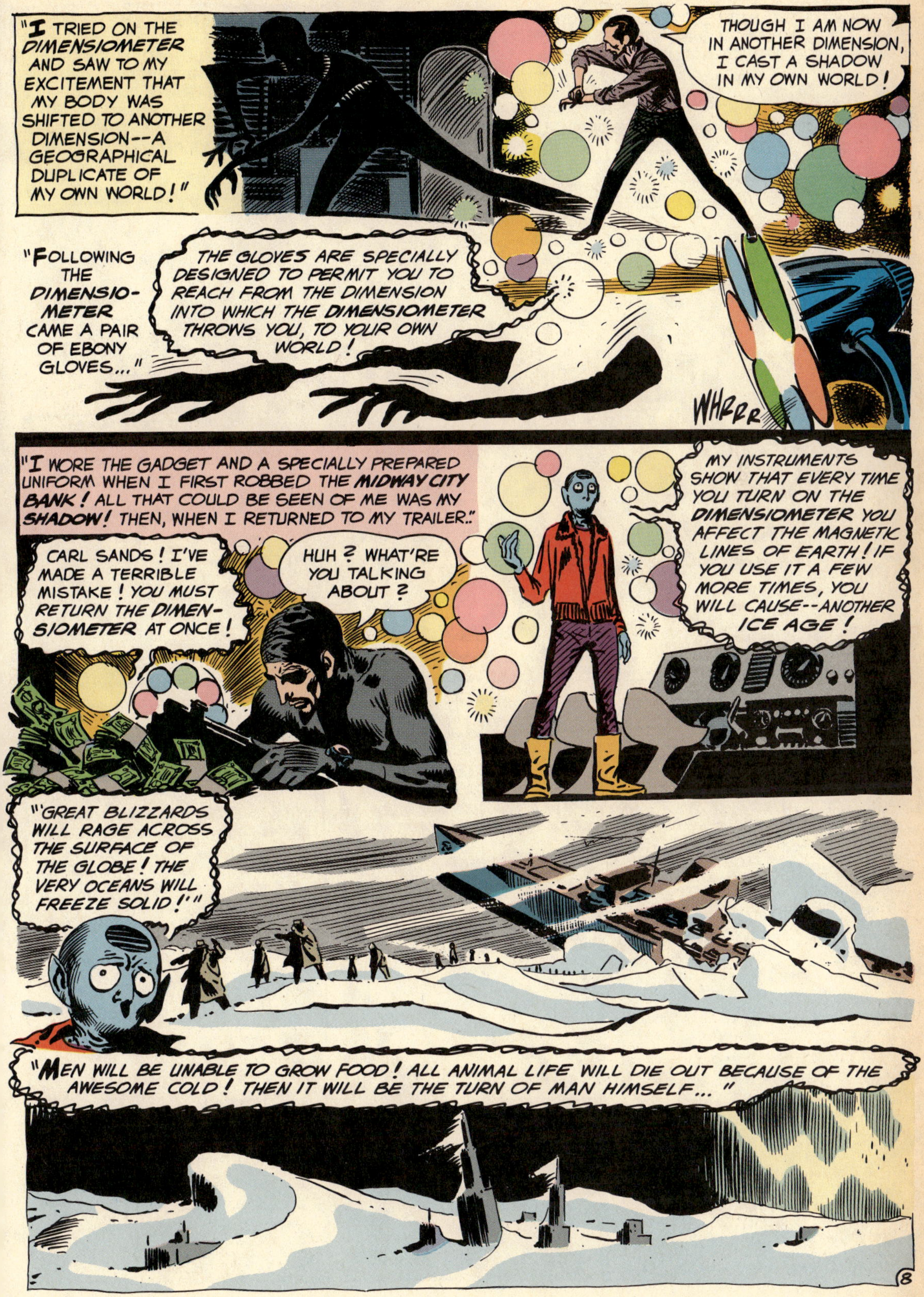
"I TRIED ON THE DIMENSIOMETER AND SAW TO MY EXCITEMENT THAT MY BODY WAS SHIFTED TO ANOTHER DIMENSION--A GEOGRAPHICAL DUPLICATE OF MY OWN WORLD!"
THOUGH I AM NOW IN ANOTHER DIMENSION, I CAST A SHADOW IN MY OWN WORLD!
"FOLLOWING THE DIMENSIOMETER CAME A PAIR OF EBONY GLOVES..."
THE GLOVES ARE SPECIALLY DESIGNED TO PERMIT YOU TO REACH FROM THE DIMENSION INTO WHICH THE DIMENSIOMETER THROWS YOU, TO YOUR OWN WORLD!
WHRRR
"I WORE THE GADGET AND A SPECIALLY PREPARED UNIFORM WHEN I FIRST ROBBED THE MIDWAY CITY BANK! ALL THAT COULD BE SEEN OF ME WAS MY SHADOW! THEN, WHEN I RETURNED TO MY TRAILER."
CARL SANDS! I'VE MADE A TERRIBLE MISTAKE! YOU MUST RETURN THE DIMENSIOMETER AT ONCE!
HUH? WHAT'RE YOU TALKING ABOUT?
MY INSTRUMENTS SHOW THAT EVERY TIME YOU TURN ON THE DIMENSIOMETER YOU AFFECT THE MAGNETIC LINES OF EARTH! IF YOU USE IT A FEW MORE TIMES, YOU WILL CAUSE--ANOTHER ICE AGE!
"GREAT BLIZZARDS WILL RAGE ACROSS THE SURFACE OF THE GLOBE! THE VERY OCEANS WILL FREEZE SOLID!"
"MEN WILL BE UNABLE TO GROW FOOD! ALL ANIMAL LIFE WILL DIE OUT BECAUSE OF THE AWESOME COLD! THEN IT WILL BE THE TURN OF MAN HIMSELF..."
8

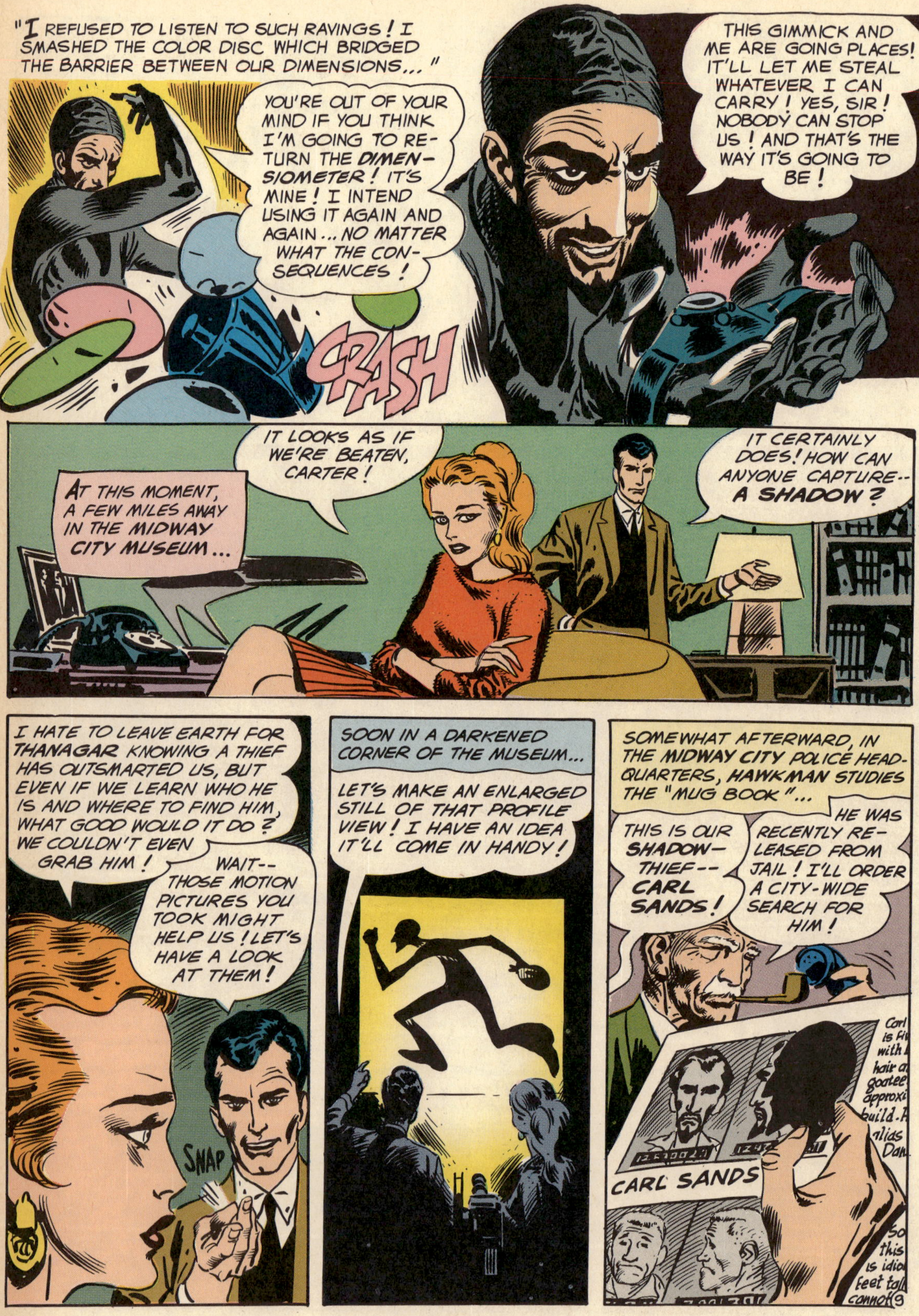
"I REFUSED TO LISTEN TO SUCH RAVINGS! I SMASHED THE COLOR DISC WHICH BRIDGED THE BARRIER BETWEEN OUR DIMENSIONS..."
YOU'RE OUT OF YOUR MIND IF YOU THINK I'M GOING TO RETURN THE DIMENSIOMETER! IT'S MINE! I INTEND USING IT AGAIN AND AGAIN... NO MATTER WHAT THE CONSEQUENCES!
CRASH
THIS GIMMICK AND ME ARE GOING PLACES! IT'LL LET ME STEAL WHATEVER I CAN CARRY! YES, SIR! NOBODY CAN STOP US! AND THAT'S THE WAY IT'S GOING TO BE!
AT THIS MOMENT, A FEW MILES AWAY IN THE MIDWAY CITY MUSEUM...
IT LOOKS AS IF WE'RE BEATEN, CARTER!
IT CERTAINLY DOES! HOW CAN ANYONE CAPTURE-- A SHADOW?
I HATE TO LEAVE EARTH FOR THANAGAR KNOWING A THIEF HAS OUTSMARTED US, BUT EVEN IF WE LEARN WHO HE IS AND WHERE TO FIND HIM, WHAT GOOD WOULD IT DO? WE COULDN'T EVEN GRAB HIM!
WAIT-- THOSE MOTION PICTURES YOU TOOK MIGHT HELP US! LET'S HAVE A LOOK AT THEM!
SNAP
SOON IN A DARKENED CORNER OF THE MUSEUM...
LET'S MAKE AN ENLARGED STILL OF THAT PROFILE VIEW! I HAVE AN IDEA IT'LL COME IN HANDY!
SOMEWHAT AFTERWARD, IN THE MIDWAY CITY POLICE HEADQUARTERS, HAWKMAN STUDIES THE "MUG BOOK"...
THIS IS OUR SHADOW-THIEF-- CARL SANDS!
HE WAS RECENTLY RELEASED FROM JAIL! I'LL ORDER A CITY-WIDE SEARCH FOR HIM!
CARL SANDS
9

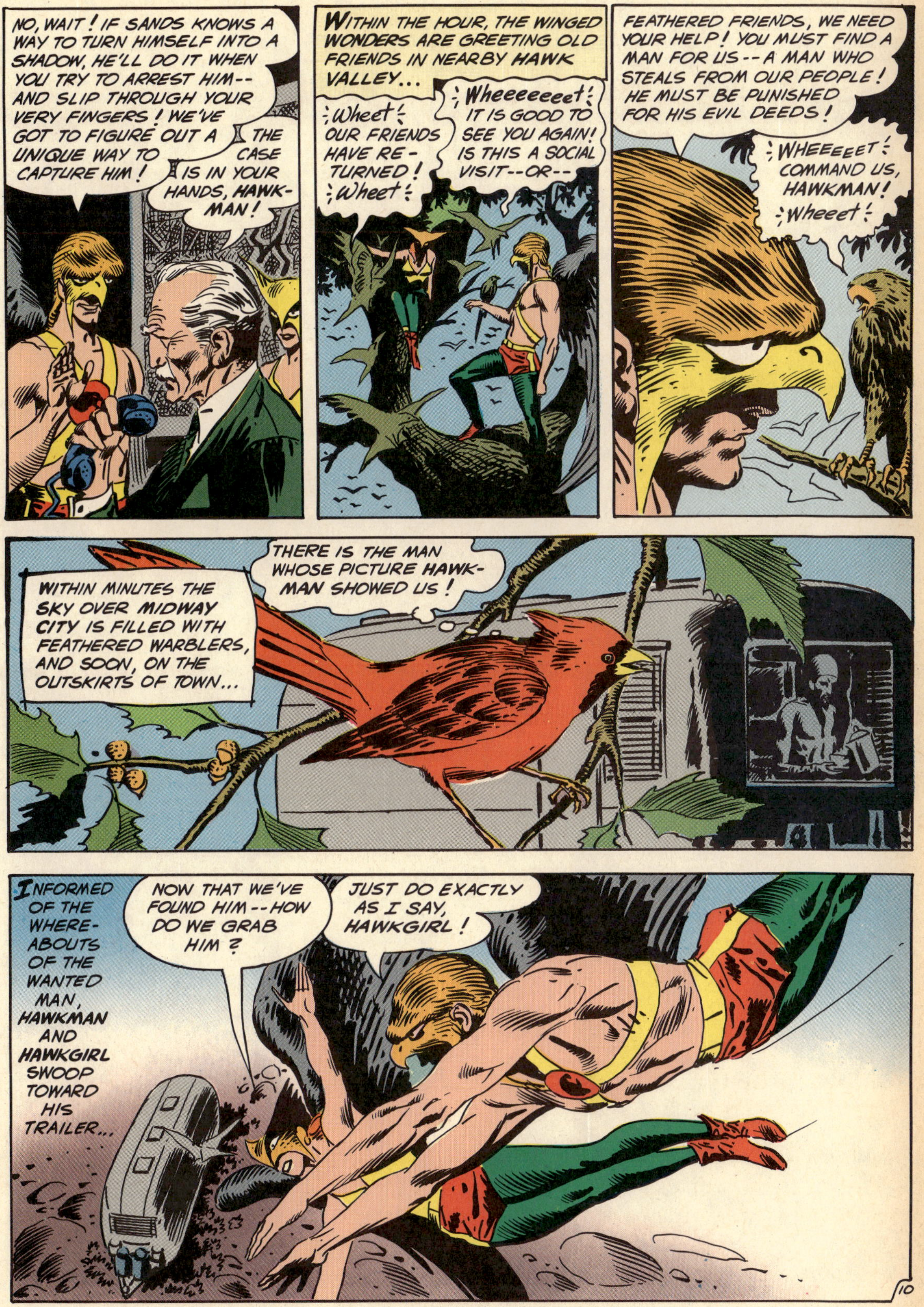
NO, WAIT! IF SANDS KNOWS A WAY TO TURN HIMSELF INTO A SHADOW, HE'LL DO IT WHEN YOU TRY TO ARREST HIM-- AND SLIP THROUGH YOUR VERY FINGERS! WE'VE GOT TO FIGURE OUT A UNIQUE WAY TO CAPTURE HIM!
THE CASE IS IN YOUR HANDS, HAWK-MAN!
WITHIN THE HOUR, THE WINGED WONDERS ARE GREETING OLD FRIENDS IN NEARBY HAWK VALLEY...
Wheet OUR FRIENDS HAVE RE-TURNED! Wheet
Wheeeeeeet! IT IS GOOD TO SEE YOU AGAIN! IS THIS A SOCIAL VISIT--OR--
FEATHERED FRIENDS, WE NEED YOUR HELP! YOU MUST FIND A MAN FOR US--A MAN WHO STEALS FROM OUR PEOPLE! HE MUST BE PUNISHED FOR HIS EVIL DEEDS!
WHEEEEEET COMMAND US, HAWKMAN! Wheeet
WITHIN MINUTES THE SKY OVER MIDWAY CITY IS FILLED WITH FEATHERED WARBLERS, AND SOON, ON THE OUTSKIRTS OF TOWN...
THERE IS THE MAN WHOSE PICTURE HAWK-MAN SHOWED US!
INFORMED OF THE WHERE-ABOUTS OF THE WANTED MAN, HAWKMAN AND HAWKGIRL SWOOP TOWARD HIS TRAILER...
NOW THAT WE'VE FOUND HIM--HOW DO WE GRAB HIM?
JUST DO EXACTLY AS I SAY, HAWKGIRL!
10

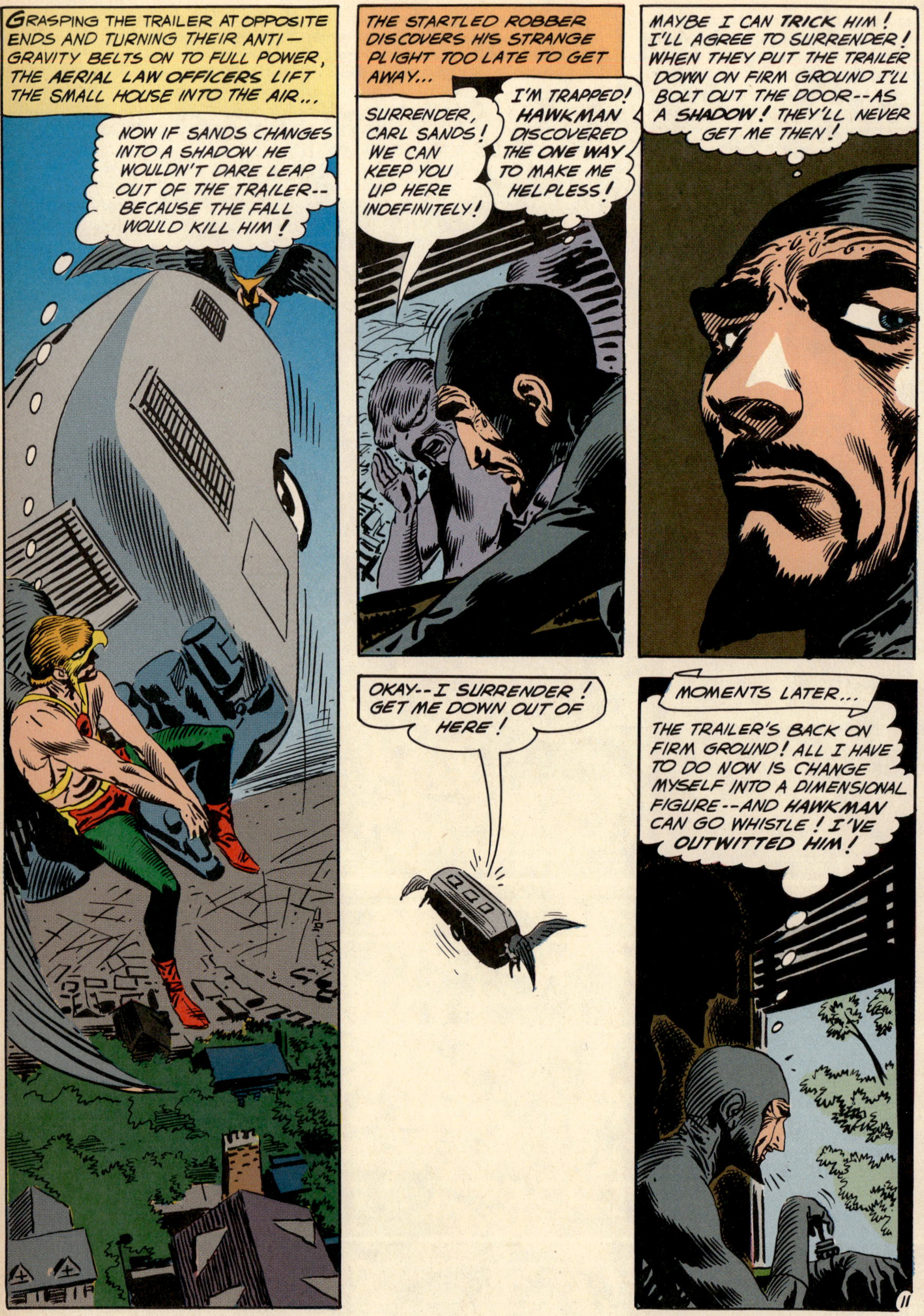
GRASPING THE TRAILER AT OPPOSITE ENDS AND TURNING THEIR ANTI-GRAVITY BELTS ON TO FULL POWER, THE AERIAL LAW OFFICERS LIFT THE SMALL HOUSE INTO THE AIR...
NOW IF SANDS CHANGES INTO A SHADOW HE WOULDN'T DARE LEAP OUT OF THE TRAILER--BECAUSE THE FALL WOULD KILL HIM!
THE STARTLED ROBBER DISCOVERS HIS STRANGE PLIGHT TOO LATE TO GET AWAY...
SURRENDER, CARL SANDS! WE CAN KEEP YOU UP HERE INDEFINITELY!
I'M TRAPPED! HAWKMAN DISCOVERED THE ONE WAY TO MAKE ME HELPLESS!
MAYBE I CAN TRICK HIM! I'LL AGREE TO SURRENDER! WHEN THEY PUT THE TRAILER DOWN ON FIRM GROUND I'LL BOLT OUT THE DOOR--AS A SHADOW! THEY'LL NEVER GET ME THEN!
OKAY--I SURRENDER! GET ME DOWN OUT OF HERE!
MOMENTS LATER...
THE TRAILER'S BACK ON FIRM GROUND! ALL I HAVE TO DO NOW IS CHANGE MYSELF INTO A DIMENSIONAL FIGURE--AND HAWKMAN CAN GO WHISTLE! I'VE OUTWITTED HIM!
11

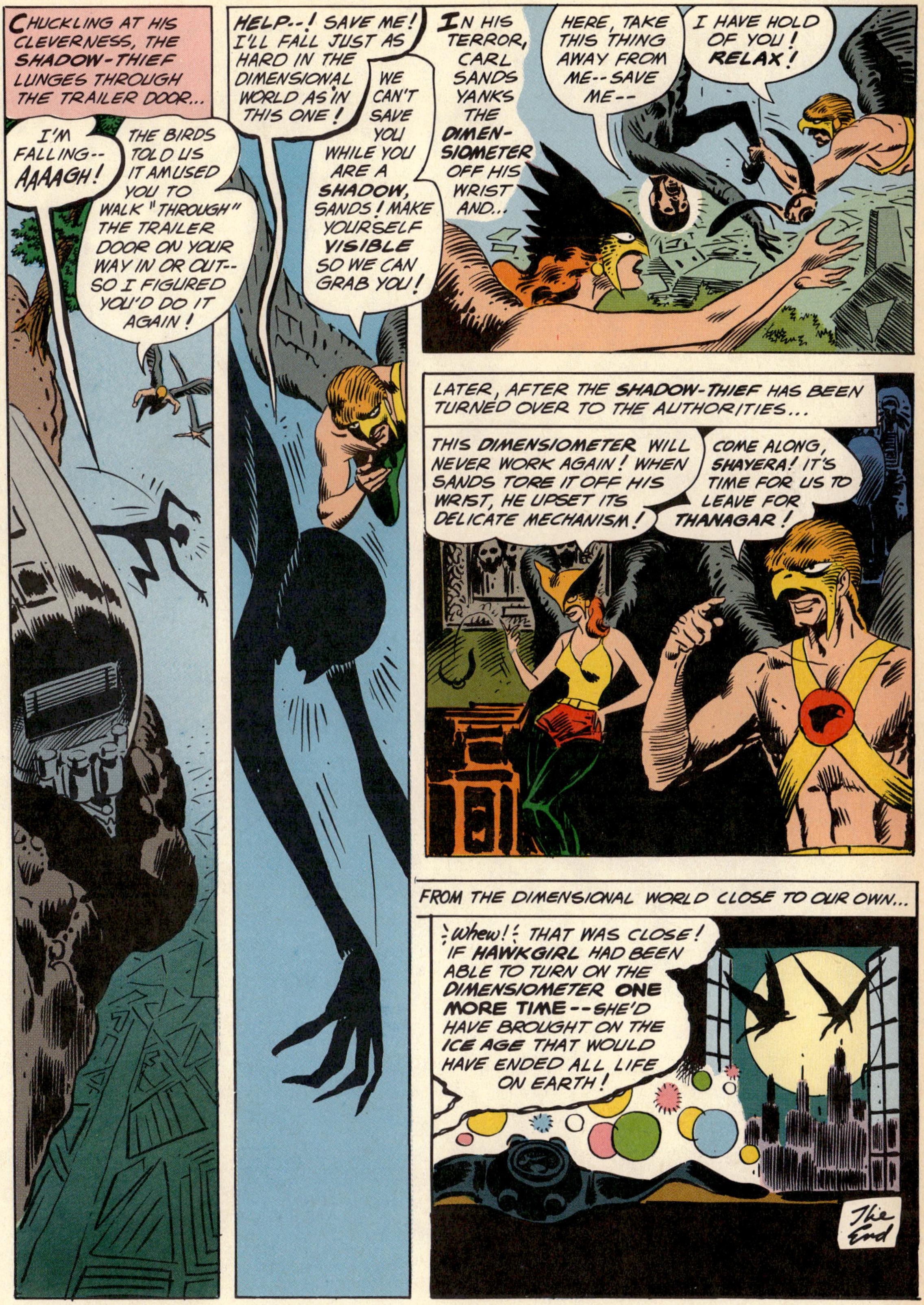
CHUCKLING AT HIS CLEVERNESS, THE SHADOW-THIEF LUNGES THROUGH THE TRAILER DOOR...
I'M FALLING-- AAAAGH!
THE BIRDS TOLD US IT AMUSED YOU TO WALK "THROUGH" THE TRAILER DOOR ON YOUR WAY IN OR OUT-- SO I FIGURED YOU'D DO IT AGAIN!
HELP--! SAVE ME! I'LL FALL JUST AS HARD IN THE DIMENSIONAL WORLD AS IN THIS ONE!
WE CAN'T SAVE YOU WHILE YOU ARE A SHADOW, SANDS! MAKE YOURSELF VISIBLE SO WE CAN GRAB YOU!
IN HIS TERROR, CARL SANDS YANKS THE DIMENSIOMETER OFF HIS WRIST AND...
HERE, TAKE THIS THING AWAY FROM ME-- SAVE ME--
I HAVE HOLD OF YOU! RELAX!
LATER, AFTER THE SHADOW-THIEF HAS BEEN TURNED OVER TO THE AUTHORITIES...
THIS DIMENSIOMETER WILL NEVER WORK AGAIN! WHEN SANDS TORE IT OFF HIS WRIST, HE UPSET ITS DELICATE MECHANISM!
COME ALONG, SHAYERA! IT'S TIME FOR US TO LEAVE FOR THANAGAR!
FROM THE DIMENSIONAL WORLD CLOSE TO OUR OWN...
Whew! THAT WAS CLOSE! IF HAWKGIRL HAD BEEN ABLE TO TURN ON THE DIMENSIOMETER ONE MORE TIME-- SHE'D HAVE BROUGHT ON THE ICE AGE THAT WOULD HAVE ENDED ALL LIFE ON EARTH!
The End

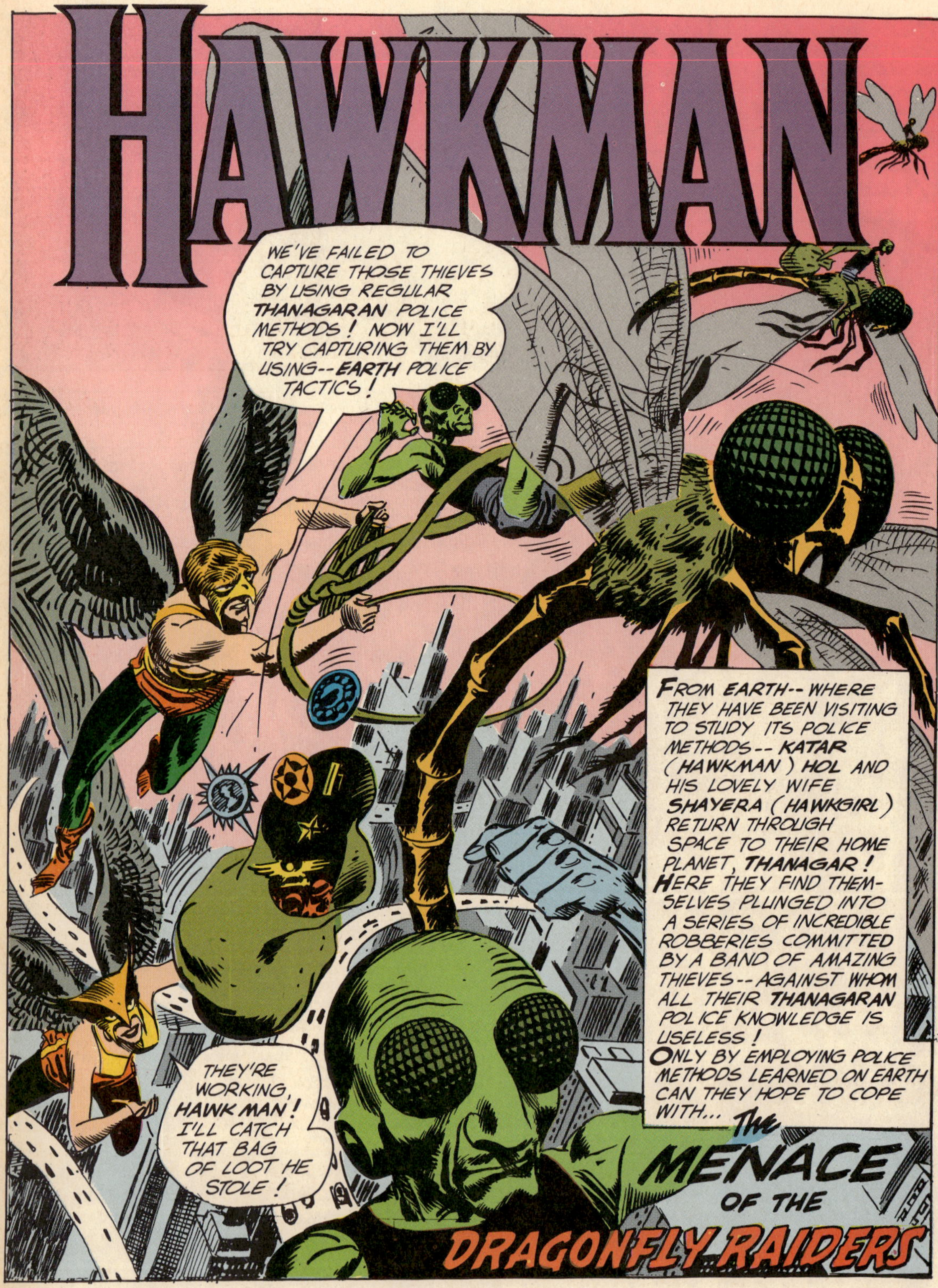
HAWKMAN
WE'VE FAILED TO CAPTURE THOSE THIEVES BY USING REGULAR THANAGARAN POLICE METHODS! NOW I'LL TRY CAPTURING THEM BY USING--EARTH POLICE TACTICS!
FROM EARTH--WHERE THEY HAVE BEEN VISITING TO STUDY ITS POLICE METHODS--KATAR (HAWKMAN) HOL AND HIS LOVELY WIFE SHAYERA (HAWKGIRL) RETURN THROUGH SPACE TO THEIR HOME PLANET, THANAGAR! HERE THEY FIND THEMSELVES PLUNGED INTO A SERIES OF INCREDIBLE ROBBERIES COMMITTED BY A BAND OF AMAZING THIEVES--AGAINST WHOM ALL THEIR THANAGARAN POLICE KNOWLEDGE IS USELESS!
ONLY BY EMPLOYING POLICE METHODS LEARNED ON EARTH CAN THEY HOPE TO COPE WITH...
THEY'RE WORKING, HAWKMAN! I'LL CATCH THAT BAG OF LOOT HE STOLE!
The MENACE OF THE DRAGONFLY RAIDERS

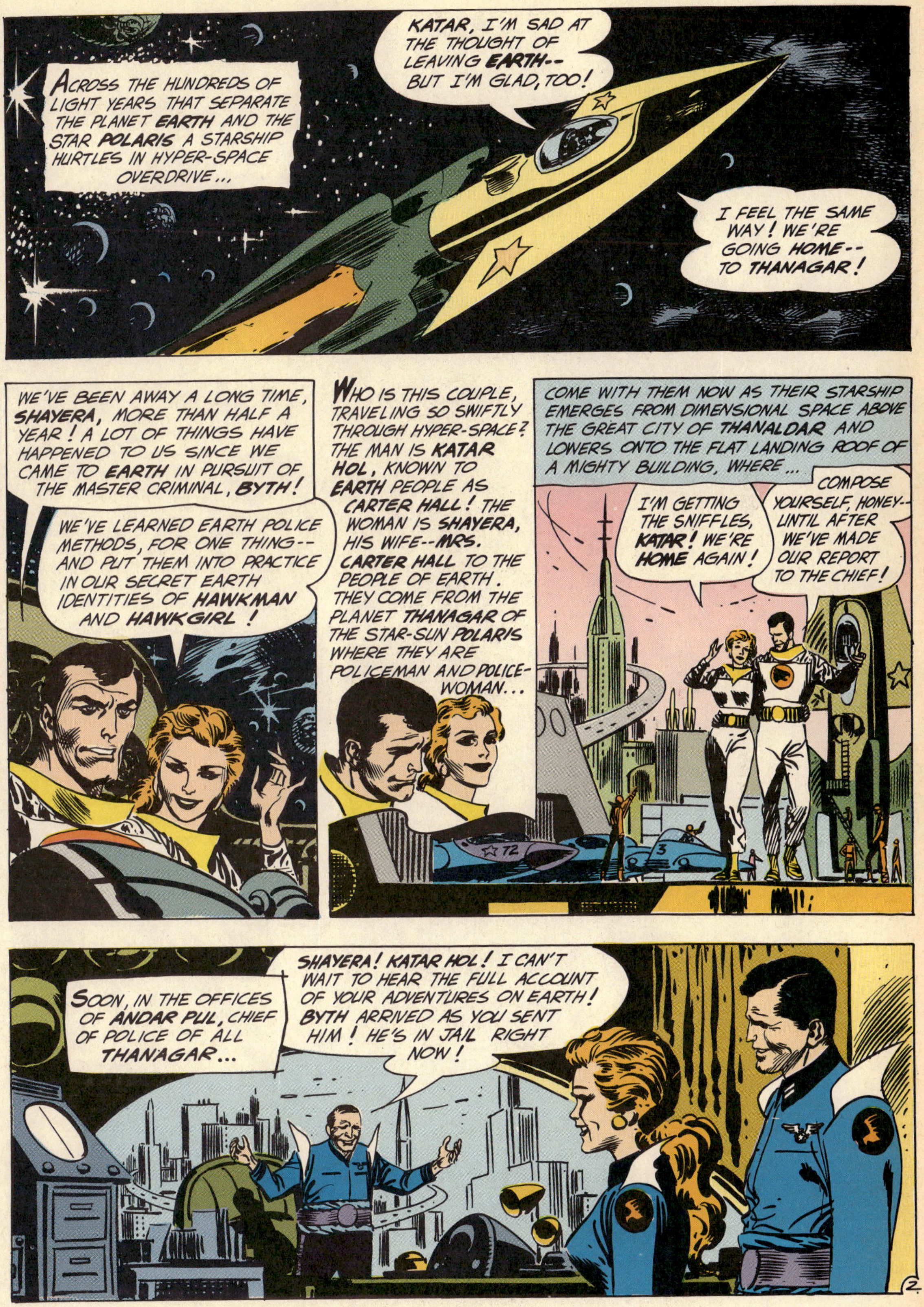
ACROSS THE HUNDREDS OF LIGHT YEARS THAT SEPARATE THE PLANET EARTH AND THE STAR POLARIS A STARSHIP HURTLES IN HYPER-SPACE OVERDRIVE...
KATAR, I'M SAD AT THE THOUGHT OF LEAVING EARTH-- BUT I'M GLAD, TOO!
I FEEL THE SAME WAY! WE'RE GOING HOME-- TO THANAGAR!
WE'VE BEEN AWAY A LONG TIME, SHAYERA, MORE THAN HALF A YEAR! A LOT OF THINGS HAVE HAPPENED TO US SINCE WE CAME TO EARTH IN PURSUIT OF THE MASTER CRIMINAL, BYTH!
WE'VE LEARNED EARTH POLICE METHODS, FOR ONE THING-- AND PUT THEM INTO PRACTICE IN OUR SECRET EARTH IDENTITIES OF HAWKMAN AND HAWKGIRL!
WHO IS THIS COUPLE, TRAVELING SO SWIFTLY THROUGH HYPER-SPACE? THE MAN IS KATAR HOL, KNOWN TO EARTH PEOPLE AS CARTER HALL! THE WOMAN IS SHAYERA, HIS WIFE--MRS. CARTER HALL TO THE PEOPLE OF EARTH. THEY COME FROM THE PLANET THANAGAR OF THE STAR-SUN POLARIS WHERE THEY ARE POLICEMAN AND POLICE-WOMAN...
COME WITH THEM NOW AS THEIR STARSHIP EMERGES FROM DIMENSIONAL SPACE ABOVE THE GREAT CITY OF THANALDAR AND LOWERS ONTO THE FLAT LANDING ROOF OF A MIGHTY BUILDING, WHERE...
I'M GETTING THE SNIFFLES, KATAR! WE'RE HOME AGAIN!
COMPOSE YOURSELF, HONEY-- UNTIL AFTER WE'VE MADE OUR REPORT TO THE CHIEF!
SOON, IN THE OFFICES OF ANDAR PUL, CHIEF OF POLICE OF ALL THANAGAR...
SHAYERA! KATAR HOL! I CAN'T WAIT TO HEAR THE FULL ACCOUNT OF YOUR ADVENTURES ON EARTH! BYTH ARRIVED AS YOU SENT HIM! HE'S IN JAIL RIGHT NOW!
2.

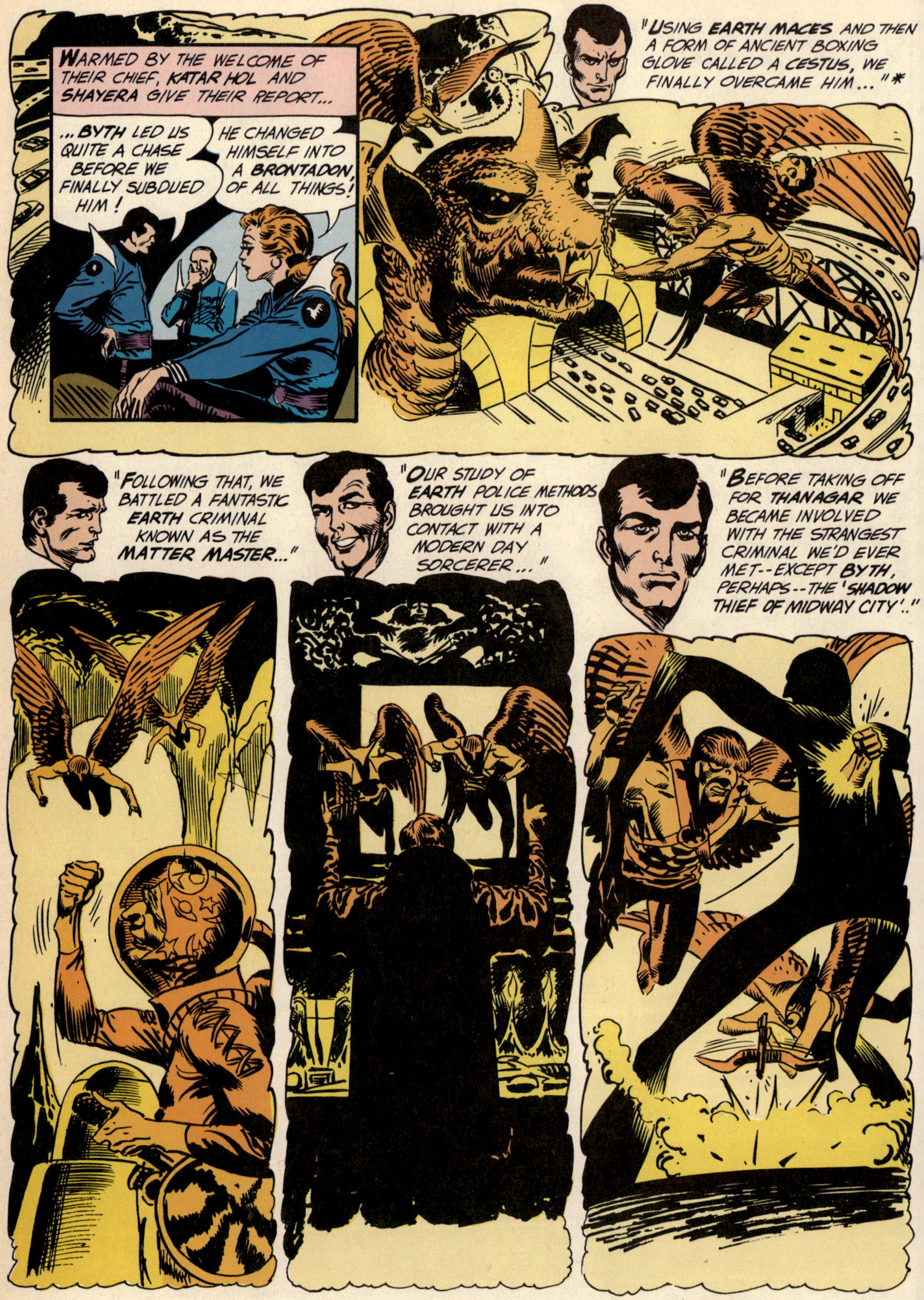
WARMED BY THE WELCOME OF THEIR CHIEF, KATAR HOL AND SHAYERA GIVE THEIR REPORT...
...BYTH LED US QUITE A CHASE BEFORE WE FINALLY SUBDUED HIM!
HE CHANGED HIMSELF INTO A BRONTADON, OF ALL THINGS!
"USING EARTH MACES AND THEN A FORM OF ANCIENT BOXING GLOVE CALLED A CESTUS, WE FINALLY OVERCAME HIM..." *
"FOLLOWING THAT, WE BATTLED A FANTASTIC EARTH CRIMINAL KNOWN AS THE MATTER MASTER..."
"OUR STUDY OF EARTH POLICE METHODS BROUGHT US INTO CONTACT WITH A MODERN DAY SORCERER..."
"BEFORE TAKING OFF FOR THANAGAR WE BECAME INVOLVED WITH THE STRANGEST CRIMINAL WE'D EVER MET--EXCEPT BYTH, PERHAPS--THE 'SHADOW THIEF OF MIDWAY CITY'."

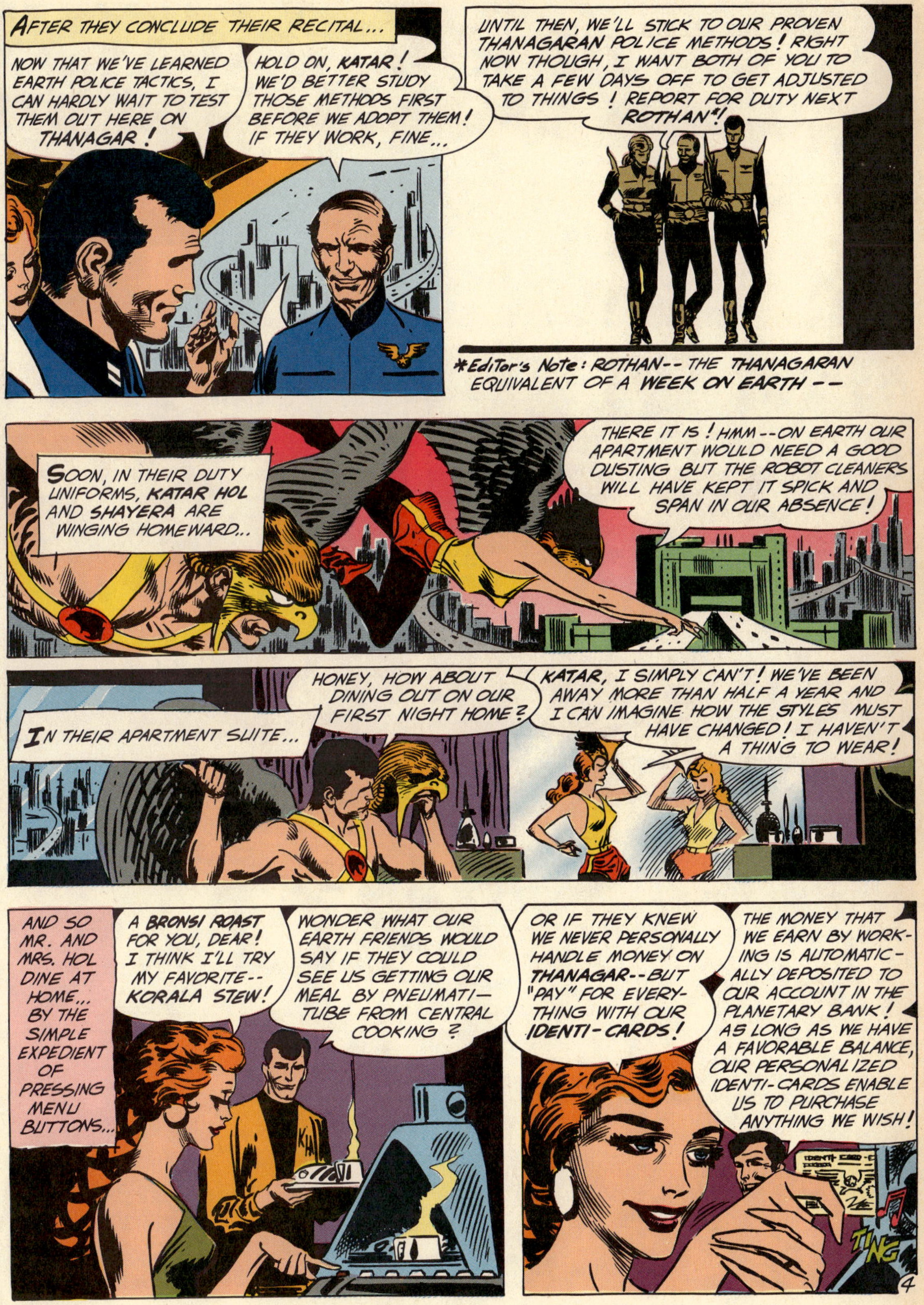
AFTER THEY CONCLUDE THEIR RECITAL...
NOW THAT WE'VE LEARNED EARTH POLICE TACTICS, I CAN HARDLY WAIT TO TEST THEM OUT HERE ON THANAGAR!
HOLD ON, KATAR! WE'D BETTER STUDY THOSE METHODS FIRST BEFORE WE ADOPT THEM! IF THEY WORK, FINE...
UNTIL THEN, WE'LL STICK TO OUR PROVEN THANAGARAN POLICE METHODS! RIGHT NOW THOUGH, I WANT BOTH OF YOU TO TAKE A FEW DAYS OFF TO GET ADJUSTED TO THINGS! REPORT FOR DUTY NEXT ROTHAN*!
*Editor's Note: ROTHAN-- THE THANAGARAN EQUIVALENT OF A WEEK ON EARTH --
SOON, IN THEIR DUTY UNIFORMS, KATAR HOL AND SHAYERA ARE WINGING HOMEWARD...
THERE IT IS! HMM--ON EARTH OUR APARTMENT WOULD NEED A GOOD DUSTING BUT THE ROBOT CLEANERS WILL HAVE KEPT IT SPICK AND SPAN IN OUR ABSENCE!
IN THEIR APARTMENT SUITE...
HONEY, HOW ABOUT DINING OUT ON OUR FIRST NIGHT HOME?
KATAR, I SIMPLY CAN'T! WE'VE BEEN AWAY MORE THAN HALF A YEAR AND I CAN IMAGINE HOW THE STYLES MUST HAVE CHANGED! I HAVEN'T A THING TO WEAR!
AND SO MR. AND MRS. HOL DINE AT HOME... BY THE SIMPLE EXPEDIENT OF PRESSING MENU BUTTONS...
A BRONSI ROAST FOR YOU, DEAR! I THINK I'LL TRY MY FAVORITE-- KORALA STEW!
WONDER WHAT OUR EARTH FRIENDS WOULD SAY IF THEY COULD SEE US GETTING OUR MEAL BY PNEUMATI-TUBE FROM CENTRAL COOKING?
OR IF THEY KNEW WE NEVER PERSONALLY HANDLE MONEY ON THANAGAR--BUT "PAY" FOR EVERY-THING WITH OUR IDENTI-CARDS!
THE MONEY THAT WE EARN BY WORK-ING IS AUTOMATIC-ALLY DEPOSITED TO OUR ACCOUNT IN THE PLANETARY BANK! AS LONG AS WE HAVE A FAVORABLE BALANCE, OUR PERSONALIZED IDENTI-CARDS ENABLE US TO PURCHASE ANYTHING WE WISH!
TING
4

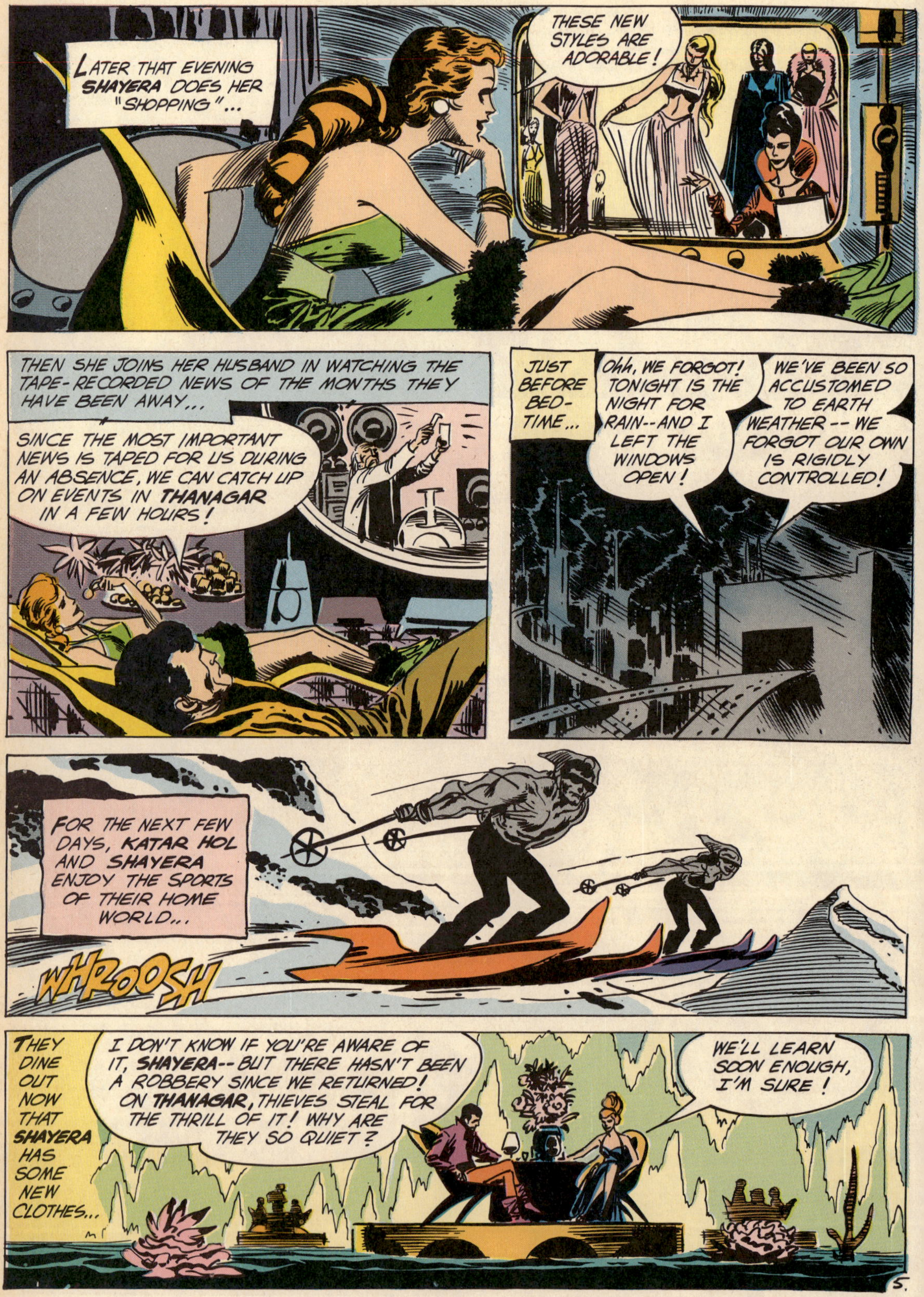
LATER THAT EVENING SHAYERA DOES HER "SHOPPING"...
THESE NEW STYLES ARE ADORABLE!
THEN SHE JOINS HER HUSBAND IN WATCHING THE TAPE-RECORDED NEWS OF THE MONTHS THEY HAVE BEEN AWAY...
SINCE THE MOST IMPORTANT NEWS IS TAPED FOR US DURING AN ABSENCE, WE CAN CATCH UP ON EVENTS IN THANAGAR IN A FEW HOURS!
JUST BEFORE BED-TIME...
Ohh, WE FORGOT! TONIGHT IS THE NIGHT FOR RAIN--AND I LEFT THE WINDOWS OPEN!
WE'VE BEEN SO ACCUSTOMED TO EARTH WEATHER -- WE FORGOT OUR OWN IS RIGIDLY CONTROLLED!
FOR THE NEXT FEW DAYS, KATAR HOL AND SHAYERA ENJOY THE SPORTS OF THEIR HOME WORLD...
WHROOSH
THEY DINE OUT NOW THAT SHAYERA HAS SOME NEW CLOTHES...
I DON'T KNOW IF YOU'RE AWARE OF IT, SHAYERA-- BUT THERE HASN'T BEEN A ROBBERY SINCE WE RETURNED! ON THANAGAR, THIEVES STEAL FOR THE THRILL OF IT! WHY ARE THEY SO QUIET?
WE'LL LEARN SOON ENOUGH, I'M SURE!
5.

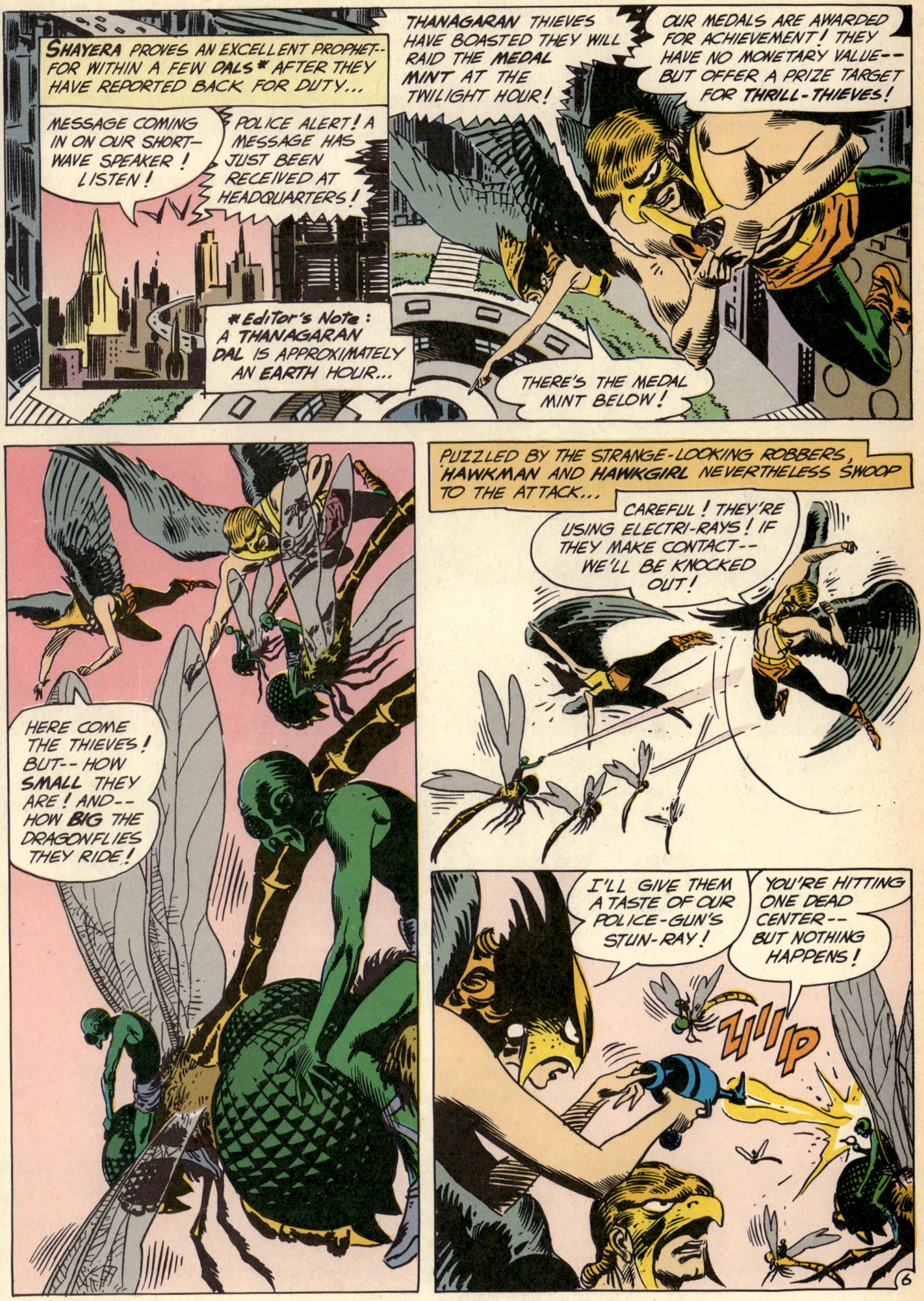
SHAYERA PROVES AN EXCELLENT PROPHET-- FOR WITHIN A FEW DALS* AFTER THEY HAVE REPORTED BACK FOR DUTY...
MESSAGE COMING IN ON OUR SHORT-WAVE SPEAKER! LISTEN!
POLICE ALERT! A MESSAGE HAS JUST BEEN RECEIVED AT HEADQUARTERS!
*Editor's Note: A THANAGARAN DAL IS APPROXIMATELY AN EARTH HOUR...
THANAGARAN THIEVES HAVE BOASTED THEY WILL RAID THE MEDAL MINT AT THE TWILIGHT HOUR!
OUR MEDALS ARE AWARDED FOR ACHIEVEMENT! THEY HAVE NO MONETARY VALUE-- BUT OFFER A PRIZE TARGET FOR THRILL-THIEVES!
THERE'S THE MEDAL MINT BELOW!
HERE COME THE THIEVES! BUT-- HOW SMALL THEY ARE! AND-- HOW BIG THE DRAGONFLIES THEY RIDE!
PUZZLED BY THE STRANGE-LOOKING ROBBERS, HAWKMAN AND HAWKGIRL NEVERTHELESS SWOOP TO THE ATTACK...
CAREFUL! THEY'RE USING ELECTRI-RAYS! IF THEY MAKE CONTACT-- WE'LL BE KNOCKED OUT!
I'LL GIVE THEM A TASTE OF OUR POLICE-GUN'S STUN-RAY!
YOU'RE HITTING ONE DEAD CENTER-- BUT NOTHING HAPPENS!
ZZIIP
6

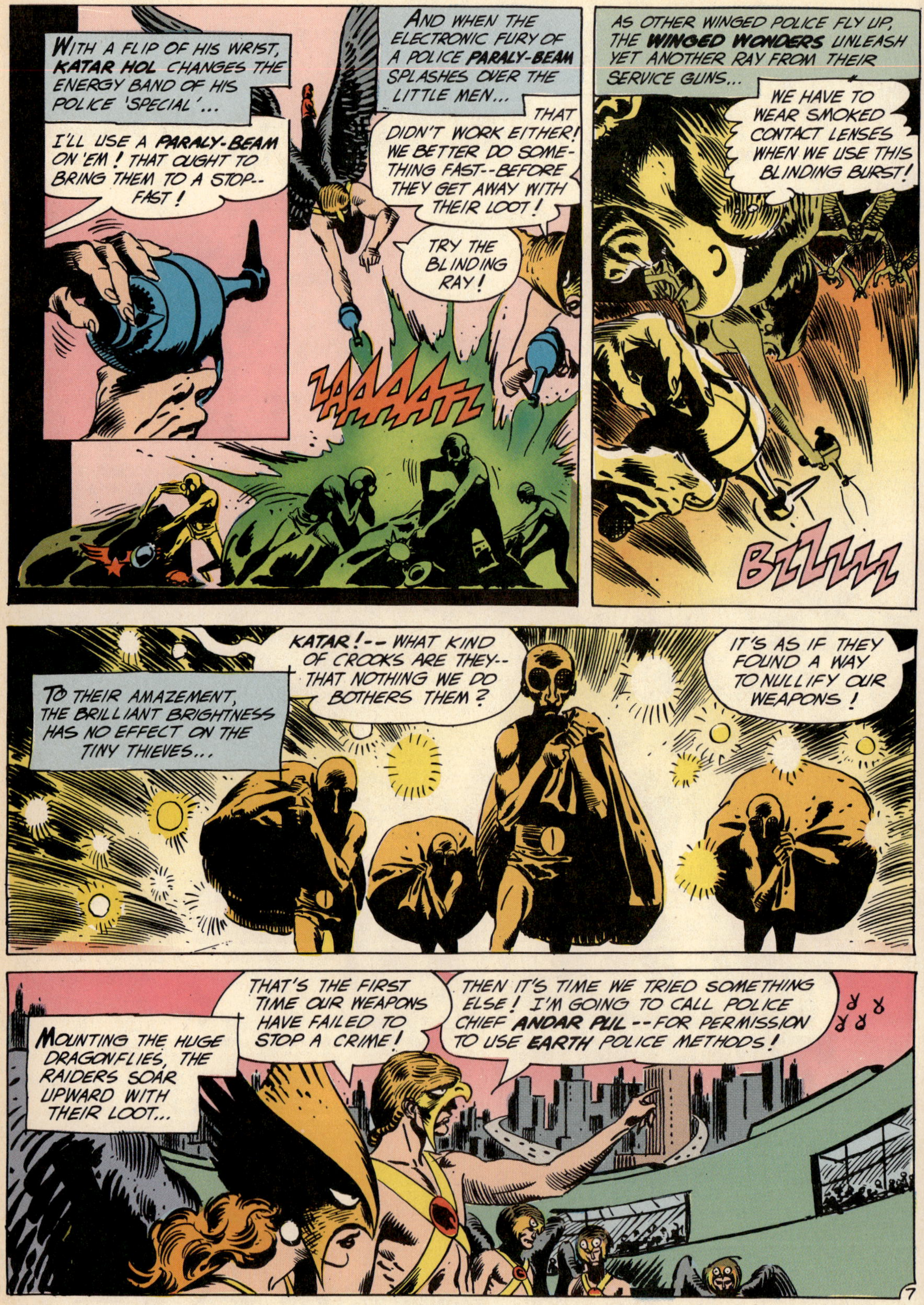
WITH A FLIP OF HIS WRIST, KATAR HOL CHANGES THE ENERGY BAND OF HIS POLICE 'SPECIAL'...
I'LL USE A PARALY-BEAM ON 'EM! THAT OUGHT TO BRING THEM TO A STOP--FAST!
AND WHEN THE ELECTRONIC FURY OF A POLICE PARALY-BEAM SPLASHES OVER THE LITTLE MEN...
THAT DIDN'T WORK EITHER! WE BETTER DO SOMETHING FAST--BEFORE THEY GET AWAY WITH THEIR LOOT!
TRY THE BLINDING RAY!
ZAAAATZ
AS OTHER WINGED POLICE FLY UP, THE WINGED WONDERS UNLEASH YET ANOTHER RAY FROM THEIR SERVICE GUNS...
WE HAVE TO WEAR SMOKED CONTACT LENSES WHEN WE USE THIS BLINDING BURST!
BZZZZZ
TO THEIR AMAZEMENT, THE BRILLIANT BRIGHTNESS HAS NO EFFECT ON THE TINY THIEVES...
KATAR!-- WHAT KIND OF CROOKS ARE THEY--THAT NOTHING WE DO BOTHERS THEM?
IT'S AS IF THEY FOUND A WAY TO NULLIFY OUR WEAPONS!
MOUNTING THE HUGE DRAGONFLIES, THE RAIDERS SOAR UPWARD WITH THEIR LOOT...
THAT'S THE FIRST TIME OUR WEAPONS HAVE FAILED TO STOP A CRIME!
THEN IT'S TIME WE TRIED SOMETHING ELSE! I'M GOING TO CALL POLICE CHIEF ANDAR PUL--FOR PERMISSION TO USE EARTH POLICE METHODS!
RRRR
7

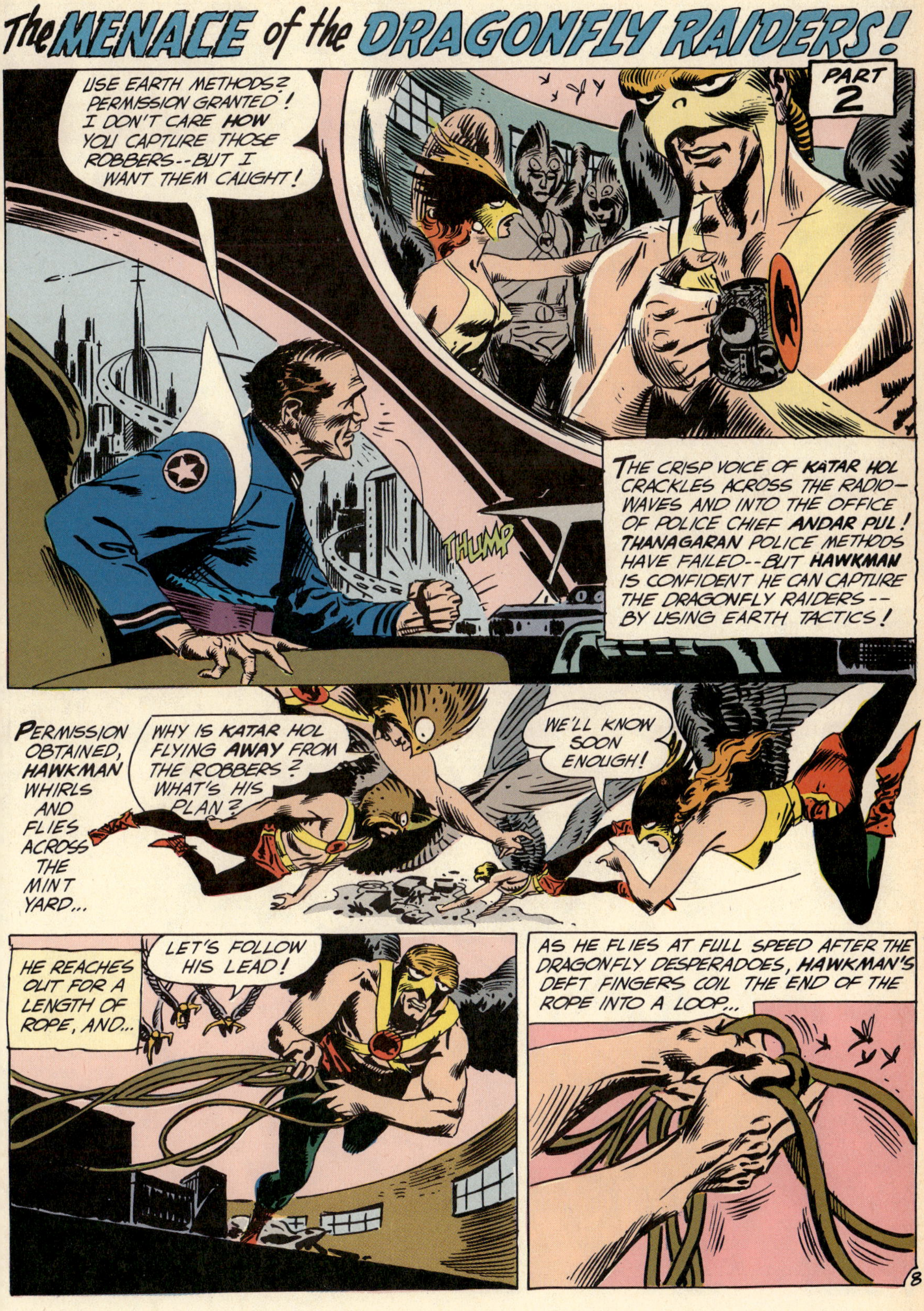
The MENACE of the DRAGONFLY RAIDERS!
PART 2
USE EARTH METHODS? PERMISSION GRANTED! I DON'T CARE HOW YOU CAPTURE THOSE ROBBERS--BUT I WANT THEM CAUGHT!
THUMP
THE CRISP VOICE OF KATAR HOL CRACKLES ACROSS THE RADIO-WAVES AND INTO THE OFFICE OF POLICE CHIEF ANDAR PUL! THANAGARAN POLICE METHODS HAVE FAILED--BUT HAWKMAN IS CONFIDENT HE CAN CAPTURE THE DRAGONFLY RAIDERS--BY USING EARTH TACTICS!
PERMISSION OBTAINED, HAWKMAN WHIRLS AND FLIES ACROSS THE MINT YARD...
WHY IS KATAR HOL FLYING AWAY FROM THE ROBBERS? WHAT'S HIS PLAN?
WE'LL KNOW SOON ENOUGH!
HE REACHES OUT FOR A LENGTH OF ROPE, AND...
LET'S FOLLOW HIS LEAD!
AS HE FLIES AT FULL SPEED AFTER THE DRAGONFLY DESPERADOES, HAWKMAN'S DEFT FINGERS COIL THE END OF THE ROPE INTO A LOOP...
8

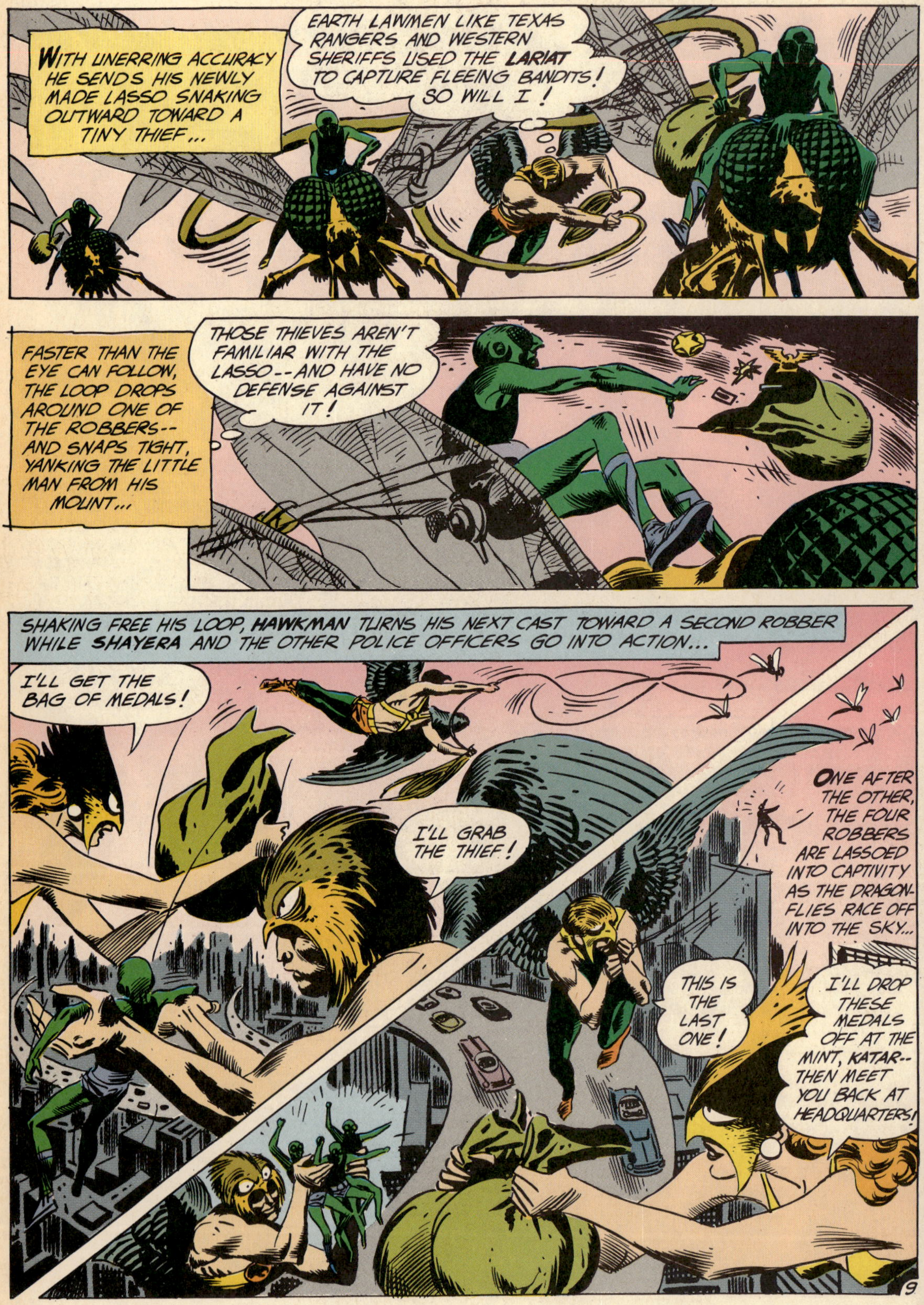

WITH UNERRING ACCURACY HE SENDS HIS NEWLY MADE LASSO SNAKING OUTWARD TOWARD A TINY THIEF...
EARTH LAWMEN LIKE TEXAS RANGERS AND WESTERN SHERIFFS USED THE LARIAT TO CAPTURE FLEEING BANDITS! SO WILL I!
FASTER THAN THE EYE CAN FOLLOW, THE LOOP DROPS AROUND ONE OF THE ROBBERS-- AND SNAPS TIGHT, YANKING THE LITTLE MAN FROM HIS MOUNT...
THOSE THIEVES AREN'T FAMILIAR WITH THE LASSO--AND HAVE NO DEFENSE AGAINST IT!
SHAKING FREE HIS LOOP, HAWKMAN TURNS HIS NEXT CAST TOWARD A SECOND ROBBER WHILE SHAYERA AND THE OTHER POLICE OFFICERS GO INTO ACTION...
I'LL GET THE BAG OF MEDALS!
I'LL GRAB THE THIEF!
ONE AFTER THE OTHER, THE FOUR ROBBERS ARE LASSOED INTO CAPTIVITY AS THE DRAGON-FLIES RACE OFF INTO THE SKY...
THIS IS THE LAST ONE!
I'LL DROP THESE MEDALS OFF AT THE MINT, KATAR-- THEN MEET YOU BACK AT HEADQUARTERS!
9

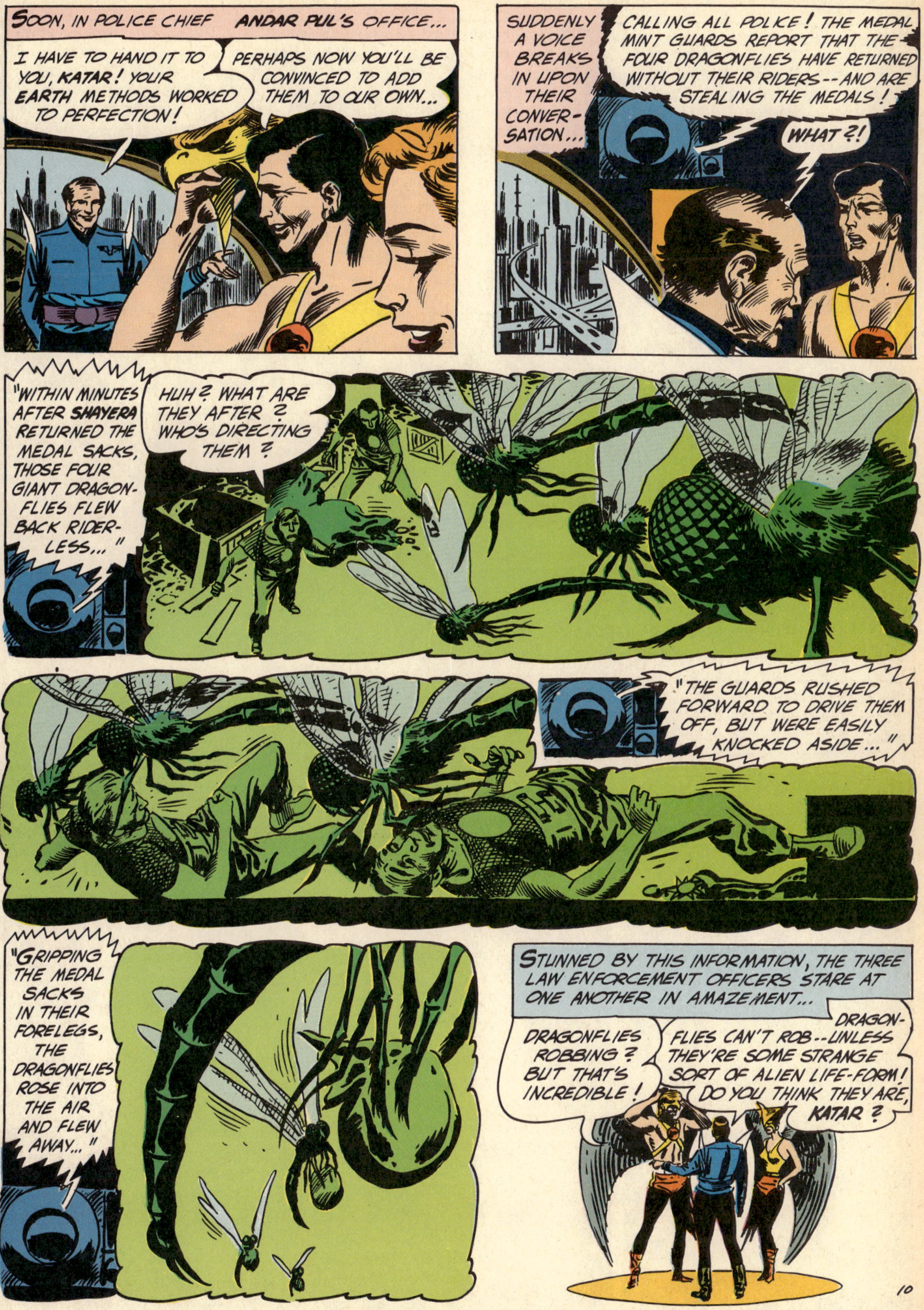
SOON, IN POLICE CHIEF ANDAR PUL'S OFFICE...
I HAVE TO HAND IT TO YOU, KATAR! YOUR EARTH METHODS WORKED TO PERFECTION!
PERHAPS NOW YOU'LL BE CONVINCED TO ADD THEM TO OUR OWN...
SUDDENLY A VOICE BREAKS IN UPON THEIR CONVERSATION...
CALLING ALL POLICE! THE MEDAL MINT GUARDS REPORT THAT THE FOUR DRAGONFLIES HAVE RETURNED WITHOUT THEIR RIDERS--AND ARE STEALING THE MEDALS!
WHAT ?!
"WITHIN MINUTES AFTER SHAYERA RETURNED THE MEDAL SACKS, THOSE FOUR GIANT DRAGONFLIES FLEW BACK RIDERLESS..."
HUH? WHAT ARE THEY AFTER? WHO'S DIRECTING THEM?
"THE GUARDS RUSHED FORWARD TO DRIVE THEM OFF, BUT WERE EASILY KNOCKED ASIDE..."
"GRIPPING THE MEDAL SACKS IN THEIR FORELEGS, THE DRAGONFLIES ROSE INTO THE AIR AND FLEW AWAY..."
STUNNED BY THIS INFORMATION, THE THREE LAW ENFORCEMENT OFFICERS STARE AT ONE ANOTHER IN AMAZEMENT...
DRAGONFLIES ROBBING? BUT THAT'S INCREDIBLE!
DRAGONFLIES CAN'T ROB--UNLESS THEY'RE SOME STRANGE SORT OF ALIEN LIFE-FORM! DO YOU THINK THEY ARE, KATAR?
10

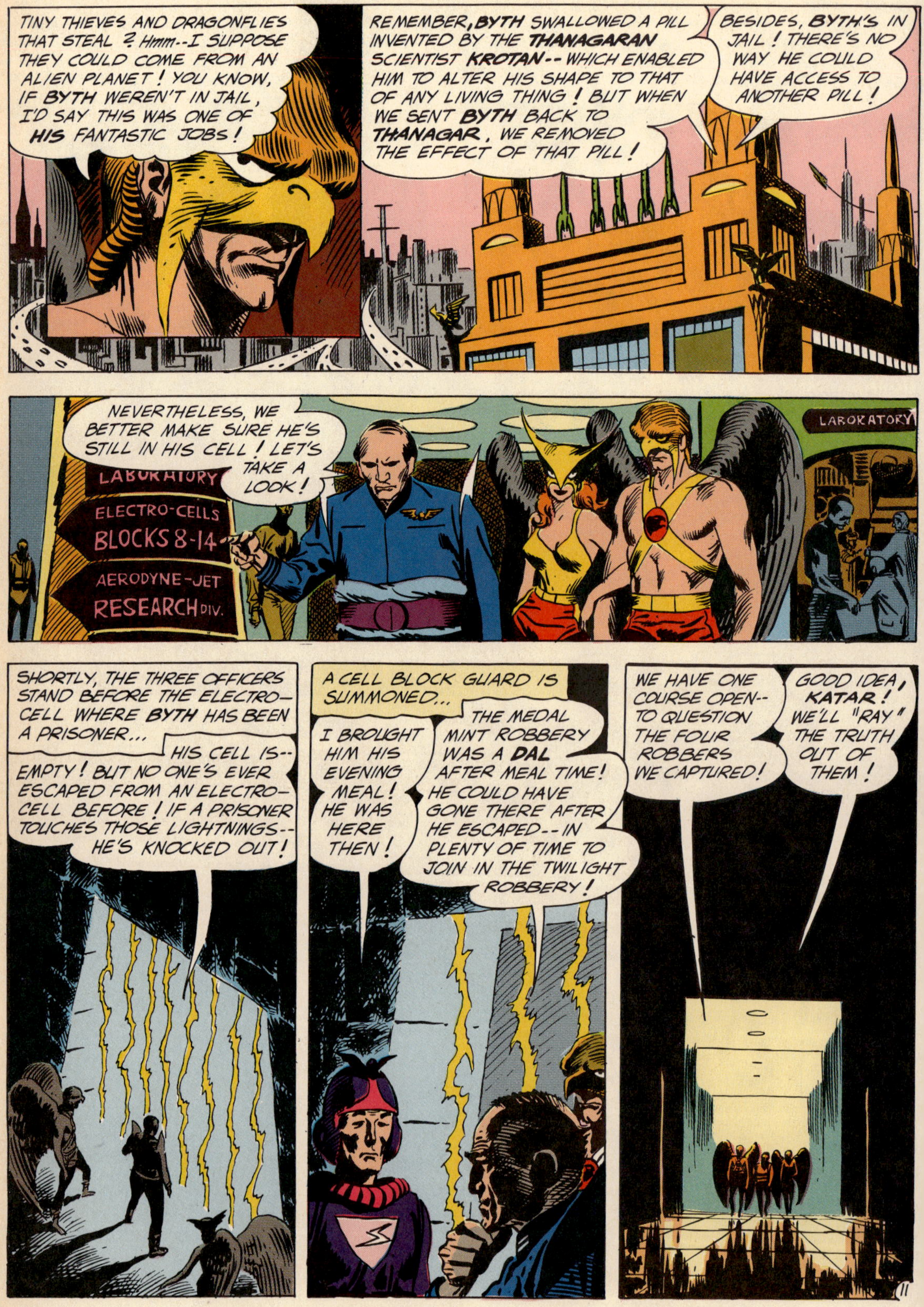
TINY THIEVES AND DRAGONFLIES THAT STEAL ? Hmm--I SUPPOSE THEY COULD COME FROM AN ALIEN PLANET! YOU KNOW, IF BYTH WEREN'T IN JAIL, I'D SAY THIS WAS ONE OF HIS FANTASTIC JOBS!
REMEMBER, BYTH SWALLOWED A PILL INVENTED BY THE THANAGARAN SCIENTIST KROTAN-- WHICH ENABLED HIM TO ALTER HIS SHAPE TO THAT OF ANY LIVING THING! BUT WHEN WE SENT BYTH BACK TO THANAGAR, WE REMOVED THE EFFECT OF THAT PILL!
BESIDES, BYTH'S IN JAIL! THERE'S NO WAY HE COULD HAVE ACCESS TO ANOTHER PILL!
NEVERTHELESS, WE BETTER MAKE SURE HE'S STILL IN HIS CELL! LET'S TAKE A LOOK!
LABORATORY
ELECTRO-CELLS
BLOCKS 8-14
AERODYNE-JET
RESEARCH DIV.
LABORATORY
SHORTLY, THE THREE OFFICERS STAND BEFORE THE ELECTRO-CELL WHERE BYTH HAS BEEN A PRISONER...
HIS CELL IS-- EMPTY! BUT NO ONE'S EVER ESCAPED FROM AN ELECTRO-CELL BEFORE! IF A PRISONER TOUCHES THOSE LIGHTNINGS-- HE'S KNOCKED OUT!
A CELL BLOCK GUARD IS SUMMONED...
I BROUGHT HIM HIS EVENING MEAL! HE WAS HERE THEN!
THE MEDAL MINT ROBBERY WAS A DAL AFTER MEAL TIME! HE COULD HAVE GONE THERE AFTER HE ESCAPED-- IN PLENTY OF TIME TO JOIN IN THE TWILIGHT ROBBERY!
WE HAVE ONE COURSE OPEN-- TO QUESTION THE FOUR ROBBERS WE CAPTURED!
GOOD IDEA, KATAR! WE'LL "RAY" THE TRUTH OUT OF THEM!
11

BROUGHT TO THE INTERROGATION ROOM AND FACED BY A BATTERY OF TRUTH-RAY LAMPS, THE FOUR ROBBERS REMAIN SILENT...

I CAN'T UNDERSTAND IT! THOSE RAYS SHOULD FORCE THEM TO TELL THE TRUTH!

NOTHING AFFECTS THEM! OUR POLICE-GUNS! OUR TRUTH RAYS! THEY DON'T SEEM *HUMAN*!

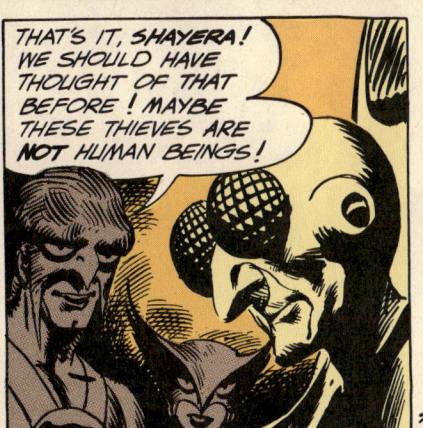

THAT'S IT, **SHAYERA**! WE SHOULD HAVE THOUGHT OF THAT BEFORE! MAYBE THESE THIEVES ARE **NOT** HUMAN BEINGS!

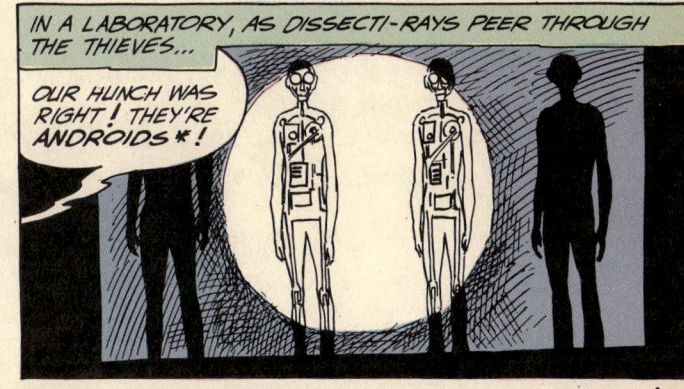

IN A LABORATORY, AS DISSECTI-RAYS PEER THROUGH THE THIEVES...

OUR HUNCH WAS RIGHT! THEY'RE ANDROIDS*!

*Editor's Note: AN ANDROID IS A HUMAN-LIKE ROBOT!

IT WAS ALL A TRICK TO DRAW OUR ATTENTION TO THEM WHILE THE **REAL** ROBBERS-- THE DRAGONFLIES-- GOT AWAY! WHEN THE POLICE LEFT-- ALL THE DRAGONFLIES HAD TO DO WAS RETURN AND STEAL THE MEDALS UNOPPOSED!

NOW IF ONLY WE COULD FIGURE HOW **BYTH** ESCAPED!

AS A PRISONER HE WAS ENTITLED TO RECEIVE VISITORS-- BUT A GUARD WAS ALWAYS CLOSE BY TO PREVENT ANYTHING BEING GIVEN HIM AND AT THE SAME TIME TO OVERHEAR WHAT WAS SAID!

HOW INDEED COULD **BYTH** HAVE ESCAPED SUCH A SEEMINGLY ESCAPE-PROOF CELL?
UNABLE TO SPEAK WITH-- OR RECEIVE ANYTHING FROM-- HIS FEW VISITORS, AND PENNED SECURELY INSIDE BY ELECTRIC BEAMS, WHAT POSSIBLE COURSE OF ACTION WAS OPEN TO HIM?

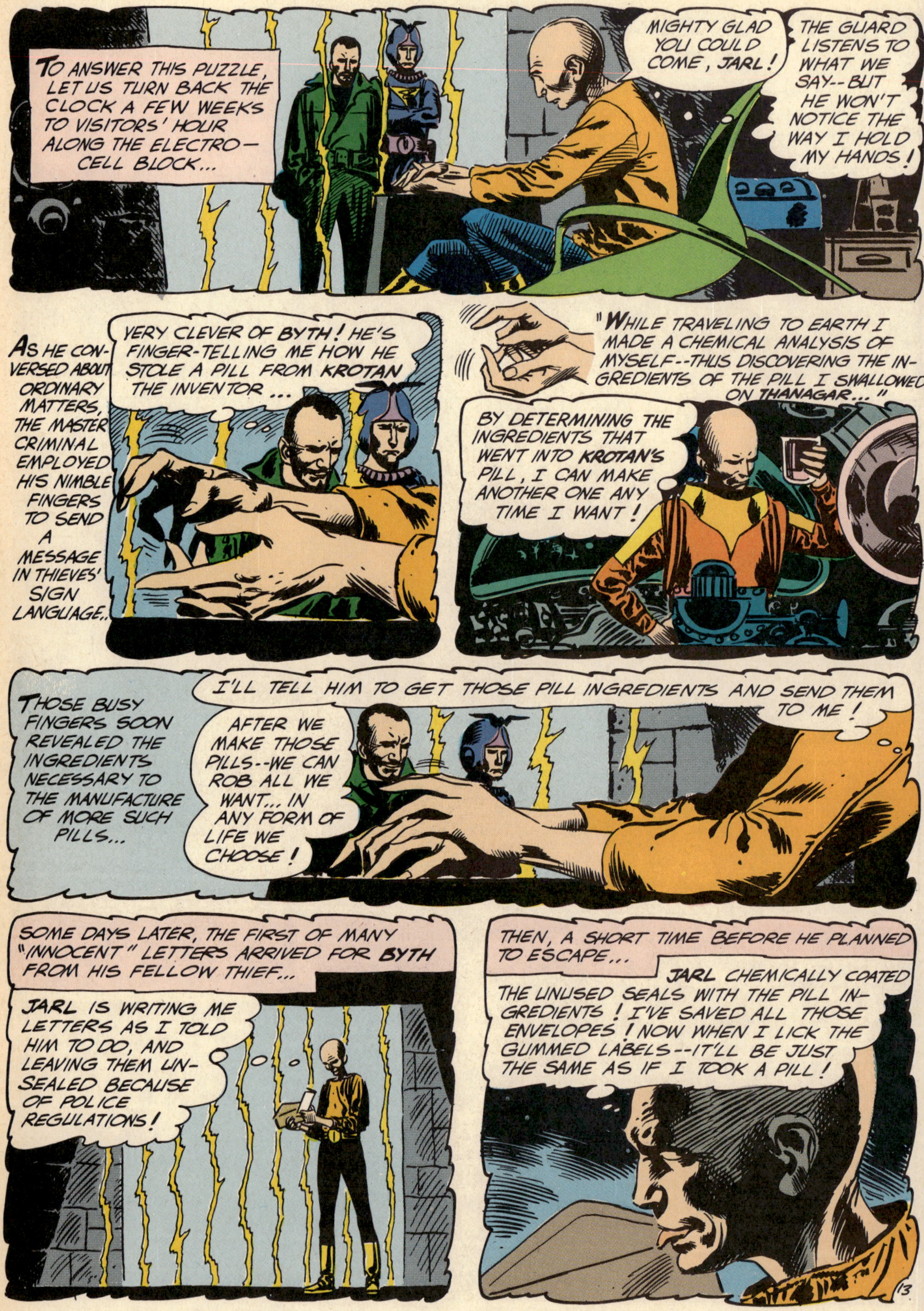
TO ANSWER THIS PUZZLE, LET US TURN BACK THE CLOCK A FEW WEEKS TO VISITORS' HOUR ALONG THE ELECTRO-CELL BLOCK...
MIGHTY GLAD YOU COULD COME, JARL!
THE GUARD LISTENS TO WHAT WE SAY--BUT HE WON'T NOTICE THE WAY I HOLD MY HANDS!
AS HE CONVERSED ABOUT ORDINARY MATTERS, THE MASTER CRIMINAL EMPLOYED HIS NIMBLE FINGERS TO SEND A MESSAGE IN THIEVES' SIGN LANGUAGE...
VERY CLEVER OF BYTH! HE'S FINGER-TELLING ME HOW HE STOLE A PILL FROM KROTAN THE INVENTOR...
"WHILE TRAVELING TO EARTH I MADE A CHEMICAL ANALYSIS OF MYSELF--THUS DISCOVERING THE INGREDIENTS OF THE PILL I SWALLOWED ON THANAGAR..."
BY DETERMINING THE INGREDIENTS THAT WENT INTO KROTAN'S PILL, I CAN MAKE ANOTHER ONE ANY TIME I WANT!
THOSE BUSY FINGERS SOON REVEALED THE INGREDIENTS NECESSARY TO THE MANUFACTURE OF MORE SUCH PILLS...
I'LL TELL HIM TO GET THOSE PILL INGREDIENTS AND SEND THEM TO ME!
AFTER WE MAKE THOSE PILLS--WE CAN ROB ALL WE WANT... IN ANY FORM OF LIFE WE CHOOSE!
SOME DAYS LATER, THE FIRST OF MANY "INNOCENT" LETTERS ARRIVED FOR BYTH FROM HIS FELLOW THIEF...
JARL IS WRITING ME LETTERS AS I TOLD HIM TO DO, AND LEAVING THEM UNSEALED BECAUSE OF POLICE REGULATIONS!
THEN, A SHORT TIME BEFORE HE PLANNED TO ESCAPE...
JARL CHEMICALLY COATED THE UNUSED SEALS WITH THE PILL INGREDIENTS! I'VE SAVED ALL THOSE ENVELOPES! NOW WHEN I LICK THE GUMMED LABELS--IT'LL BE JUST THE SAME AS IF I TOOK A PILL!
13

HAWKMAN 95

THE PILL INGREDIENTS ENABLED BYTH TO ALTER HIS BODY INTO THAT OF A VANDALUSIAN DRILLER MOLE...

MY EVENING MEAL! THE GUARD WON'T BE BACK FOR OVER A DAL...PLENTY OF TIME FOR ME TO GET AWAY!

SOON HE WAS BORING THROUGH THE SOLID CONCRETE OF THE CELL-FLOOR BENEATH HIS COT SO IT WOULD NOT BE EASILY NOTICED...

SOON I'LL JOIN JARL AND THE TWO FELLOW THIEVES HE'S SELECTED TO HELP US ROB THE MEDAL MINT!

AND SO IT WAS THAT, HAVING FOOLED THE POLICE BY MASQUERADING AS DRAGONFLIES, BYTH AND HIS COMPANIONS MADE OFF WITH THE MEDALS..

THIS IS ONLY THE BEGINNING! HAVING SWALLOWED THE PILL INGREDIENTS WE CAN PLAN BIGGER AND BETTER ROBBERIES!

REALIZING THEY HAVE BEEN DUPED, KATAR HOL AND SHAYERA, TOGETHER WITH THEIR POLICE CHIEF, ARE UNDERSTANDABLY ANGRY...

SO BYTH GOT AWAY WITH IT! AND LIKE ALL HIS KIND-- GOT PLENTY OF THRILLS FROM FOOLING US!

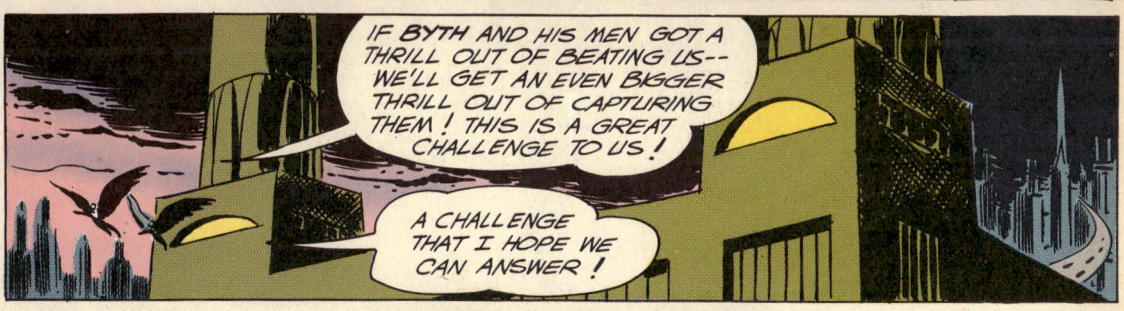

IF BYTH AND HIS MEN GOT A THRILL OUT OF BEATING US-- WE'LL GET AN EVEN BIGGER THRILL OUT OF CAPTURING THEM! THIS IS A GREAT CHALLENGE TO US!

A CHALLENGE THAT I HOPE WE CAN ANSWER!

KATAR, IT'S NO USE GOING HOME! I KNOW YOU! WITH BYTH ON YOUR MIND, YOU JUST WON'T SLEEP!

YOU'RE RIGHT, HONEY! HMM-- I KNOW JUST THE PLACE TO GO!

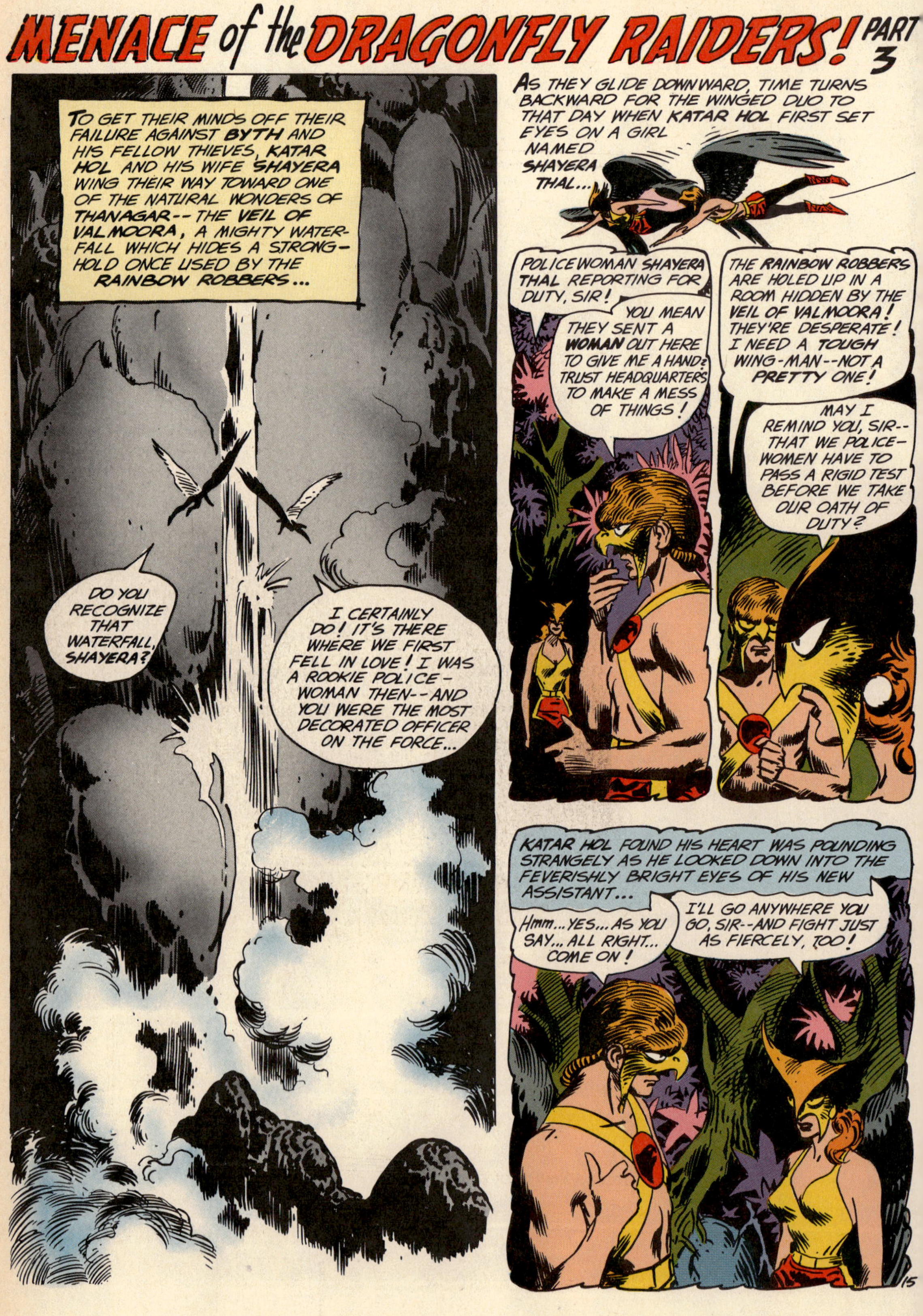
MENACE of the DRAGONFLY RAIDERS! PART 3
TO GET THEIR MINDS OFF THEIR FAILURE AGAINST BYTH AND HIS FELLOW THIEVES, KATAR HOL AND HIS WIFE SHAYERA WING THEIR WAY TOWARD ONE OF THE NATURAL WONDERS OF THANAGAR--THE VEIL OF VALMOORA, A MIGHTY WATER-FALL WHICH HIDES A STRONG-HOLD ONCE USED BY THE RAINBOW ROBBERS...
DO YOU RECOGNIZE THAT WATERFALL, SHAYERA?
I CERTAINLY DO! IT'S THERE WHERE WE FIRST FELL IN LOVE! I WAS A ROOKIE POLICE-WOMAN THEN--AND YOU WERE THE MOST DECORATED OFFICER ON THE FORCE...
AS THEY GLIDE DOWNWARD, TIME TURNS BACKWARD FOR THE WINGED DUO TO THAT DAY WHEN KATAR HOL FIRST SET EYES ON A GIRL NAMED SHAYERA THAL...
POLICEWOMAN SHAYERA THAL REPORTING FOR DUTY, SIR!
YOU MEAN THEY SENT A WOMAN OUT HERE TO GIVE ME A HAND? TRUST HEADQUARTERS TO MAKE A MESS OF THINGS!
THE RAINBOW ROBBERS ARE HOLED UP IN A ROOM HIDDEN BY THE VEIL OF VALMOORA! THEY'RE DESPERATE! I NEED A TOUGH WING-MAN--NOT A PRETTY ONE!
MAY I REMIND YOU, SIR--THAT WE POLICE-WOMEN HAVE TO PASS A RIGID TEST BEFORE WE TAKE OUR OATH OF DUTY?
KATAR HOL FOUND HIS HEART WAS POUNDING STRANGELY AS HE LOOKED DOWN INTO THE FEVERISHLY BRIGHT EYES OF HIS NEW ASSISTANT...
Hmm...YES...AS YOU SAY...ALL RIGHT...COME ON!
I'LL GO ANYWHERE YOU GO, SIR--AND FIGHT JUST AS FIERCELY, TOO!
15

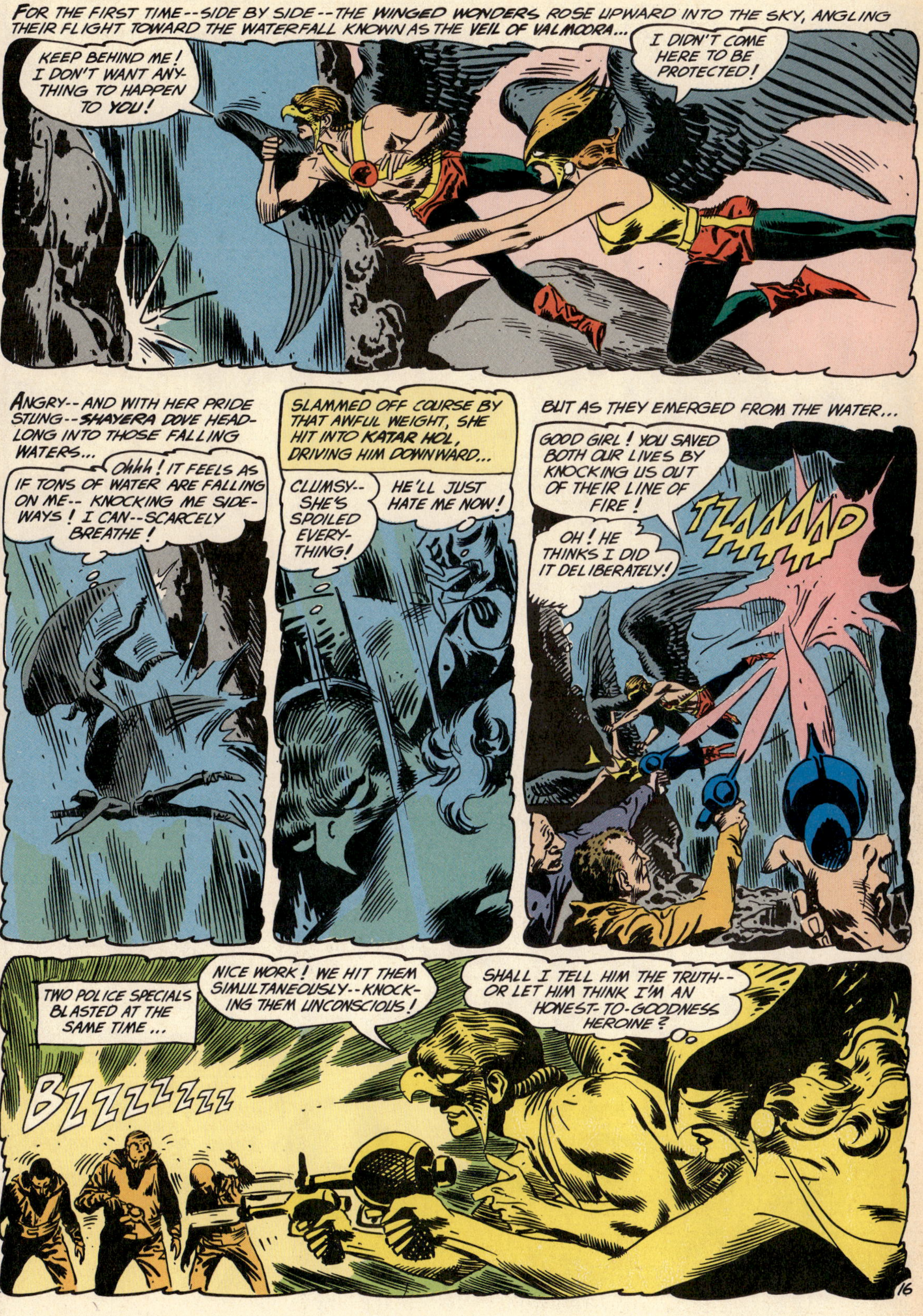
FOR THE FIRST TIME--SIDE BY SIDE--THE WINGED WONDERS ROSE UPWARD INTO THE SKY, ANGLING THEIR FLIGHT TOWARD THE WATERFALL KNOWN AS THE VEIL OF VALMOORA...
KEEP BEHIND ME! I DON'T WANT ANY-THING TO HAPPEN TO YOU!
I DIDN'T COME HERE TO BE PROTECTED!
ANGRY--AND WITH HER PRIDE STUNG--SHAYERA DOVE HEAD-LONG INTO THOSE FALLING WATERS...
Ohhh! IT FEELS AS IF TONS OF WATER ARE FALLING ON ME--KNOCKING ME SIDE-WAYS! I CAN--SCARCELY BREATHE!
SLAMMED OFF COURSE BY THAT AWFUL WEIGHT, SHE HIT INTO KATAR HOL, DRIVING HIM DOWNWARD...
CLUMSY--SHE'S SPOILED EVERY-THING!
HE'LL JUST HATE ME NOW!
BUT AS THEY EMERGED FROM THE WATER...
GOOD GIRL! YOU SAVED BOTH OUR LIVES BY KNOCKING US OUT OF THEIR LINE OF FIRE!
OH! HE THINKS I DID IT DELIBERATELY!
TZAAAAAP
TWO POLICE SPECIALS BLASTED AT THE SAME TIME...
NICE WORK! WE HIT THEM SIMULTANEOUSLY--KNOCK-ING THEM UNCONSCIOUS!
SHALL I TELL HIM THE TRUTH--OR LET HIM THINK I'M AN HONEST-TO-GOODNESS HEROINE?
BZZZZZZZ
16

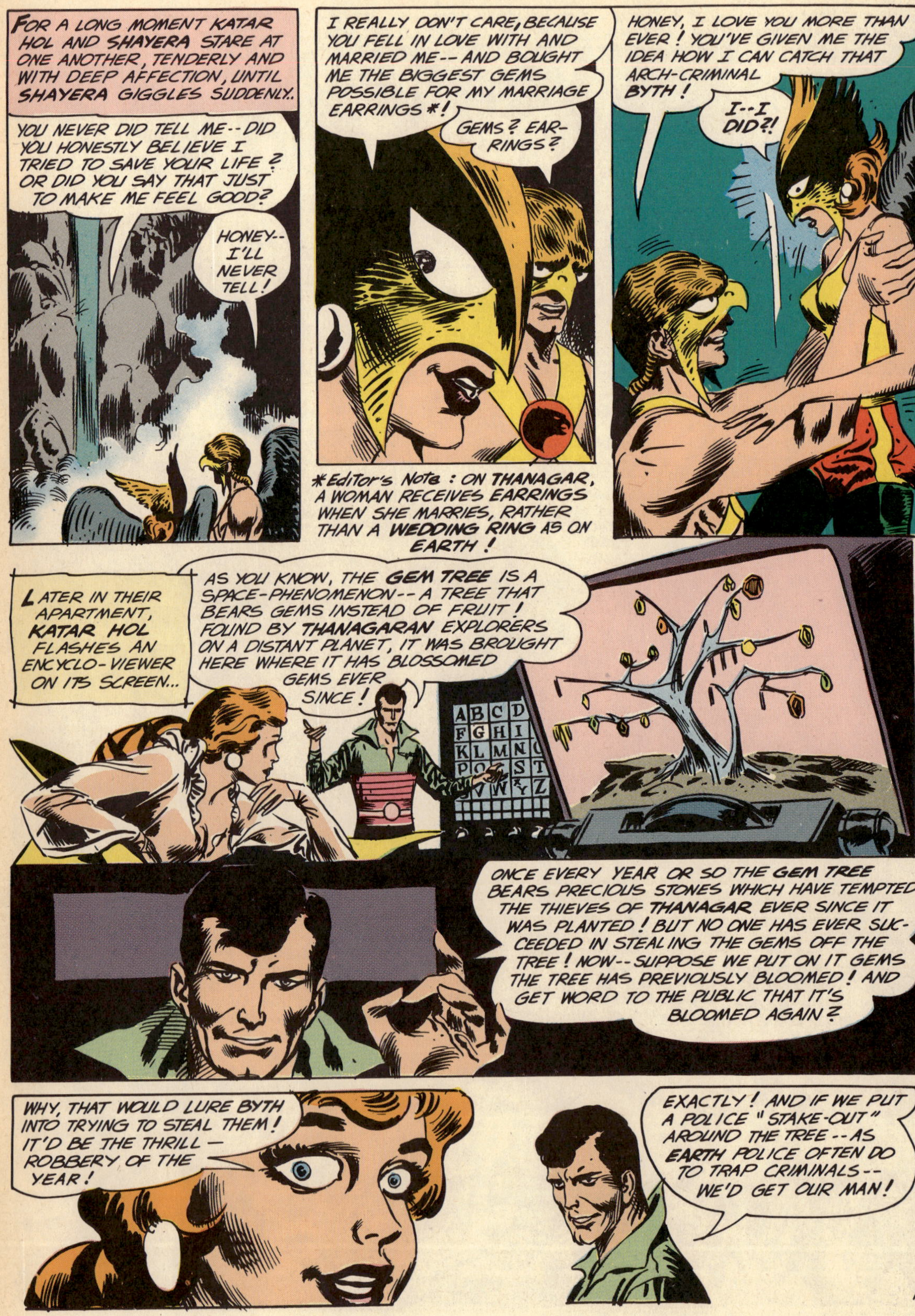
FOR A LONG MOMENT KATAR HOL AND SHAYERA STARE AT ONE ANOTHER, TENDERLY AND WITH DEEP AFFECTION, UNTIL SHAYERA GIGGLES SUDDENLY.
YOU NEVER DID TELL ME--DID YOU HONESTLY BELIEVE I TRIED TO SAVE YOUR LIFE? OR DID YOU SAY THAT JUST TO MAKE ME FEEL GOOD?
HONEY--I'LL NEVER TELL!
I REALLY DON'T CARE, BECAUSE YOU FELL IN LOVE WITH AND MARRIED ME--AND BOUGHT ME THE BIGGEST GEMS POSSIBLE FOR MY MARRIAGE EARRINGS*!
GEMS? EAR-RINGS?
*Editor's Note: ON THANAGAR, A WOMAN RECEIVES EARRINGS WHEN SHE MARRIES, RATHER THAN A WEDDING RING AS ON EARTH!
HONEY, I LOVE YOU MORE THAN EVER! YOU'VE GIVEN ME THE IDEA HOW I CAN CATCH THAT ARCH-CRIMINAL BYTH!
I--I DID?!
LATER IN THEIR APARTMENT, KATAR HOL FLASHES AN ENCYCLO-VIEWER ON ITS SCREEN...
AS YOU KNOW, THE GEM TREE IS A SPACE-PHENOMENON--A TREE THAT BEARS GEMS INSTEAD OF FRUIT! FOUND BY THANAGARAN EXPLORERS ON A DISTANT PLANET, IT WAS BROUGHT HERE WHERE IT HAS BLOSSOMED GEMS EVER SINCE!
ONCE EVERY YEAR OR SO THE GEM TREE BEARS PRECIOUS STONES WHICH HAVE TEMPTED THE THIEVES OF THANAGAR EVER SINCE IT WAS PLANTED! BUT NO ONE HAS EVER SUC-CEEDED IN STEALING THE GEMS OFF THE TREE! NOW--SUPPOSE WE PUT ON IT GEMS THE TREE HAS PREVIOUSLY BLOOMED! AND GET WORD TO THE PUBLIC THAT IT'S BLOOMED AGAIN?
WHY, THAT WOULD LURE BYTH INTO TRYING TO STEAL THEM! IT'D BE THE THRILL—ROBBERY OF THE YEAR!
EXACTLY! AND IF WE PUT A POLICE "STAKE-OUT" AROUND THE TREE--AS EARTH POLICE OFTEN DO TO TRAP CRIMINALS--WE'D GET OUR MAN!

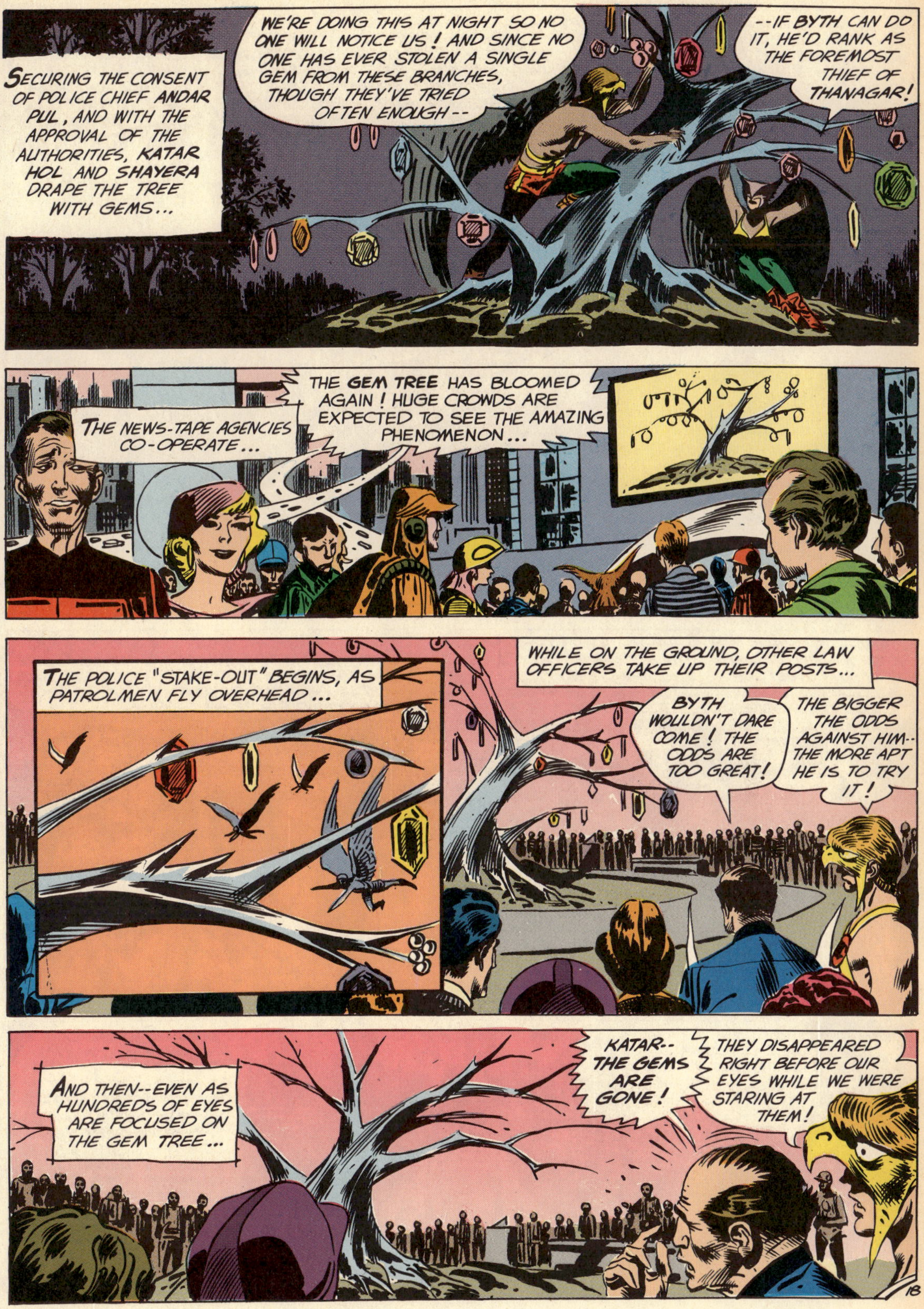
SECURING THE CONSENT OF POLICE CHIEF ANDAR PUL, AND WITH THE APPROVAL OF THE AUTHORITIES, KATAR HOL AND SHAYERA DRAPE THE TREE WITH GEMS...
WE'RE DOING THIS AT NIGHT SO NO ONE WILL NOTICE US! AND SINCE NO ONE HAS EVER STOLEN A SINGLE GEM FROM THESE BRANCHES, THOUGH THEY'VE TRIED OFTEN ENOUGH--
--IF BYTH CAN DO IT, HE'D RANK AS THE FOREMOST THIEF OF THANAGAR!
THE NEWS-TAPE AGENCIES CO-OPERATE...
THE GEM TREE HAS BLOOMED AGAIN! HUGE CROWDS ARE EXPECTED TO SEE THE AMAZING PHENOMENON...
THE POLICE "STAKE-OUT" BEGINS, AS PATROLMEN FLY OVERHEAD...
WHILE ON THE GROUND, OTHER LAW OFFICERS TAKE UP THEIR POSTS...
BYTH WOULDN'T DARE COME! THE ODDS ARE TOO GREAT!
THE BIGGER THE ODDS AGAINST HIM-- THE MORE APT HE IS TO TRY IT!
AND THEN--EVEN AS HUNDREDS OF EYES ARE FOCUSED ON THE GEM TREE...
KATAR-- THE GEMS ARE GONE!
THEY DISAPPEARED RIGHT BEFORE OUR EYES WHILE WE WERE STARING AT THEM!
18

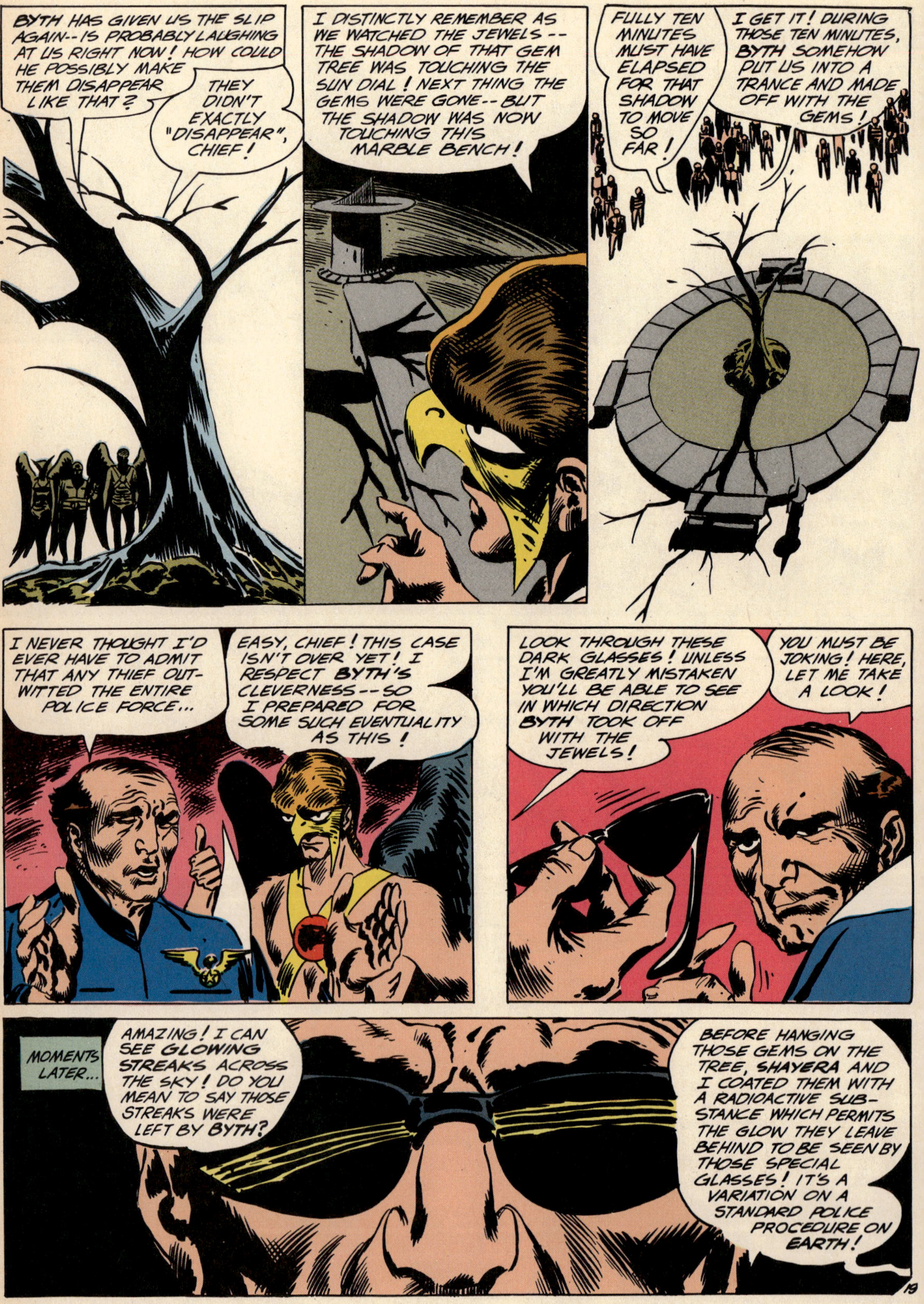
BYTH HAS GIVEN US THE SLIP AGAIN--IS PROBABLY LAUGHING AT US RIGHT NOW! HOW COULD HE POSSIBLY MAKE THEM DISAPPEAR LIKE THAT?
THEY DIDN'T EXACTLY "DISAPPEAR", CHIEF!
I DISTINCTLY REMEMBER AS WE WATCHED THE JEWELS--THE SHADOW OF THAT GEM TREE WAS TOUCHING THE SUN DIAL! NEXT THING THE GEMS WERE GONE--BUT THE SHADOW WAS NOW TOUCHING THIS MARBLE BENCH!
FULLY TEN MINUTES MUST HAVE ELAPSED FOR THAT SHADOW TO MOVE SO FAR!
I GET IT! DURING THOSE TEN MINUTES, BYTH SOMEHOW PUT US INTO A TRANCE AND MADE OFF WITH THE GEMS!
I NEVER THOUGHT I'D EVER HAVE TO ADMIT THAT ANY THIEF OUT-WITTED THE ENTIRE POLICE FORCE...
EASY, CHIEF! THIS CASE ISN'T OVER YET! I RESPECT BYTH'S CLEVERNESS--SO I PREPARED FOR SOME SUCH EVENTUALITY AS THIS!
LOOK THROUGH THESE DARK GLASSES! UNLESS I'M GREATLY MISTAKEN YOU'LL BE ABLE TO SEE IN WHICH DIRECTION BYTH TOOK OFF WITH THE JEWELS!
YOU MUST BE JOKING! HERE, LET ME TAKE A LOOK!
MOMENTS LATER...
AMAZING! I CAN SEE GLOWING STREAKS ACROSS THE SKY! DO YOU MEAN TO SAY THOSE STREAKS WERE LEFT BY BYTH?
BEFORE HANGING THOSE GEMS ON THE TREE, SHAYERA AND I COATED THEM WITH A RADIOACTIVE SUB-STANCE WHICH PERMITS THE GLOW THEY LEAVE BEHIND TO BE SEEN BY THOSE SPECIAL GLASSES! IT'S A VARIATION ON A STANDARD POLICE PROCEDURE ON EARTH!
19

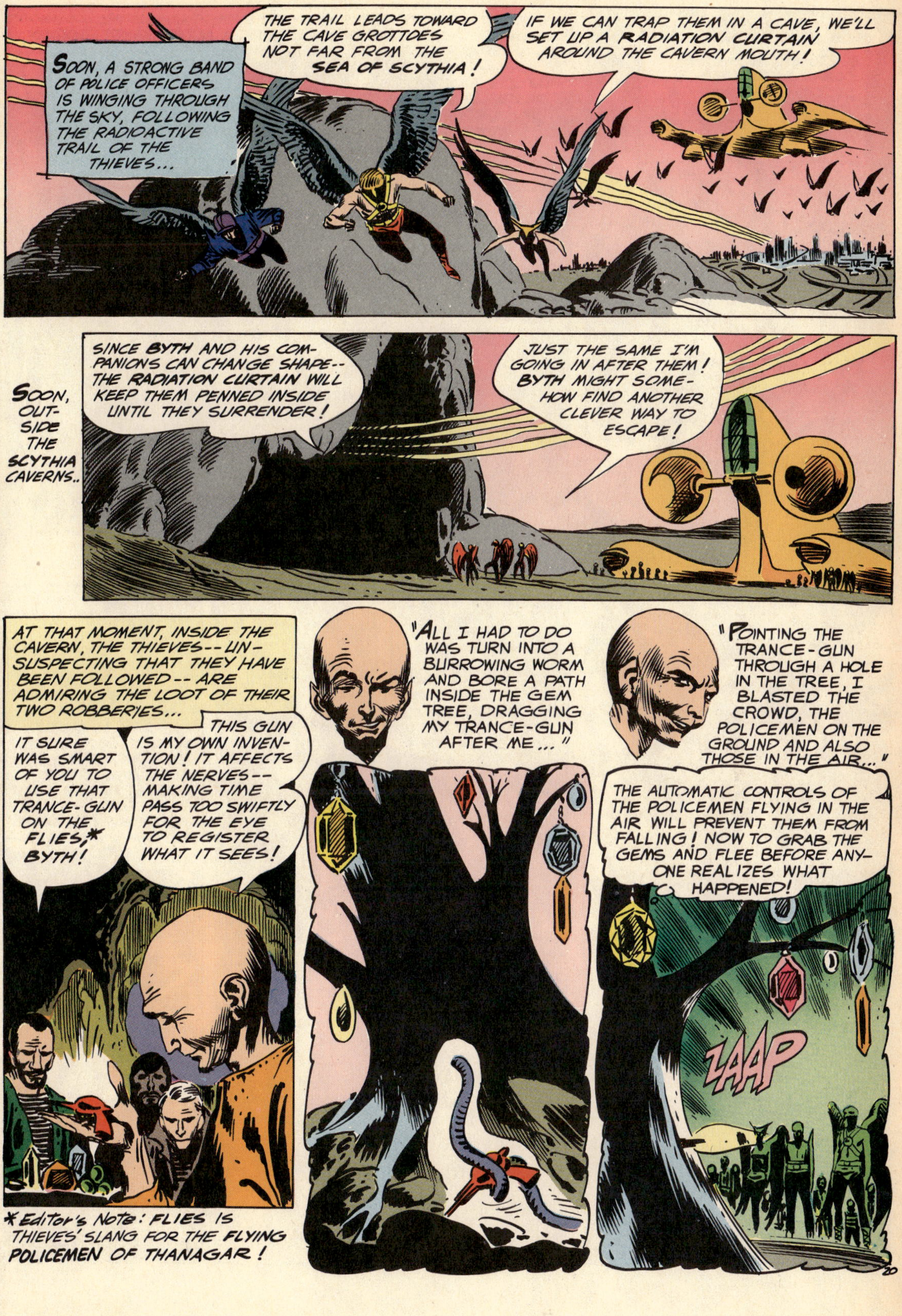
SOON, A STRONG BAND OF POLICE OFFICERS IS WINGING THROUGH THE SKY, FOLLOWING THE RADIOACTIVE TRAIL OF THE THIEVES...
THE TRAIL LEADS TOWARD THE CAVE GROTTOES NOT FAR FROM THE SEA OF SCYTHIA!
IF WE CAN TRAP THEM IN A CAVE, WE'LL SET UP A RADIATION CURTAIN AROUND THE CAVERN MOUTH!
SOON, OUTSIDE THE SCYTHIA CAVERNS..
SINCE BYTH AND HIS COMPANIONS CAN CHANGE SHAPE-- THE RADIATION CURTAIN WILL KEEP THEM PENNED INSIDE UNTIL THEY SURRENDER!
JUST THE SAME I'M GOING IN AFTER THEM! BYTH MIGHT SOMEHOW FIND ANOTHER CLEVER WAY TO ESCAPE!
AT THAT MOMENT, INSIDE THE CAVERN, THE THIEVES-- UNSUSPECTING THAT THEY HAVE BEEN FOLLOWED-- ARE ADMIRING THE LOOT OF THEIR TWO ROBBERIES...
IT SURE WAS SMART OF YOU TO USE THAT TRANCE-GUN ON THE FLIES,* BYTH!
THIS GUN IS MY OWN INVENTION! IT AFFECTS THE NERVES-- MAKING TIME PASS TOO SWIFTLY FOR THE EYE TO REGISTER WHAT IT SEES!
"ALL I HAD TO DO WAS TURN INTO A BURROWING WORM AND BORE A PATH INSIDE THE GEM TREE, DRAGGING MY TRANCE-GUN AFTER ME..."
"POINTING THE TRANCE-GUN THROUGH A HOLE IN THE TREE, I BLASTED THE CROWD, THE POLICEMEN ON THE GROUND AND ALSO THOSE IN THE AIR..."
THE AUTOMATIC CONTROLS OF THE POLICEMEN FLYING IN THE AIR WILL PREVENT THEM FROM FALLING! NOW TO GRAB THE GEMS AND FLEE BEFORE ANYONE REALIZES WHAT HAPPENED!
ZAAP
*Editor's Note: FLIES IS THIEVES' SLANG FOR THE FLYING POLICEMEN OF THANAGAR!
20

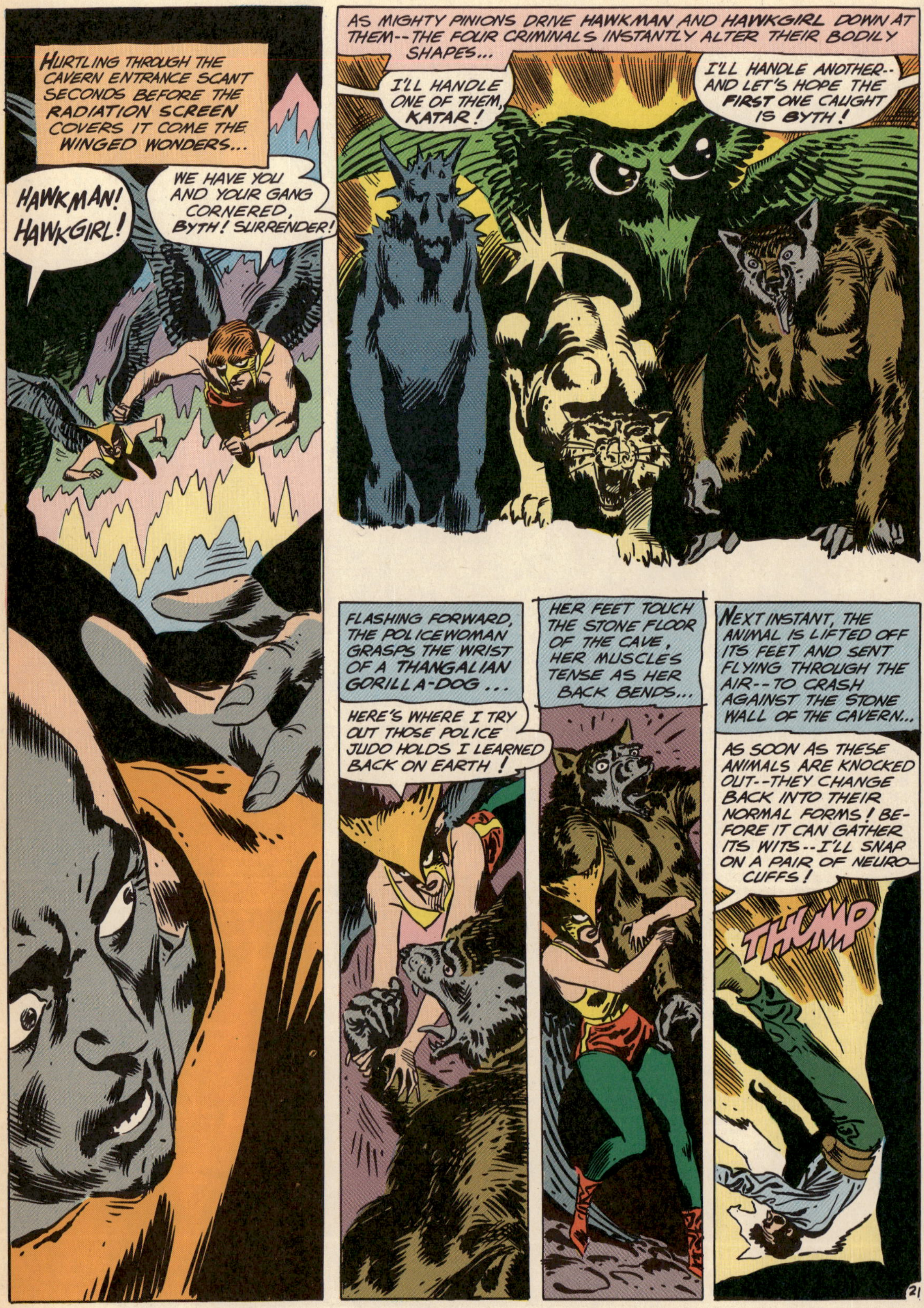

HURTLING THROUGH THE CAVERN ENTRANCE SCANT SECONDS BEFORE THE RADIATION SCREEN COVERS IT COME THE WINGED WONDERS...
HAWKMAN! HAWKGIRL!
WE HAVE YOU AND YOUR GANG CORNERED, BYTH! SURRENDER!
AS MIGHTY PINIONS DRIVE HAWKMAN AND HAWKGIRL DOWN AT THEM--THE FOUR CRIMINALS INSTANTLY ALTER THEIR BODILY SHAPES...
I'LL HANDLE ONE OF THEM, KATAR!
I'LL HANDLE ANOTHER--AND LET'S HOPE THE FIRST ONE CAUGHT IS BYTH!
FLASHING FORWARD, THE POLICEWOMAN GRASPS THE WRIST OF A THANGALIAN GORILLA-DOG...
HERE'S WHERE I TRY OUT THOSE POLICE JUDO HOLDS I LEARNED BACK ON EARTH!
HER FEET TOUCH THE STONE FLOOR OF THE CAVE, HER MUSCLES TENSE AS HER BACK BENDS...
NEXT INSTANT, THE ANIMAL IS LIFTED OFF ITS FEET AND SENT FLYING THROUGH THE AIR--TO CRASH AGAINST THE STONE WALL OF THE CAVERN...
AS SOON AS THESE ANIMALS ARE KNOCKED OUT--THEY CHANGE BACK INTO THEIR NORMAL FORMS! BEFORE IT CAN GATHER ITS WITS--I'LL SNAP ON A PAIR OF NEURO-CUFFS!
THUMP
21

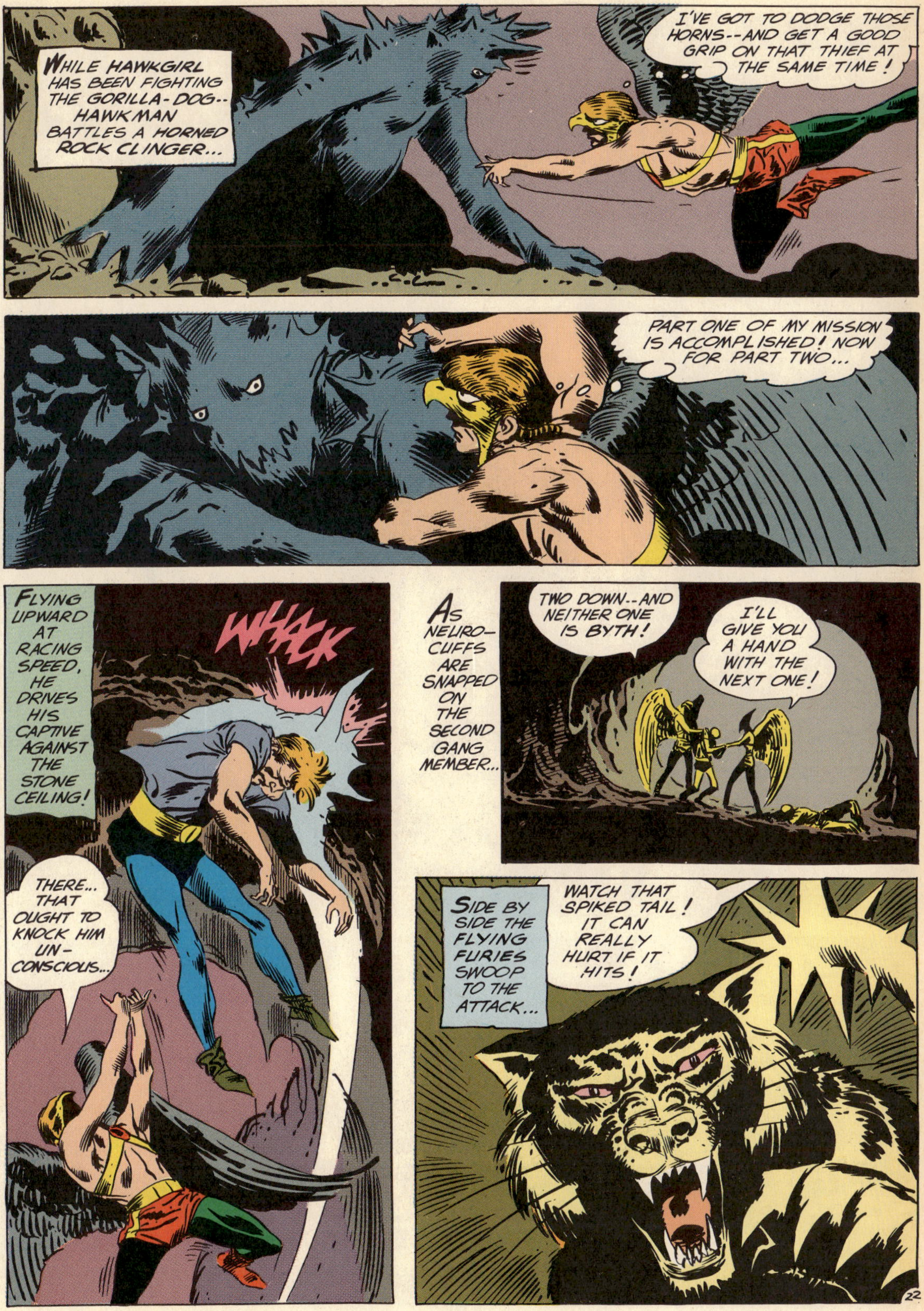
WHILE HAWKGIRL HAS BEEN FIGHTING THE GORILLA-DOG-- HAWKMAN BATTLES A HORNED ROCK CLINGER...
I'VE GOT TO DODGE THOSE HORNS--AND GET A GOOD GRIP ON THAT THIEF AT THE SAME TIME!
PART ONE OF MY MISSION IS ACCOMPLISHED! NOW FOR PART TWO...
FLYING UPWARD AT RACING SPEED, HE DRIVES HIS CAPTIVE AGAINST THE STONE CEILING!
WHACK
THERE... THAT OUGHT TO KNOCK HIM UN-CONSCIOUS...
AS NEURO-CUFFS ARE SNAPPED ON THE SECOND GANG MEMBER...
TWO DOWN--AND NEITHER ONE IS BYTH!
I'LL GIVE YOU A HAND WITH THE NEXT ONE!
SIDE BY SIDE THE FLYING FURIES SWOOP TO THE ATTACK...
WATCH THAT SPIKED TAIL! IT CAN REALLY HURT IF IT HITS!
22

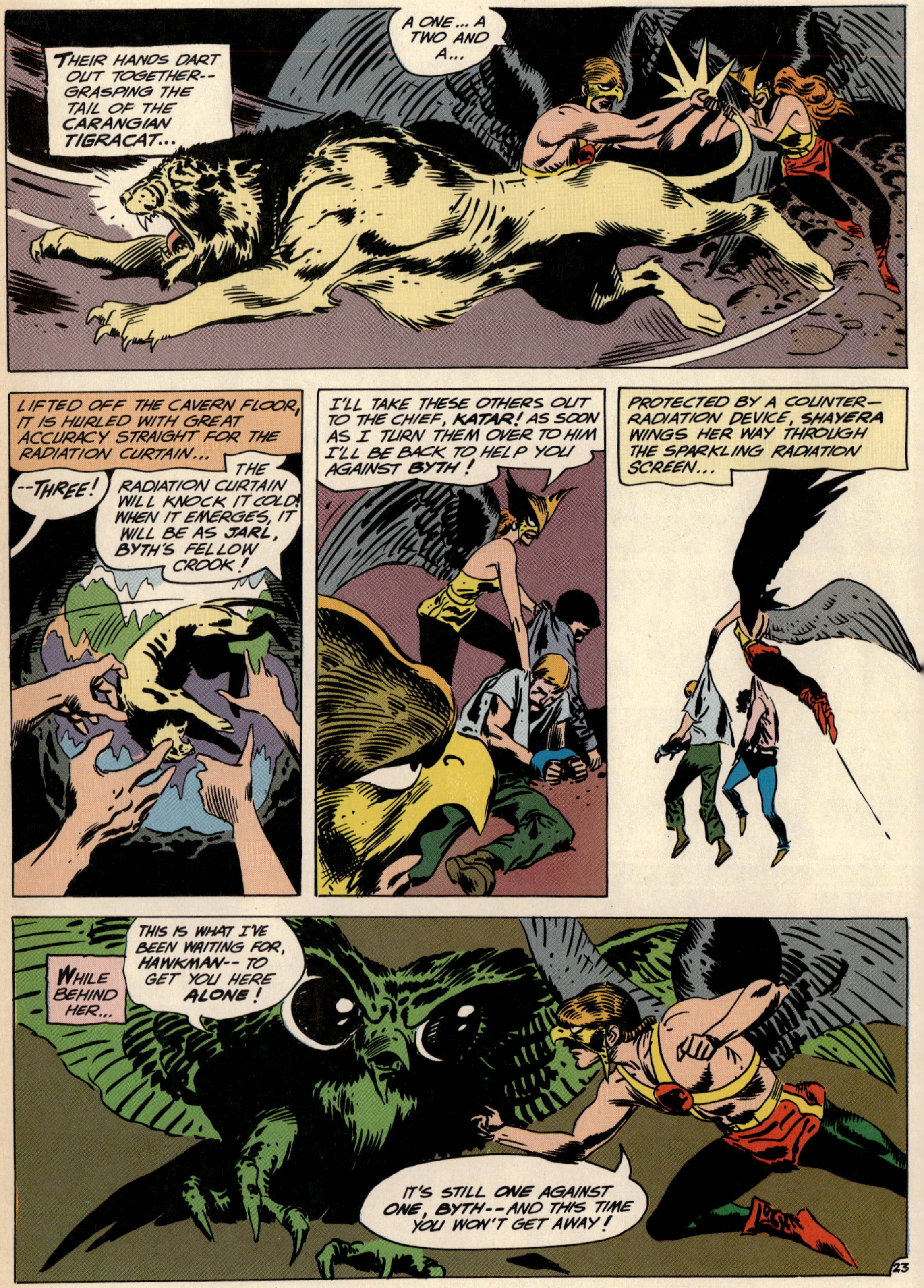
THEIR HANDS DART OUT TOGETHER-- GRASPING THE TAIL OF THE CARANGIAN TIGRACAT...
A ONE... A TWO AND A...
LIFTED OFF THE CAVERN FLOOR, IT IS HURLED WITH GREAT ACCURACY STRAIGHT FOR THE RADIATION CURTAIN...
--THREE!
THE RADIATION CURTAIN WILL KNOCK IT COLD! WHEN IT EMERGES, IT WILL BE AS JARL, BYTH'S FELLOW CROOK!
I'LL TAKE THESE OTHERS OUT TO THE CHIEF, KATAR! AS SOON AS I TURN THEM OVER TO HIM I'LL BE BACK TO HELP YOU AGAINST BYTH!
PROTECTED BY A COUNTER-RADIATION DEVICE, SHAYERA WINGS HER WAY THROUGH THE SPARKLING RADIATION SCREEN...
WHILE BEHIND HER...
THIS IS WHAT I'VE BEEN WAITING FOR, HAWKMAN-- TO GET YOU HERE ALONE!
IT'S STILL ONE AGAINST ONE, BYTH--AND THIS TIME YOU WON'T GET AWAY!
23

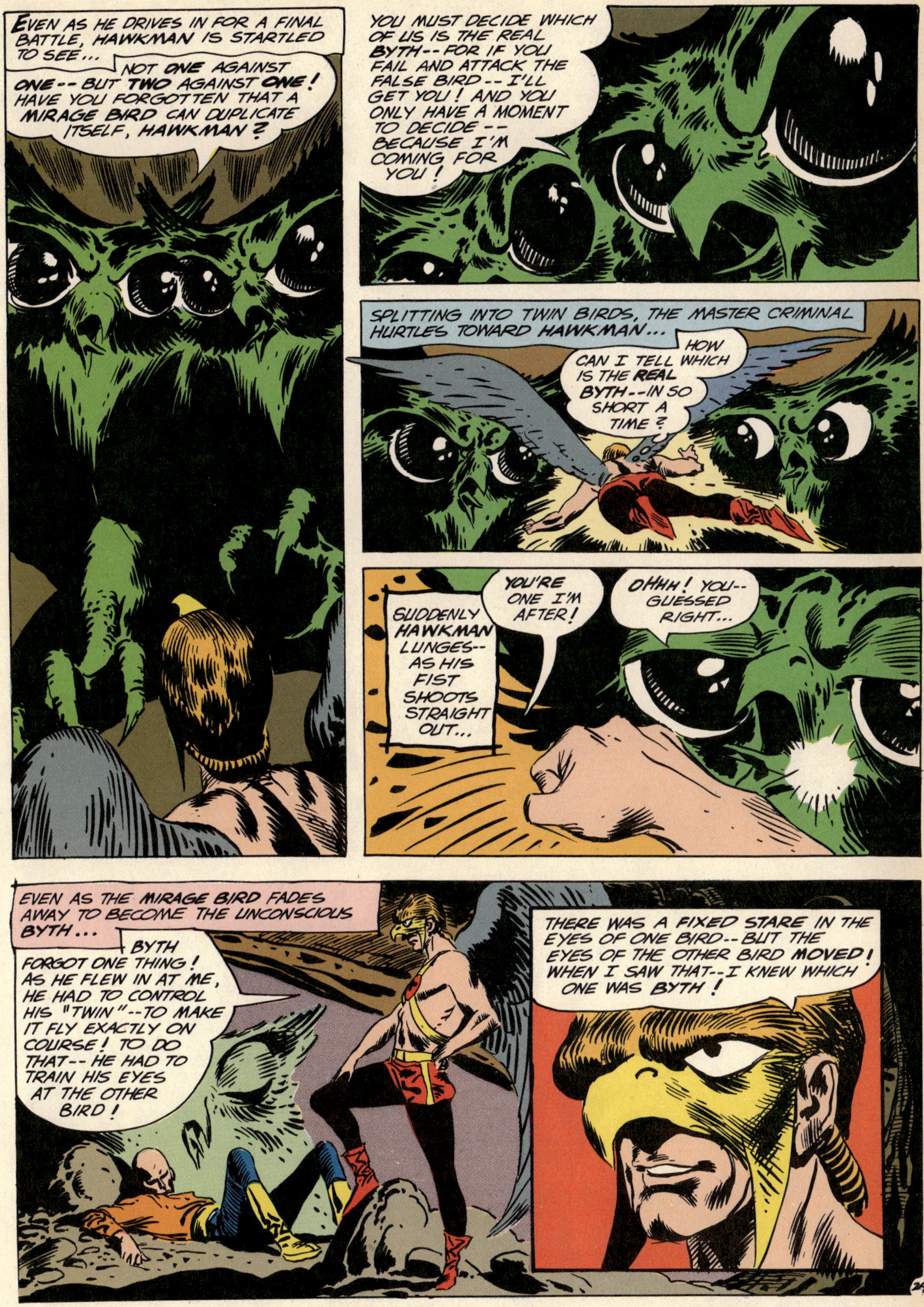
EVEN AS HE DRIVES IN FOR A FINAL BATTLE, HAWKMAN IS STARTLED TO SEE...
NOT ONE AGAINST ONE-- BUT TWO AGAINST ONE! HAVE YOU FORGOTTEN THAT A MIRAGE BIRD CAN DUPLICATE ITSELF, HAWKMAN?
YOU MUST DECIDE WHICH OF US IS THE REAL BYTH-- FOR IF YOU FAIL AND ATTACK THE FALSE BIRD -- I'LL GET YOU! AND YOU ONLY HAVE A MOMENT TO DECIDE -- BECAUSE I'M COMING FOR YOU!
SPLITTING INTO TWIN BIRDS, THE MASTER CRIMINAL HURTLES TOWARD HAWKMAN...
HOW CAN I TELL WHICH IS THE REAL BYTH--IN SO SHORT A TIME?
SUDDENLY HAWKMAN LUNGES-- AS HIS FIST SHOOTS STRAIGHT OUT...
YOU'RE ONE I'M AFTER!
OHHH! YOU-- GUESSED RIGHT...
EVEN AS THE MIRAGE BIRD FADES AWAY TO BECOME THE UNCONSCIOUS BYTH...
BYTH FORGOT ONE THING! AS HE FLEW IN AT ME, HE HAD TO CONTROL HIS "TWIN"--TO MAKE IT FLY EXACTLY ON COURSE! TO DO THAT-- HE HAD TO TRAIN HIS EYES AT THE OTHER BIRD!
THERE WAS A FIXED STARE IN THE EYES OF ONE BIRD--BUT THE EYES OF THE OTHER BIRD MOVED! WHEN I SAW THAT--I KNEW WHICH ONE WAS BYTH!
24

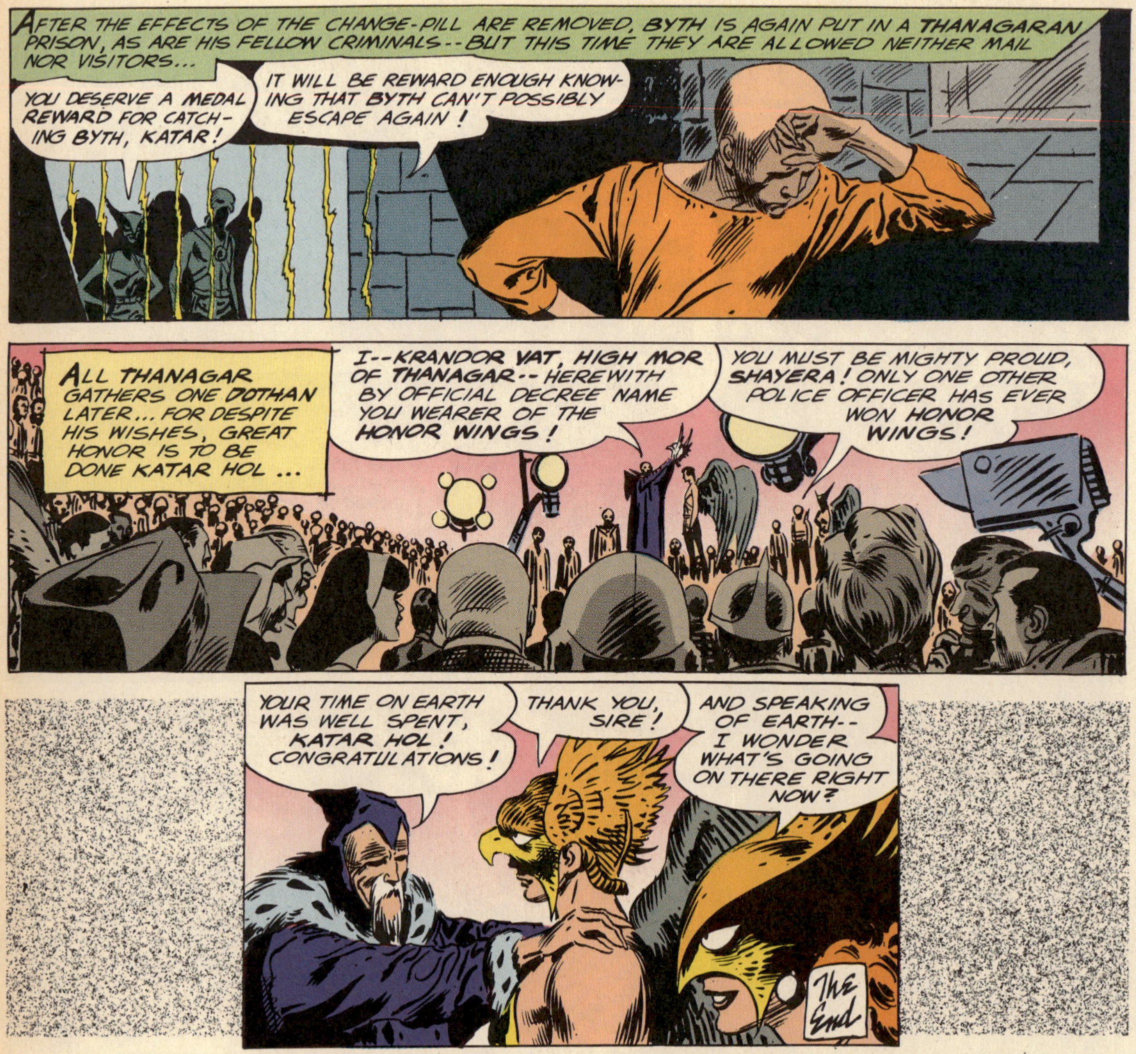
AFTER THE EFFECTS OF THE CHANGE-PILL ARE REMOVED, BYTH IS AGAIN PUT IN A THANAGARAN PRISON, AS ARE HIS FELLOW CRIMINALS--BUT THIS TIME THEY ARE ALLOWED NEITHER MAIL NOR VISITORS...
YOU DESERVE A MEDAL REWARD FOR CATCHING BYTH, KATAR!
IT WILL BE REWARD ENOUGH KNOWING THAT BYTH CAN'T POSSIBLY ESCAPE AGAIN!
ALL THANAGAR GATHERS ONE DOTHAN LATER... FOR DESPITE HIS WISHES, GREAT HONOR IS TO BE DONE KATAR HOL...
I--KRANDOR VAT, HIGH MOR OF THANAGAR--HEREWITH BY OFFICIAL DECREE NAME YOU WEARER OF THE HONOR WINGS!
YOU MUST BE MIGHTY PROUD, SHAYERA! ONLY ONE OTHER POLICE OFFICER HAS EVER WON HONOR WINGS!
YOUR TIME ON EARTH WAS WELL SPENT, KATAR HOL! CONGRATULATIONS!
THANK YOU, SIRE!
AND SPEAKING OF EARTH--I WONDER WHAT'S GOING ON THERE RIGHT NOW?
THE END

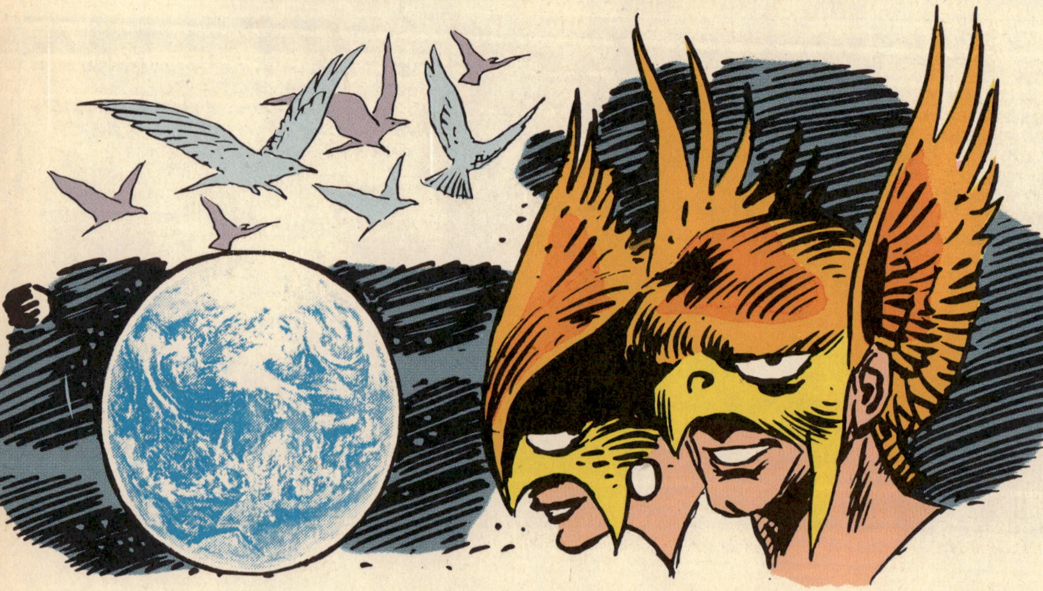

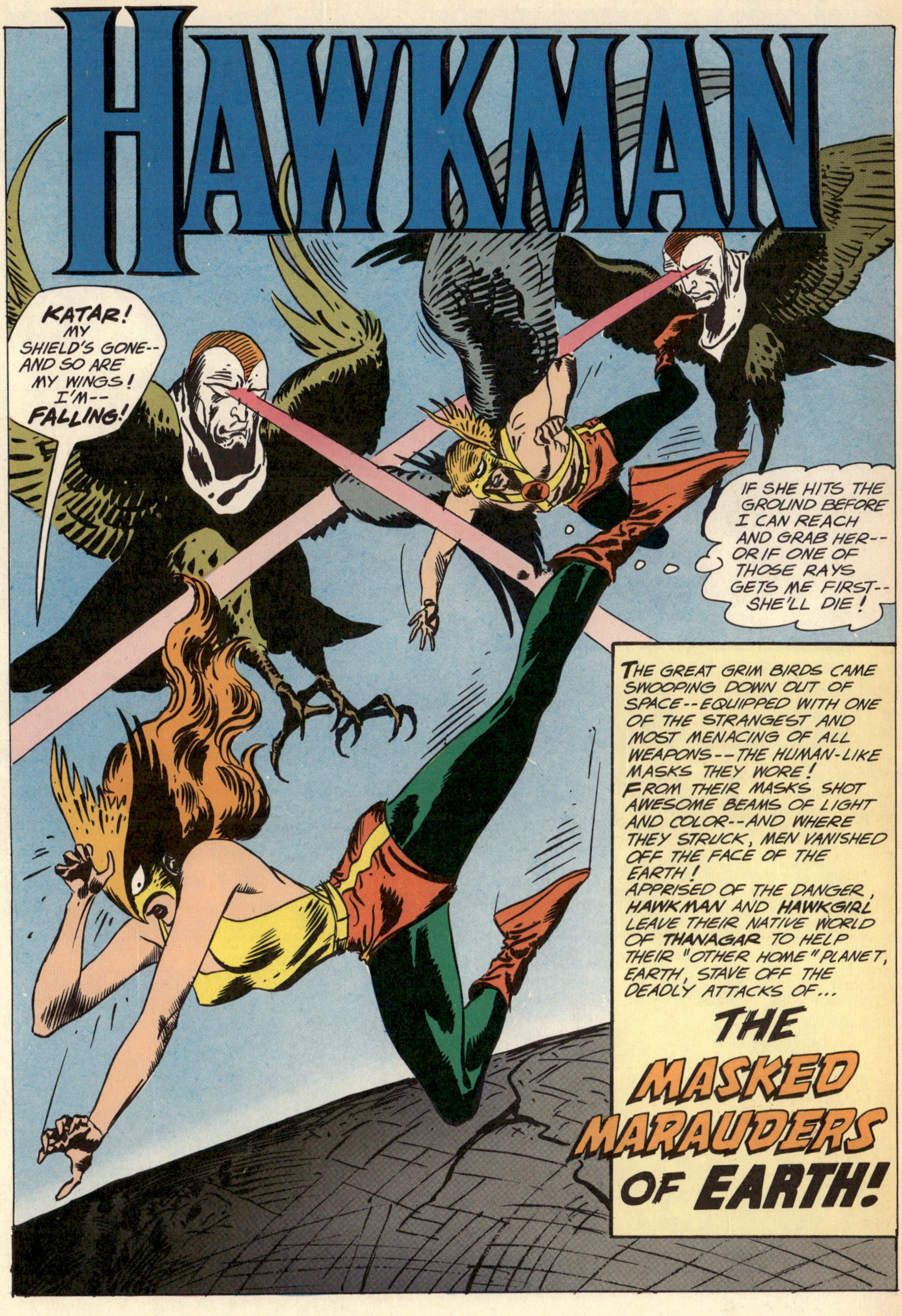
HAWKMAN
KATAR! MY SHIELD'S GONE-- AND SO ARE MY WINGS! I'M-- FALLING!
IF SHE HITS THE GROUND BEFORE I CAN REACH AND GRAB HER-- OR IF ONE OF THOSE RAYS GETS ME FIRST-- SHE'LL DIE!
THE GREAT GRIM BIRDS CAME SWOOPING DOWN OUT OF SPACE--EQUIPPED WITH ONE OF THE STRANGEST AND MOST MENACING OF ALL WEAPONS--THE HUMAN-LIKE MASKS THEY WORE!
FROM THEIR MASKS SHOT AWESOME BEAMS OF LIGHT AND COLOR--AND WHERE THEY STRUCK, MEN VANISHED OFF THE FACE OF THE EARTH!
APPRISED OF THE DANGER, HAWKMAN AND HAWKGIRL LEAVE THEIR NATIVE WORLD OF THANAGAR TO HELP THEIR "OTHER HOME" PLANET, EARTH, STAVE OFF THE DEADLY ATTACKS OF...
THE MASKED MARAUDERS OF EARTH!

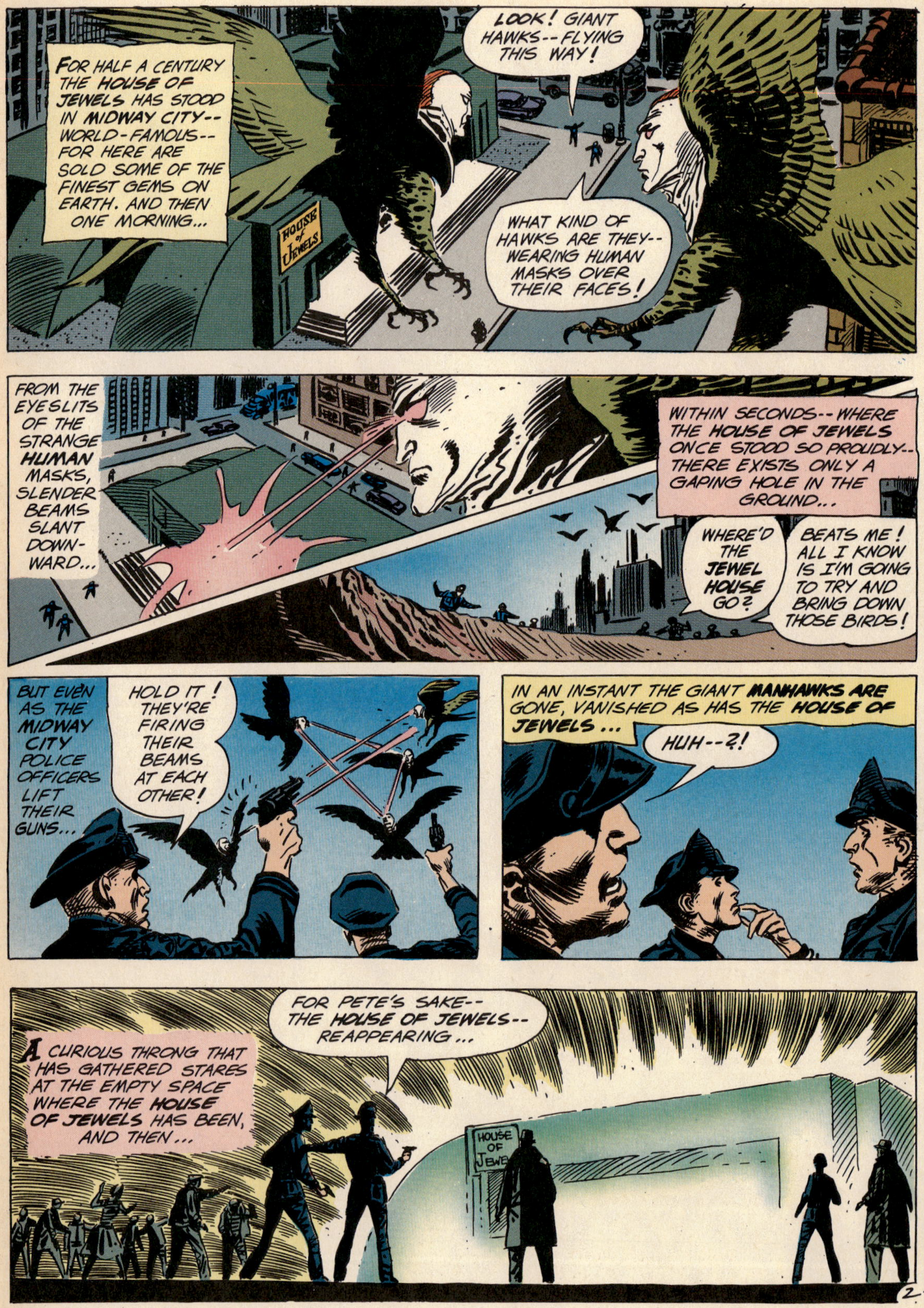
FOR HALF A CENTURY THE HOUSE OF JEWELS HAS STOOD IN MIDWAY CITY-- WORLD-FAMOUS-- FOR HERE ARE SOLD SOME OF THE FINEST GEMS ON EARTH. AND THEN ONE MORNING...
LOOK! GIANT HAWKS-- FLYING THIS WAY!
HOUSE of JEWELS
WHAT KIND OF HAWKS ARE THEY-- WEARING HUMAN MASKS OVER THEIR FACES!
FROM THE EYESLITS OF THE STRANGE HUMAN MASKS, SLENDER BEAMS SLANT DOWNWARD...
WITHIN SECONDS-- WHERE THE HOUSE OF JEWELS ONCE STOOD SO PROUDLY-- THERE EXISTS ONLY A GAPING HOLE IN THE GROUND...
WHERE'D THE JEWEL HOUSE GO?
BEATS ME! ALL I KNOW IS I'M GOING TO TRY AND BRING DOWN THOSE BIRDS!
BUT EVEN AS THE MIDWAY CITY POLICE OFFICERS LIFT THEIR GUNS...
HOLD IT! THEY'RE FIRING THEIR BEAMS AT EACH OTHER!
IN AN INSTANT THE GIANT MANHAWKS ARE GONE, VANISHED AS HAS THE HOUSE OF JEWELS...
HUH--?!
A CURIOUS THRONG THAT HAS GATHERED STARES AT THE EMPTY SPACE WHERE THE HOUSE OF JEWELS HAS BEEN, AND THEN...
FOR PETE'S SAKE-- THE HOUSE OF JEWELS-- REAPPEARING...
HOUSE OF JEWE
2

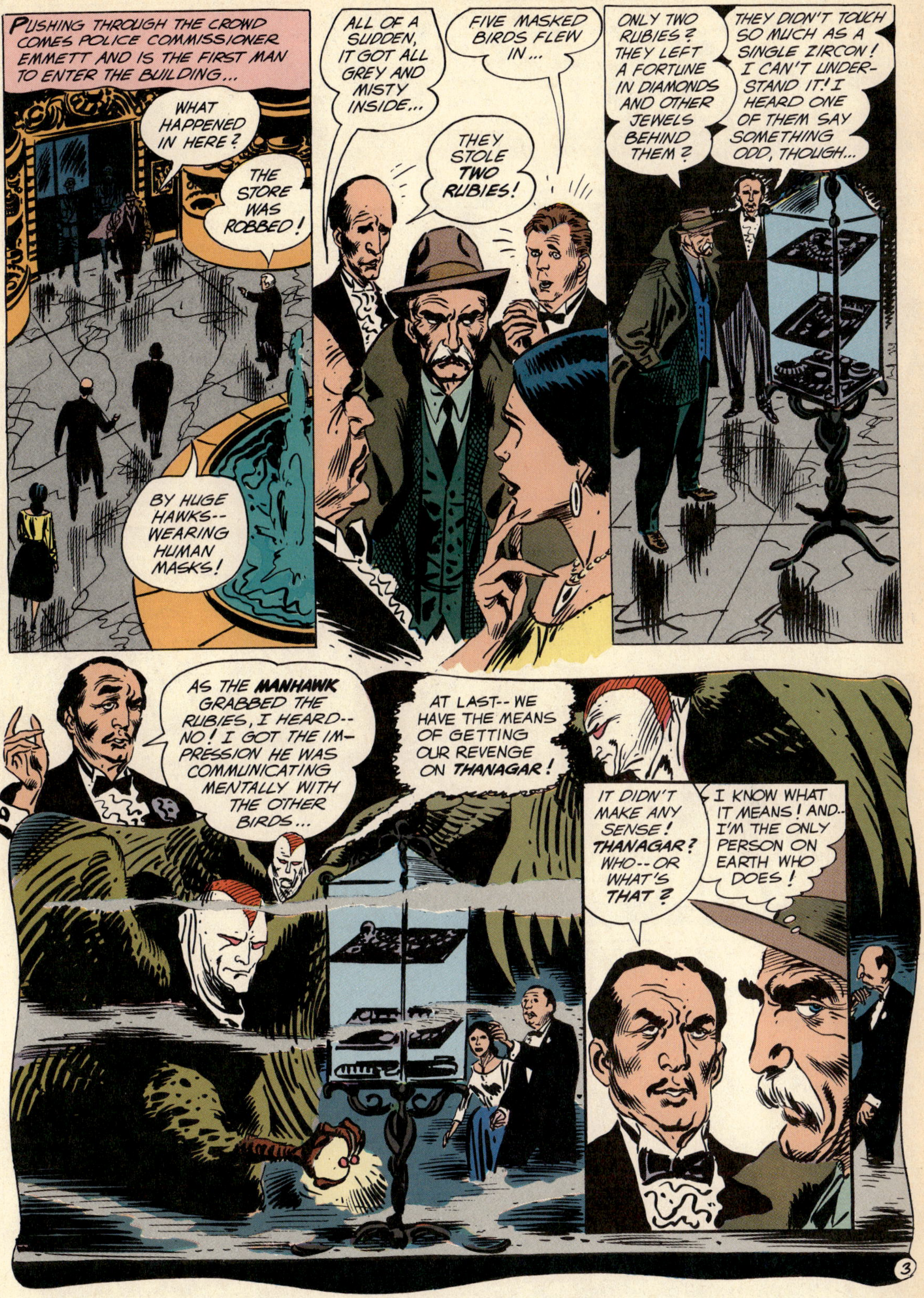
PUSHING THROUGH THE CROWD COMES POLICE COMMISSIONER EMMETT AND IS THE FIRST MAN TO ENTER THE BUILDING...
WHAT HAPPENED IN HERE?
THE STORE WAS ROBBED!
BY HUGE HAWKS-- WEARING HUMAN MASKS!
ALL OF A SUDDEN, IT GOT ALL GREY AND MISTY INSIDE...
FIVE MASKED BIRDS FLEW IN...
THEY STOLE TWO RUBIES!
ONLY TWO RUBIES? THEY LEFT A FORTUNE IN DIAMONDS AND OTHER JEWELS BEHIND THEM?
THEY DIDN'T TOUCH SO MUCH AS A SINGLE ZIRCON! I CAN'T UNDERSTAND IT! I HEARD ONE OF THEM SAY SOMETHING ODD, THOUGH...
AS THE MANHAWK GRABBED THE RUBIES, I HEARD-- NO! I GOT THE IMPRESSION HE WAS COMMUNICATING MENTALLY WITH THE OTHER BIRDS...
AT LAST-- WE HAVE THE MEANS OF GETTING OUR REVENGE ON THANAGAR!
IT DIDN'T MAKE ANY SENSE! THANAGAR? WHO--OR WHAT'S THAT?
I KNOW WHAT IT MEANS! AND.. I'M THE ONLY PERSON ON EARTH WHO DOES!
3

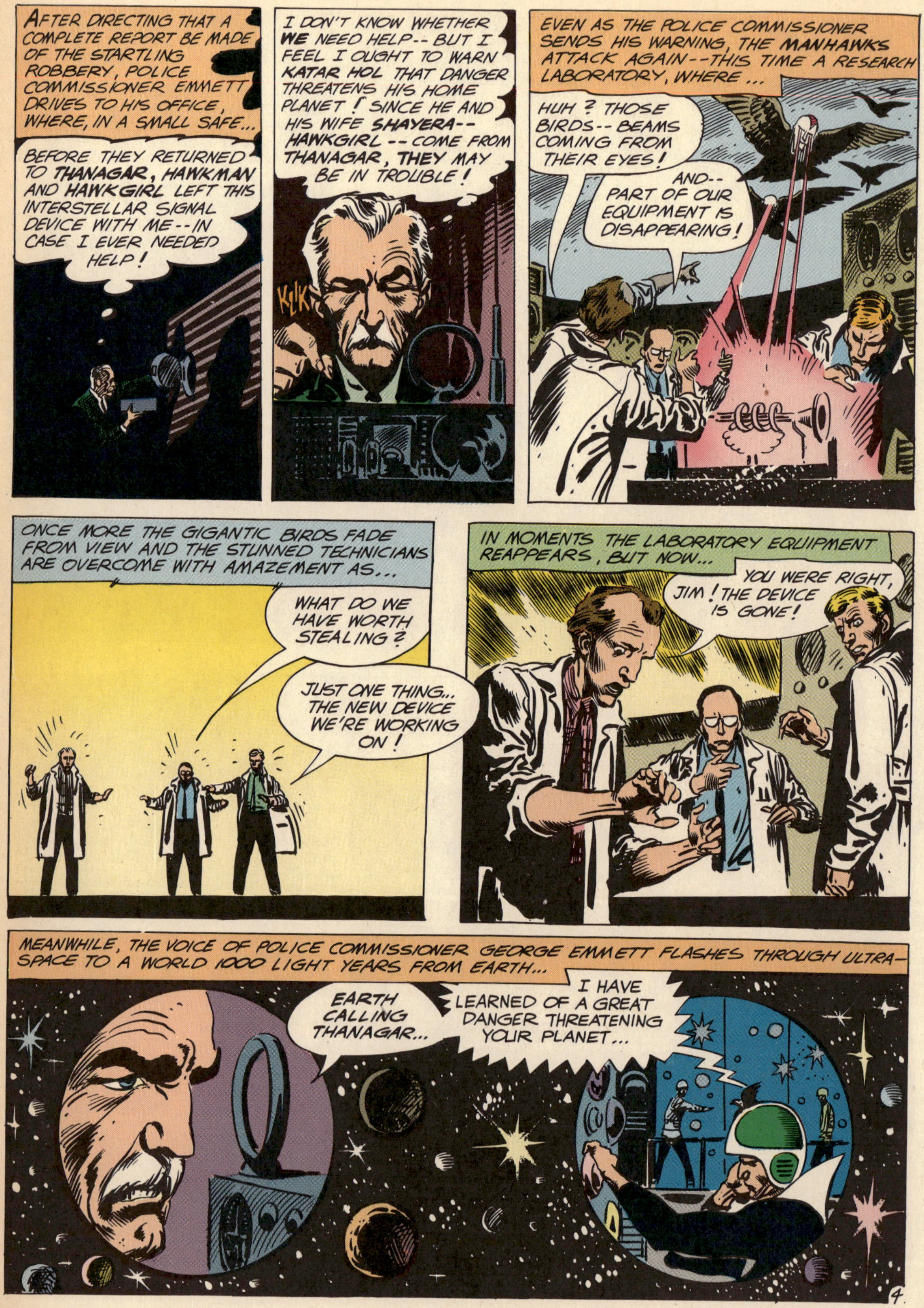
AFTER DIRECTING THAT A COMPLETE REPORT BE MADE OF THE STARTLING ROBBERY, POLICE COMMISSIONER EMMETT DRIVES TO HIS OFFICE, WHERE, IN A SMALL SAFE...
BEFORE THEY RETURNED TO THANAGAR, HAWKMAN AND HAWKGIRL LEFT THIS INTERSTELLAR SIGNAL DEVICE WITH ME--IN CASE I EVER NEEDED HELP!
I DON'T KNOW WHETHER WE NEED HELP-- BUT I FEEL I OUGHT TO WARN KATAR HOL THAT DANGER THREATENS HIS HOME PLANET! SINCE HE AND HIS WIFE SHAYERA-- HAWKGIRL -- COME FROM THANAGAR, THEY MAY BE IN TROUBLE!
KLIK
EVEN AS THE POLICE COMMISSIONER SENDS HIS WARNING, THE MANHAWKS ATTACK AGAIN--THIS TIME A RESEARCH LABORATORY, WHERE ...
HUH? THOSE BIRDS-- BEAMS COMING FROM THEIR EYES!
AND-- PART OF OUR EQUIPMENT IS DISAPPEARING!
ONCE MORE THE GIGANTIC BIRDS FADE FROM VIEW AND THE STUNNED TECHNICIANS ARE OVERCOME WITH AMAZEMENT AS...
WHAT DO WE HAVE WORTH STEALING?
JUST ONE THING... THE NEW DEVICE WE'RE WORKING ON!
IN MOMENTS THE LABORATORY EQUIPMENT REAPPEARS, BUT NOW...
YOU WERE RIGHT, JIM! THE DEVICE IS GONE!
MEANWHILE, THE VOICE OF POLICE COMMISSIONER GEORGE EMMETT FLASHES THROUGH ULTRA-SPACE TO A WORLD 1000 LIGHT YEARS FROM EARTH...
EARTH CALLING THANAGAR...
I HAVE LEARNED OF A GREAT DANGER THREATENING YOUR PLANET...
4.

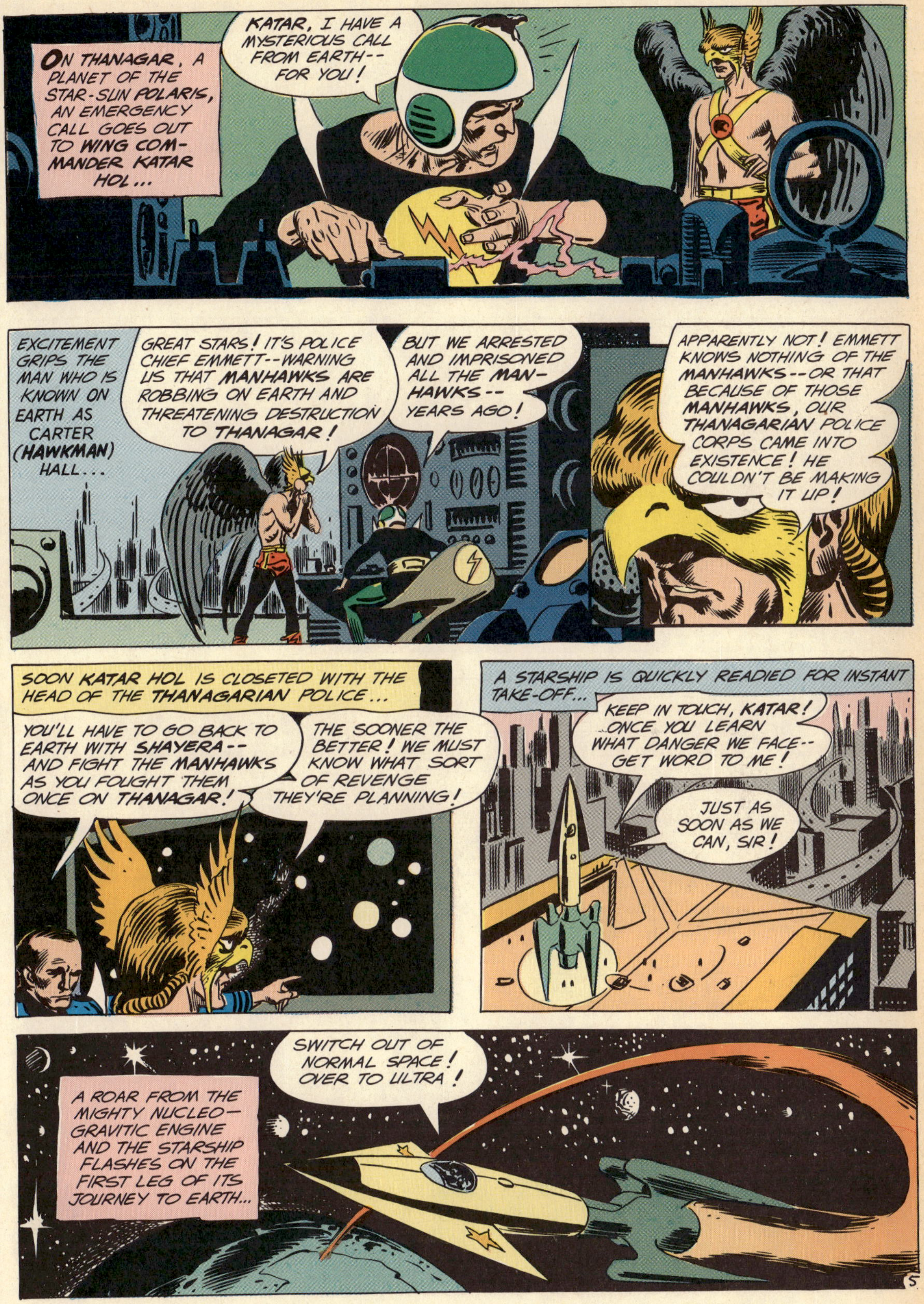
ON THANAGAR, A PLANET OF THE STAR-SUN POLARIS, AN EMERGENCY CALL GOES OUT TO WING COMMANDER KATAR HOL...
KATAR, I HAVE A MYSTERIOUS CALL FROM EARTH-- FOR YOU!
EXCITEMENT GRIPS THE MAN WHO IS KNOWN ON EARTH AS CARTER (HAWKMAN) HALL...
GREAT STARS! IT'S POLICE CHIEF EMMETT--WARNING US THAT MANHAWKS ARE ROBBING ON EARTH AND THREATENING DESTRUCTION TO THANAGAR!
BUT WE ARRESTED AND IMPRISONED ALL THE MAN-HAWKS-- YEARS AGO!
APPARENTLY NOT! EMMETT KNOWS NOTHING OF THE MANHAWKS--OR THAT BECAUSE OF THOSE MANHAWKS, OUR THANAGARIAN POLICE CORPS CAME INTO EXISTENCE! HE COULDN'T BE MAKING IT UP!
SOON KATAR HOL IS CLOSETED WITH THE HEAD OF THE THANAGARIAN POLICE...
YOU'LL HAVE TO GO BACK TO EARTH WITH SHAYERA-- AND FIGHT THE MANHAWKS AS YOU FOUGHT THEM ONCE ON THANAGAR!
THE SOONER THE BETTER! WE MUST KNOW WHAT SORT OF REVENGE THEY'RE PLANNING!
A STARSHIP IS QUICKLY READIED FOR INSTANT TAKE-OFF...
KEEP IN TOUCH, KATAR! ONCE YOU LEARN WHAT DANGER WE FACE-- GET WORD TO ME!
JUST AS SOON AS WE CAN, SIR!
A ROAR FROM THE MIGHTY NUCLEO-GRAVITIC ENGINE AND THE STARSHIP FLASHES ON THE FIRST LEG OF ITS JOURNEY TO EARTH...
SWITCH OUT OF NORMAL SPACE! OVER TO ULTRA!
5

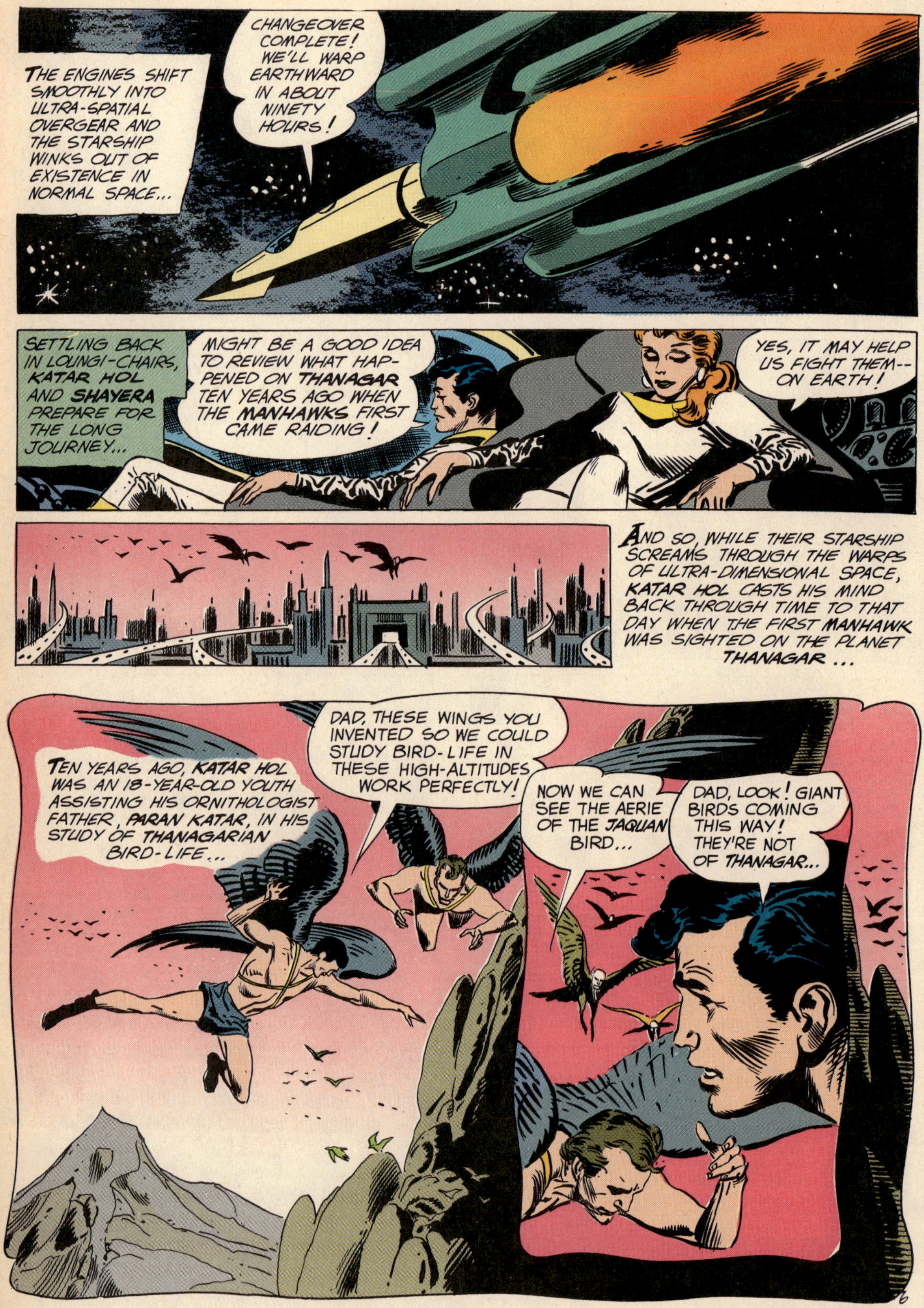
THE ENGINES SHIFT SMOOTHLY INTO ULTRA-SPATIAL OVERGEAR AND THE STARSHIP WINKS OUT OF EXISTENCE IN NORMAL SPACE...
CHANGEOVER COMPLETE! WE'LL WARP EARTHWARD IN ABOUT NINETY HOURS!
SETTLING BACK IN LOUNGI-CHAIRS, KATAR HOL AND SHAYERA PREPARE FOR THE LONG JOURNEY...
MIGHT BE A GOOD IDEA TO REVIEW WHAT HAPPENED ON THANAGAR TEN YEARS AGO WHEN THE MANHAWKS FIRST CAME RAIDING!
YES, IT MAY HELP US FIGHT THEM-- ON EARTH!
AND SO, WHILE THEIR STARSHIP SCREAMS THROUGH THE WARPS OF ULTRA-DIMENSIONAL SPACE, KATAR HOL CASTS HIS MIND BACK THROUGH TIME TO THAT DAY WHEN THE FIRST MANHAWK WAS SIGHTED ON THE PLANET THANAGAR ...
TEN YEARS AGO, KATAR HOL WAS AN 18-YEAR-OLD YOUTH ASSISTING HIS ORNITHOLOGIST FATHER, PARAN KATAR, IN HIS STUDY OF THANAGARIAN BIRD-LIFE...
DAD, THESE WINGS YOU INVENTED SO WE COULD STUDY BIRD-LIFE IN THESE HIGH-ALTITUDES WORK PERFECTLY!
NOW WE CAN SEE THE AERIE OF THE JAQUAN BIRD...
DAD, LOOK! GIANT BIRDS COMING THIS WAY! THEY'RE NOT OF THANAGAR...
6

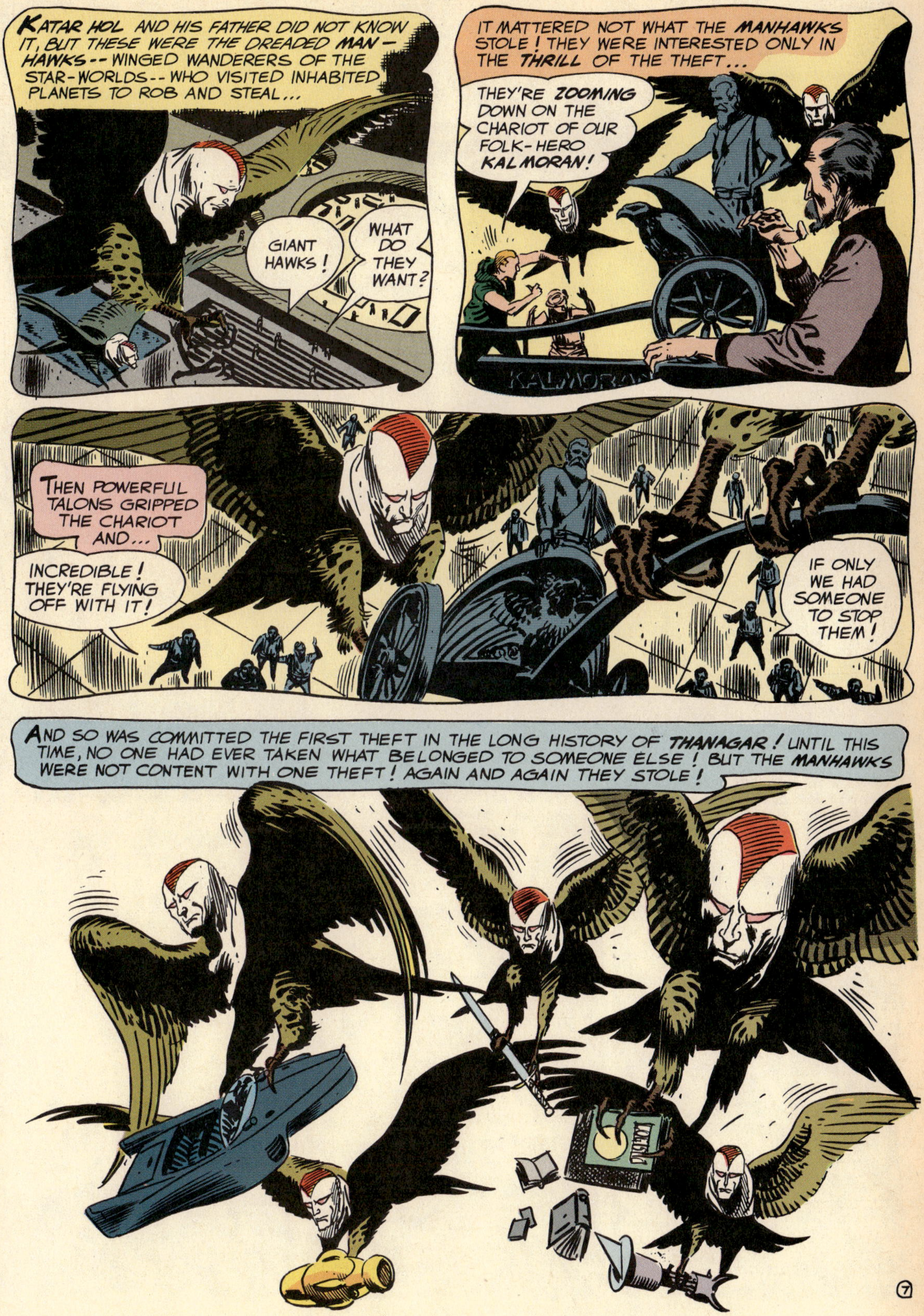
KATAR HOL AND HIS FATHER DID NOT KNOW IT, BUT THESE WERE THE DREADED MAN-HAWKS -- WINGED WANDERERS OF THE STAR-WORLDS -- WHO VISITED INHABITED PLANETS TO ROB AND STEAL...
GIANT HAWKS!
WHAT DO THEY WANT?
IT MATTERED NOT WHAT THE MANHAWKS STOLE! THEY WERE INTERESTED ONLY IN THE THRILL OF THE THEFT...
THEY'RE ZOOMING DOWN ON THE CHARIOT OF OUR FOLK-HERO KALMORAN!
THEN POWERFUL TALONS GRIPPED THE CHARIOT AND...
INCREDIBLE! THEY'RE FLYING OFF WITH IT!
IF ONLY WE HAD SOMEONE TO STOP THEM!
AND SO WAS COMMITTED THE FIRST THEFT IN THE LONG HISTORY OF THANAGAR! UNTIL THIS TIME, NO ONE HAD EVER TAKEN WHAT BELONGED TO SOMEONE ELSE! BUT THE MANHAWKS WERE NOT CONTENT WITH ONE THEFT! AGAIN AND AGAIN THEY STOLE!
7

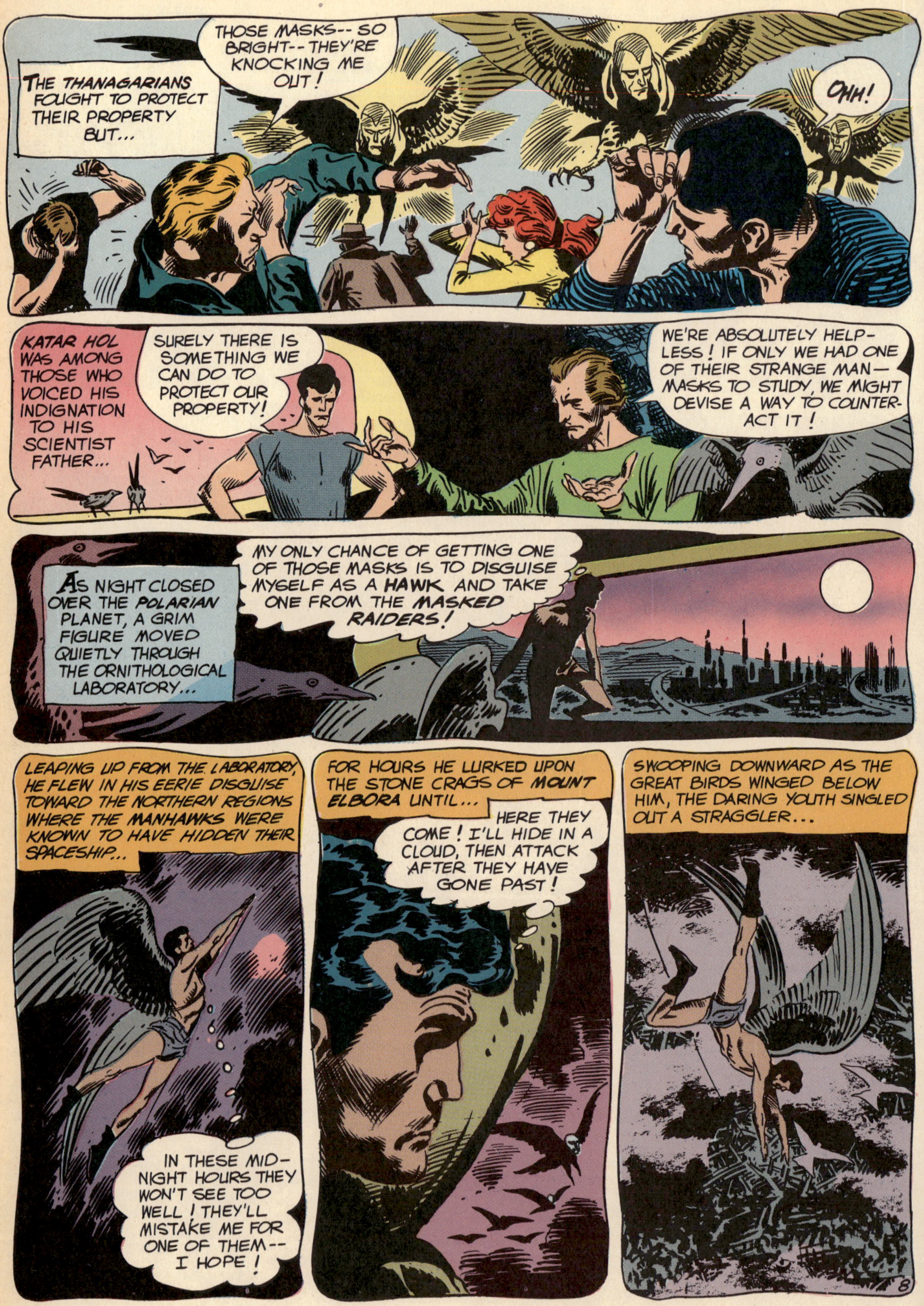
THE THANAGARIANS FOUGHT TO PROTECT THEIR PROPERTY BUT...
THOSE MASKS-- SO BRIGHT-- THEY'RE KNOCKING ME OUT!
OHH!
KATAR HOL WAS AMONG THOSE WHO VOICED HIS INDIGNATION TO HIS SCIENTIST FATHER...
SURELY THERE IS SOMETHING WE CAN DO TO PROTECT OUR PROPERTY!
WE'RE ABSOLUTELY HELPLESS! IF ONLY WE HAD ONE OF THEIR STRANGE MAN-MASKS TO STUDY, WE MIGHT DEVISE A WAY TO COUNTERACT IT!
AS NIGHT CLOSED OVER THE POLARIAN PLANET, A GRIM FIGURE MOVED QUIETLY THROUGH THE ORNITHOLOGICAL LABORATORY...
MY ONLY CHANCE OF GETTING ONE OF THOSE MASKS IS TO DISGUISE MYSELF AS A HAWK AND TAKE ONE FROM THE MASKED RAIDERS!
LEAPING UP FROM THE LABORATORY, HE FLEW IN HIS EERIE DISGUISE TOWARD THE NORTHERN REGIONS WHERE THE MANHAWKS WERE KNOWN TO HAVE HIDDEN THEIR SPACESHIP...
IN THESE MIDNIGHT HOURS THEY WON'T SEE TOO WELL! THEY'LL MISTAKE ME FOR ONE OF THEM-- I HOPE!
FOR HOURS HE LURKED UPON THE STONE CRAGS OF MOUNT ELBORA UNTIL...
HERE THEY COME! I'LL HIDE IN A CLOUD, THEN ATTACK AFTER THEY HAVE GONE PAST!
SWOOPING DOWNWARD AS THE GREAT BIRDS WINGED BELOW HIM, THE DARING YOUTH SINGLED OUT A STRAGGLER...
8

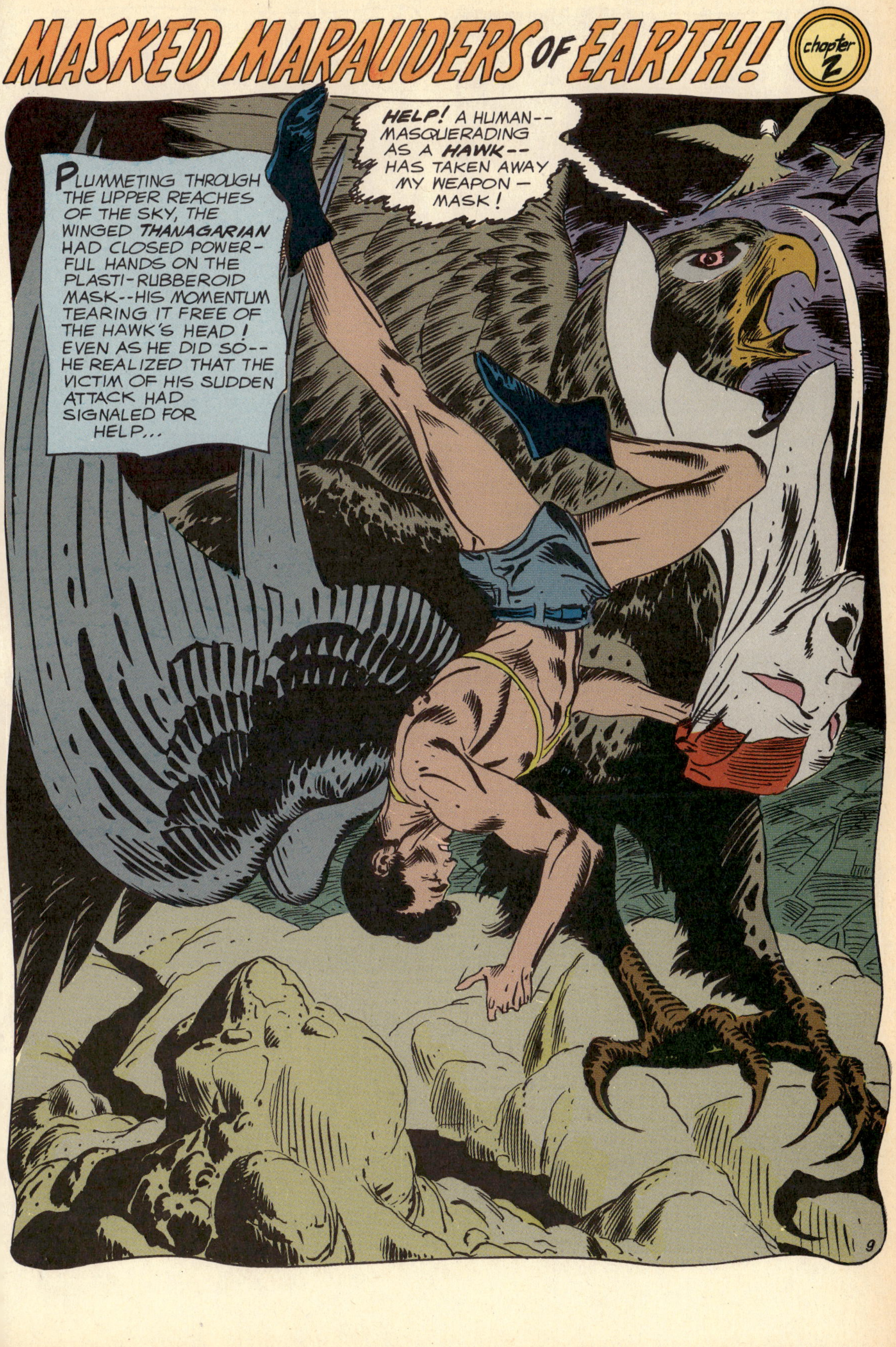
MASKED MARAUDERS OF EARTH!
chapter 2
PLUMMETING THROUGH THE UPPER REACHES OF THE SKY, THE WINGED THANAGARIAN HAD CLOSED POWERFUL HANDS ON THE PLASTI-RUBBEROID MASK--HIS MOMENTUM TEARING IT FREE OF THE HAWK'S HEAD! EVEN AS HE DID SO-- HE REALIZED THAT THE VICTIM OF HIS SUDDEN ATTACK HAD SIGNALED FOR HELP...
HELP! A HUMAN-- MASQUERADING AS A HAWK-- HAS TAKEN AWAY MY WEAPON-MASK!
9

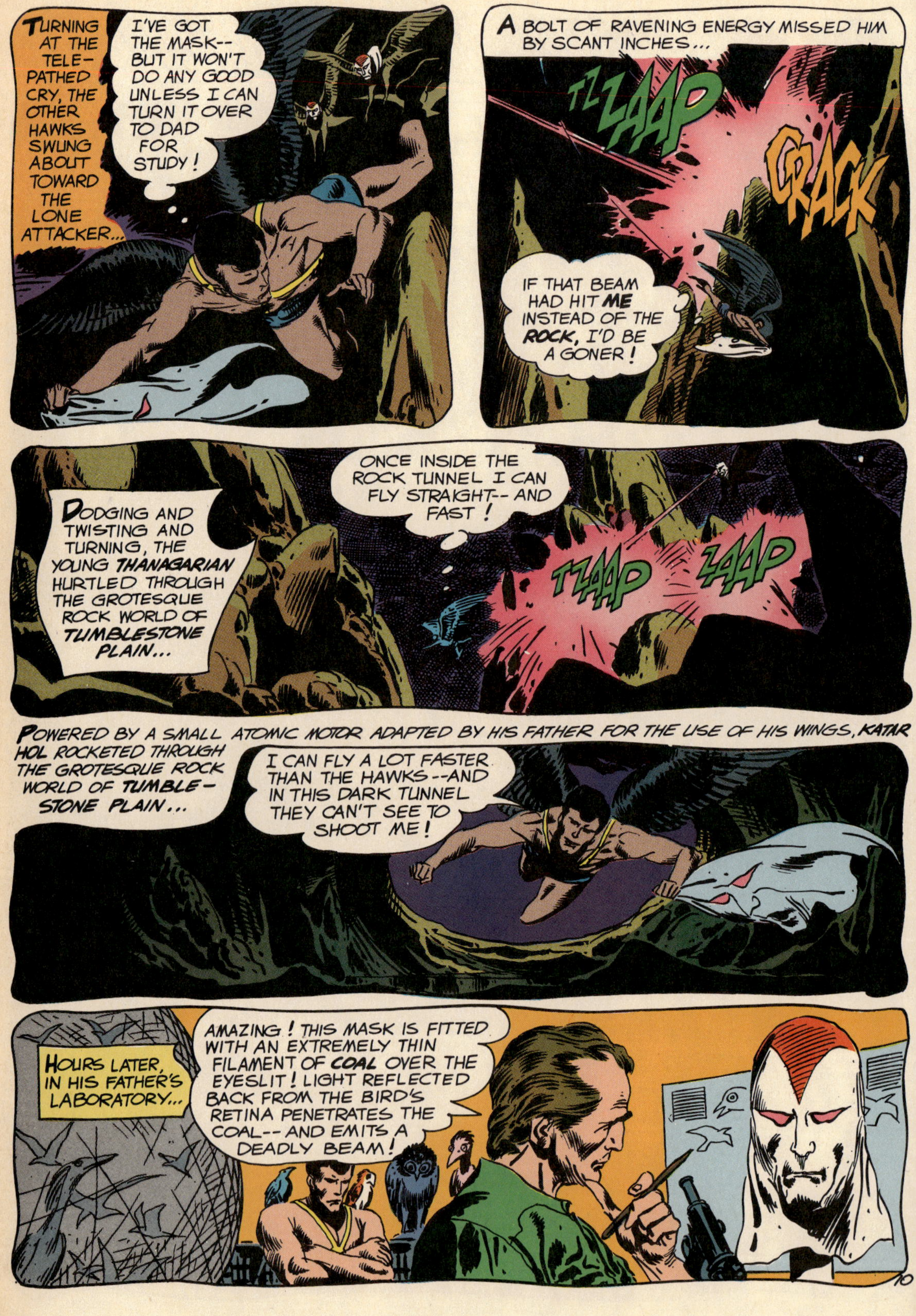
TURNING AT THE TELE-PATHED CRY, THE OTHER HAWKS SWUNG ABOUT TOWARD THE LONE ATTACKER...
I'VE GOT THE MASK-- BUT IT WON'T DO ANY GOOD UNLESS I CAN TURN IT OVER TO DAD FOR STUDY!
A BOLT OF RAVENING ENERGY MISSED HIM BY SCANT INCHES...
TZZAAP
CRACK
IF THAT BEAM HAD HIT ME INSTEAD OF THE ROCK, I'D BE A GONER!
DODGING AND TWISTING AND TURNING, THE YOUNG THANAGARIAN HURTLED THROUGH THE GROTESQUE ROCK WORLD OF TUMBLESTONE PLAIN...
ONCE INSIDE THE ROCK TUNNEL I CAN FLY STRAIGHT-- AND FAST!
TZAAP
ZAAP
POWERED BY A SMALL ATOMIC MOTOR ADAPTED BY HIS FATHER FOR THE USE OF HIS WINGS, KATAR HOL ROCKETED THROUGH THE GROTESQUE ROCK WORLD OF TUMBLE-STONE PLAIN...
I CAN FLY A LOT FASTER THAN THE HAWKS--AND IN THIS DARK TUNNEL THEY CAN'T SEE TO SHOOT ME!
HOURS LATER, IN HIS FATHER'S LABORATORY...
AMAZING! THIS MASK IS FITTED WITH AN EXTREMELY THIN FILAMENT OF COAL OVER THE EYESLIT! LIGHT REFLECTED BACK FROM THE BIRD'S RETINA PENETRATES THE COAL-- AND EMITS A DEADLY BEAM!
10

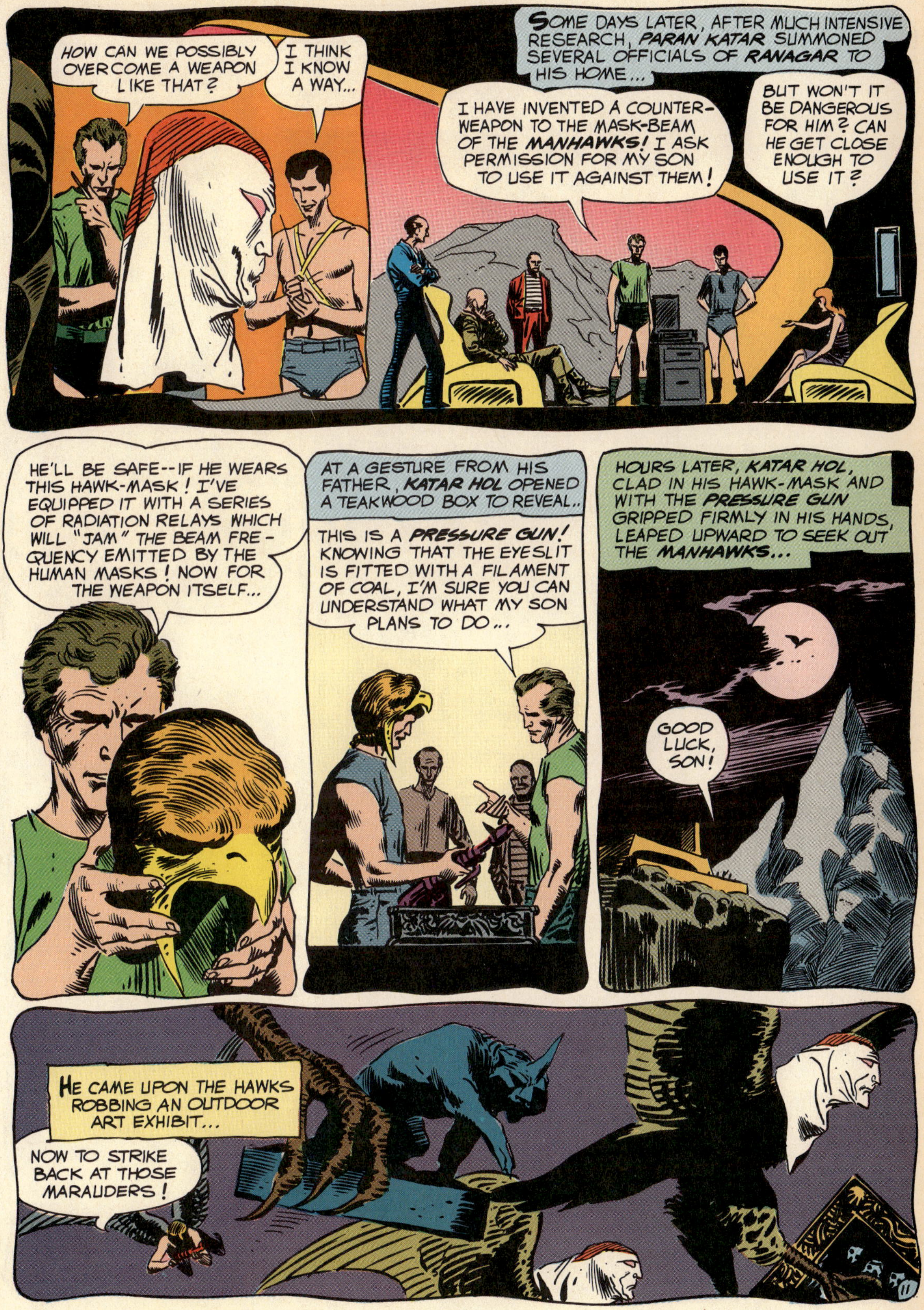
HOW CAN WE POSSIBLY OVERCOME A WEAPON LIKE THAT?
I THINK I KNOW A WAY...
SOME DAYS LATER, AFTER MUCH INTENSIVE RESEARCH, PARAN KATAR SUMMONED SEVERAL OFFICIALS OF RANAGAR TO HIS HOME...
I HAVE INVENTED A COUNTER-WEAPON TO THE MASK-BEAM OF THE MANHAWKS! I ASK PERMISSION FOR MY SON TO USE IT AGAINST THEM!
BUT WON'T IT BE DANGEROUS FOR HIM? CAN HE GET CLOSE ENOUGH TO USE IT?
HE'LL BE SAFE--IF HE WEARS THIS HAWK-MASK! I'VE EQUIPPED IT WITH A SERIES OF RADIATION RELAYS WHICH WILL "JAM" THE BEAM FRE-QUENCY EMITTED BY THE HUMAN MASKS! NOW FOR THE WEAPON ITSELF...
AT A GESTURE FROM HIS FATHER, KATAR HOL OPENED A TEAKWOOD BOX TO REVEAL..
THIS IS A PRESSURE GUN! KNOWING THAT THE EYESLIT IS FITTED WITH A FILAMENT OF COAL, I'M SURE YOU CAN UNDERSTAND WHAT MY SON PLANS TO DO...
HOURS LATER, KATAR HOL, CLAD IN HIS HAWK-MASK AND WITH THE PRESSURE GUN GRIPPED FIRMLY IN HIS HANDS, LEAPED UPWARD TO SEEK OUT THE MANHAWKS...
GOOD LUCK, SON!
HE CAME UPON THE HAWKS ROBBING AN OUTDOOR ART EXHIBIT...
NOW TO STRIKE BACK AT THOSE MARAUDERS!
11

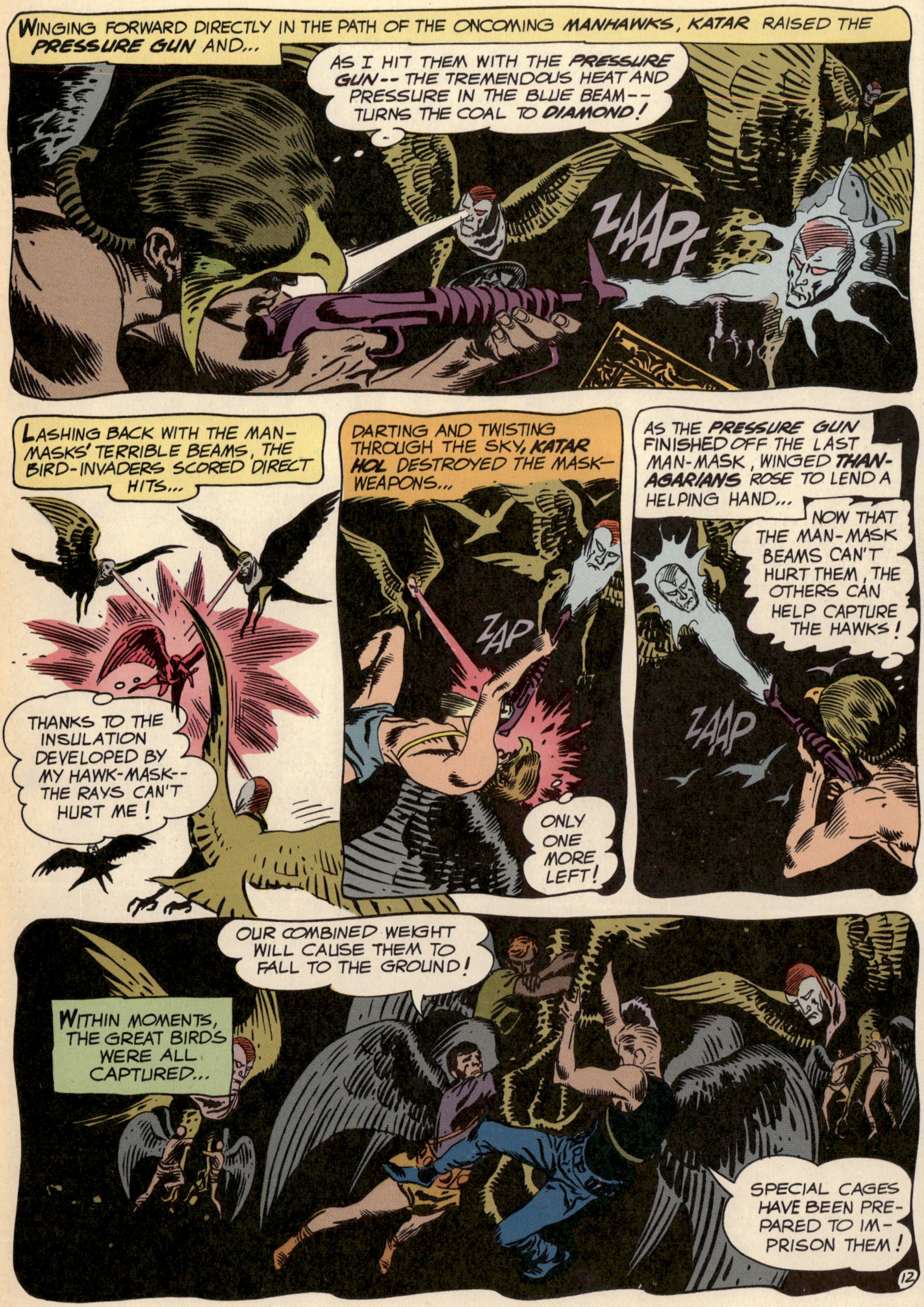
WINGING FORWARD DIRECTLY IN THE PATH OF THE ONCOMING MANHAWKS, KATAR RAISED THE PRESSURE GUN AND...
AS I HIT THEM WITH THE PRESSURE GUN -- THE TREMENDOUS HEAT AND PRESSURE IN THE BLUE BEAM -- TURNS THE COAL TO DIAMOND!
ZAAPF
LASHING BACK WITH THE MAN-MASKS' TERRIBLE BEAMS, THE BIRD-INVADERS SCORED DIRECT HITS...
THANKS TO THE INSULATION DEVELOPED BY MY HAWK-MASK-- THE RAYS CAN'T HURT ME!
DARTING AND TWISTING THROUGH THE SKY, KATAR HOL DESTROYED THE MASK-WEAPONS...
ZAP
ONLY ONE MORE LEFT!
AS THE PRESSURE GUN FINISHED OFF THE LAST MAN-MASK, WINGED THANAGARIANS ROSE TO LEND A HELPING HAND...
NOW THAT THE MAN-MASK BEAMS CAN'T HURT THEM, THE OTHERS CAN HELP CAPTURE THE HAWKS!
ZAAP
OUR COMBINED WEIGHT WILL CAUSE THEM TO FALL TO THE GROUND!
WITHIN MOMENTS, THE GREAT BIRDS WERE ALL CAPTURED...
SPECIAL CAGES HAVE BEEN PREPARED TO IMPRISON THEM!
12

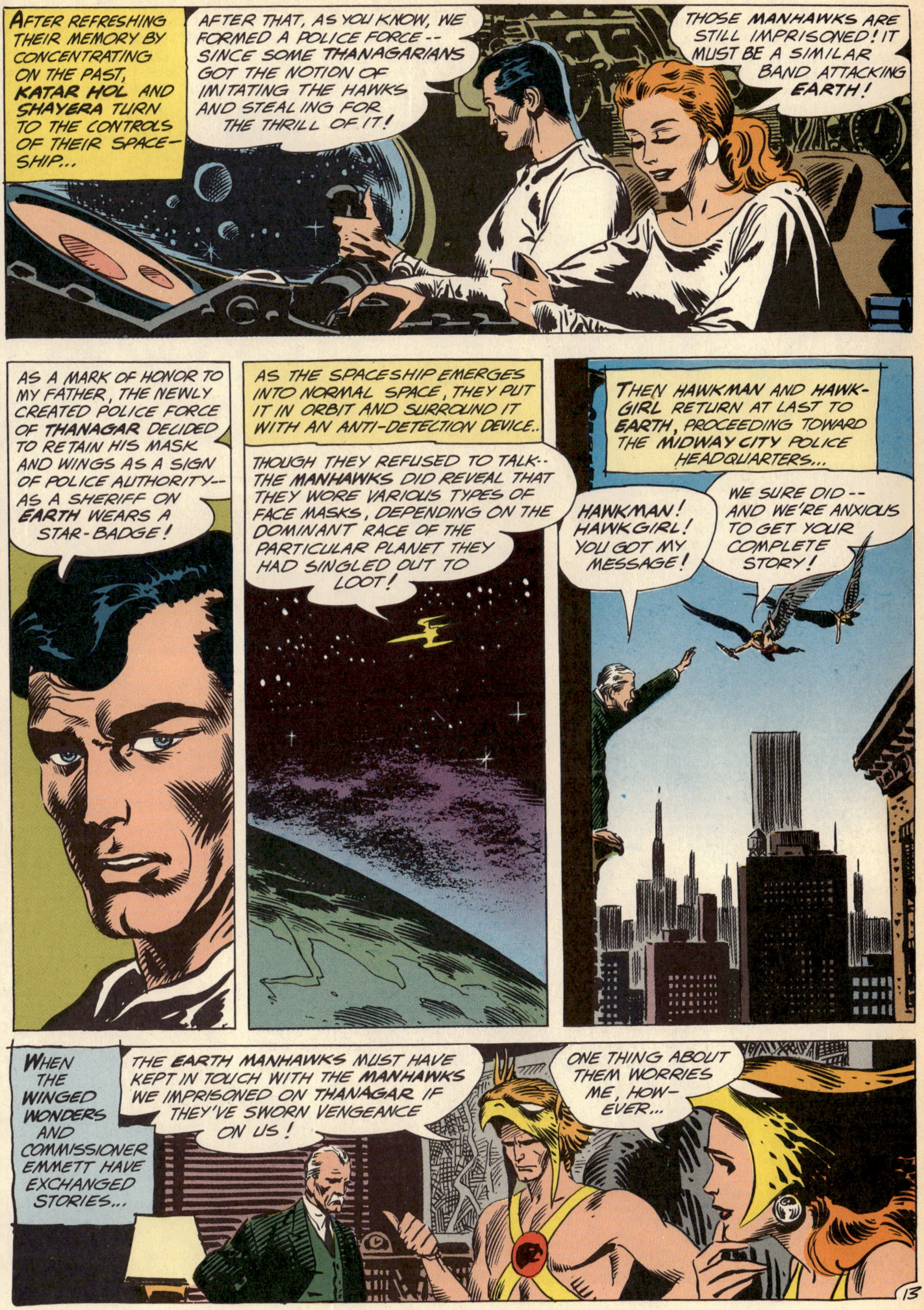
AFTER REFRESHING THEIR MEMORY BY CONCENTRATING ON THE PAST, KATAR HOL AND SHAYERA TURN TO THE CONTROLS OF THEIR SPACE-SHIP...
AFTER THAT, AS YOU KNOW, WE FORMED A POLICE FORCE -- SINCE SOME THANAGARIANS GOT THE NOTION OF IMITATING THE HAWKS AND STEALING FOR THE THRILL OF IT!
THOSE MANHAWKS ARE STILL IMPRISONED! IT MUST BE A SIMILAR BAND ATTACKING EARTH!
AS A MARK OF HONOR TO MY FATHER, THE NEWLY CREATED POLICE FORCE OF THANAGAR DECIDED TO RETAIN HIS MASK AND WINGS AS A SIGN OF POLICE AUTHORITY-- AS A SHERIFF ON EARTH WEARS A STAR-BADGE!
AS THE SPACESHIP EMERGES INTO NORMAL SPACE, THEY PUT IT IN ORBIT AND SURROUND IT WITH AN ANTI-DETECTION DEVICE..
THOUGH THEY REFUSED TO TALK-- THE MANHAWKS DID REVEAL THAT THEY WORE VARIOUS TYPES OF FACE MASKS, DEPENDING ON THE DOMINANT RACE OF THE PARTICULAR PLANET THEY HAD SINGLED OUT TO LOOT!
THEN HAWKMAN AND HAWK-GIRL RETURN AT LAST TO EARTH, PROCEEDING TOWARD THE MIDWAY CITY POLICE HEADQUARTERS...
HAWKMAN! HAWKGIRL! YOU GOT MY MESSAGE!
WE SURE DID -- AND WE'RE ANXIOUS TO GET YOUR COMPLETE STORY!
WHEN THE WINGED WONDERS AND COMMISSIONER EMMETT HAVE EXCHANGED STORIES...
THE EARTH MANHAWKS MUST HAVE KEPT IN TOUCH WITH THE MANHAWKS WE IMPRISONED ON THANAGAR IF THEY'VE SWORN VENGEANCE ON US!
ONE THING ABOUT THEM WORRIES ME, HOW-EVER...
13

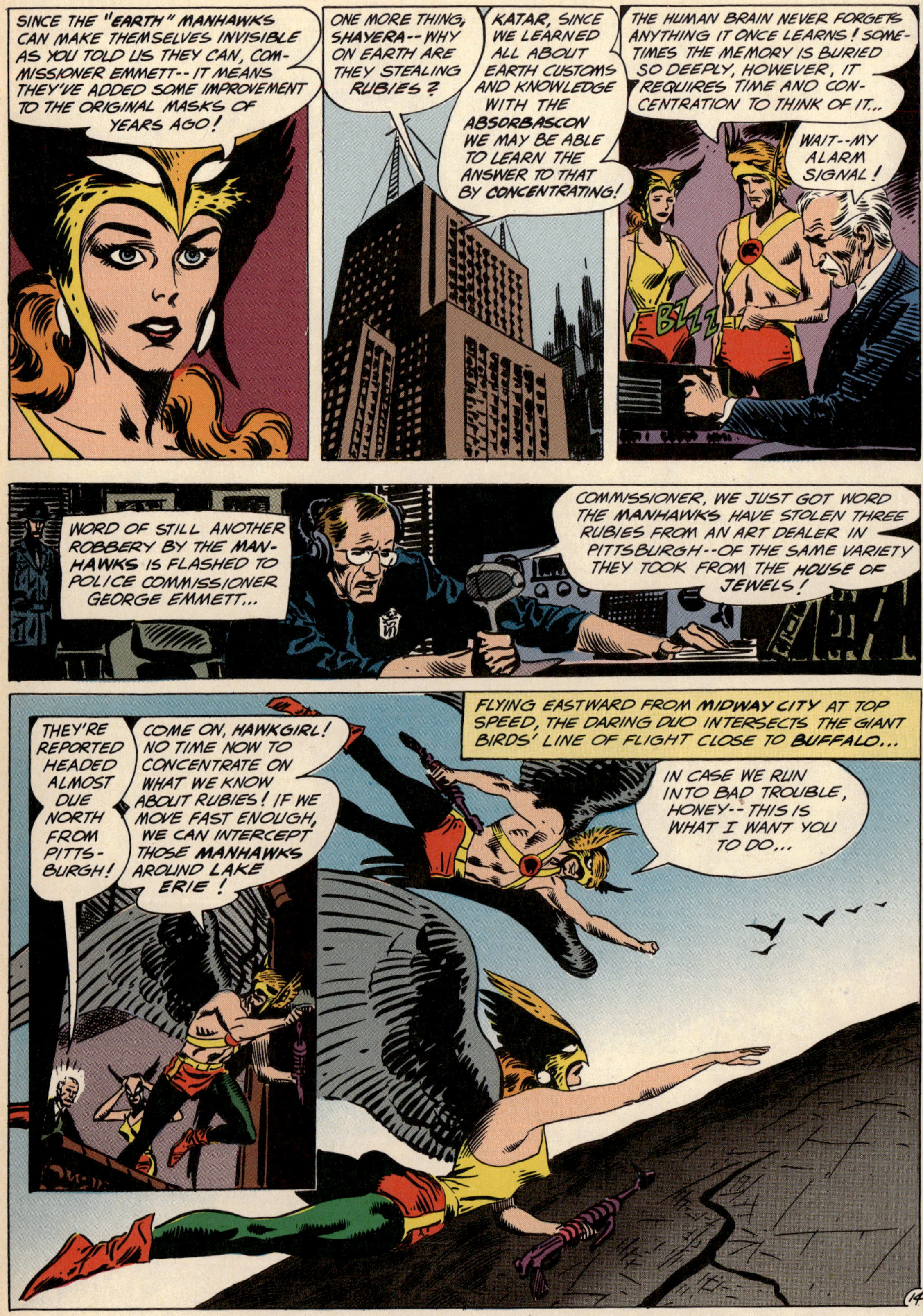
SINCE THE "EARTH" MANHAWKS CAN MAKE THEMSELVES INVISIBLE AS YOU TOLD US THEY CAN, COMMISSIONER EMMETT-- IT MEANS THEY'VE ADDED SOME IMPROVEMENT TO THE ORIGINAL MASKS OF YEARS AGO!
ONE MORE THING, SHAYERA-- WHY ON EARTH ARE THEY STEALING RUBIES?
KATAR, SINCE WE LEARNED ALL ABOUT EARTH CUSTOMS AND KNOWLEDGE WITH THE ABSORBASCON WE MAY BE ABLE TO LEARN THE ANSWER TO THAT BY CONCENTRATING!
THE HUMAN BRAIN NEVER FORGETS ANYTHING IT ONCE LEARNS! SOMETIMES THE MEMORY IS BURIED SO DEEPLY, HOWEVER, IT REQUIRES TIME AND CONCENTRATION TO THINK OF IT...
WAIT--MY ALARM SIGNAL!
BZZZ
WORD OF STILL ANOTHER ROBBERY BY THE MANHAWKS IS FLASHED TO POLICE COMMISSIONER GEORGE EMMETT...
COMMISSIONER, WE JUST GOT WORD THE MANHAWKS HAVE STOLEN THREE RUBIES FROM AN ART DEALER IN PITTSBURGH--OF THE SAME VARIETY THEY TOOK FROM THE HOUSE OF JEWELS!
THEY'RE REPORTED HEADED ALMOST DUE NORTH FROM PITTSBURGH!
COME ON, HAWKGIRL! NO TIME NOW TO CONCENTRATE ON WHAT WE KNOW ABOUT RUBIES! IF WE MOVE FAST ENOUGH, WE CAN INTERCEPT THOSE MANHAWKS AROUND LAKE ERIE!
FLYING EASTWARD FROM MIDWAY CITY AT TOP SPEED, THE DARING DUO INTERSECTS THE GIANT BIRDS' LINE OF FLIGHT CLOSE TO BUFFALO...
IN CASE WE RUN INTO BAD TROUBLE, HONEY-- THIS IS WHAT I WANT YOU TO DO...
14

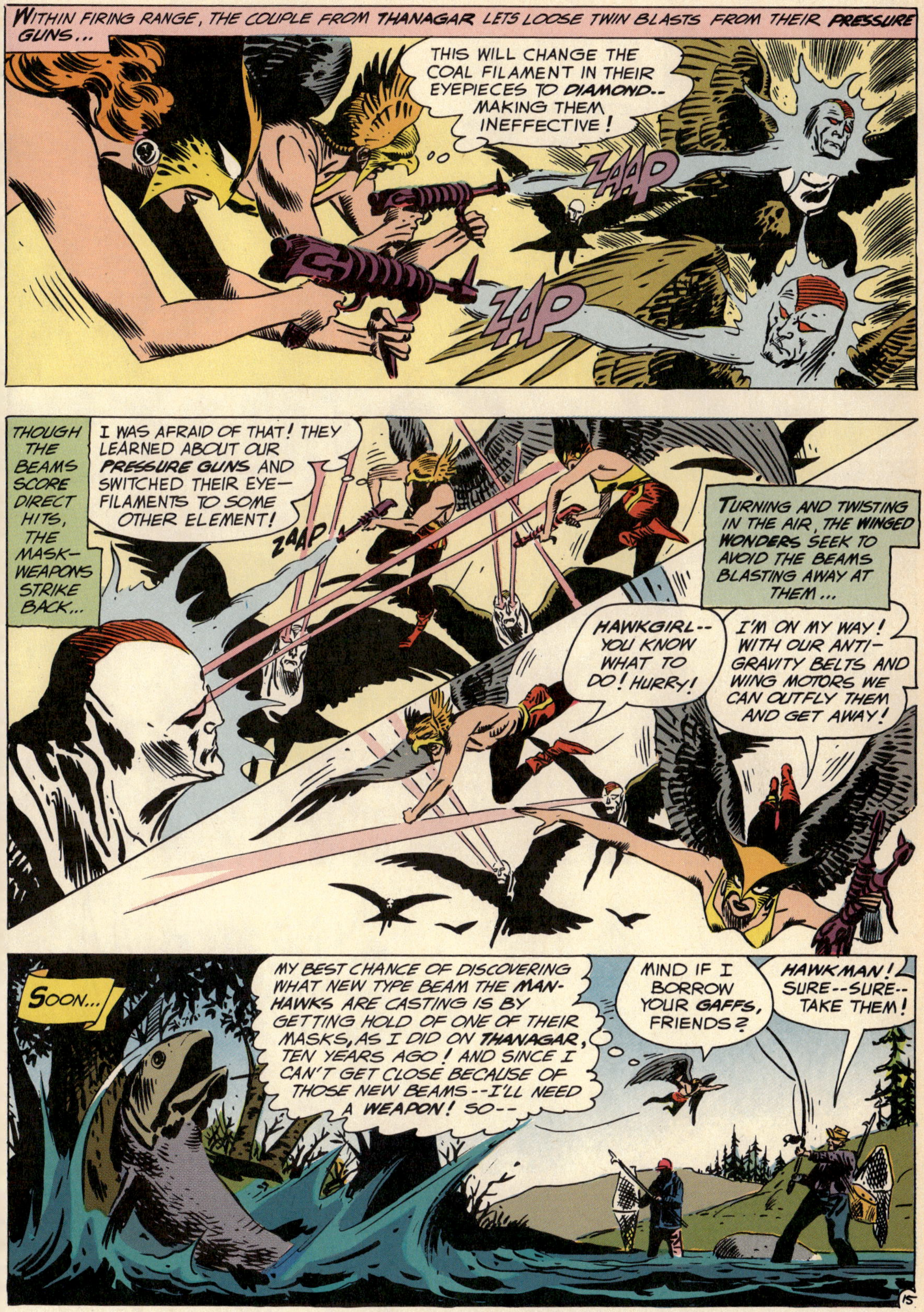
WITHIN FIRING RANGE, THE COUPLE FROM THANAGAR LETS LOOSE TWIN BLASTS FROM THEIR PRESSURE GUNS...
THIS WILL CHANGE THE COAL FILAMENT IN THEIR EYEPIECES TO DIAMOND-- MAKING THEM INEFFECTIVE!
ZAAP
ZAP
THOUGH THE BEAMS SCORE DIRECT HITS, THE MASK-WEAPONS STRIKE BACK...
I WAS AFRAID OF THAT! THEY LEARNED ABOUT OUR PRESSURE GUNS AND SWITCHED THEIR EYE-FILAMENTS TO SOME OTHER ELEMENT!
ZAAP
TURNING AND TWISTING IN THE AIR, THE WINGED WONDERS SEEK TO AVOID THE BEAMS BLASTING AWAY AT THEM...
HAWKGIRL-- YOU KNOW WHAT TO DO! HURRY!
I'M ON MY WAY! WITH OUR ANTI-GRAVITY BELTS AND WING MOTORS WE CAN OUTFLY THEM AND GET AWAY!
SOON...
MY BEST CHANCE OF DISCOVERING WHAT NEW TYPE BEAM THE MAN-HAWKS ARE CASTING IS BY GETTING HOLD OF ONE OF THEIR MASKS, AS I DID ON THANAGAR, TEN YEARS AGO! AND SINCE I CAN'T GET CLOSE BECAUSE OF THOSE NEW BEAMS--I'LL NEED A WEAPON! SO--
MIND IF I BORROW YOUR GAFFS, FRIENDS?
HAWKMAN! SURE--SURE-- TAKE THEM!
15

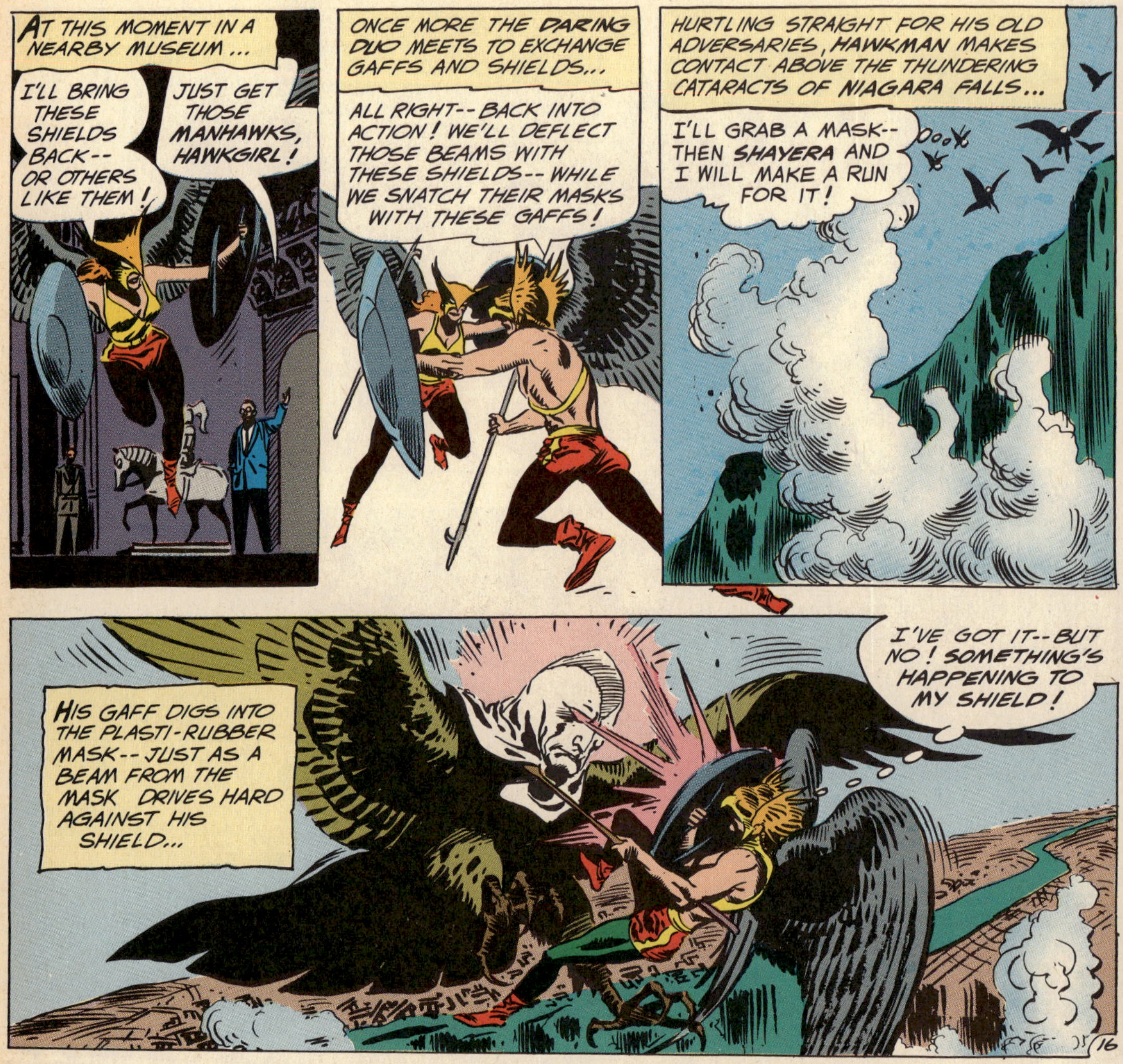
AT THIS MOMENT IN A NEARBY MUSEUM ...
I'LL BRING THESE SHIELDS BACK-- OR OTHERS LIKE THEM!
JUST GET THOSE MANHAWKS, HAWKGIRL!
ONCE MORE THE DARING DUO MEETS TO EXCHANGE GAFFS AND SHIELDS...
ALL RIGHT-- BACK INTO ACTION! WE'LL DEFLECT THOSE BEAMS WITH THESE SHIELDS-- WHILE WE SNATCH THEIR MASKS WITH THESE GAFFS!
HURTLING STRAIGHT FOR HIS OLD ADVERSARIES, HAWKMAN MAKES CONTACT ABOVE THE THUNDERING CATARACTS OF NIAGARA FALLS...
I'LL GRAB A MASK-- THEN SHAYERA AND I WILL MAKE A RUN FOR IT!
HIS GAFF DIGS INTO THE PLASTI-RUBBER MASK-- JUST AS A BEAM FROM THE MASK DRIVES HARD AGAINST HIS SHIELD...
I'VE GOT IT-- BUT NO! SOMETHING'S HAPPENING TO MY SHIELD!
16

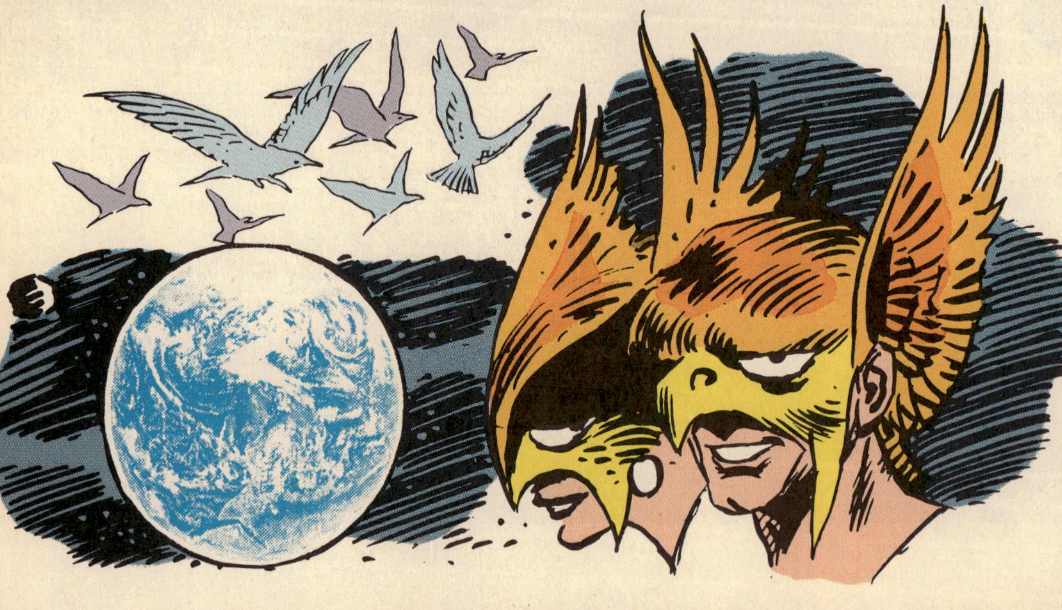

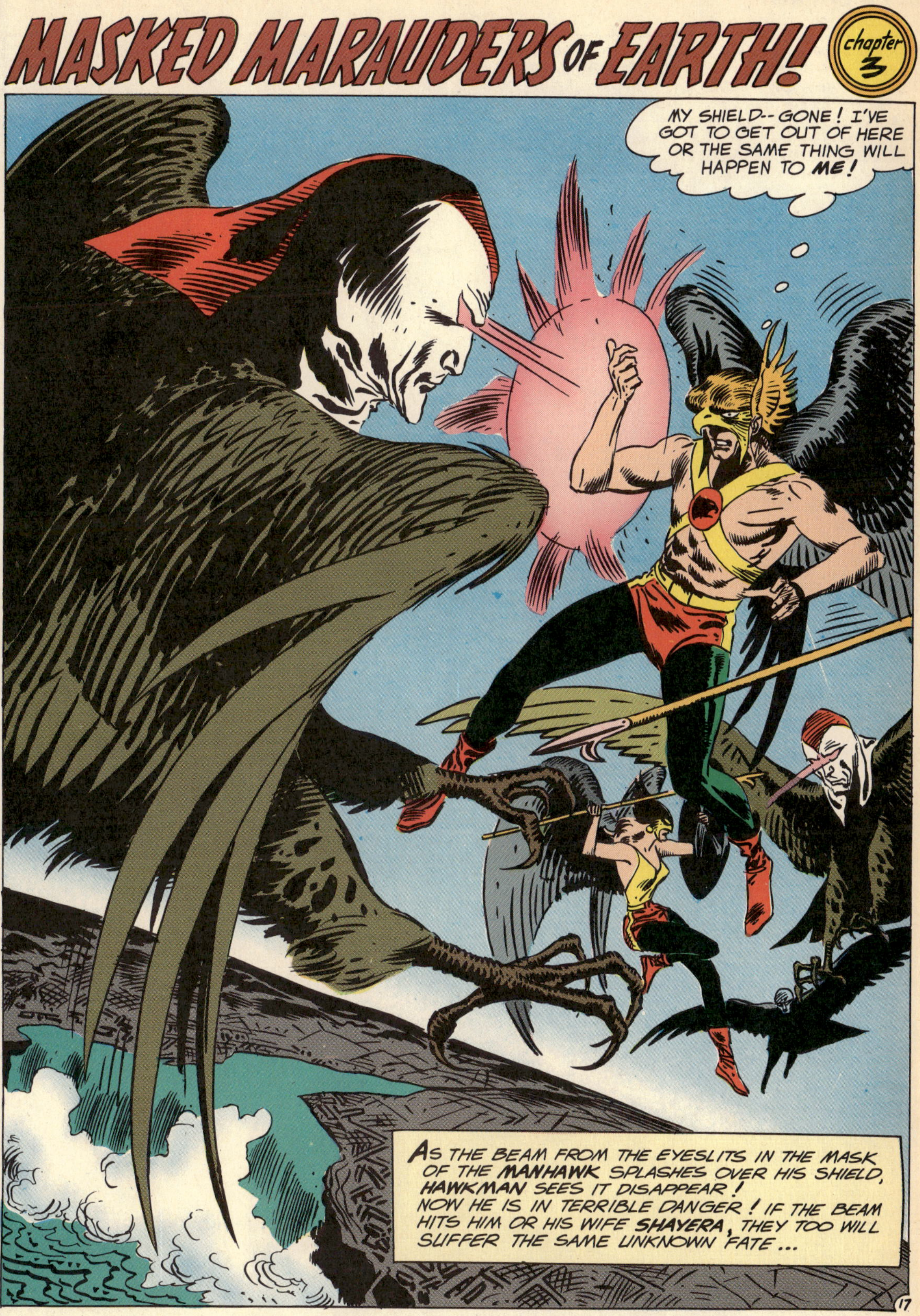
MASKED MARAUDERS OF EARTH!
chapter 3
MY SHIELD-- GONE! I'VE GOT TO GET OUT OF HERE OR THE SAME THING WILL HAPPEN TO **ME**!
AS THE BEAM FROM THE EYESLITS IN THE MASK OF THE **MANHAWK** SPLASHES OVER HIS SHIELD, **HAWKMAN** SEES IT DISAPPEAR! NOW HE IS IN TERRIBLE DANGER! IF THE BEAM HITS HIM OR HIS WIFE **SHAYERA**, THEY TOO WILL SUFFER THE SAME UNKNOWN FATE...
17

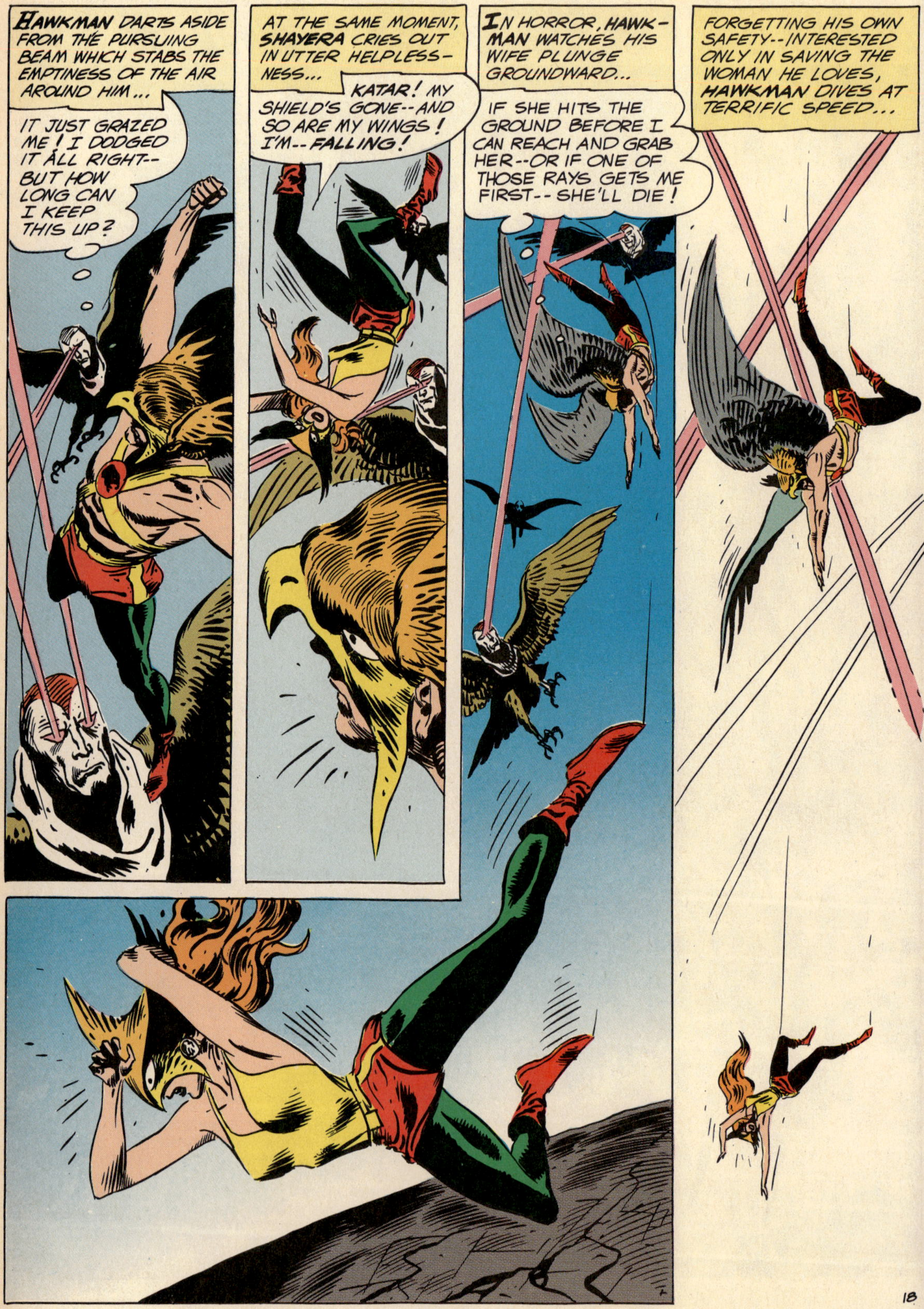

HAWKMAN DARTS ASIDE FROM THE PURSUING BEAM WHICH STABS THE EMPTINESS OF THE AIR AROUND HIM...
IT JUST GRAZED ME! I DODGED IT ALL RIGHT-- BUT HOW LONG CAN I KEEP THIS UP?
AT THE SAME MOMENT, SHAYERA CRIES OUT IN UTTER HELPLESS-NESS...
KATAR! MY SHIELD'S GONE--AND SO ARE MY WINGS! I'M--FALLING!
IN HORROR, HAWK-MAN WATCHES HIS WIFE PLUNGE GROUNDWARD...
IF SHE HITS THE GROUND BEFORE I CAN REACH AND GRAB HER--OR IF ONE OF THOSE RAYS GETS ME FIRST-- SHE'LL DIE!
FORGETTING HIS OWN SAFETY--INTERESTED ONLY IN SAVING THE WOMAN HE LOVES, HAWKMAN DIVES AT TERRIFIC SPEED...

TUMBLING AND TWISTING -- CAUGHT BY THE TUG OF GRAVITY AND DRAGGED TOWARD HER DOOM -- HAWKGIRL PLUMMETS DOWNWARD AS HAWKMAN FLASHES BETWEEN THE TERRIBLE RAYS OF THE MASK-WEAPONS IN HIS DESPERATE RACE TO SAVE HER...
DRIVEN TO DESPAIR BY THE SIGHT WHICH CONFRONTS HIM, HE HURTLES WILDLY DOWNWARD--AND CAROMS INTO HER, SCANT INCHES FROM THE STONE EDGE OF A JUTTING ROCK...
DARLING-- OH, I THOUGHT YOU'D NEVER MAKE IT!
NOW BEGINS HIS UPWARD CLIMB--STRAIGHT INTO THE TEETH OF THOSE GRIM AND DEADLY BEAMS...
I--I CAN'T LOOK!
RELAX, HONEY! LEAVE THIS TO ME! I'VE GOT TO FLY-- AS I NEVER HAVE BEFORE!
TRAPPED IN THE SKY--SURROUNDED BY THE AWESOME SHAFTS OF DEADLY LIGHT-- HE AND THE WOMAN HE LOVES FACE APPARENT DEFEAT, WHEN SUDDENLY...
HOLD ON! WE HAVE ONE SLIM HOPE FOR LIFE--AND I MEAN TO TAKE IT!
HIS KEEN EYES HAVING SIGHTED THE MISTY VEIL THAT SURROUNDS THE THUNDERING, TUMBLING WATERS OF NIAGARA FALLS, HE ANGLES HIS FLIGHT IN ITS DIRECTION...
ONCE INSIDE THOSE MISTS--THEY WON'T BE ABLE TO SEE US!
19

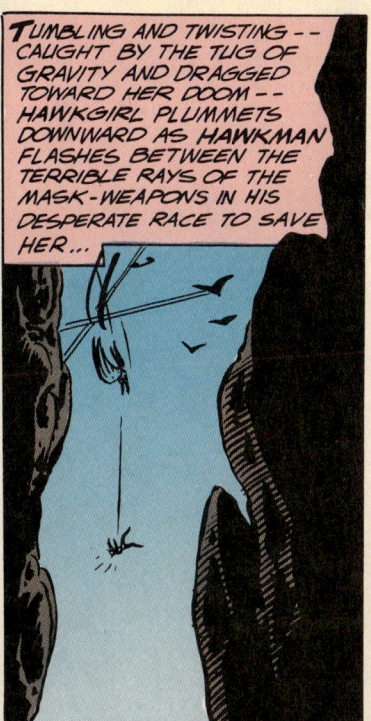

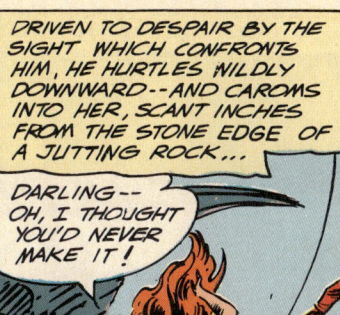

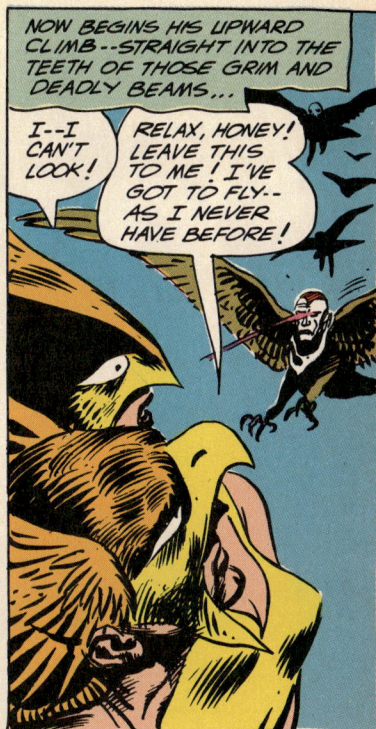

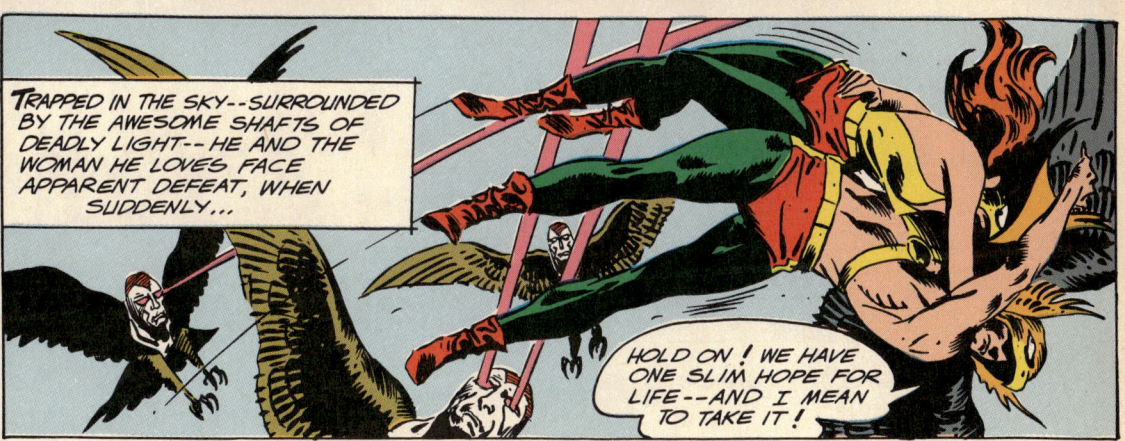

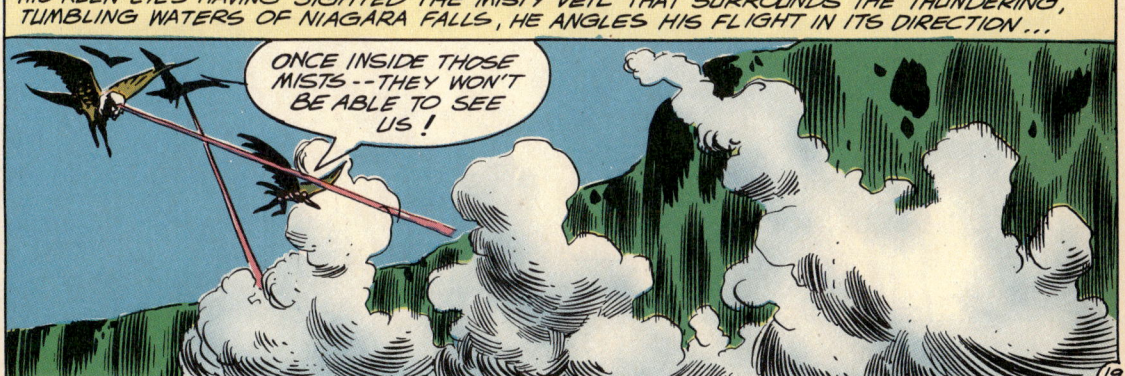

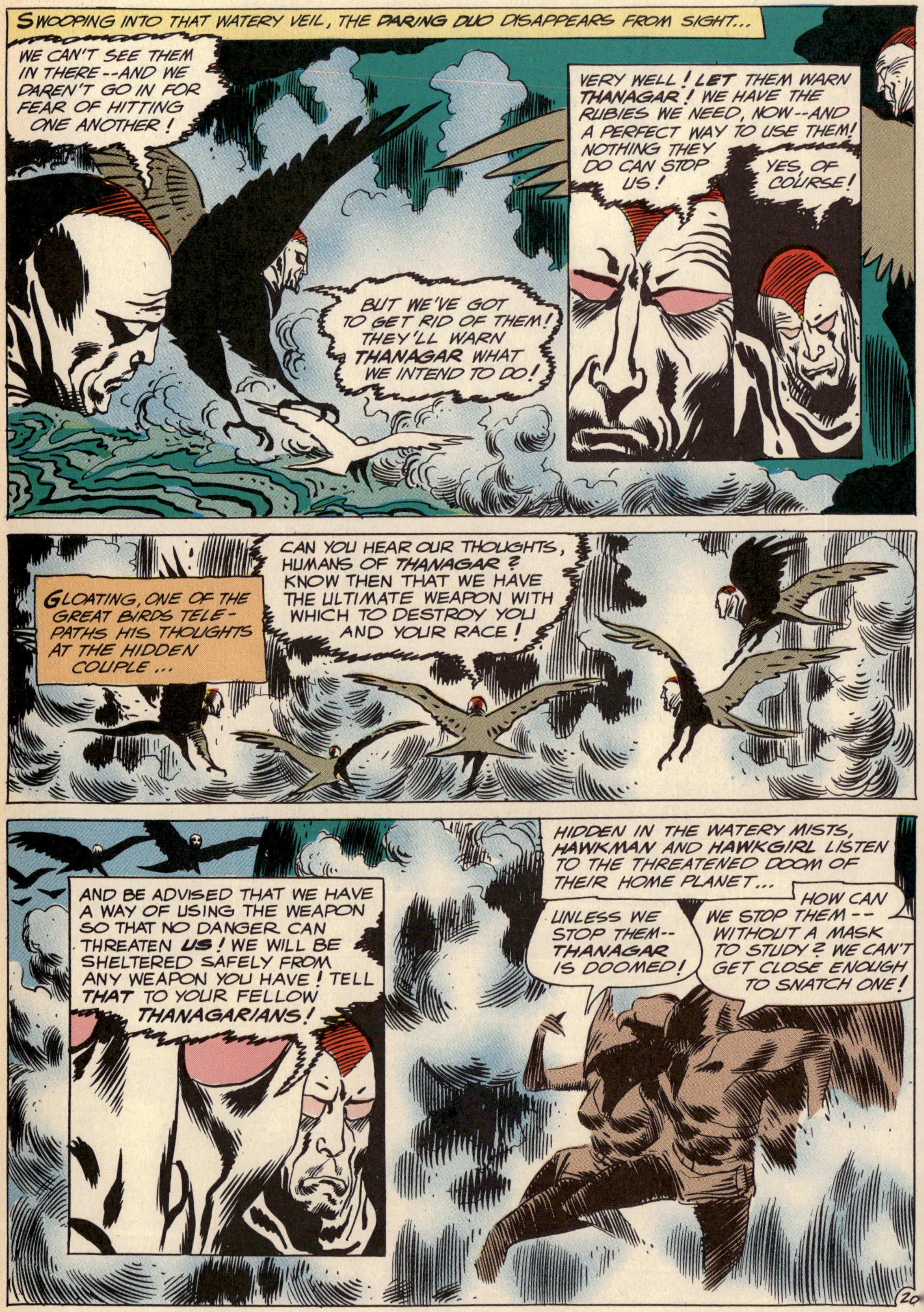
SWOOPING INTO THAT WATERY VEIL, THE DARING DUO DISAPPEARS FROM SIGHT...
WE CAN'T SEE THEM IN THERE--AND WE DAREN'T GO IN FOR FEAR OF HITTING ONE ANOTHER!
BUT WE'VE GOT TO GET RID OF THEM! THEY'LL WARN THANAGAR WHAT WE INTEND TO DO!
VERY WELL! LET THEM WARN THANAGAR! WE HAVE THE RUBIES WE NEED, NOW--AND A PERFECT WAY TO USE THEM! NOTHING THEY DO CAN STOP US!
YES, OF COURSE!
GLOATING, ONE OF THE GREAT BIRDS TELE-PATHS HIS THOUGHTS AT THE HIDDEN COUPLE...
CAN YOU HEAR OUR THOUGHTS, HUMANS OF THANAGAR? KNOW THEN THAT WE HAVE THE ULTIMATE WEAPON WITH WHICH TO DESTROY YOU AND YOUR RACE!
AND BE ADVISED THAT WE HAVE A WAY OF USING THE WEAPON SO THAT NO DANGER CAN THREATEN US! WE WILL BE SHELTERED SAFELY FROM ANY WEAPON YOU HAVE! TELL THAT TO YOUR FELLOW THANAGARIANS!
HIDDEN IN THE WATERY MISTS, HAWKMAN AND HAWKGIRL LISTEN TO THE THREATENED DOOM OF THEIR HOME PLANET...
UNLESS WE STOP THEM--THANAGAR IS DOOMED!
HOW CAN WE STOP THEM--WITHOUT A MASK TO STUDY? WE CAN'T GET CLOSE ENOUGH TO SNATCH ONE!
20

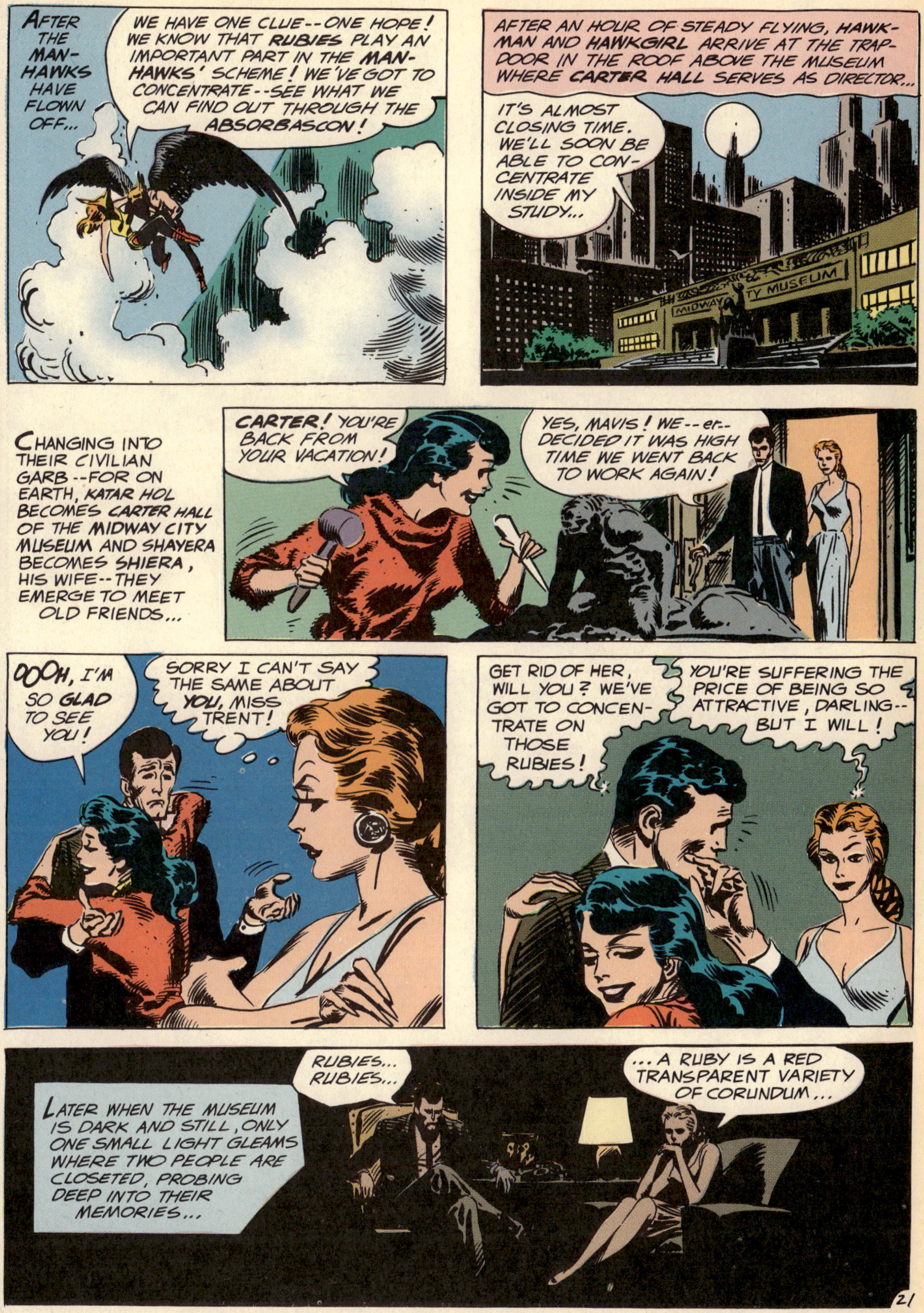
AFTER THE MAN-HAWKS HAVE FLOWN OFF...
WE HAVE ONE CLUE--ONE HOPE! WE KNOW THAT RUBIES PLAY AN IMPORTANT PART IN THE MAN-HAWKS' SCHEME! WE'VE GOT TO CONCENTRATE--SEE WHAT WE CAN FIND OUT THROUGH THE ABSORBASCON!
AFTER AN HOUR OF STEADY FLYING, HAWK-MAN AND HAWKGIRL ARRIVE AT THE TRAP-DOOR IN THE ROOF ABOVE THE MUSEUM WHERE CARTER HALL SERVES AS DIRECTOR...
IT'S ALMOST CLOSING TIME. WE'LL SOON BE ABLE TO CON-CENTRATE INSIDE MY STUDY...
MIDWAY CITY MUSEUM
CHANGING INTO THEIR CIVILIAN GARB--FOR ON EARTH, KATAR HOL BECOMES CARTER HALL OF THE MIDWAY CITY MUSEUM AND SHAYERA BECOMES SHIERA, HIS WIFE--THEY EMERGE TO MEET OLD FRIENDS...
CARTER! YOU'RE BACK FROM YOUR VACATION!
YES, MAVIS! WE--er--DECIDED IT WAS HIGH TIME WE WENT BACK TO WORK AGAIN!
OOOH, I'M SO GLAD TO SEE YOU!
SORRY I CAN'T SAY THE SAME ABOUT YOU, MISS TRENT!
GET RID OF HER, WILL YOU? WE'VE GOT TO CONCEN-TRATE ON THOSE RUBIES!
YOU'RE SUFFERING THE PRICE OF BEING SO ATTRACTIVE, DARLING--BUT I WILL!
LATER WHEN THE MUSEUM IS DARK AND STILL, ONLY ONE SMALL LIGHT GLEAMS WHERE TWO PEOPLE ARE CLOSETED, PROBING DEEP INTO THEIR MEMORIES...
RUBIES... RUBIES...
...A RUBY IS A RED TRANSPARENT VARIETY OF CORUNDUM...
21

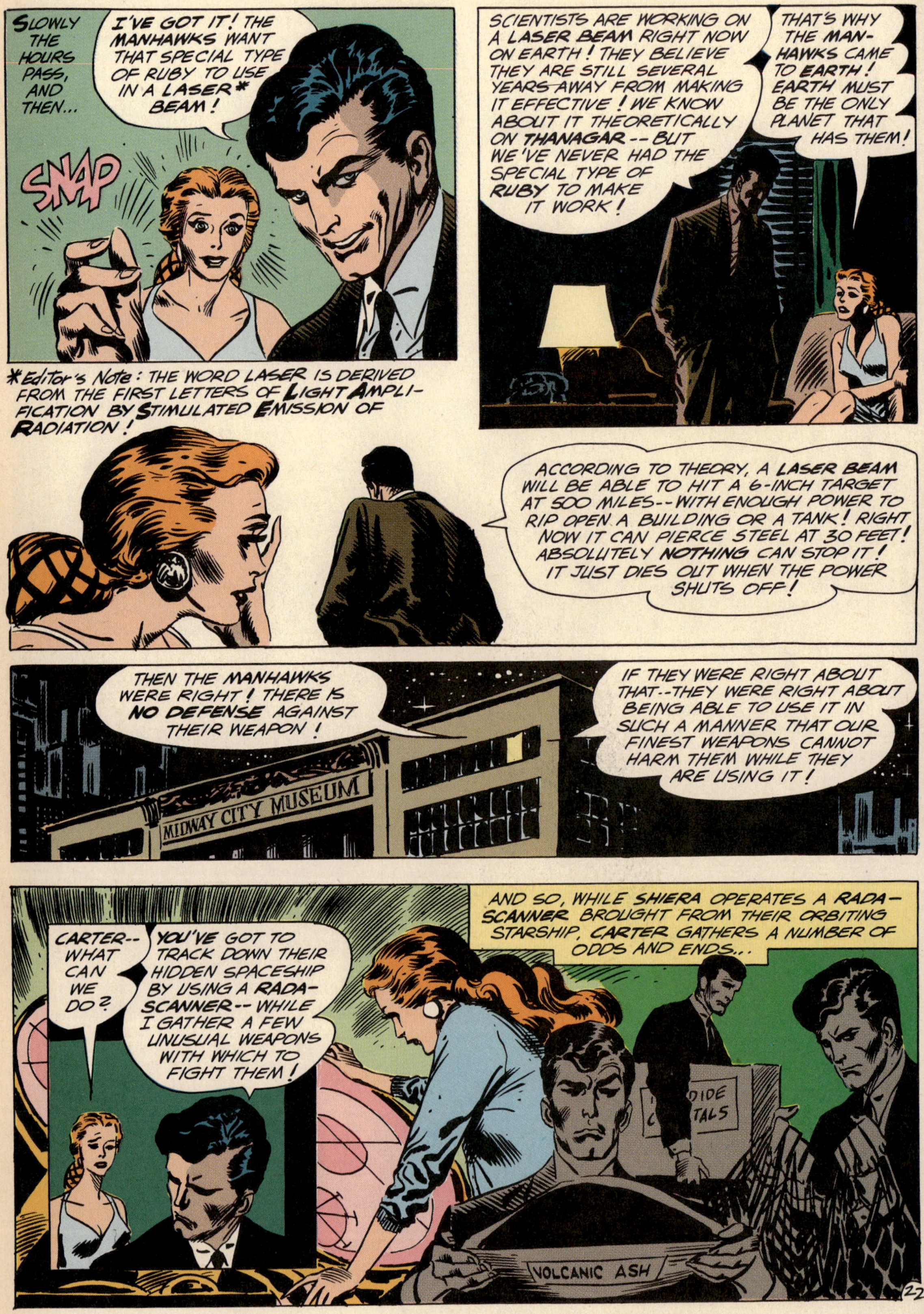
SLOWLY THE HOURS PASS, AND THEN...
I'VE GOT IT! THE MANHAWKS WANT THAT SPECIAL TYPE OF RUBY TO USE IN A LASER* BEAM!
SNAP
*Editor's Note: THE WORD LASER IS DERIVED FROM THE FIRST LETTERS OF LIGHT AMPLIFICATION BY STIMULATED EMISSION OF RADIATION!
SCIENTISTS ARE WORKING ON A LASER BEAM RIGHT NOW ON EARTH! THEY BELIEVE THEY ARE STILL SEVERAL YEARS AWAY FROM MAKING IT EFFECTIVE! WE KNOW ABOUT IT THEORETICALLY ON THANAGAR -- BUT WE'VE NEVER HAD THE SPECIAL TYPE OF RUBY TO MAKE IT WORK!
THAT'S WHY THE MANHAWKS CAME TO EARTH! EARTH MUST BE THE ONLY PLANET THAT HAS THEM!
ACCORDING TO THEORY, A LASER BEAM WILL BE ABLE TO HIT A 6-INCH TARGET AT 500 MILES--WITH ENOUGH POWER TO RIP OPEN A BUILDING OR A TANK! RIGHT NOW IT CAN PIERCE STEEL AT 30 FEET! ABSOLUTELY NOTHING CAN STOP IT! IT JUST DIES OUT WHEN THE POWER SHUTS OFF!
THEN THE MANHAWKS WERE RIGHT! THERE IS NO DEFENSE AGAINST THEIR WEAPON!
MIDWAY CITY MUSEUM
IF THEY WERE RIGHT ABOUT THAT--THEY WERE RIGHT ABOUT BEING ABLE TO USE IT IN SUCH A MANNER THAT OUR FINEST WEAPONS CANNOT HARM THEM WHILE THEY ARE USING IT!
CARTER-- WHAT CAN WE DO?
YOU'VE GOT TO TRACK DOWN THEIR HIDDEN SPACESHIP BY USING A RADA-SCANNER-- WHILE I GATHER A FEW UNUSUAL WEAPONS WITH WHICH TO FIGHT THEM!
AND SO, WHILE SHIERA OPERATES A RADA-SCANNER BROUGHT FROM THEIR ORBITING STARSHIP, CARTER GATHERS A NUMBER OF ODDS AND ENDS...
VOLCANIC ASH
22

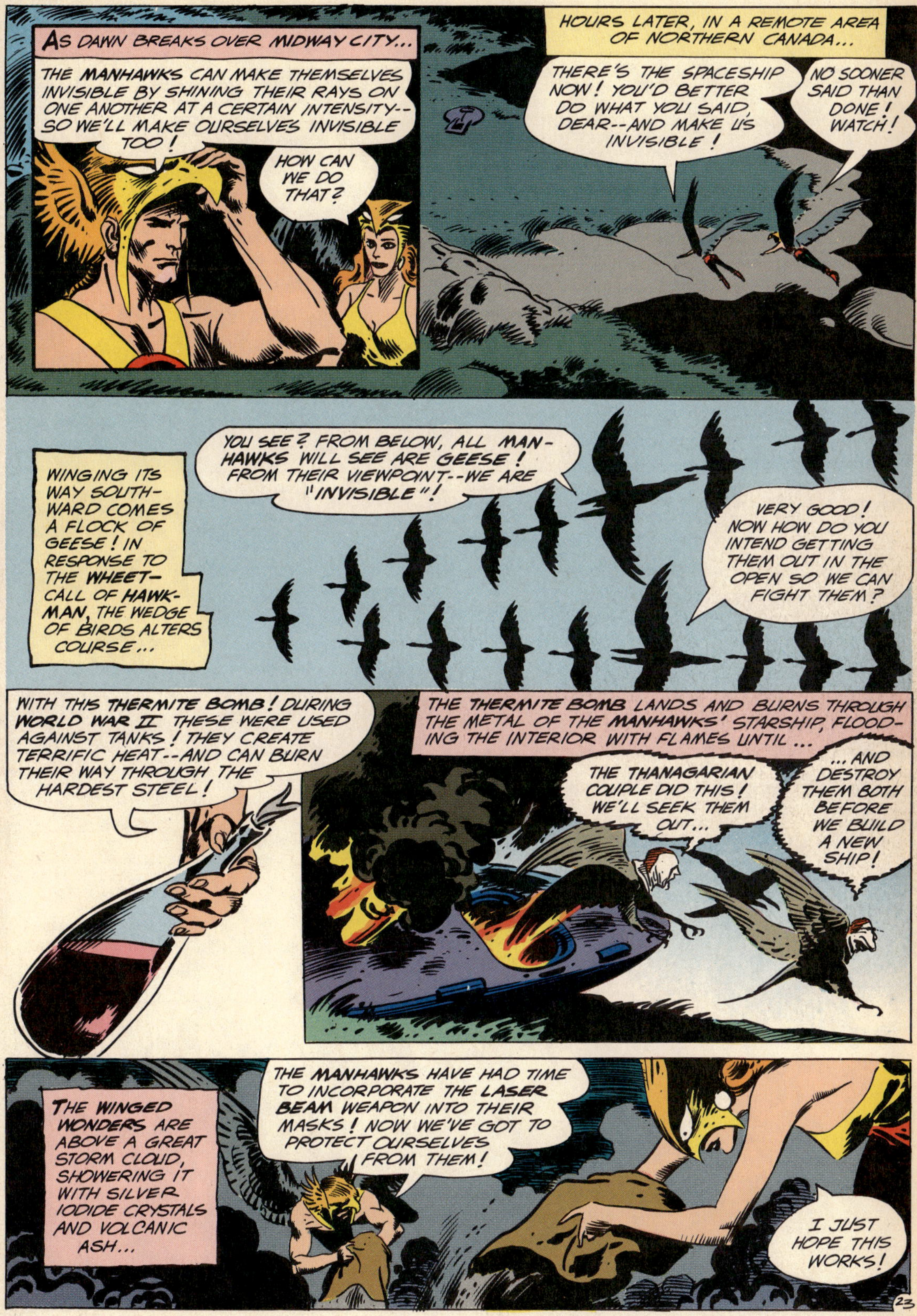
AS DAWN BREAKS OVER MIDWAY CITY...
THE MANHAWKS CAN MAKE THEMSELVES INVISIBLE BY SHINING THEIR RAYS ON ONE ANOTHER AT A CERTAIN INTENSITY--SO WE'LL MAKE OURSELVES INVISIBLE TOO!
HOW CAN WE DO THAT?
HOURS LATER, IN A REMOTE AREA OF NORTHERN CANADA...
THERE'S THE SPACESHIP NOW! YOU'D BETTER DO WHAT YOU SAID, DEAR--AND MAKE US INVISIBLE!
NO SOONER SAID THAN DONE! WATCH!
WINGING ITS WAY SOUTHWARD COMES A FLOCK OF GEESE! IN RESPONSE TO THE WHEET-CALL OF HAWKMAN, THE WEDGE OF BIRDS ALTERS COURSE...
YOU SEE? FROM BELOW, ALL MANHAWKS WILL SEE ARE GEESE! FROM THEIR VIEWPOINT--WE ARE "INVISIBLE"!
VERY GOOD! NOW HOW DO YOU INTEND GETTING THEM OUT IN THE OPEN SO WE CAN FIGHT THEM?
WITH THIS THERMITE BOMB! DURING WORLD WAR II THESE WERE USED AGAINST TANKS! THEY CREATE TERRIFIC HEAT--AND CAN BURN THEIR WAY THROUGH THE HARDEST STEEL!
THE THERMITE BOMB LANDS AND BURNS THROUGH THE METAL OF THE MANHAWKS' STARSHIP, FLOODING THE INTERIOR WITH FLAMES UNTIL...
THE THANAGARIAN COUPLE DID THIS! WE'LL SEEK THEM OUT...
...AND DESTROY THEM BOTH BEFORE WE BUILD A NEW SHIP!
THE WINGED WONDERS ARE ABOVE A GREAT STORM CLOUD, SHOWERING IT WITH SILVER IODIDE CRYSTALS AND VOLCANIC ASH...
THE MANHAWKS HAVE HAD TIME TO INCORPORATE THE LASER BEAM WEAPON INTO THEIR MASKS! NOW WE'VE GOT TO PROTECT OURSELVES FROM THEM!
I JUST HOPE THIS WORKS!
23

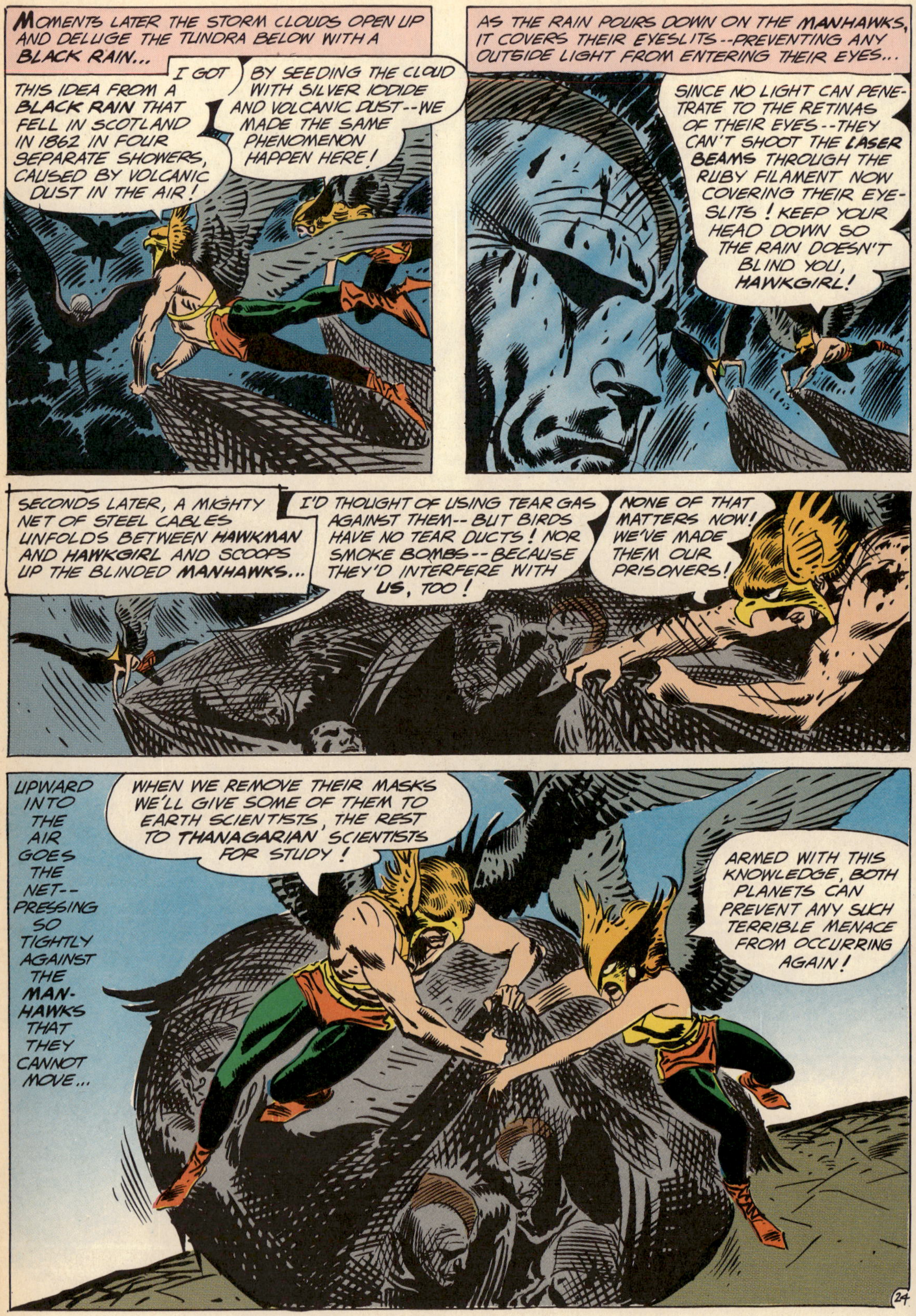
MOMENTS LATER THE STORM CLOUDS OPEN UP AND DELUGE THE TUNDRA BELOW WITH A BLACK RAIN...
I GOT THIS IDEA FROM A BLACK RAIN THAT FELL IN SCOTLAND IN 1862 IN FOUR SEPARATE SHOWERS, CAUSED BY VOLCANIC DUST IN THE AIR!
BY SEEDING THE CLOUD WITH SILVER IODIDE AND VOLCANIC DUST--WE MADE THE SAME PHENOMENON HAPPEN HERE!
AS THE RAIN POURS DOWN ON THE MANHAWKS, IT COVERS THEIR EYESLITS--PREVENTING ANY OUTSIDE LIGHT FROM ENTERING THEIR EYES...
SINCE NO LIGHT CAN PENETRATE TO THE RETINAS OF THEIR EYES--THEY CAN'T SHOOT THE LASER BEAMS THROUGH THE RUBY FILAMENT NOW COVERING THEIR EYESLITS! KEEP YOUR HEAD DOWN SO THE RAIN DOESN'T BLIND YOU, HAWKGIRL!
SECONDS LATER, A MIGHTY NET OF STEEL CABLES UNFOLDS BETWEEN HAWKMAN AND HAWKGIRL AND SCOOPS UP THE BLINDED MANHAWKS...
I'D THOUGHT OF USING TEAR GAS AGAINST THEM-- BUT BIRDS HAVE NO TEAR DUCTS! NOR SMOKE BOMBS--BECAUSE THEY'D INTERFERE WITH US, TOO!
NONE OF THAT MATTERS NOW! WE'VE MADE THEM OUR PRISONERS!
UPWARD INTO THE AIR GOES THE NET--PRESSING SO TIGHTLY AGAINST THE MAN-HAWKS THAT THEY CANNOT MOVE...
WHEN WE REMOVE THEIR MASKS WE'LL GIVE SOME OF THEM TO EARTH SCIENTISTS, THE REST TO THANAGARIAN SCIENTISTS FOR STUDY!
ARMED WITH THIS KNOWLEDGE, BOTH PLANETS CAN PREVENT ANY SUCH TERRIBLE MENACE FROM OCCURRING AGAIN!
24

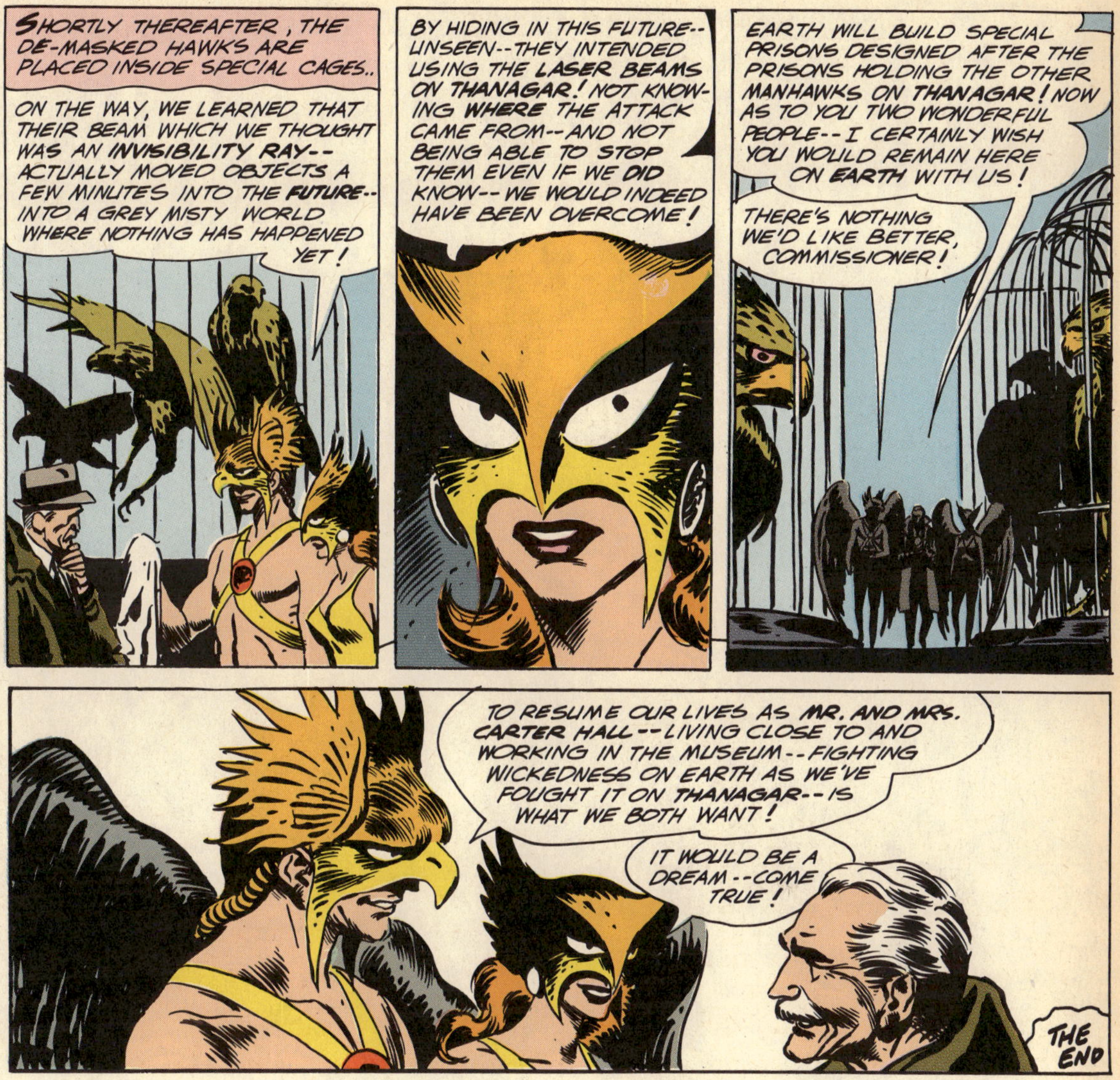
SHORTLY THEREAFTER, THE DE-MASKED HAWKS ARE PLACED INSIDE SPECIAL CAGES..
ON THE WAY, WE LEARNED THAT THEIR BEAM WHICH WE THOUGHT WAS AN INVISIBILITY RAY-- ACTUALLY MOVED OBJECTS A FEW MINUTES INTO THE FUTURE-- INTO A GREY MISTY WORLD WHERE NOTHING HAS HAPPENED YET!
BY HIDING IN THIS FUTURE-- UNSEEN--THEY INTENDED USING THE LASER BEAMS ON THANAGAR! NOT KNOWING WHERE THE ATTACK CAME FROM--AND NOT BEING ABLE TO STOP THEM EVEN IF WE DID KNOW--WE WOULD INDEED HAVE BEEN OVERCOME!
EARTH WILL BUILD SPECIAL PRISONS DESIGNED AFTER THE PRISONS HOLDING THE OTHER MANHAWKS ON THANAGAR! NOW AS TO YOU TWO WONDERFUL PEOPLE--I CERTAINLY WISH YOU WOULD REMAIN HERE ON EARTH WITH US!
THERE'S NOTHING WE'D LIKE BETTER, COMMISSIONER!
TO RESUME OUR LIVES AS MR. AND MRS. CARTER HALL--LIVING CLOSE TO AND WORKING IN THE MUSEUM--FIGHTING WICKEDNESS ON EARTH AS WE'VE FOUGHT IT ON THANAGAR--IS WHAT WE BOTH WANT!
IT WOULD BE A DREAM--COME TRUE!
THE END

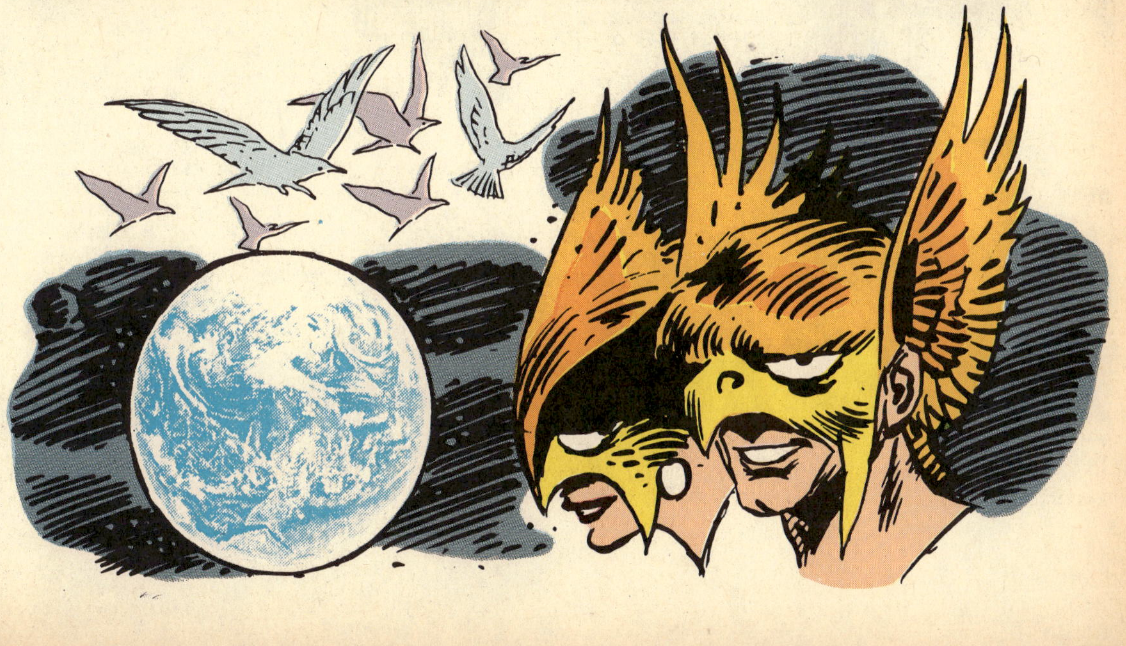

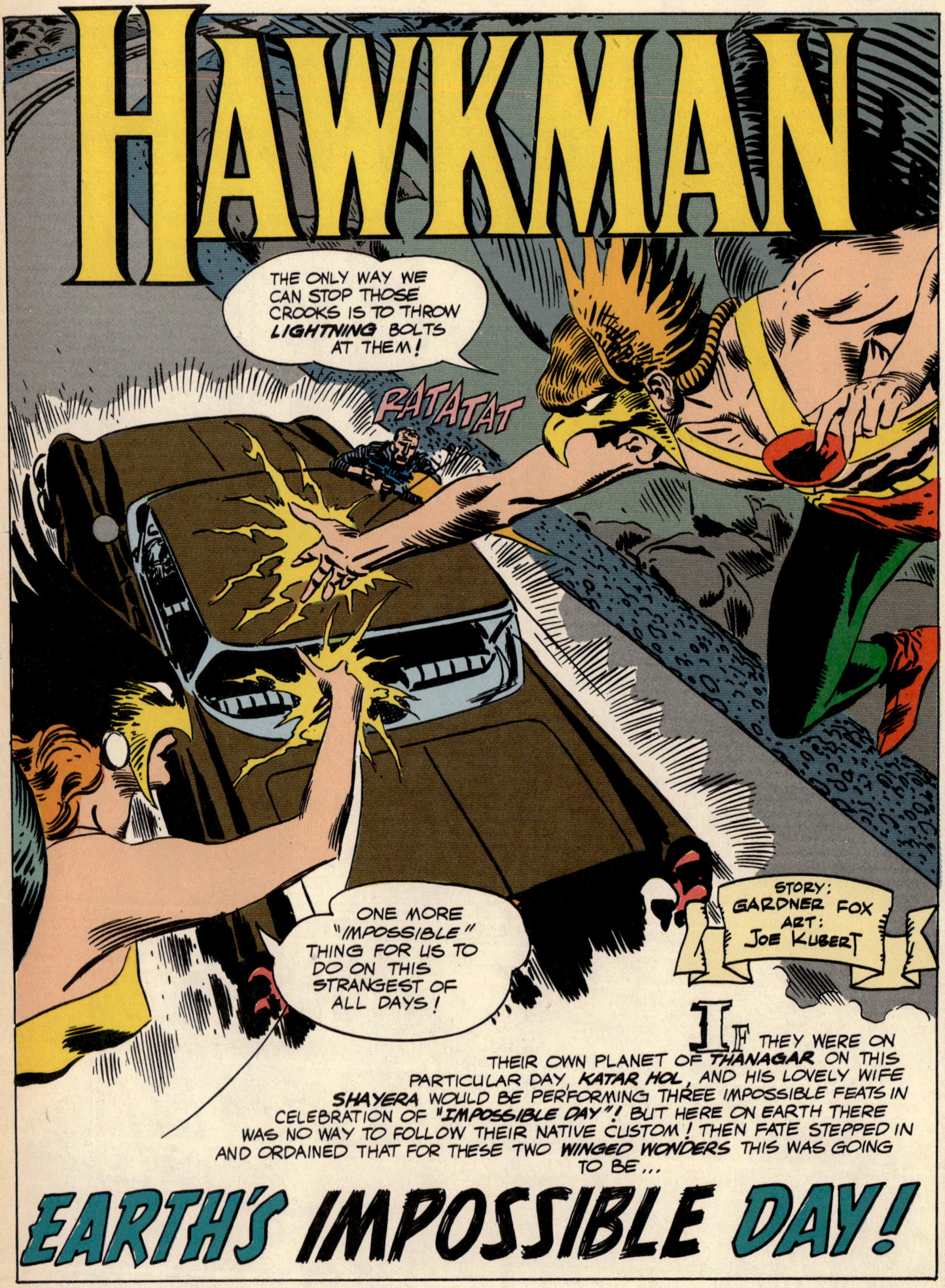
HAWKMAN
THE ONLY WAY WE CAN STOP THOSE CROOKS IS TO THROW LIGHTNING BOLTS AT THEM!
RATATAT
ONE MORE "IMPOSSIBLE" THING FOR US TO DO ON THIS STRANGEST OF ALL DAYS!
STORY: GARDNER FOX ART: JOE KUBERT
IF THEY WERE ON THEIR OWN PLANET OF THANAGAR ON THIS PARTICULAR DAY, KATAR HOL, AND HIS LOVELY WIFE SHAYERA WOULD BE PERFORMING THREE IMPOSSIBLE FEATS IN CELEBRATION OF "IMPOSSIBLE DAY"! BUT HERE ON EARTH THERE WAS NO WAY TO FOLLOW THEIR NATIVE CUSTOM! THEN FATE STEPPED IN AND ORDAINED THAT FOR THESE TWO WINGED WONDERS THIS WAS GOING TO BE...
EARTH'S IMPOSSIBLE DAY!

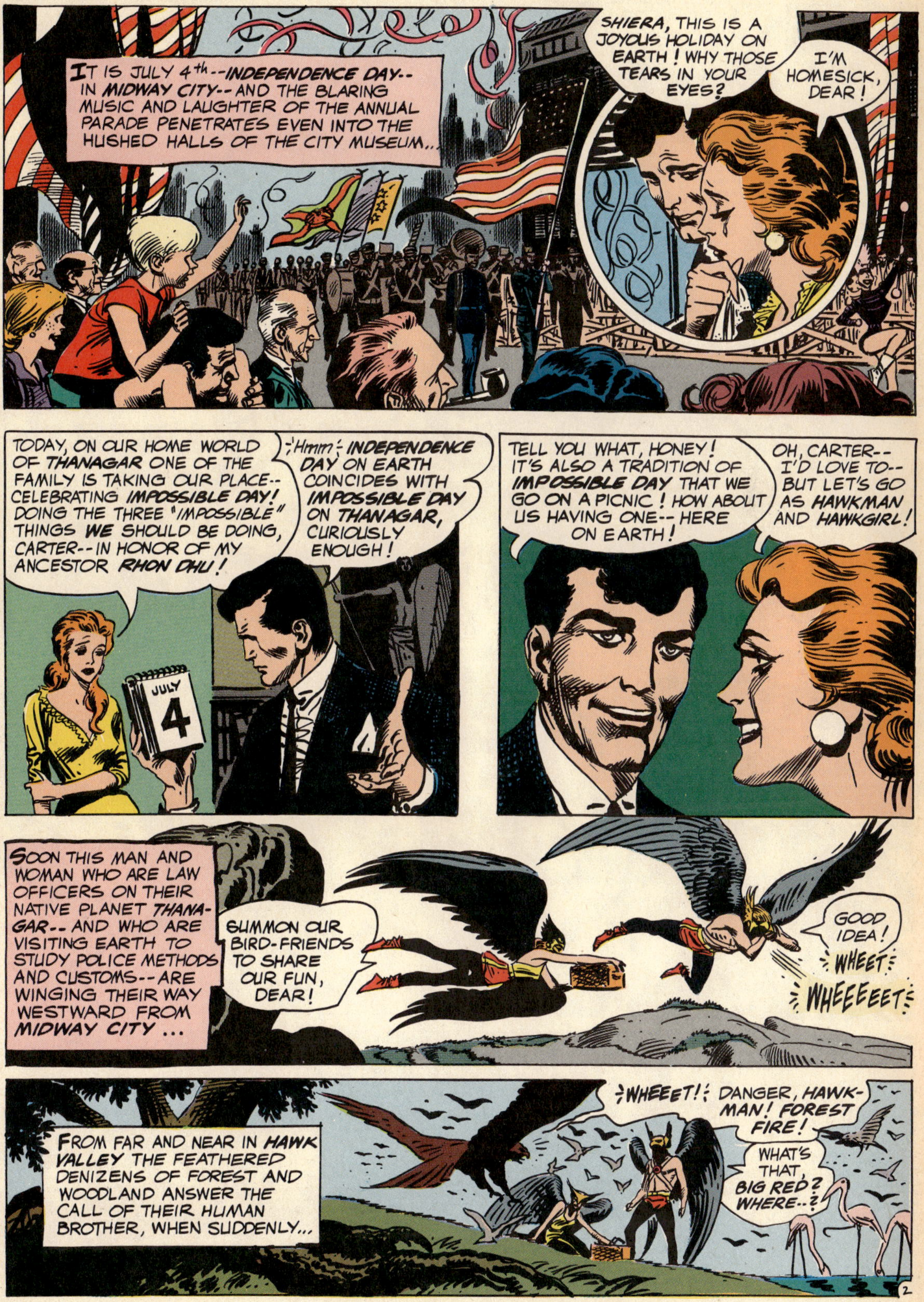
IT IS JULY 4th--INDEPENDENCE DAY--IN MIDWAY CITY--AND THE BLARING MUSIC AND LAUGHTER OF THE ANNUAL PARADE PENETRATES EVEN INTO THE HUSHED HALLS OF THE CITY MUSEUM...
SHIERA, THIS IS A JOYOUS HOLIDAY ON EARTH! WHY THOSE TEARS IN YOUR EYES?
I'M HOMESICK, DEAR!
TODAY, ON OUR HOME WORLD OF THANAGAR ONE OF THE FAMILY IS TAKING OUR PLACE--CELEBRATING IMPOSSIBLE DAY! DOING THE THREE "IMPOSSIBLE" THINGS WE SHOULD BE DOING, CARTER--IN HONOR OF MY ANCESTOR RHON DHU!
Hmm - INDEPENDENCE DAY ON EARTH COINCIDES WITH IMPOSSIBLE DAY ON THANAGAR, CURIOUSLY ENOUGH!
JULY
4
TELL YOU WHAT, HONEY! IT'S ALSO A TRADITION OF IMPOSSIBLE DAY THAT WE GO ON A PICNIC! HOW ABOUT US HAVING ONE--HERE ON EARTH!
OH, CARTER--I'D LOVE TO--BUT LET'S GO AS HAWKMAN AND HAWKGIRL!
SOON THIS MAN AND WOMAN WHO ARE LAW OFFICERS ON THEIR NATIVE PLANET THANAGAR--AND WHO ARE VISITING EARTH TO STUDY POLICE METHODS AND CUSTOMS--ARE WINGING THEIR WAY WESTWARD FROM MIDWAY CITY...
SUMMON OUR BIRD-FRIENDS TO SHARE OUR FUN, DEAR!
GOOD IDEA!
WHEET
WHEEEEET
FROM FAR AND NEAR IN HAWK VALLEY THE FEATHERED DENIZENS OF FOREST AND WOODLAND ANSWER THE CALL OF THEIR HUMAN BROTHER, WHEN SUDDENLY...
WHEEET! DANGER, HAWKMAN! FOREST FIRE!
WHAT'S THAT, BIG RED? WHERE..?
2

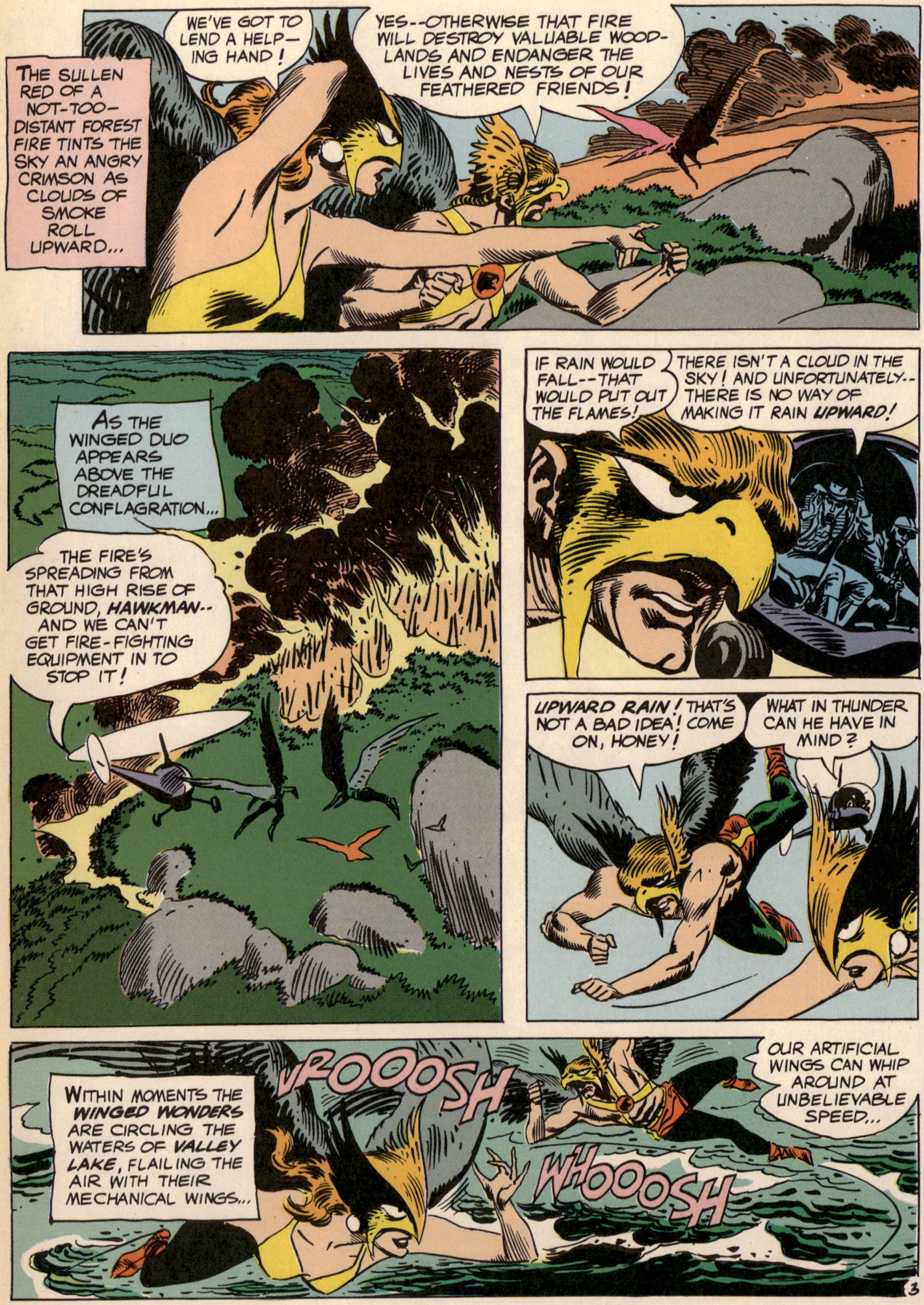

THE SULLEN RED OF A NOT-TOO-DISTANT FOREST FIRE TINTS THE SKY AN ANGRY CRIMSON AS CLOUDS OF SMOKE ROLL UPWARD...
WE'VE GOT TO LEND A HELPING HAND!
YES--OTHERWISE THAT FIRE WILL DESTROY VALUABLE WOODLANDS AND ENDANGER THE LIVES AND NESTS OF OUR FEATHERED FRIENDS!
AS THE WINGED DUO APPEARS ABOVE THE DREADFUL CONFLAGRATION...
THE FIRE'S SPREADING FROM THAT HIGH RISE OF GROUND, HAWKMAN-- AND WE CAN'T GET FIRE-FIGHTING EQUIPMENT IN TO STOP IT!
IF RAIN WOULD FALL--THAT WOULD PUT OUT THE FLAMES!
THERE ISN'T A CLOUD IN THE SKY! AND UNFORTUNATELY-- THERE IS NO WAY OF MAKING IT RAIN UPWARD!
UPWARD RAIN! THAT'S NOT A BAD IDEA! COME ON, HONEY!
WHAT IN THUNDER CAN HE HAVE IN MIND?
WITHIN MOMENTS THE WINGED WONDERS ARE CIRCLING THE WATERS OF VALLEY LAKE, FLAILING THE AIR WITH THEIR MECHANICAL WINGS...
VROOOOSH
OUR ARTIFICIAL WINGS CAN WHIP AROUND AT UNBELIEVABLE SPEED...
WHOOOOSH
3

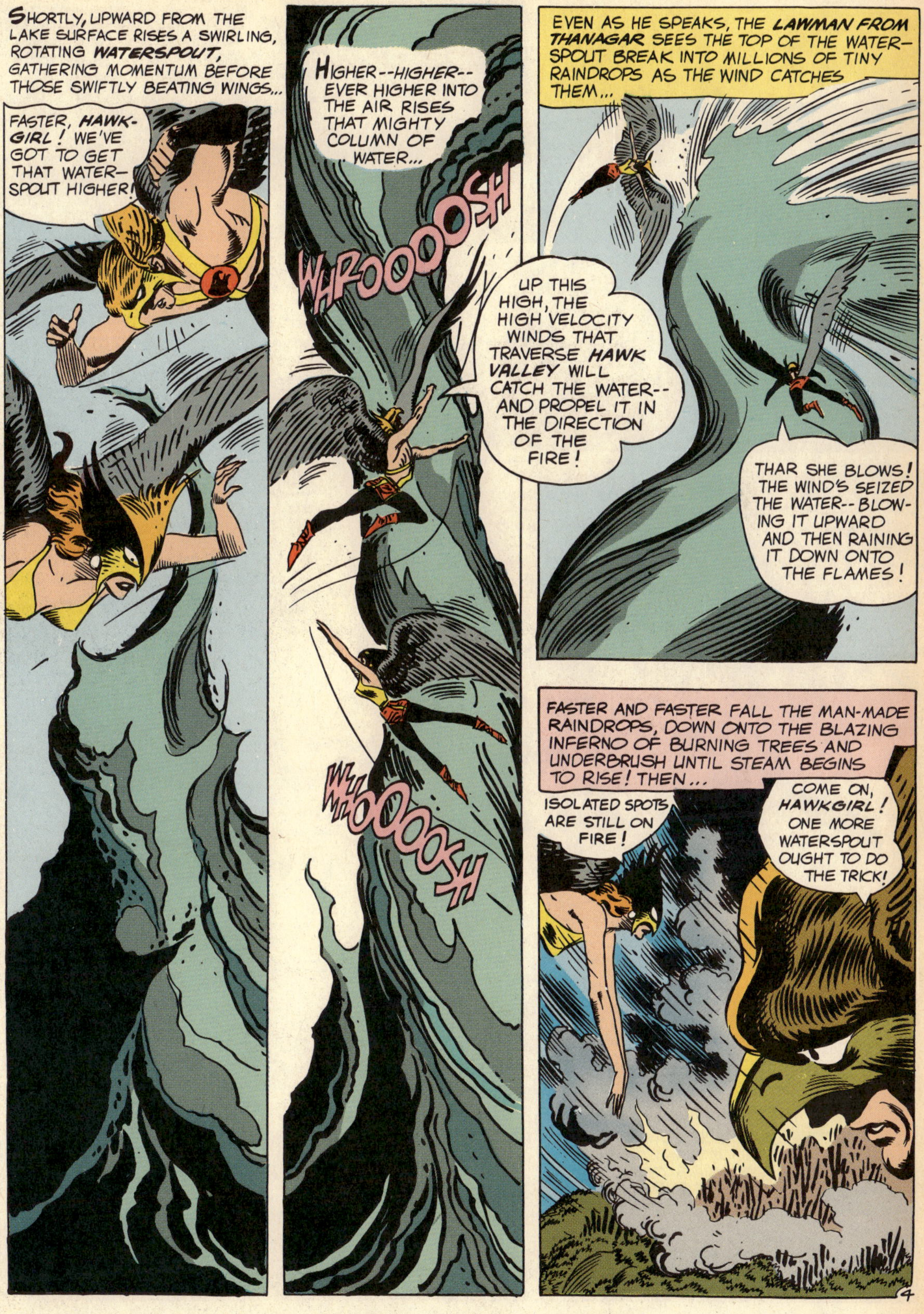
SHORTLY, UPWARD FROM THE LAKE SURFACE RISES A SWIRLING, ROTATING WATERSPOUT, GATHERING MOMENTUM BEFORE THOSE SWIFTLY BEATING WINGS...
FASTER, HAWK-GIRL! WE'VE GOT TO GET THAT WATER-SPOUT HIGHER!
HIGHER--HIGHER--EVER HIGHER INTO THE AIR RISES THAT MIGHTY COLUMN OF WATER...
WHROOOOOSH
UP THIS HIGH, THE HIGH VELOCITY WINDS THAT TRAVERSE HAWK VALLEY WILL CATCH THE WATER--AND PROPEL IT IN THE DIRECTION OF THE FIRE!
WHOOOOOSH
EVEN AS HE SPEAKS, THE LAWMAN FROM THANAGAR SEES THE TOP OF THE WATER-SPOUT BREAK INTO MILLIONS OF TINY RAINDROPS AS THE WIND CATCHES THEM...
THAR SHE BLOWS! THE WIND'S SEIZED THE WATER--BLOWING IT UPWARD AND THEN RAINING IT DOWN ONTO THE FLAMES!
FASTER AND FASTER FALL THE MAN-MADE RAINDROPS, DOWN ONTO THE BLAZING INFERNO OF BURNING TREES AND UNDERBRUSH UNTIL STEAM BEGINS TO RISE! THEN...
ISOLATED SPOTS ARE STILL ON FIRE!
COME ON, HAWKGIRL! ONE MORE WATERSPOUT OUGHT TO DO THE TRICK!
4

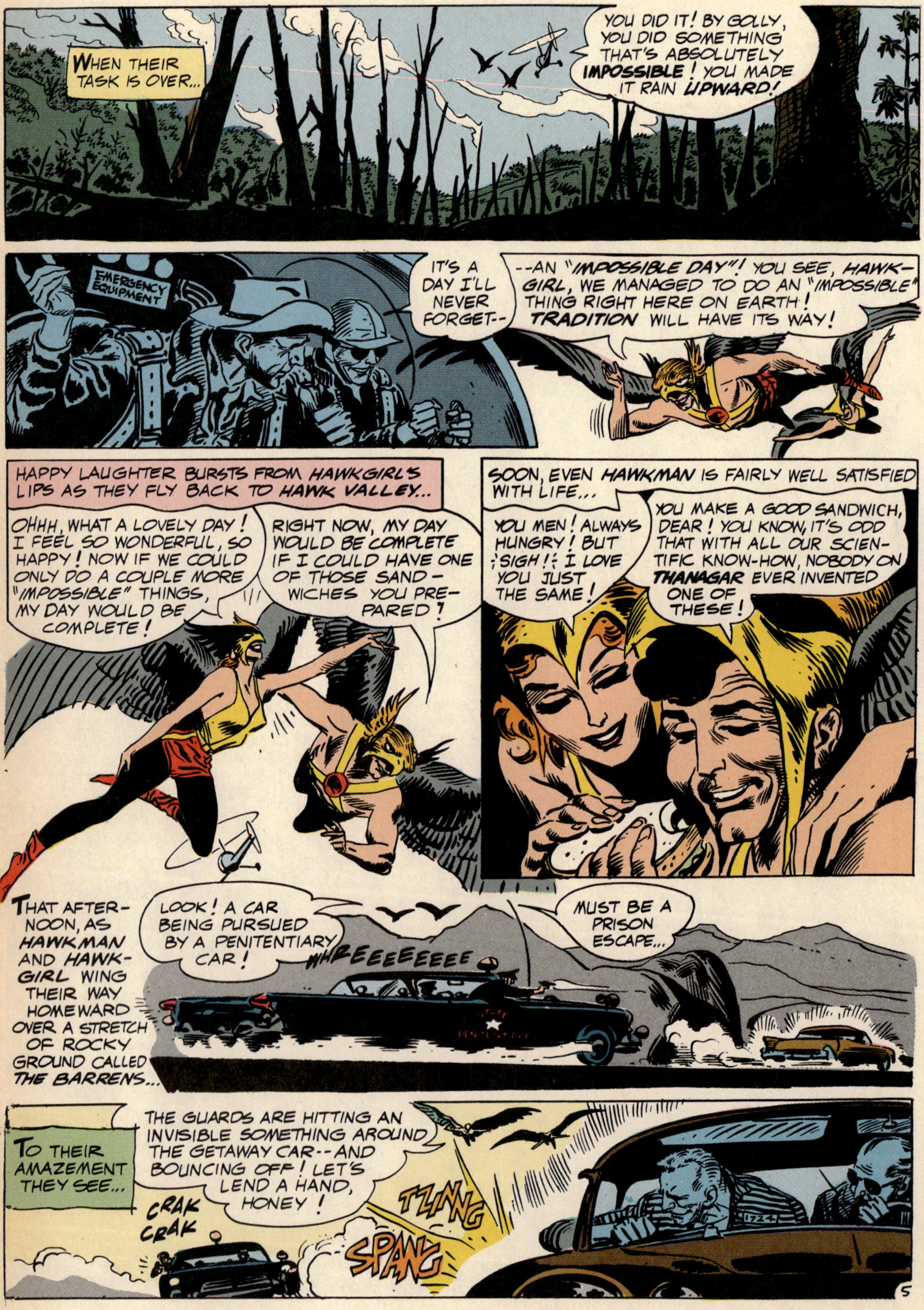
WHEN THEIR TASK IS OVER...
YOU DID IT! BY GOLLY, YOU DID SOMETHING THAT'S ABSOLUTELY IMPOSSIBLE! YOU MADE IT RAIN UPWARD!
EMERGENCY EQUIPMENT
IT'S A DAY I'LL NEVER FORGET--
--AN "IMPOSSIBLE DAY"! YOU SEE, HAWK-GIRL, WE MANAGED TO DO AN "IMPOSSIBLE" THING RIGHT HERE ON EARTH! TRADITION WILL HAVE ITS WAY!
HAPPY LAUGHTER BURSTS FROM HAWKGIRL'S LIPS AS THEY FLY BACK TO HAWK VALLEY...
OHHH, WHAT A LOVELY DAY! I FEEL SO WONDERFUL, SO HAPPY! NOW IF WE COULD ONLY DO A COUPLE MORE "IMPOSSIBLE" THINGS, MY DAY WOULD BE COMPLETE!
RIGHT NOW, MY DAY WOULD BE COMPLETE IF I COULD HAVE ONE OF THOSE SAND-WICHES YOU PRE-PARED!
SOON, EVEN HAWKMAN IS FAIRLY WELL SATISFIED WITH LIFE...
YOU MEN! ALWAYS HUNGRY! BUT :SIGH!: I LOVE YOU JUST THE SAME!
YOU MAKE A GOOD SANDWICH, DEAR! YOU KNOW, IT'S ODD THAT WITH ALL OUR SCIEN-TIFIC KNOW-HOW, NOBODY ON THANAGAR EVER INVENTED ONE OF THESE!
THAT AFTER-NOON, AS HAWKMAN AND HAWK-GIRL WING THEIR WAY HOMEWARD OVER A STRETCH OF ROCKY GROUND CALLED THE BARRENS...
LOOK! A CAR BEING PURSUED BY A PENITENTIARY CAR!
MUST BE A PRISON ESCAPE...
WHREEEEEEEEE
TO THEIR AMAZEMENT THEY SEE...
THE GUARDS ARE HITTING AN INVISIBLE SOMETHING AROUND THE GETAWAY CAR--AND BOUNCING OFF! LET'S LEND A HAND, HONEY!
CRAK CRAK
TZING
SPANG
5

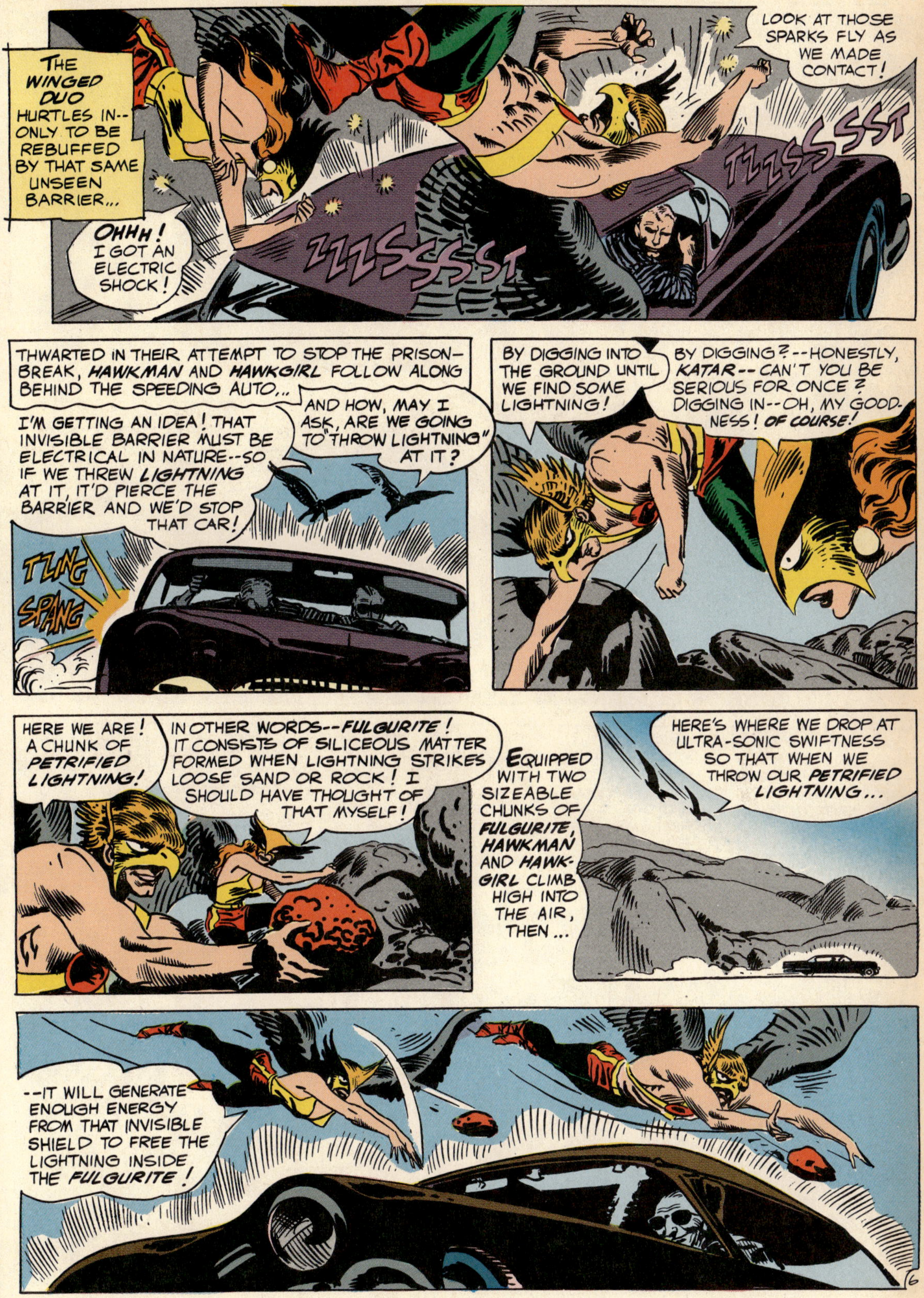
THE WINGED DUO HURTLES IN-- ONLY TO BE REBUFFED BY THAT SAME UNSEEN BARRIER...
LOOK AT THOSE SPARKS FLY AS WE MADE CONTACT!
OHHH! I GOT AN ELECTRIC SHOCK!
ZZZSSSSST
TZZZSSSSST
THWARTED IN THEIR ATTEMPT TO STOP THE PRISON-BREAK, HAWKMAN AND HAWKGIRL FOLLOW ALONG BEHIND THE SPEEDING AUTO...
I'M GETTING AN IDEA! THAT INVISIBLE BARRIER MUST BE ELECTRICAL IN NATURE--SO IF WE THREW LIGHTNING AT IT, IT'D PIERCE THE BARRIER AND WE'D STOP THAT CAR!
AND HOW, MAY I ASK, ARE WE GOING TO "THROW LIGHTNING" AT IT?
TZING
SPANG
BY DIGGING INTO THE GROUND UNTIL WE FIND SOME LIGHTNING!
BY DIGGING?--HONESTLY, KATAR--CAN'T YOU BE SERIOUS FOR ONCE? DIGGING IN--OH, MY GOODNESS! OF COURSE!
HERE WE ARE! A CHUNK OF PETRIFIED LIGHTNING!
IN OTHER WORDS--FULGURITE! IT CONSISTS OF SILICEOUS MATTER FORMED WHEN LIGHTNING STRIKES LOOSE SAND OR ROCK! I SHOULD HAVE THOUGHT OF THAT MYSELF!
EQUIPPED WITH TWO SIZEABLE CHUNKS OF FULGURITE, HAWKMAN AND HAWKGIRL CLIMB HIGH INTO THE AIR, THEN...
HERE'S WHERE WE DROP AT ULTRA-SONIC SWIFTNESS SO THAT WHEN WE THROW OUR PETRIFIED LIGHTNING...
--IT WILL GENERATE ENOUGH ENERGY FROM THAT INVISIBLE SHIELD TO FREE THE LIGHTNING INSIDE THE FULGURITE!
6

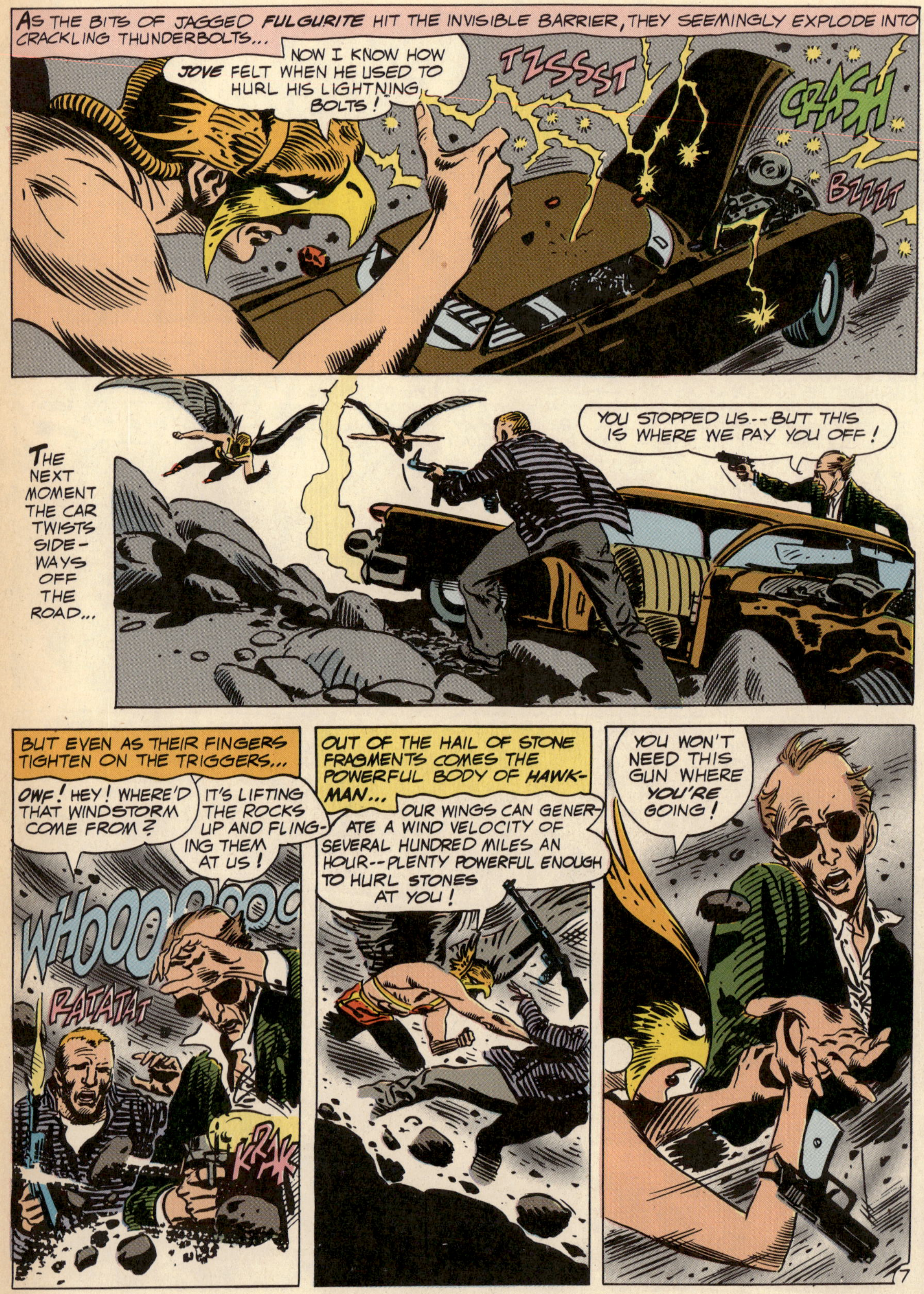
AS THE BITS OF JAGGED FULGURITE HIT THE INVISIBLE BARRIER, THEY SEEMINGLY EXPLODE INTO CRACKLING THUNDERBOLTS...
NOW I KNOW HOW JOVE FELT WHEN HE USED TO HURL HIS LIGHTNING BOLTS!
TZSSSST
CRASH
BZZZT
THE NEXT MOMENT THE CAR TWISTS SIDE-WAYS OFF THE ROAD...
YOU STOPPED US--BUT THIS IS WHERE WE PAY YOU OFF!
BUT EVEN AS THEIR FINGERS TIGHTEN ON THE TRIGGERS...
OWF! HEY! WHERE'D THAT WINDSTORM COME FROM?
IT'S LIFTING THE ROCKS UP AND FLING-ING THEM AT US!
WHOOOOOOO
RATATAT
KRAK
OUT OF THE HAIL OF STONE FRAGMENTS COMES THE POWERFUL BODY OF HAWK-MAN...
OUR WINGS CAN GENER-ATE A WIND VELOCITY OF SEVERAL HUNDRED MILES AN HOUR--PLENTY POWERFUL ENOUGH TO HURL STONES AT YOU!
YOU WON'T NEED THIS GUN WHERE YOU'RE GOING!
7

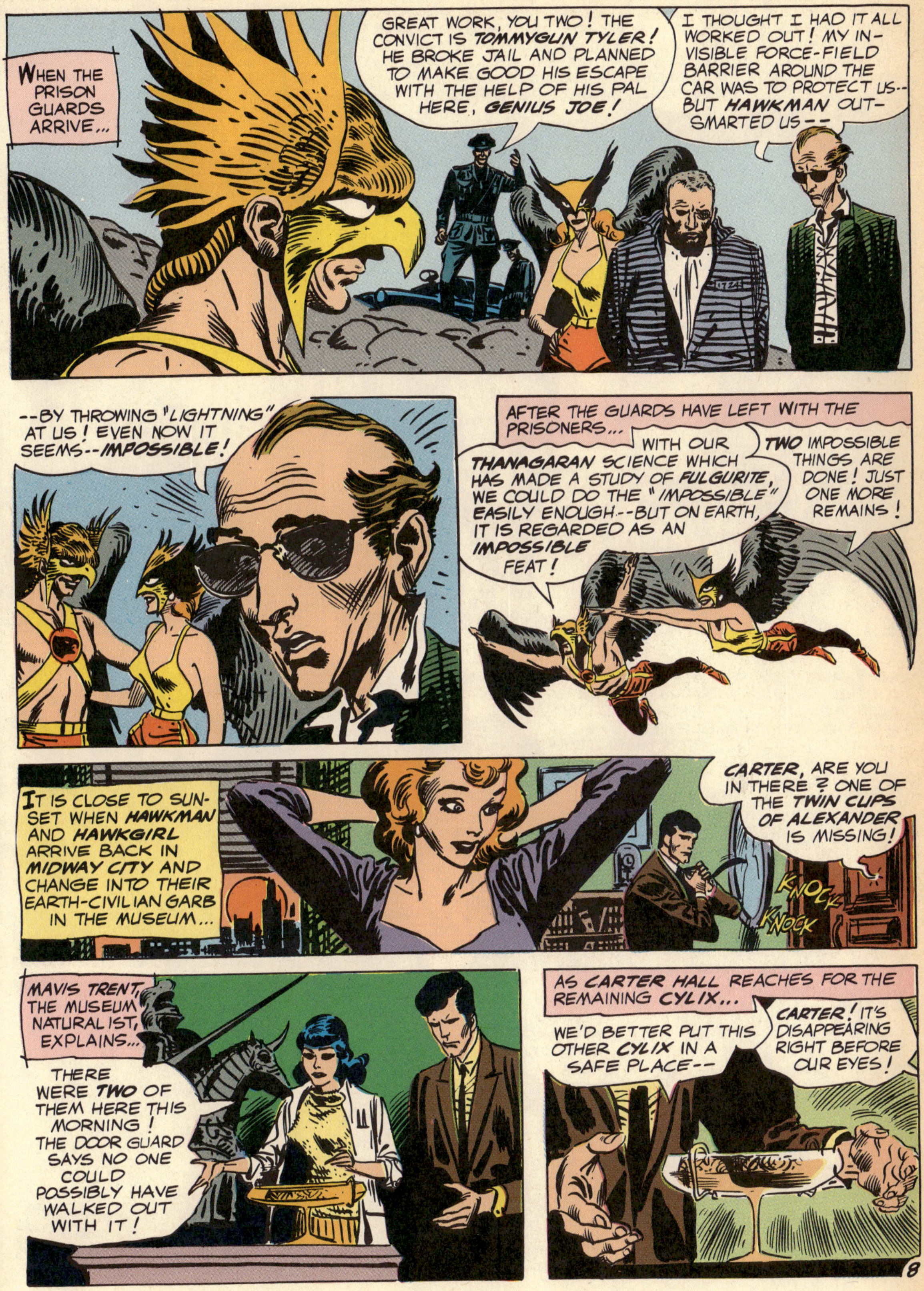
WHEN THE PRISON GUARDS ARRIVE...
GREAT WORK, YOU TWO! THE CONVICT IS TOMMYGUN TYLER! HE BROKE JAIL AND PLANNED TO MAKE GOOD HIS ESCAPE WITH THE HELP OF HIS PAL HERE, GENIUS JOE!
I THOUGHT I HAD IT ALL WORKED OUT! MY INVISIBLE FORCE-FIELD BARRIER AROUND THE CAR WAS TO PROTECT US--BUT HAWKMAN OUTSMARTED US--
--BY THROWING "LIGHTNING" AT US! EVEN NOW IT SEEMS--IMPOSSIBLE!
AFTER THE GUARDS HAVE LEFT WITH THE PRISONERS...
WITH OUR THANAGARAN SCIENCE WHICH HAS MADE A STUDY OF FULGURITE, WE COULD DO THE "IMPOSSIBLE" EASILY ENOUGH--BUT ON EARTH, IT IS REGARDED AS AN IMPOSSIBLE FEAT!
TWO IMPOSSIBLE THINGS ARE DONE! JUST ONE MORE REMAINS!
IT IS CLOSE TO SUNSET WHEN HAWKMAN AND HAWKGIRL ARRIVE BACK IN MIDWAY CITY AND CHANGE INTO THEIR EARTH-CIVILIAN GARB IN THE MUSEUM...
CARTER, ARE YOU IN THERE? ONE OF THE TWIN CUPS OF ALEXANDER IS MISSING!
KNOCK
KNOCK
MAVIS TRENT, THE MUSEUM NATURALIST, EXPLAINS...
THERE WERE TWO OF THEM HERE THIS MORNING! THE DOOR GUARD SAYS NO ONE COULD POSSIBLY HAVE WALKED OUT WITH IT!
AS CARTER HALL REACHES FOR THE REMAINING CYLIX...
WE'D BETTER PUT THIS OTHER CYLIX IN A SAFE PLACE--
CARTER! IT'S DISAPPEARING RIGHT BEFORE OUR EYES!
8

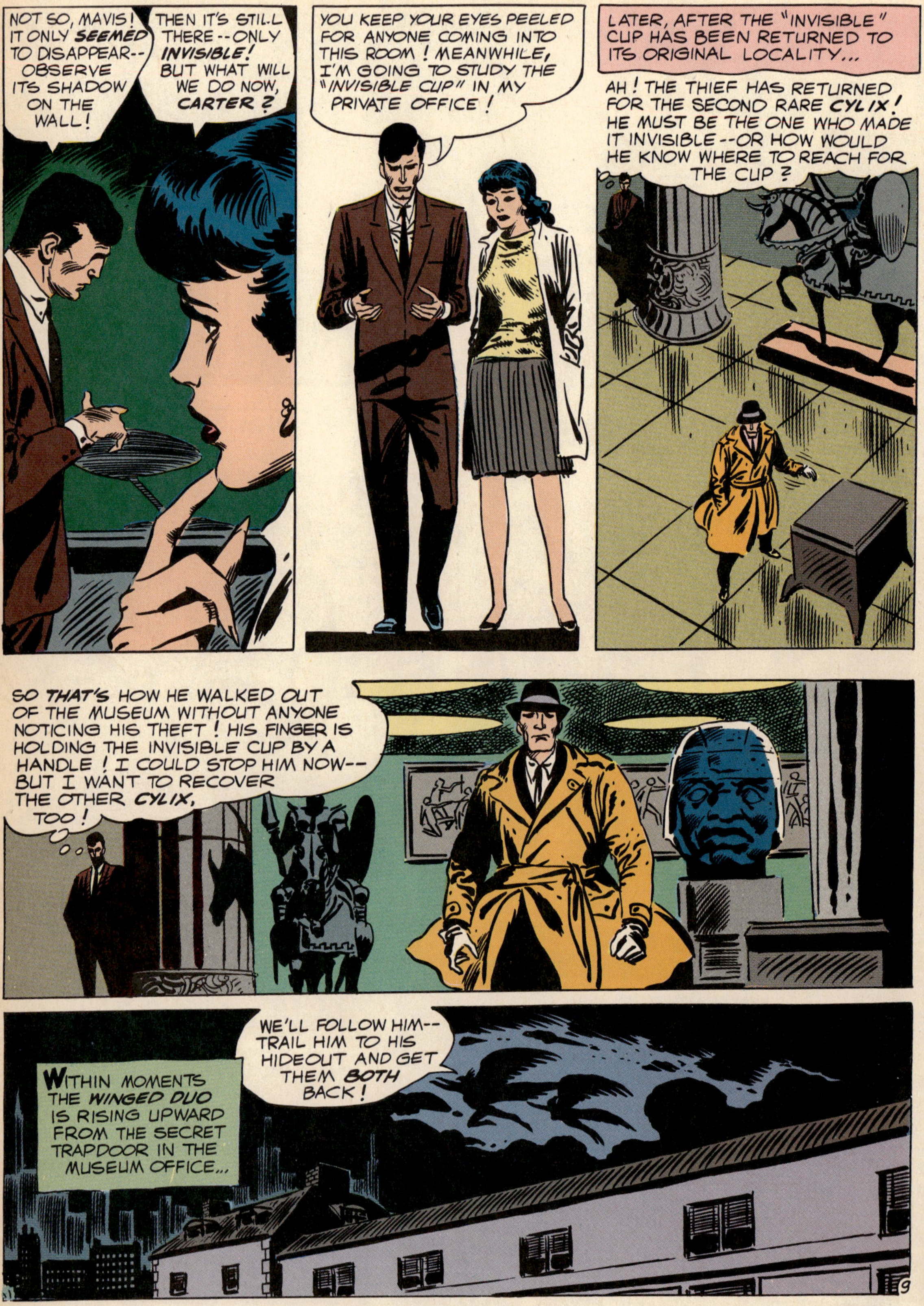
NOT SO, MAVIS! IT ONLY SEEMED TO DISAPPEAR-- OBSERVE ITS SHADOW ON THE WALL!
THEN IT'S STILL THERE--ONLY INVISIBLE! BUT WHAT WILL WE DO NOW, CARTER?
YOU KEEP YOUR EYES PEELED FOR ANYONE COMING INTO THIS ROOM! MEANWHILE, I'M GOING TO STUDY THE "INVISIBLE CUP" IN MY PRIVATE OFFICE!
LATER, AFTER THE "INVISIBLE" CUP HAS BEEN RETURNED TO ITS ORIGINAL LOCALITY...
AH! THE THIEF HAS RETURNED FOR THE SECOND RARE CYLIX! HE MUST BE THE ONE WHO MADE IT INVISIBLE--OR HOW WOULD HE KNOW WHERE TO REACH FOR THE CUP?
SO THAT'S HOW HE WALKED OUT OF THE MUSEUM WITHOUT ANYONE NOTICING HIS THEFT! HIS FINGER IS HOLDING THE INVISIBLE CUP BY A HANDLE! I COULD STOP HIM NOW--BUT I WANT TO RECOVER THE OTHER CYLIX, TOO!
WITHIN MOMENTS THE WINGED DUO IS RISING UPWARD FROM THE SECRET TRAPDOOR IN THE MUSEUM OFFICE...
WE'LL FOLLOW HIM--TRAIL HIM TO HIS HIDEOUT AND GET THEM BOTH BACK!
9

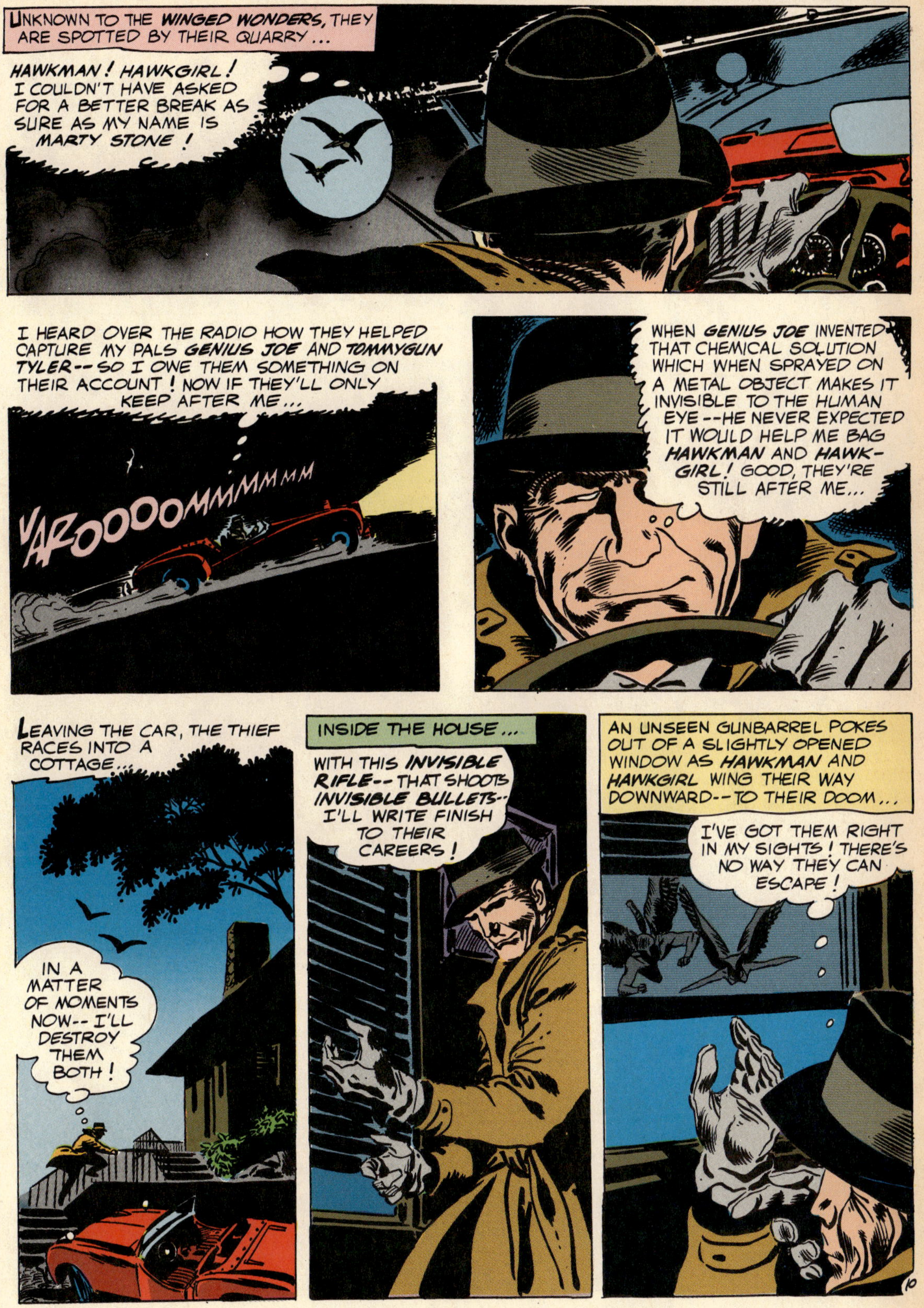
UNKNOWN TO THE WINGED WONDERS, THEY ARE SPOTTED BY THEIR QUARRY...
HAWKMAN! HAWKGIRL! I COULDN'T HAVE ASKED FOR A BETTER BREAK AS SURE AS MY NAME IS MARTY STONE!
I HEARD OVER THE RADIO HOW THEY HELPED CAPTURE MY PALS GENIUS JOE AND TOMMYGUN TYLER-- SO I OWE THEM SOMETHING ON THEIR ACCOUNT! NOW IF THEY'LL ONLY KEEP AFTER ME...
VAROOOOOMMMMMMM
WHEN GENIUS JOE INVENTED THAT CHEMICAL SOLUTION WHICH WHEN SPRAYED ON A METAL OBJECT MAKES IT INVISIBLE TO THE HUMAN EYE --HE NEVER EXPECTED IT WOULD HELP ME BAG HAWKMAN AND HAWK-GIRL! GOOD, THEY'RE STILL AFTER ME...
LEAVING THE CAR, THE THIEF RACES INTO A COTTAGE...
IN A MATTER OF MOMENTS NOW-- I'LL DESTROY THEM BOTH!
INSIDE THE HOUSE...
WITH THIS INVISIBLE RIFLE-- THAT SHOOTS INVISIBLE BULLETS-- I'LL WRITE FINISH TO THEIR CAREERS!
AN UNSEEN GUNBARREL POKES OUT OF A SLIGHTLY OPENED WINDOW AS HAWKMAN AND HAWKGIRL WING THEIR WAY DOWNWARD-- TO THEIR DOOM...
I'VE GOT THEM RIGHT IN MY SIGHTS! THERE'S NO WAY THEY CAN ESCAPE!
10

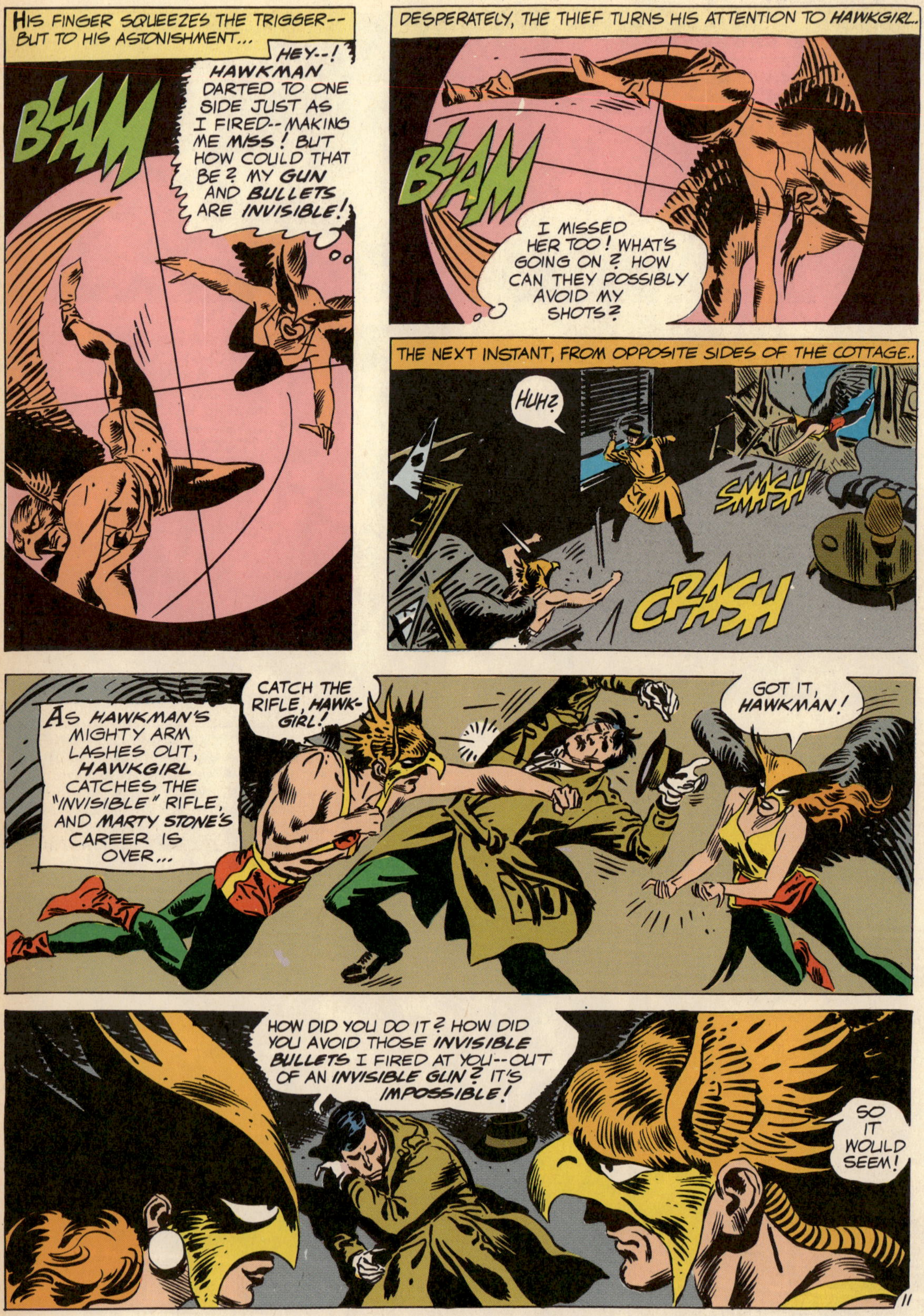
HIS FINGER SQUEEZES THE TRIGGER-- BUT TO HIS ASTONISHMENT...
BLAM
HEY--! HAWKMAN DARTED TO ONE SIDE JUST AS I FIRED--MAKING ME MISS! BUT HOW COULD THAT BE? MY GUN AND BULLETS ARE INVISIBLE!
DESPERATELY, THE THIEF TURNS HIS ATTENTION TO HAWKGIRL.
BLAM
I MISSED HER TOO! WHAT'S GOING ON? HOW CAN THEY POSSIBLY AVOID MY SHOTS?
THE NEXT INSTANT, FROM OPPOSITE SIDES OF THE COTTAGE..
HUH?
SMASH
CRASH
AS HAWKMAN'S MIGHTY ARM LASHES OUT, HAWKGIRL CATCHES THE "INVISIBLE" RIFLE, AND MARTY STONE'S CAREER IS OVER...
CATCH THE RIFLE, HAWK-GIRL!
GOT IT, HAWKMAN!
HOW DID YOU DO IT? HOW DID YOU AVOID THOSE INVISIBLE BULLETS I FIRED AT YOU--OUT OF AN INVISIBLE GUN? IT'S IMPOSSIBLE!
SO IT WOULD SEEM!
11

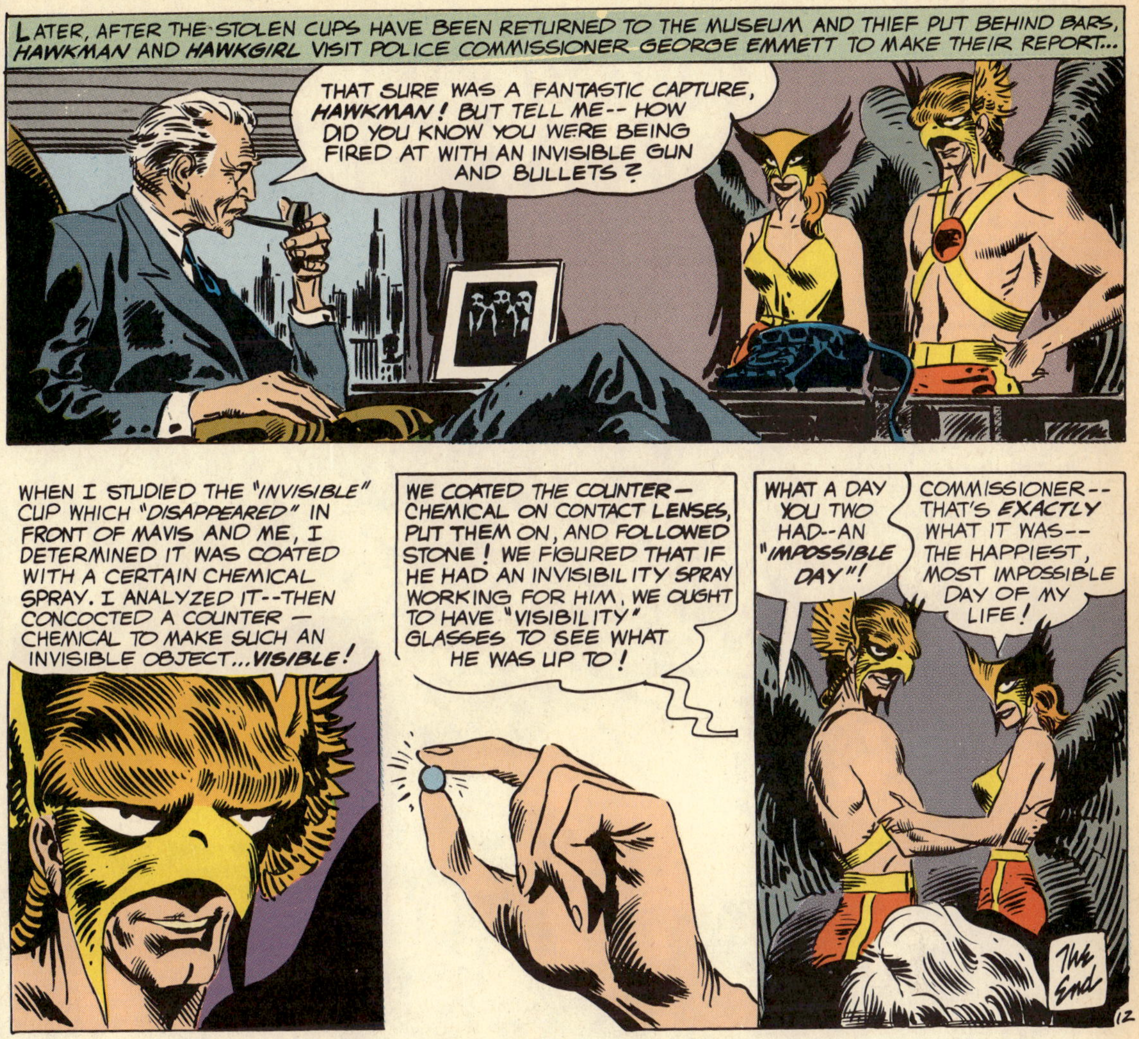
LATER, AFTER THE STOLEN CUPS HAVE BEEN RETURNED TO THE MUSEUM AND THIEF PUT BEHIND BARS, HAWKMAN AND HAWKGIRL VISIT POLICE COMMISSIONER GEORGE EMMETT TO MAKE THEIR REPORT...
THAT SURE WAS A FANTASTIC CAPTURE, HAWKMAN! BUT TELL ME-- HOW DID YOU KNOW YOU WERE BEING FIRED AT WITH AN INVISIBLE GUN AND BULLETS?
WHEN I STUDIED THE "INVISIBLE" CUP WHICH "DISAPPEARED" IN FRONT OF MAVIS AND ME, I DETERMINED IT WAS COATED WITH A CERTAIN CHEMICAL SPRAY. I ANALYZED IT--THEN CONCOCTED A COUNTER-CHEMICAL TO MAKE SUCH AN INVISIBLE OBJECT... VISIBLE!
WE COATED THE COUNTER-CHEMICAL ON CONTACT LENSES, PUT THEM ON, AND FOLLOWED STONE! WE FIGURED THAT IF HE HAD AN INVISIBILITY SPRAY WORKING FOR HIM, WE OUGHT TO HAVE "VISIBILITY" GLASSES TO SEE WHAT HE WAS UP TO!
WHAT A DAY YOU TWO HAD--AN "IMPOSSIBLE DAY"!
COMMISSIONER-- THAT'S EXACTLY WHAT IT WAS-- THE HAPPIEST, MOST IMPOSSIBLE DAY OF MY LIFE!
The End
12

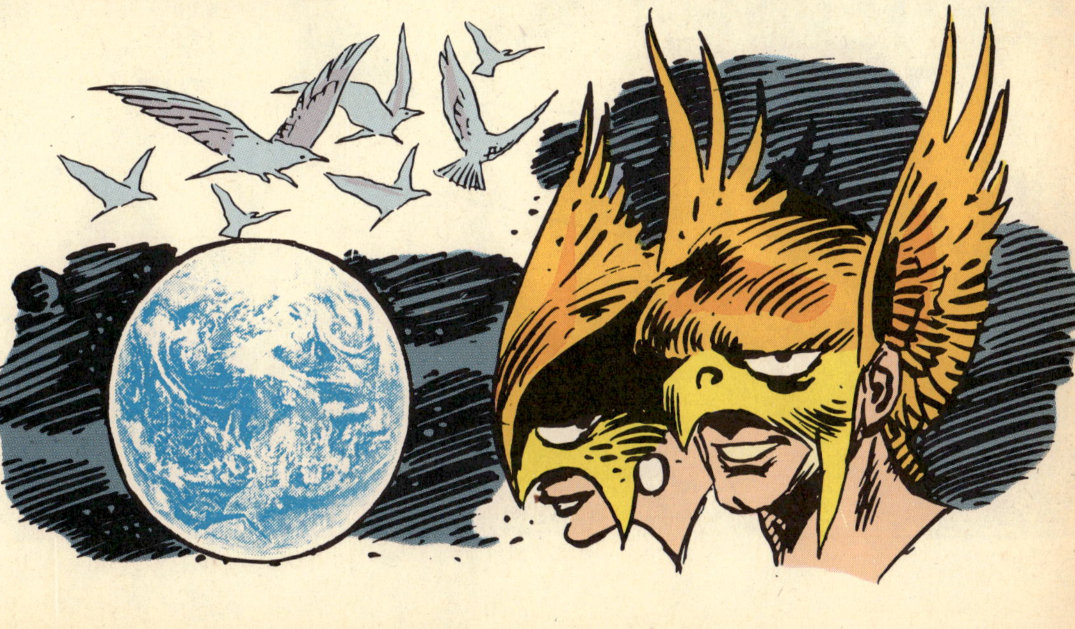

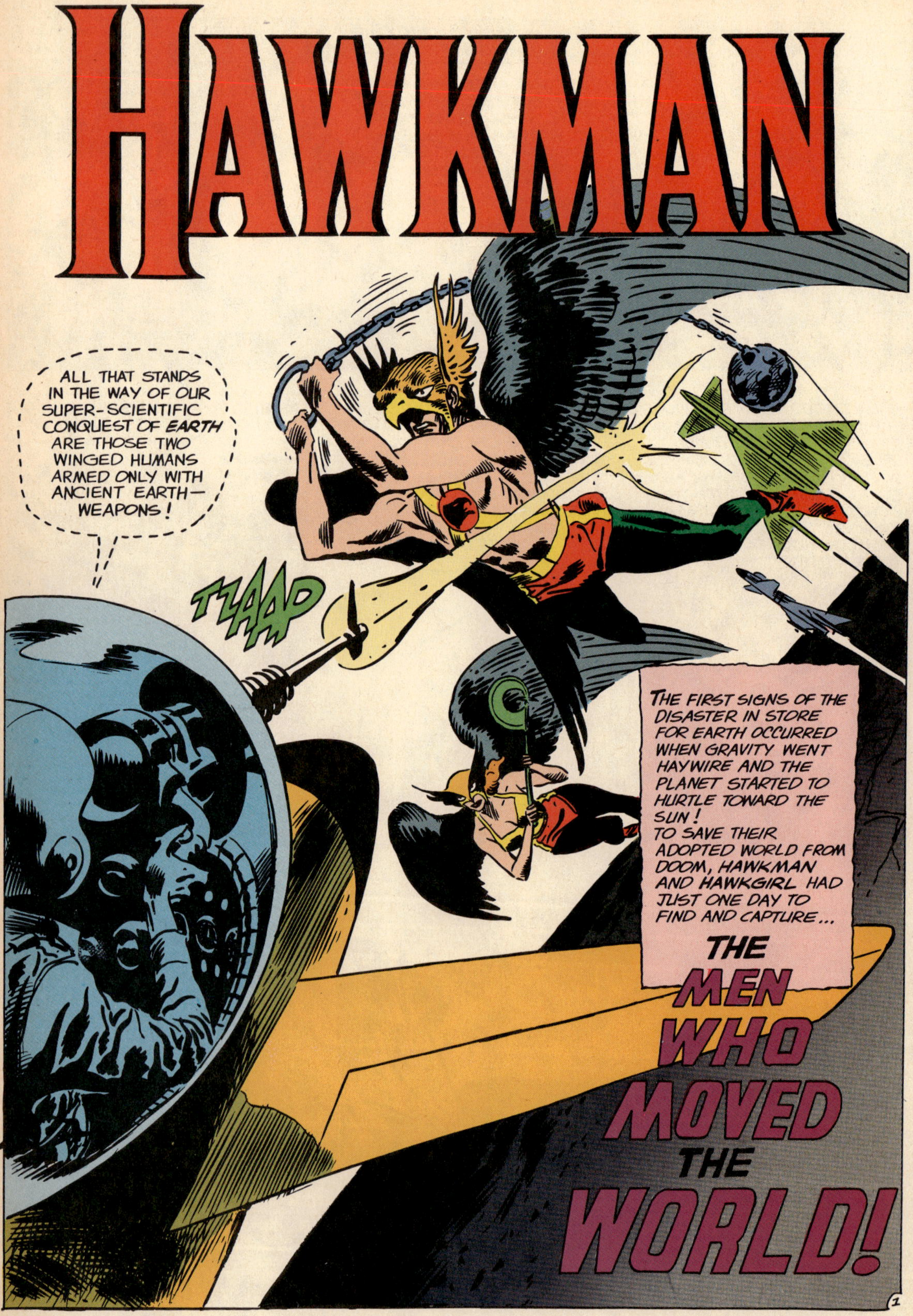
HAWKMAN
ALL THAT STANDS IN THE WAY OF OUR SUPER-SCIENTIFIC CONQUEST OF EARTH ARE THOSE TWO WINGED HUMANS ARMED ONLY WITH ANCIENT EARTH— WEAPONS!
TZAAP
THE FIRST SIGNS OF THE DISASTER IN STORE FOR EARTH OCCURRED WHEN GRAVITY WENT HAYWIRE AND THE PLANET STARTED TO HURTLE TOWARD THE SUN! TO SAVE THEIR ADOPTED WORLD FROM DOOM, HAWKMAN AND HAWKGIRL HAD JUST ONE DAY TO FIND AND CAPTURE...
THE MEN WHO MOVED THE WORLD!
1

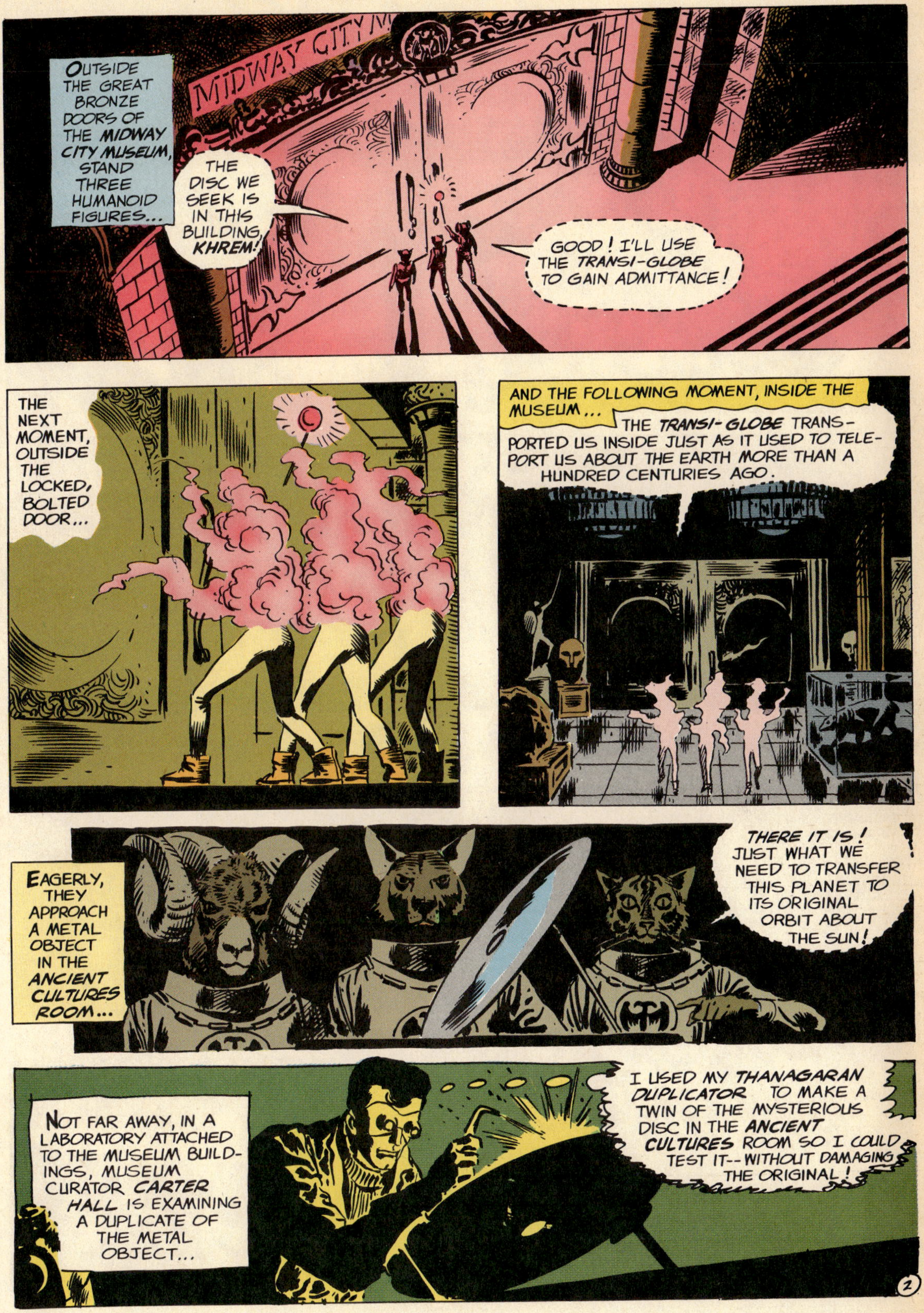
MIDWAY CITY M
OUTSIDE THE GREAT BRONZE DOORS OF THE MIDWAY CITY MUSEUM, STAND THREE HUMANOID FIGURES...
THE DISC WE SEEK IS IN THIS BUILDING, KHREM!
GOOD! I'LL USE THE TRANSI-GLOBE TO GAIN ADMITTANCE!
THE NEXT MOMENT, OUTSIDE THE LOCKED, BOLTED DOOR...
AND THE FOLLOWING MOMENT, INSIDE THE MUSEUM...
THE TRANSI-GLOBE TRANSPORTED US INSIDE JUST AS IT USED TO TELEPORT US ABOUT THE EARTH MORE THAN A HUNDRED CENTURIES AGO.
EAGERLY, THEY APPROACH A METAL OBJECT IN THE ANCIENT CULTURES ROOM...
THERE IT IS! JUST WHAT WE NEED TO TRANSFER THIS PLANET TO ITS ORIGINAL ORBIT ABOUT THE SUN!
NOT FAR AWAY, IN A LABORATORY ATTACHED TO THE MUSEUM BUILDINGS, MUSEUM CURATOR CARTER HALL IS EXAMINING A DUPLICATE OF THE METAL OBJECT...
I USED MY THANAGARAN DUPLICATOR TO MAKE A TWIN OF THE MYSTERIOUS DISC IN THE ANCIENT CULTURES ROOM SO I COULD TEST IT--WITHOUT DAMAGING THE ORIGINAL!
2

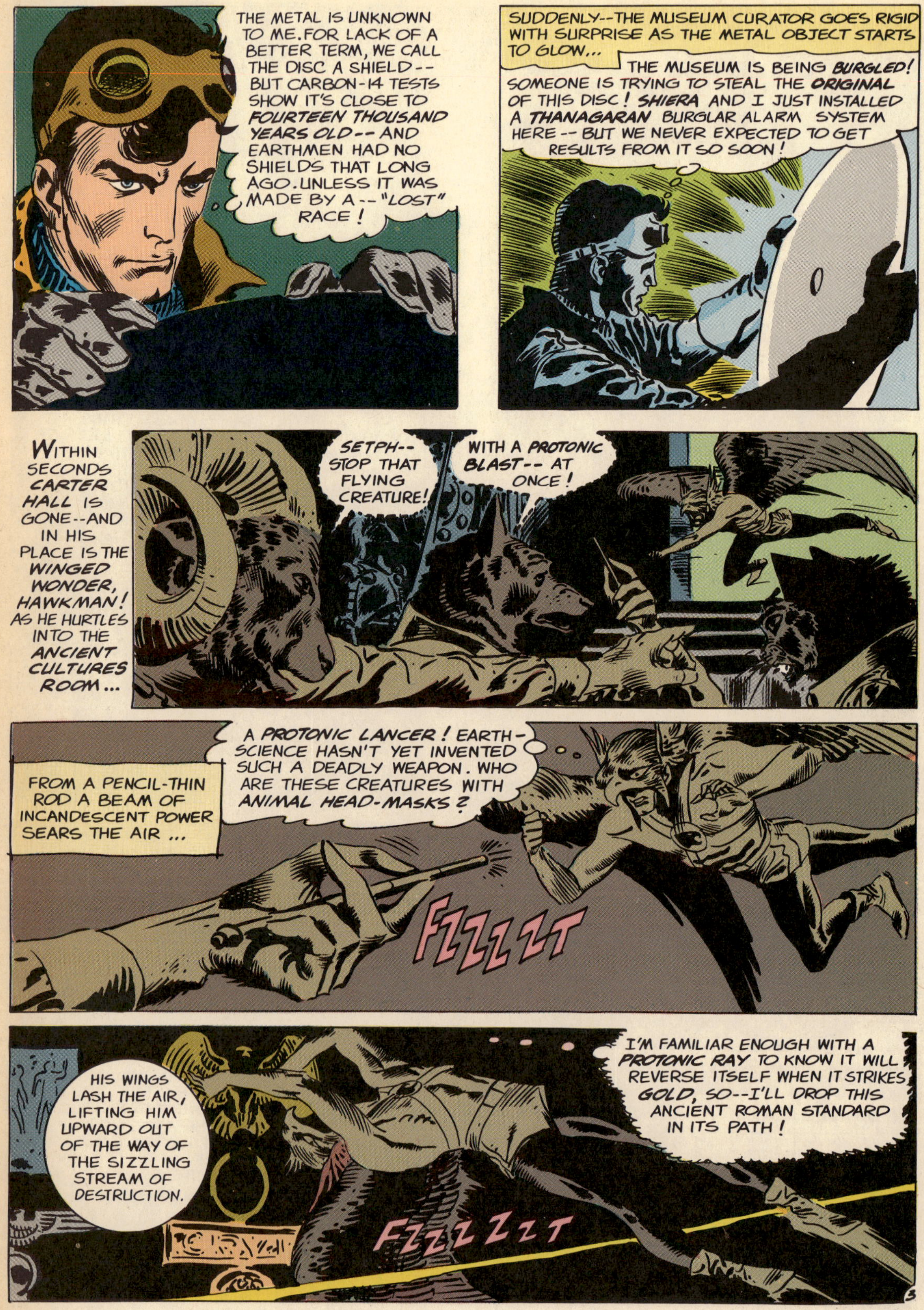
THE METAL IS UNKNOWN TO ME. FOR LACK OF A BETTER TERM, WE CALL THE DISC A SHIELD-- BUT CARBON-14 TESTS SHOW IT'S CLOSE TO FOURTEEN THOUSAND YEARS OLD-- AND EARTHMEN HAD NO SHIELDS THAT LONG AGO. UNLESS IT WAS MADE BY A -- "LOST" RACE!
SUDDENLY--THE MUSEUM CURATOR GOES RIGID WITH SURPRISE AS THE METAL OBJECT STARTS TO GLOW...
THE MUSEUM IS BEING BURGLED! SOMEONE IS TRYING TO STEAL THE ORIGINAL OF THIS DISC! SHIERA AND I JUST INSTALLED A THANAGARAN BURGLAR ALARM SYSTEM HERE -- BUT WE NEVER EXPECTED TO GET RESULTS FROM IT SO SOON!
WITHIN SECONDS CARTER HALL IS GONE--AND IN HIS PLACE IS THE WINGED WONDER, HAWKMAN! AS HE HURTLES INTO THE ANCIENT CULTURES ROOM...
SETPH-- STOP THAT FLYING CREATURE!
WITH A PROTONIC BLAST-- AT ONCE!
FROM A PENCIL-THIN ROD A BEAM OF INCANDESCENT POWER SEARS THE AIR ...
A PROTONIC LANCER! EARTH-SCIENCE HASN'T YET INVENTED SUCH A DEADLY WEAPON. WHO ARE THESE CREATURES WITH ANIMAL HEAD-MASKS?
FZZZZT
HIS WINGS LASH THE AIR, LIFTING HIM UPWARD OUT OF THE WAY OF THE SIZZLING STREAM OF DESTRUCTION.
I'M FAMILIAR ENOUGH WITH A PROTONIC RAY TO KNOW IT WILL REVERSE ITSELF WHEN IT STRIKES GOLD, SO--I'LL DROP THIS ANCIENT ROMAN STANDARD IN ITS PATH!
FZZZZZZT
3

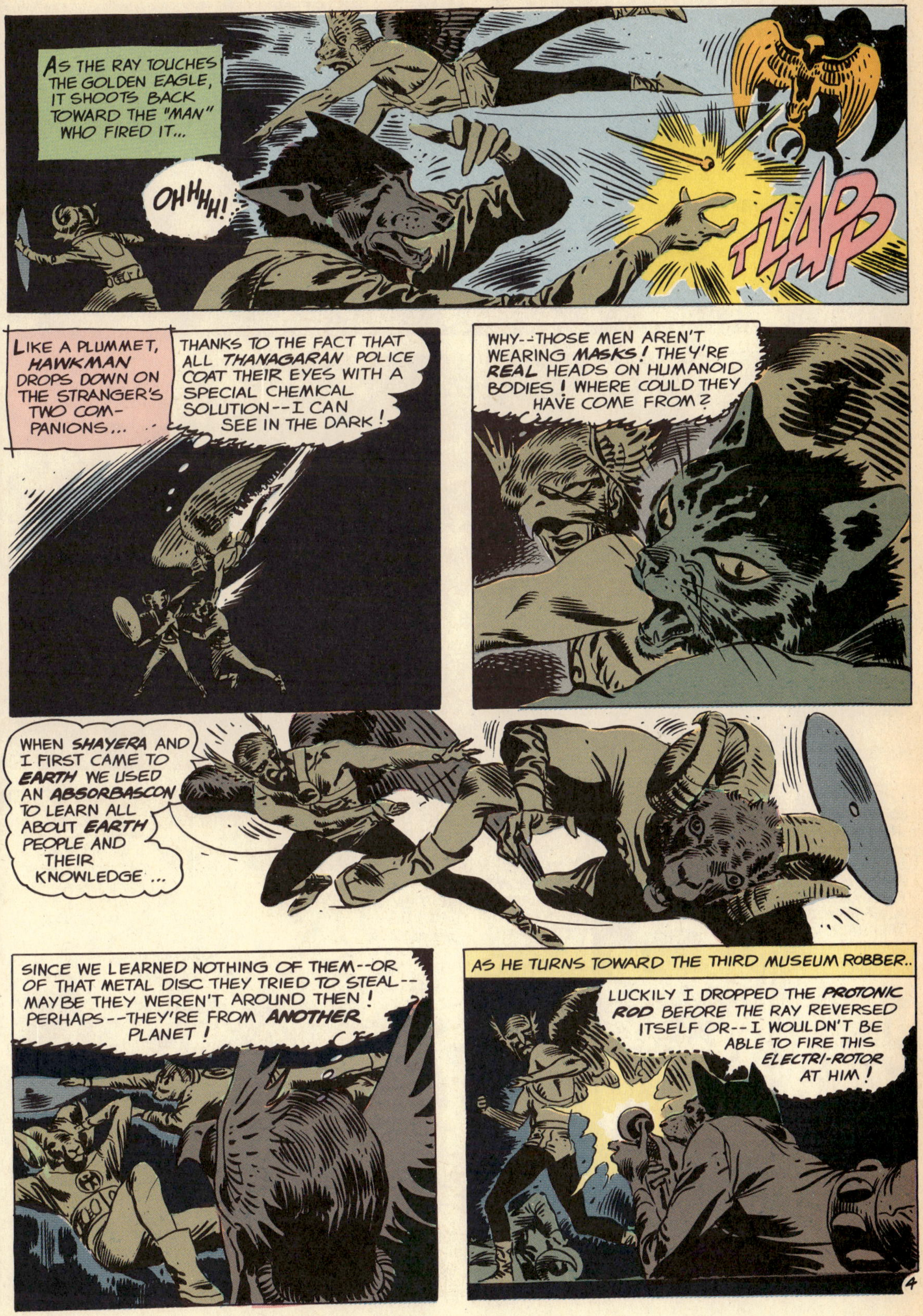
AS THE RAY TOUCHES THE GOLDEN EAGLE, IT SHOOTS BACK TOWARD THE "MAN" WHO FIRED IT...
OHHHH!
TZAPP
LIKE A PLUMMET, HAWKMAN DROPS DOWN ON THE STRANGER'S TWO COMPANIONS...
THANKS TO THE FACT THAT ALL THANAGARAN POLICE COAT THEIR EYES WITH A SPECIAL CHEMICAL SOLUTION--I CAN SEE IN THE DARK!
WHY--THOSE MEN AREN'T WEARING MASKS! THEY'RE REAL HEADS ON HUMANOID BODIES! WHERE COULD THEY HAVE COME FROM?
WHEN SHAYERA AND I FIRST CAME TO EARTH WE USED AN ABSORBASCON TO LEARN ALL ABOUT EARTH PEOPLE AND THEIR KNOWLEDGE...
SINCE WE LEARNED NOTHING OF THEM--OR OF THAT METAL DISC THEY TRIED TO STEAL--MAYBE THEY WEREN'T AROUND THEN! PERHAPS--THEY'RE FROM ANOTHER PLANET!
AS HE TURNS TOWARD THE THIRD MUSEUM ROBBER..
LUCKILY I DROPPED THE PROTONIC ROD BEFORE THE RAY REVERSED ITSELF OR--I WOULDN'T BE ABLE TO FIRE THIS ELECTRI-ROTOR AT HIM!
4

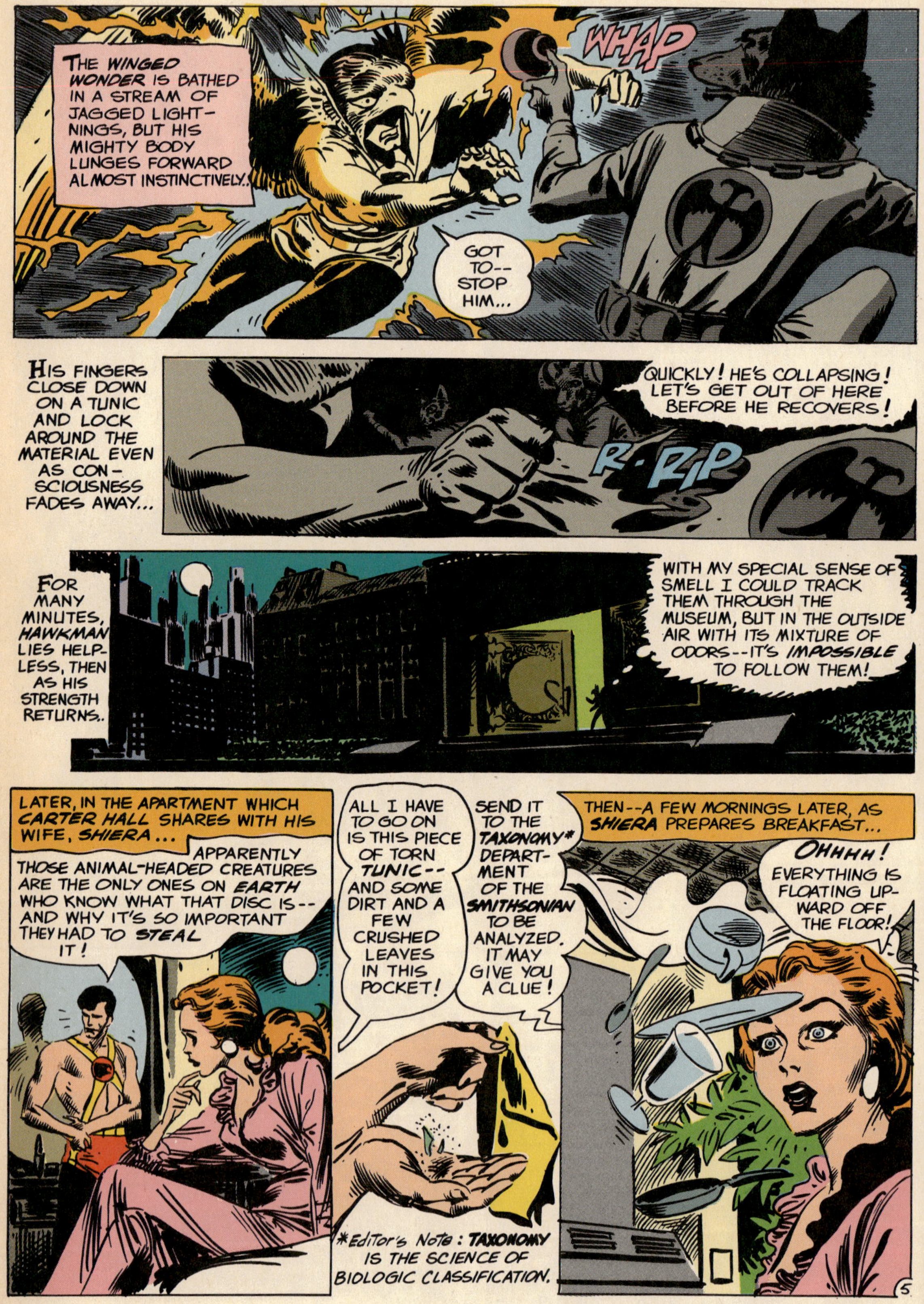
THE WINGED WONDER IS BATHED IN A STREAM OF JAGGED LIGHTNINGS, BUT HIS MIGHTY BODY LUNGES FORWARD ALMOST INSTINCTIVELY.
WHAP
GOT TO-- STOP HIM...
HIS FINGERS CLOSE DOWN ON A TUNIC AND LOCK AROUND THE MATERIAL EVEN AS CONSCIOUSNESS FADES AWAY...
QUICKLY! HE'S COLLAPSING! LET'S GET OUT OF HERE BEFORE HE RECOVERS!
R-RIP
FOR MANY MINUTES, HAWKMAN LIES HELPLESS, THEN AS HIS STRENGTH RETURNS..
WITH MY SPECIAL SENSE OF SMELL I COULD TRACK THEM THROUGH THE MUSEUM, BUT IN THE OUTSIDE AIR WITH ITS MIXTURE OF ODORS--IT'S IMPOSSIBLE TO FOLLOW THEM!
LATER, IN THE APARTMENT WHICH CARTER HALL SHARES WITH HIS WIFE, SHIERA...
APPARENTLY THOSE ANIMAL-HEADED CREATURES ARE THE ONLY ONES ON EARTH WHO KNOW WHAT THAT DISC IS--AND WHY IT'S SO IMPORTANT THEY HAD TO STEAL IT!
ALL I HAVE TO GO ON IS THIS PIECE OF TORN TUNIC--AND SOME DIRT AND A FEW CRUSHED LEAVES IN THIS POCKET!
SEND IT TO THE TAXONOMY* DEPARTMENT OF THE SMITHSONIAN TO BE ANALYZED. IT MAY GIVE YOU A CLUE!
*Editor's Note: TAXONOMY IS THE SCIENCE OF BIOLOGIC CLASSIFICATION.
THEN--A FEW MORNINGS LATER, AS SHIERA PREPARES BREAKFAST...
OHHHH! EVERYTHING IS FLOATING UPWARD OFF THE FLOOR!
5

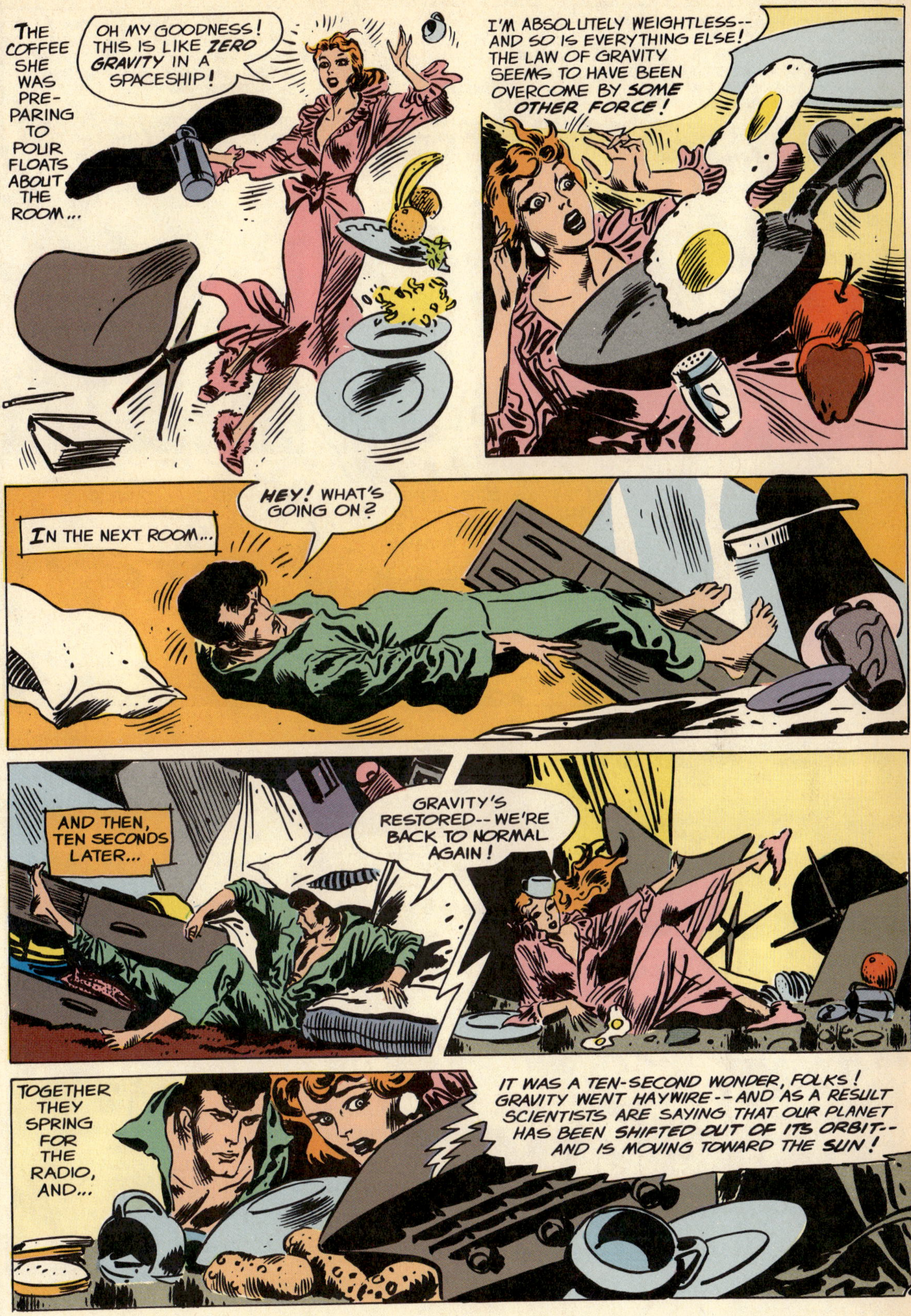
THE COFFEE SHE WAS PREPARING TO POUR FLOATS ABOUT THE ROOM...
OH MY GOODNESS! THIS IS LIKE ZERO GRAVITY IN A SPACESHIP!
I'M ABSOLUTELY WEIGHTLESS-- AND SO IS EVERYTHING ELSE! THE LAW OF GRAVITY SEEMS TO HAVE BEEN OVERCOME BY SOME OTHER FORCE!
IN THE NEXT ROOM...
HEY! WHAT'S GOING ON?
AND THEN, TEN SECONDS LATER...
GRAVITY'S RESTORED-- WE'RE BACK TO NORMAL AGAIN!
TOGETHER THEY SPRING FOR THE RADIO, AND...
IT WAS A TEN-SECOND WONDER, FOLKS! GRAVITY WENT HAYWIRE-- AND AS A RESULT SCIENTISTS ARE SAYING THAT OUR PLANET HAS BEEN SHIFTED OUT OF ITS ORBIT-- AND IS MOVING TOWARD THE SUN!
6

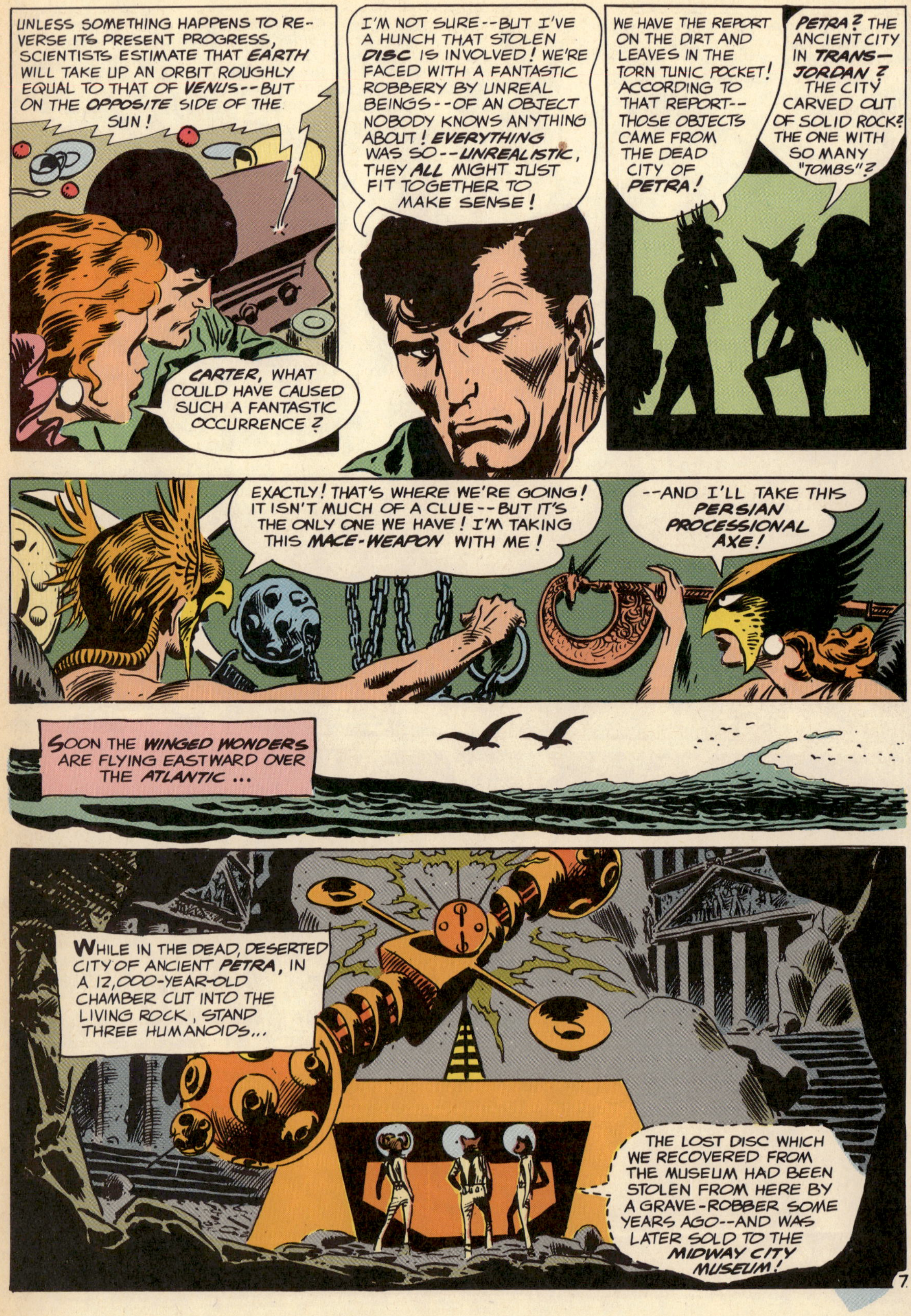

UNLESS SOMETHING HAPPENS TO REVERSE ITS PRESENT PROGRESS, SCIENTISTS ESTIMATE THAT EARTH WILL TAKE UP AN ORBIT ROUGHLY EQUAL TO THAT OF VENUS--BUT ON THE OPPOSITE SIDE OF THE SUN!
CARTER, WHAT COULD HAVE CAUSED SUCH A FANTASTIC OCCURRENCE?
I'M NOT SURE--BUT I'VE A HUNCH THAT STOLEN DISC IS INVOLVED! WE'RE FACED WITH A FANTASTIC ROBBERY BY UNREAL BEINGS--OF AN OBJECT NOBODY KNOWS ANYTHING ABOUT! EVERYTHING WAS SO--UNREALISTIC, THEY ALL MIGHT JUST FIT TOGETHER TO MAKE SENSE!
WE HAVE THE REPORT ON THE DIRT AND LEAVES IN THE TORN TUNIC POCKET! ACCORDING TO THAT REPORT--THOSE OBJECTS CAME FROM THE DEAD CITY OF PETRA!
PETRA? THE ANCIENT CITY IN TRANS-JORDAN? THE CITY CARVED OUT OF SOLID ROCK? THE ONE WITH SO MANY "TOMBS"?
EXACTLY! THAT'S WHERE WE'RE GOING! IT ISN'T MUCH OF A CLUE--BUT IT'S THE ONLY ONE WE HAVE! I'M TAKING THIS MACE-WEAPON WITH ME!
--AND I'LL TAKE THIS PERSIAN PROCESSIONAL AXE!
SOON THE WINGED WONDERS ARE FLYING EASTWARD OVER THE ATLANTIC...
WHILE IN THE DEAD, DESERTED CITY OF ANCIENT PETRA, IN A 12,000-YEAR-OLD CHAMBER CUT INTO THE LIVING ROCK, STAND THREE HUMANOIDS...
THE LOST DISC WHICH WE RECOVERED FROM THE MUSEUM HAD BEEN STOLEN FROM HERE BY A GRAVE-ROBBER SOME YEARS AGO--AND WAS LATER SOLD TO THE MIDWAY CITY MUSEUM!
7

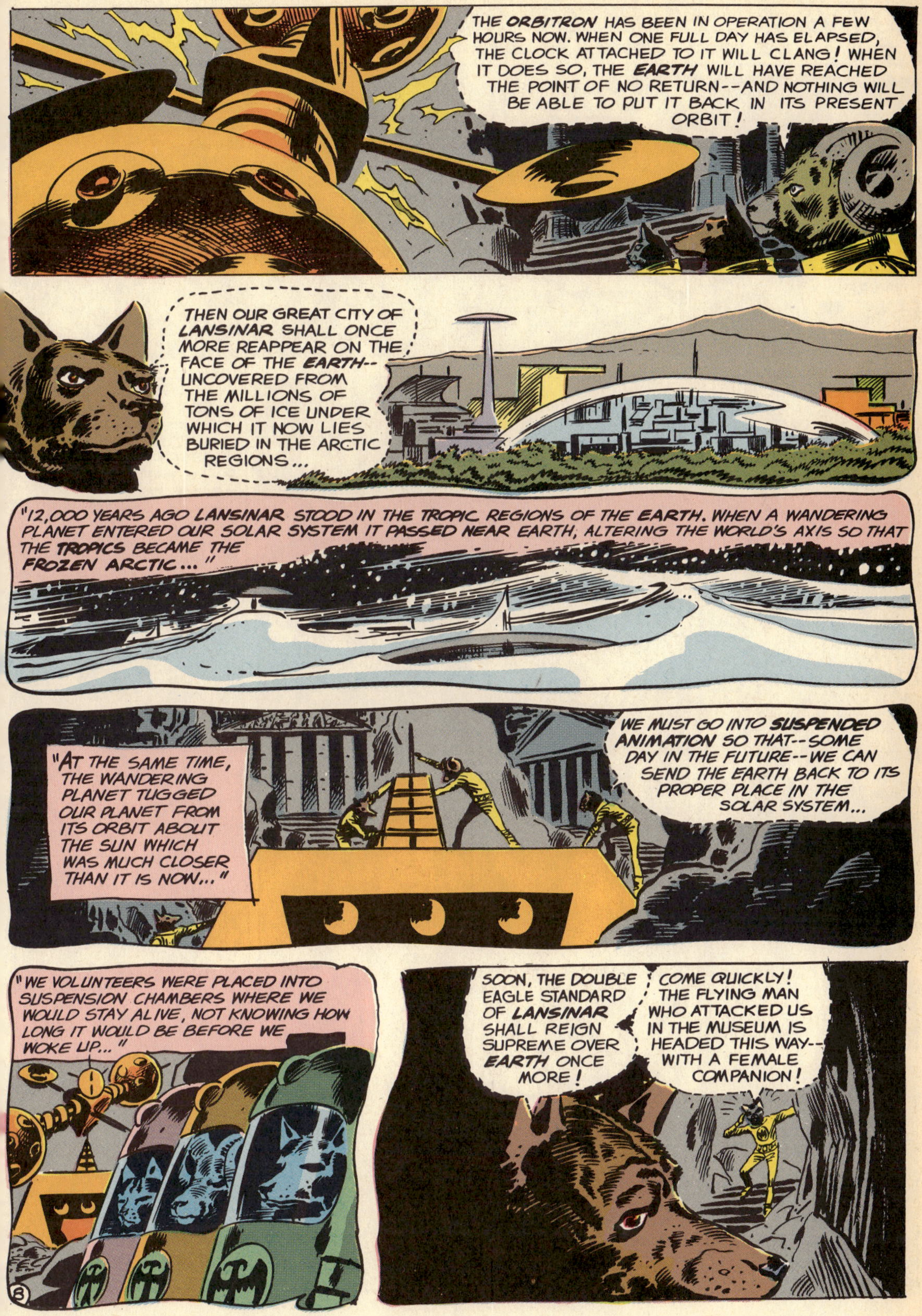
THE ORBITRON HAS BEEN IN OPERATION A FEW HOURS NOW. WHEN ONE FULL DAY HAS ELAPSED, THE CLOCK ATTACHED TO IT WILL CLANG! WHEN IT DOES SO, THE EARTH WILL HAVE REACHED THE POINT OF NO RETURN--AND NOTHING WILL BE ABLE TO PUT IT BACK IN ITS PRESENT ORBIT!
THEN OUR GREAT CITY OF LANSINAR SHALL ONCE MORE REAPPEAR ON THE FACE OF THE EARTH--UNCOVERED FROM THE MILLIONS OF TONS OF ICE UNDER WHICH IT NOW LIES BURIED IN THE ARCTIC REGIONS...
"12,000 YEARS AGO LANSINAR STOOD IN THE TROPIC REGIONS OF THE EARTH. WHEN A WANDERING PLANET ENTERED OUR SOLAR SYSTEM IT PASSED NEAR EARTH, ALTERING THE WORLD'S AXIS SO THAT THE TROPICS BECAME THE FROZEN ARCTIC..."
"AT THE SAME TIME, THE WANDERING PLANET TUGGED OUR PLANET FROM ITS ORBIT ABOUT THE SUN WHICH WAS MUCH CLOSER THAN IT IS NOW..."
WE MUST GO INTO SUSPENDED ANIMATION SO THAT--SOME DAY IN THE FUTURE--WE CAN SEND THE EARTH BACK TO ITS PROPER PLACE IN THE SOLAR SYSTEM...
"WE VOLUNTEERS WERE PLACED INTO SUSPENSION CHAMBERS WHERE WE WOULD STAY ALIVE, NOT KNOWING HOW LONG IT WOULD BE BEFORE WE WOKE UP..."
8
SOON, THE DOUBLE EAGLE STANDARD OF LANSINAR SHALL REIGN SUPREME OVER EARTH ONCE MORE!
COME QUICKLY! THE FLYING MAN WHO ATTACKED US IN THE MUSEUM IS HEADED THIS WAY--WITH A FEMALE COMPANION!

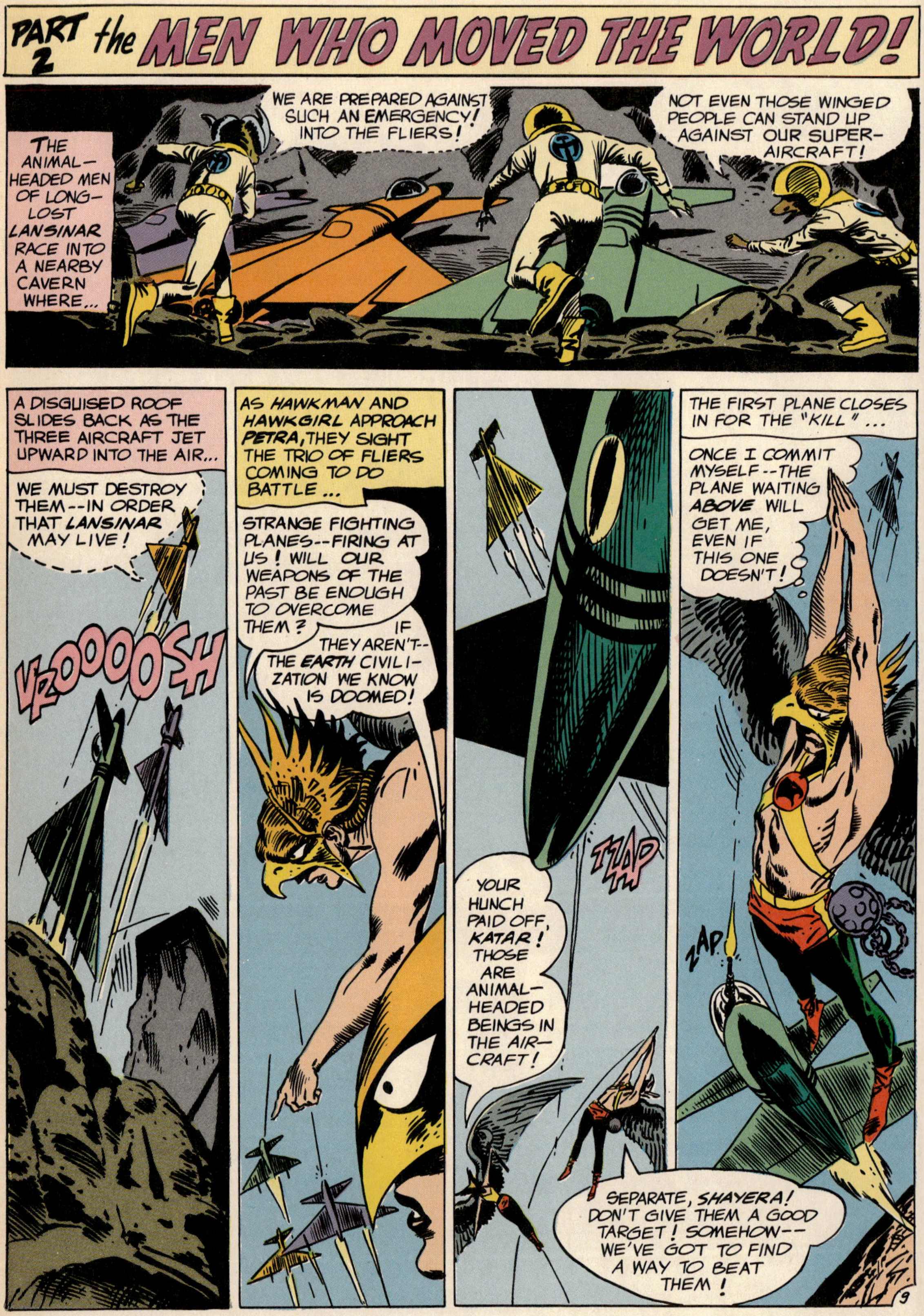
PART 2 the MEN WHO MOVED THE WORLD!
THE ANIMAL-HEADED MEN OF LONG-LOST LANSINAR RACE INTO A NEARBY CAVERN WHERE...
WE ARE PREPARED AGAINST SUCH AN EMERGENCY! INTO THE FLIERS!
NOT EVEN THOSE WINGED PEOPLE CAN STAND UP AGAINST OUR SUPER-AIRCRAFT!
A DISGUISED ROOF SLIDES BACK AS THE THREE AIRCRAFT JET UPWARD INTO THE AIR...
WE MUST DESTROY THEM--IN ORDER THAT LANSINAR MAY LIVE!
VROOOOOSH
AS HAWKMAN AND HAWKGIRL APPROACH PETRA, THEY SIGHT THE TRIO OF FLIERS COMING TO DO BATTLE...
STRANGE FIGHTING PLANES--FIRING AT US! WILL OUR WEAPONS OF THE PAST BE ENOUGH TO OVERCOME THEM?
IF THEY AREN'T--THE EARTH CIVILIZATION WE KNOW IS DOOMED!
ZZAP
YOUR HUNCH PAID OFF, KATAR! THOSE ARE ANIMAL-HEADED BEINGS IN THE AIRCRAFT!
SEPARATE, SHAYERA! DON'T GIVE THEM A GOOD TARGET! SOMEHOW--WE'VE GOT TO FIND A WAY TO BEAT THEM!
THE FIRST PLANE CLOSES IN FOR THE "KILL"...
ONCE I COMMIT MYSELF--THE PLANE WAITING ABOVE WILL GET ME, EVEN IF THIS ONE DOESN'T!
ZAP
9

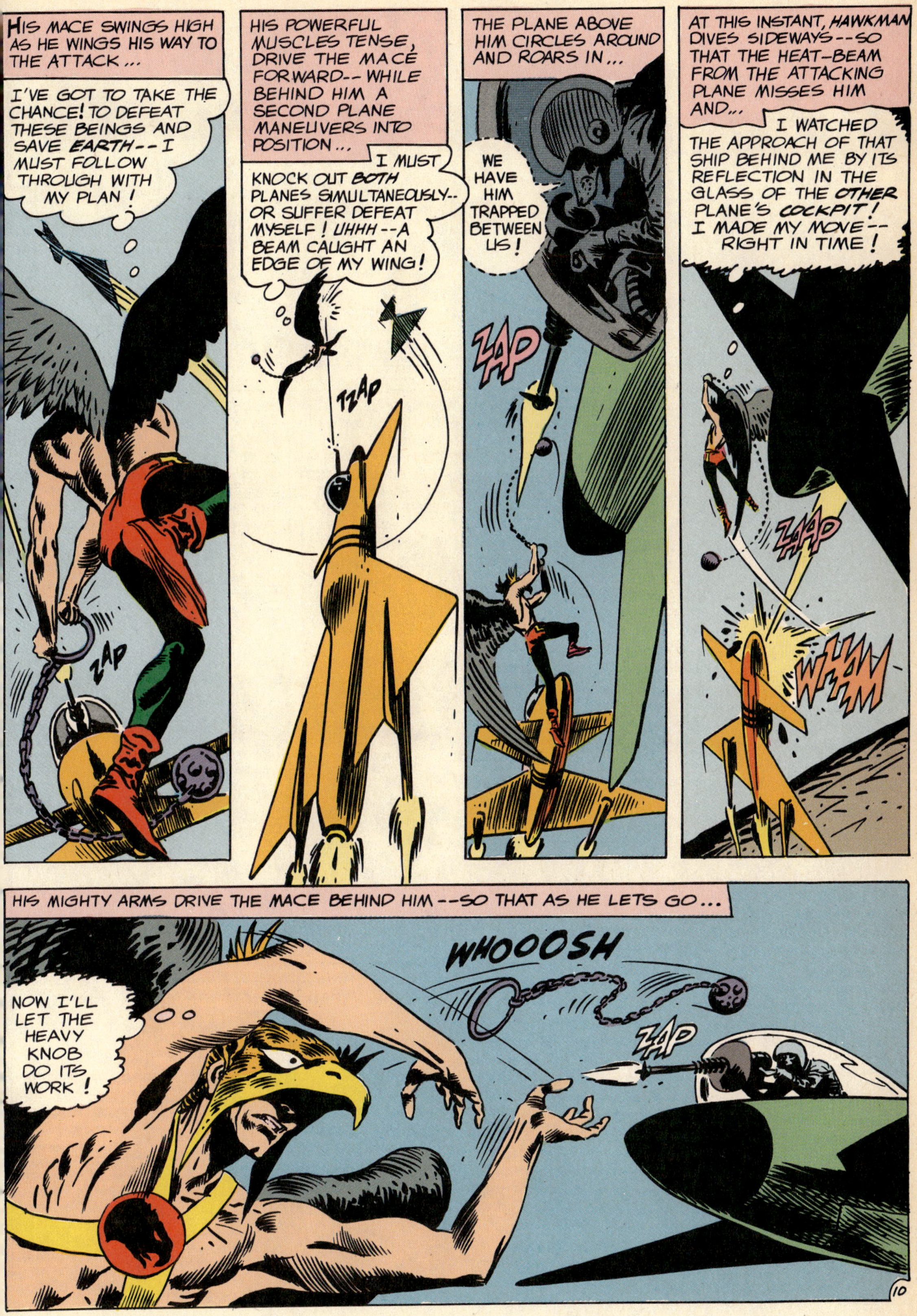
HIS MACE SWINGS HIGH AS HE WINGS HIS WAY TO THE ATTACK...
I'VE GOT TO TAKE THE CHANCE! TO DEFEAT THESE BEINGS AND SAVE EARTH--I MUST FOLLOW THROUGH WITH MY PLAN!
ZAP
HIS POWERFUL MUSCLES TENSE, DRIVE THE MACE FORWARD--WHILE BEHIND HIM A SECOND PLANE MANEUVERS INTO POSITION...
I MUST KNOCK OUT BOTH PLANES SIMULTANEOUSLY--OR SUFFER DEFEAT MYSELF! UHHH--A BEAM CAUGHT AN EDGE OF MY WING!
ZZAP
THE PLANE ABOVE HIM CIRCLES AROUND AND ROARS IN...
WE HAVE HIM TRAPPED BETWEEN US!
ZAP
AT THIS INSTANT, HAWKMAN DIVES SIDEWAYS--SO THAT THE HEAT-BEAM FROM THE ATTACKING PLANE MISSES HIM AND...
I WATCHED THE APPROACH OF THAT SHIP BEHIND ME BY ITS REFLECTION IN THE GLASS OF THE OTHER PLANE'S COCKPIT! I MADE MY MOVE--RIGHT IN TIME!
ZAAP
WHAM
HIS MIGHTY ARMS DRIVE THE MACE BEHIND HIM--SO THAT AS HE LETS GO...
NOW I'LL LET THE HEAVY KNOB DO ITS WORK!
WHOOOSH
ZAP
10

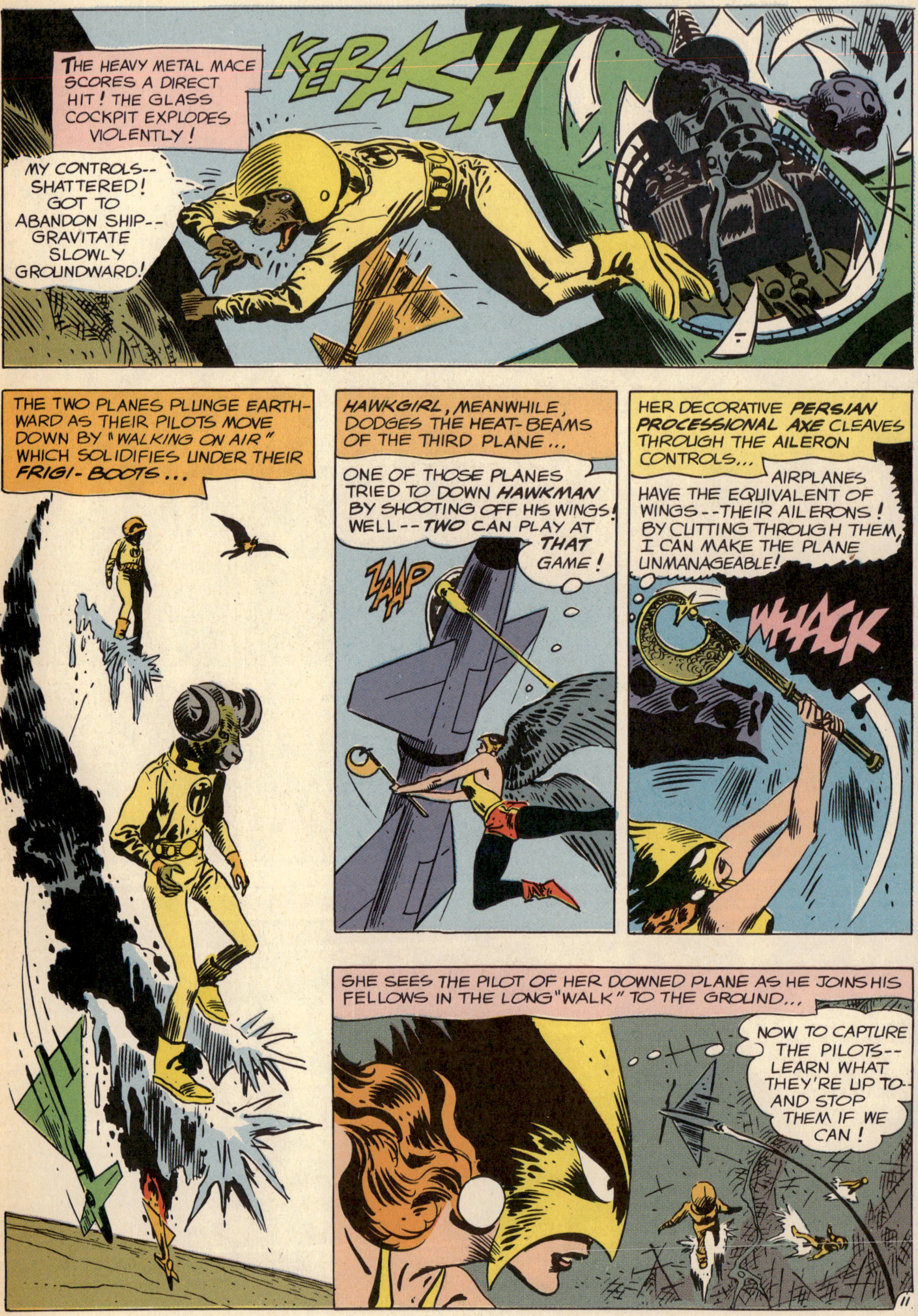
THE HEAVY METAL MACE SCORES A DIRECT HIT! THE GLASS COCKPIT EXPLODES VIOLENTLY!
KERASH
MY CONTROLS-- SHATTERED! GOT TO ABANDON SHIP-- GRAVITATE SLOWLY GROUNDWARD!
THE TWO PLANES PLUNGE EARTHWARD AS THEIR PILOTS MOVE DOWN BY "WALKING ON AIR" WHICH SOLIDIFIES UNDER THEIR FRIGI-BOOTS...
HAWKGIRL, MEANWHILE, DODGES THE HEAT-BEAMS OF THE THIRD PLANE...
ONE OF THOSE PLANES TRIED TO DOWN HAWKMAN BY SHOOTING OFF HIS WINGS! WELL--TWO CAN PLAY AT THAT GAME!
ZAAP
HER DECORATIVE PERSIAN PROCESSIONAL AXE CLEAVES THROUGH THE AILERON CONTROLS...
AIRPLANES HAVE THE EQUIVALENT OF WINGS--THEIR AILERONS! BY CUTTING THROUGH THEM, I CAN MAKE THE PLANE UNMANAGEABLE!
WHACK
SHE SEES THE PILOT OF HER DOWNED PLANE AS HE JOINS HIS FELLOWS IN THE LONG "WALK" TO THE GROUND...
NOW TO CAPTURE THE PILOTS-- LEARN WHAT THEY'RE UP TO-- AND STOP THEM IF WE CAN!
11

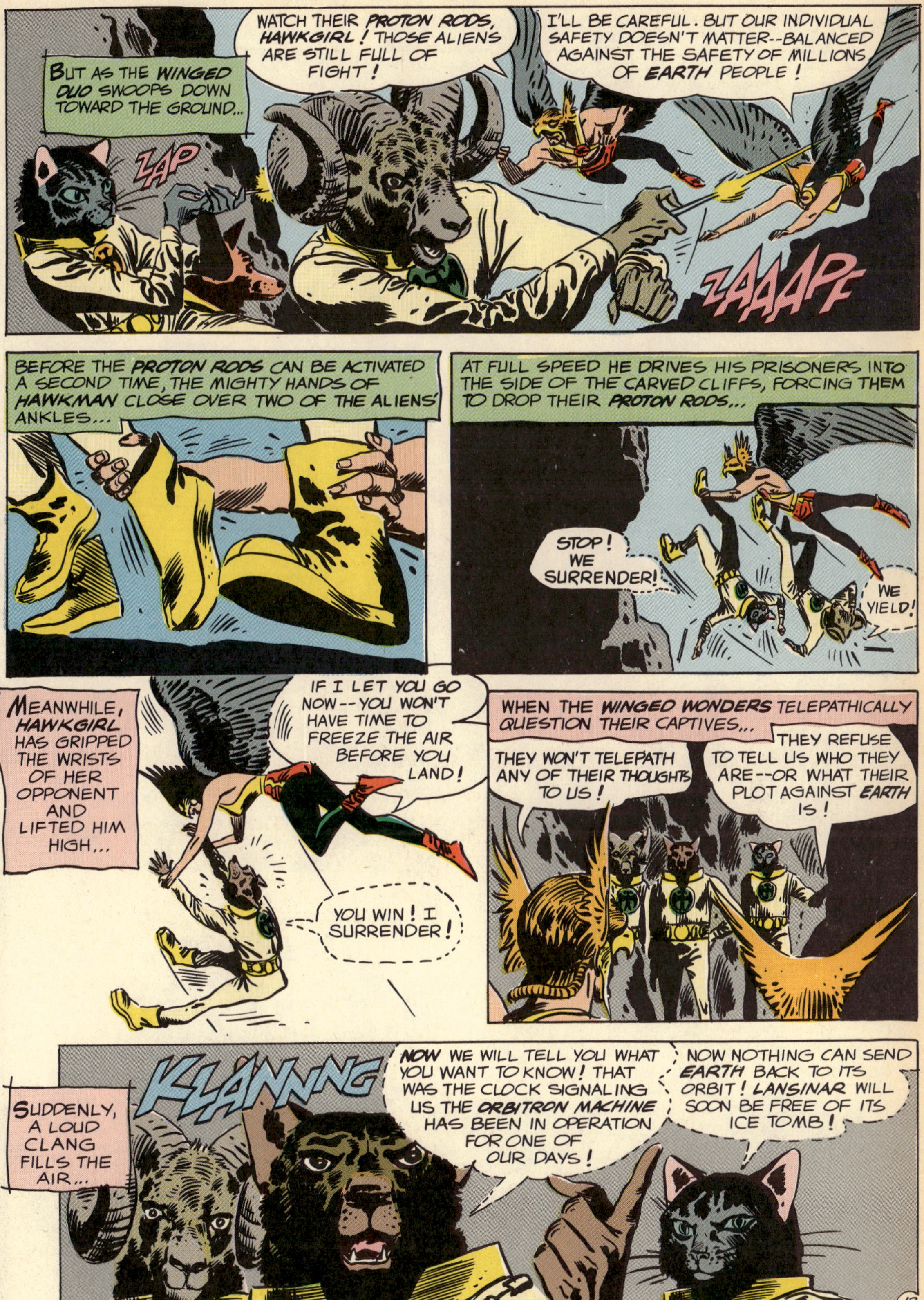

BUT AS THE WINGED DUO SWOOPS DOWN TOWARD THE GROUND...
WATCH THEIR PROTON RODS, HAWKGIRL! THOSE ALIENS ARE STILL FULL OF FIGHT!
I'LL BE CAREFUL. BUT OUR INDIVIDUAL SAFETY DOESN'T MATTER--BALANCED AGAINST THE SAFETY OF MILLIONS OF EARTH PEOPLE!
ZAP
ZAAAPF
BEFORE THE PROTON RODS CAN BE ACTIVATED A SECOND TIME, THE MIGHTY HANDS OF HAWKMAN CLOSE OVER TWO OF THE ALIENS' ANKLES...
AT FULL SPEED HE DRIVES HIS PRISONERS INTO THE SIDE OF THE CARVED CLIFFS, FORCING THEM TO DROP THEIR PROTON RODS...
STOP! WE SURRENDER!
WE YIELD!
MEANWHILE, HAWKGIRL HAS GRIPPED THE WRISTS OF HER OPPONENT AND LIFTED HIM HIGH...
IF I LET YOU GO NOW--YOU WON'T HAVE TIME TO FREEZE THE AIR BEFORE YOU LAND!
YOU WIN! I SURRENDER!
WHEN THE WINGED WONDERS TELEPATHICALLY QUESTION THEIR CAPTIVES...
THEY WON'T TELEPATH ANY OF THEIR THOUGHTS TO US!
THEY REFUSE TO TELL US WHO THEY ARE--OR WHAT THEIR PLOT AGAINST EARTH IS!
SUDDENLY, A LOUD CLANG FILLS THE AIR...
KLANNNG
NOW WE WILL TELL YOU WHAT YOU WANT TO KNOW! THAT WAS THE CLOCK SIGNALING US THE ORBITRON MACHINE HAS BEEN IN OPERATION FOR ONE OF OUR DAYS!
NOW NOTHING CAN SEND EARTH BACK TO ITS ORBIT! LANSINAR WILL SOON BE FREE OF ITS ICE TOMB!
12

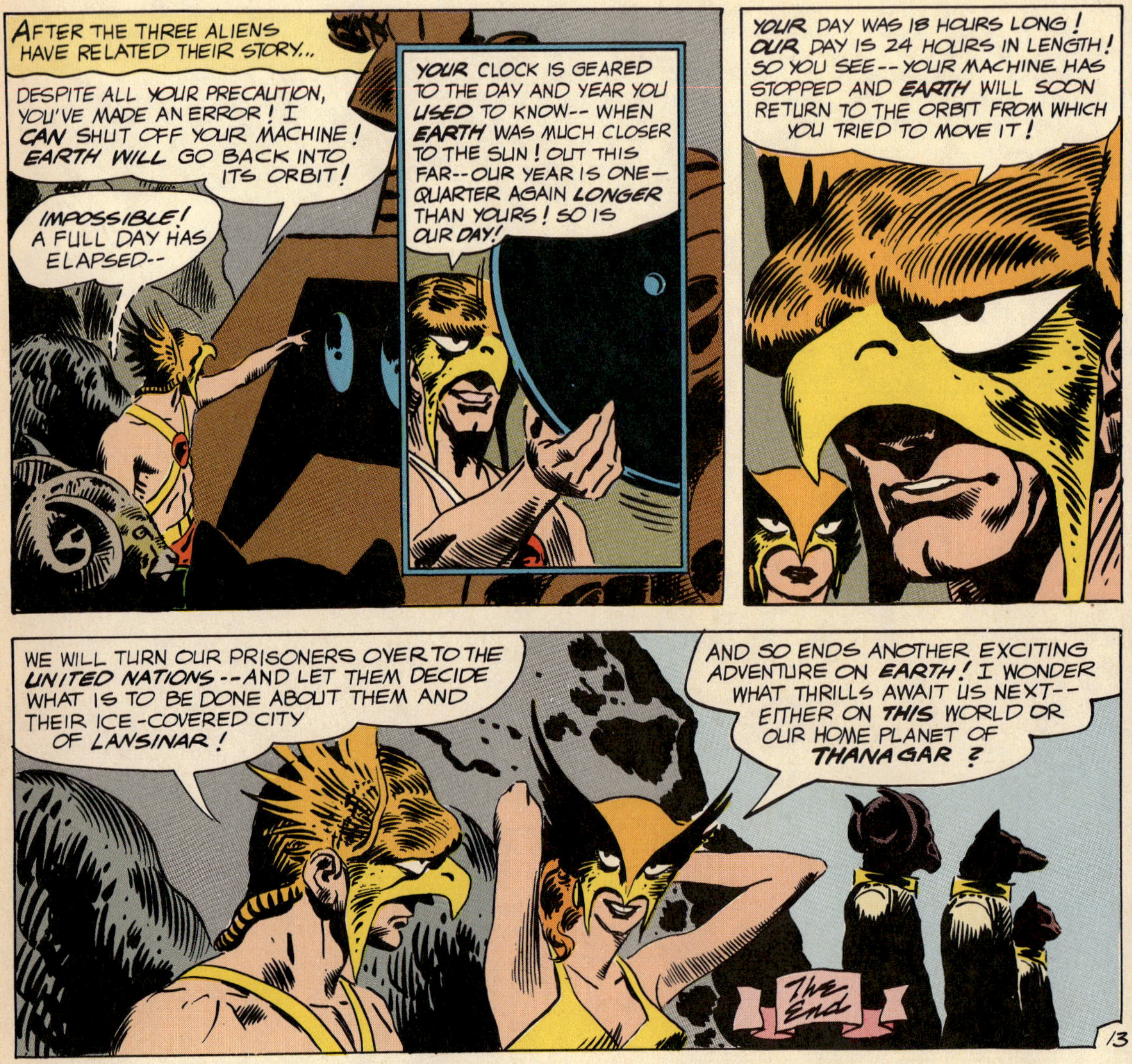
AFTER THE THREE ALIENS HAVE RELATED THEIR STORY...
DESPITE ALL YOUR PRECAUTION, YOU'VE MADE AN ERROR! I CAN SHUT OFF YOUR MACHINE! EARTH WILL GO BACK INTO ITS ORBIT!
IMPOSSIBLE! A FULL DAY HAS ELAPSED--
YOUR CLOCK IS GEARED TO THE DAY AND YEAR YOU USED TO KNOW-- WHEN EARTH WAS MUCH CLOSER TO THE SUN! OUT THIS FAR--OUR YEAR IS ONE-QUARTER AGAIN LONGER THAN YOURS! SO IS OUR DAY!
YOUR DAY WAS 18 HOURS LONG! OUR DAY IS 24 HOURS IN LENGTH! SO YOU SEE-- YOUR MACHINE HAS STOPPED AND EARTH WILL SOON RETURN TO THE ORBIT FROM WHICH YOU TRIED TO MOVE IT!
WE WILL TURN OUR PRISONERS OVER TO THE UNITED NATIONS--AND LET THEM DECIDE WHAT IS TO BE DONE ABOUT THEM AND THEIR ICE-COVERED CITY OF LANSINAR!
AND SO ENDS ANOTHER EXCITING ADVENTURE ON EARTH! I WONDER WHAT THRILLS AWAIT US NEXT-- EITHER ON THIS WORLD OR OUR HOME PLANET OF THANAGAR?
The End
13

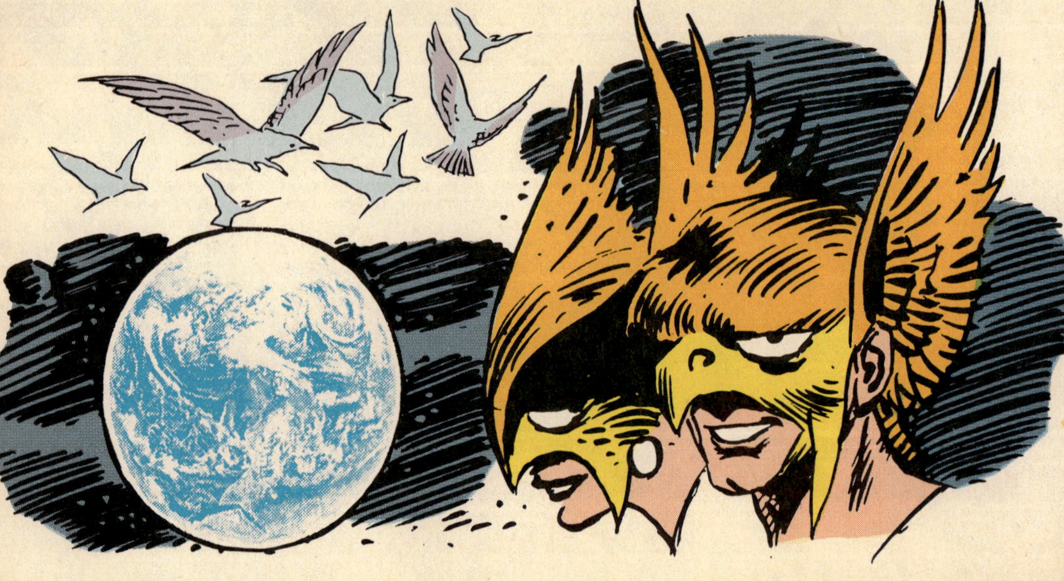

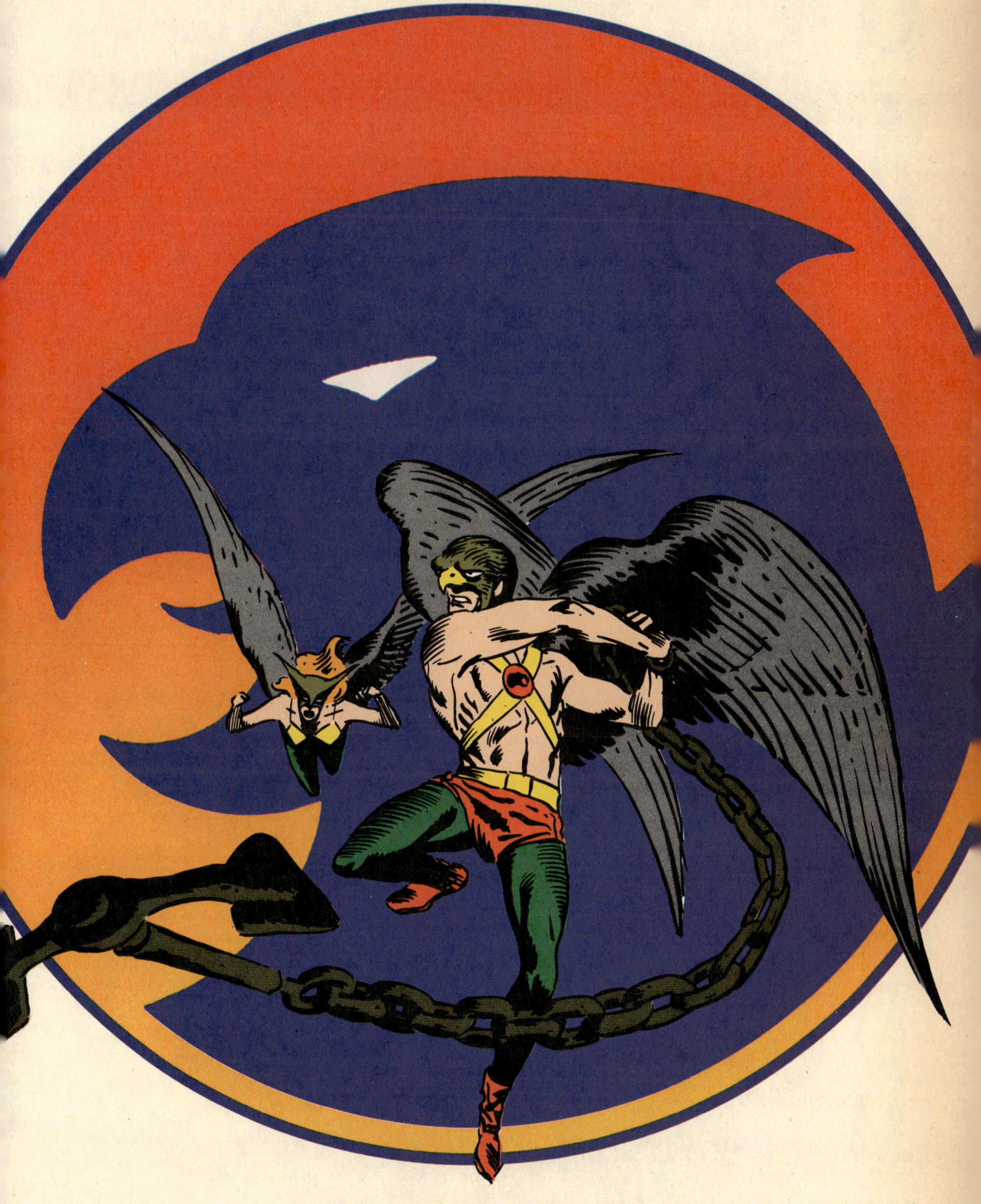

GALLERY

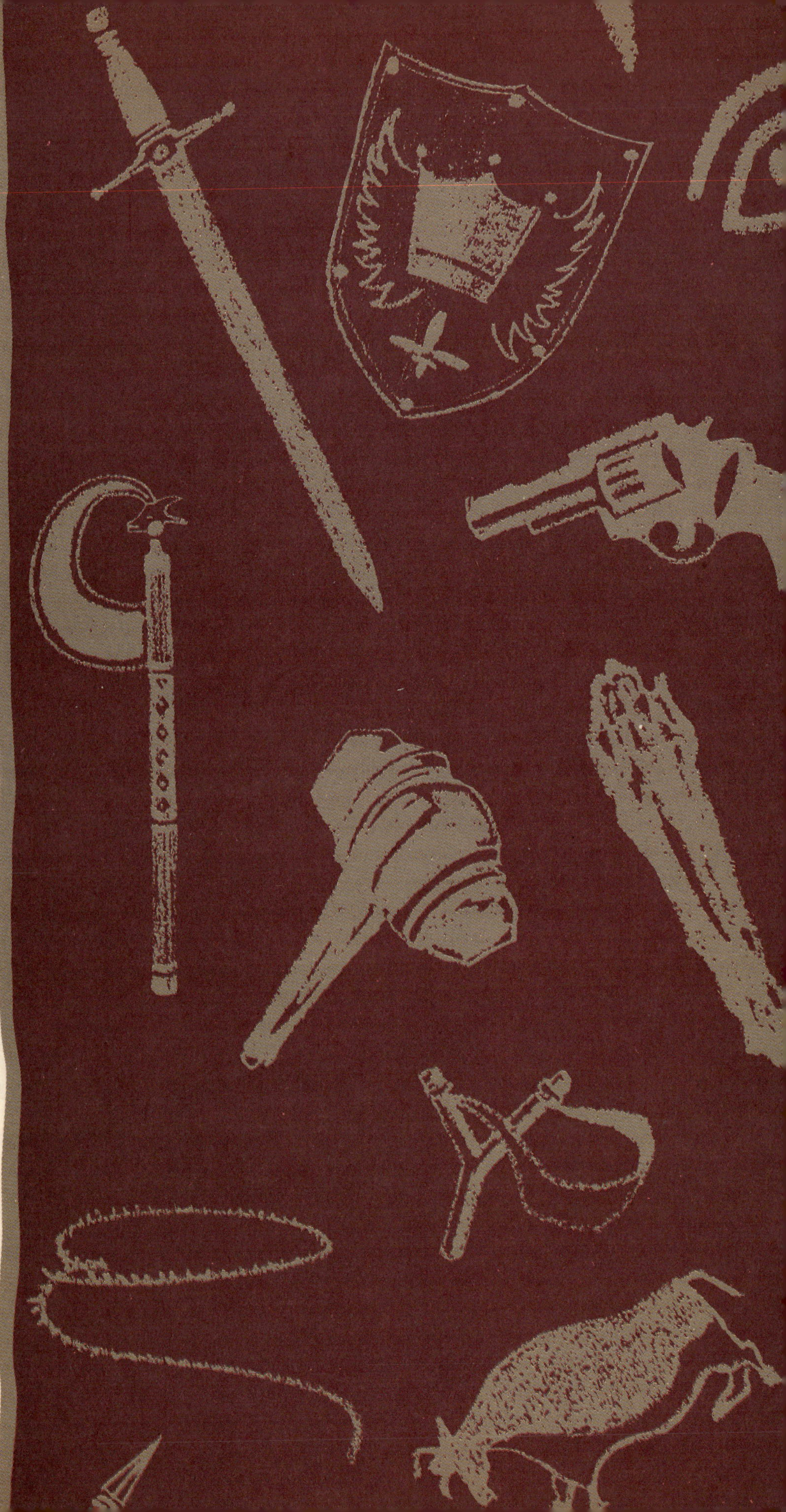

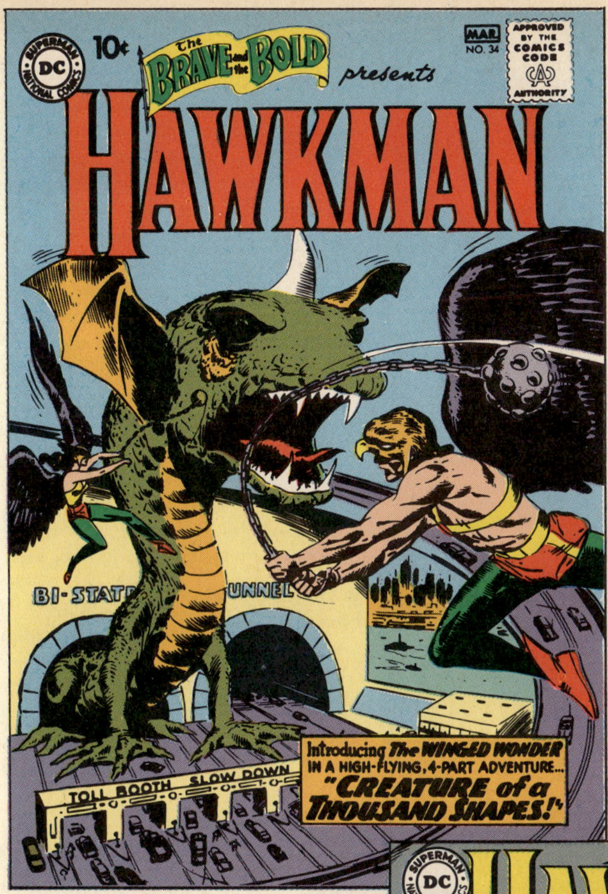
10¢
The BRAVE and the BOLD
presents
HAWKMAN
MAR. NO. 34
APPROVED BY THE COMICS CODE AUTHORITY
BI-STAT
UNNEL
TOLL BOOTH
SLOW DOWN
Introducing The WINGED WONDER IN A HIGH-FLYING, 4-PART ADVENTURE... "CREATURE of a THOUSAND SHAPES!"

There are models, icons, that we aspiring and ever-learning artists hope to someday even come close to, both as artists and as human beings—greats whose artwork makes you wonder how the hell they ever did it.

I was fortunate enough to just walk upstairs and ask.

Andy Kubert
Artist, DOC SAVAGE, ADAM STRANGE

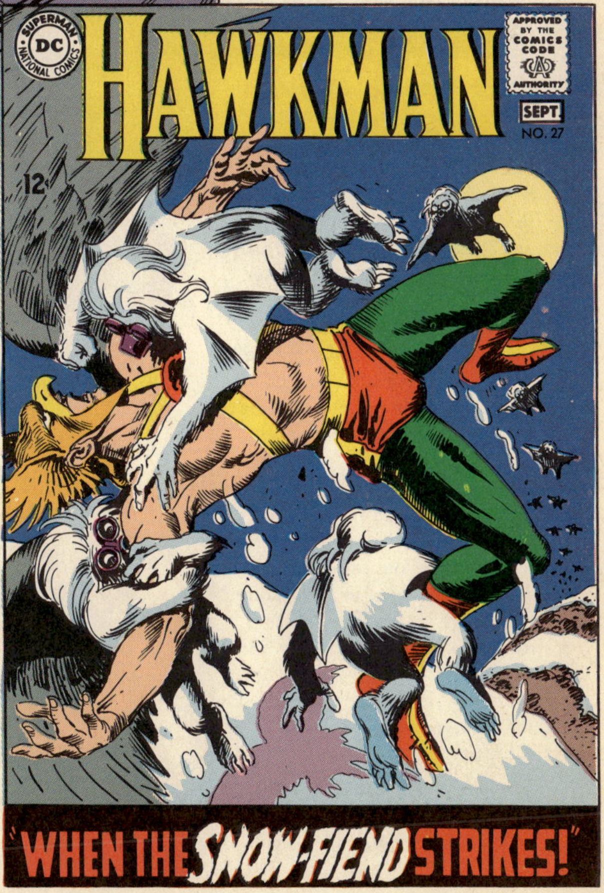
HAWKMAN
APPROVED BY THE COMICS CODE AUTHORITY
SEPT. NO. 27
12¢
WHEN THE SNOW-FIEND STRIKES!

Gardner Fox was a pro. He would be prepared to discuss stories and scripts and, when he left to write them, you could bet he'd be back when they were promised. He was a fun-loving, gentle man who will always be fondly remembered.

And Joe Kubert . . . I consider him to be the most talented artist on the horizon. Joe had a strength in his work that needed direction toward simplicity. At first, he inked all his work in the same way with no regard for texture; with a few pointers, over a period of time, he began to simplify his work and became one of the finest artists in the comics industry.

Sol Harrison,
Former President, DC Comics

the TITAN and the FURY
APPROVED BY THE COMICS CODE AUTHORITY
JULY NO. 43
THE ATOM AND HAWKMAN
12¢

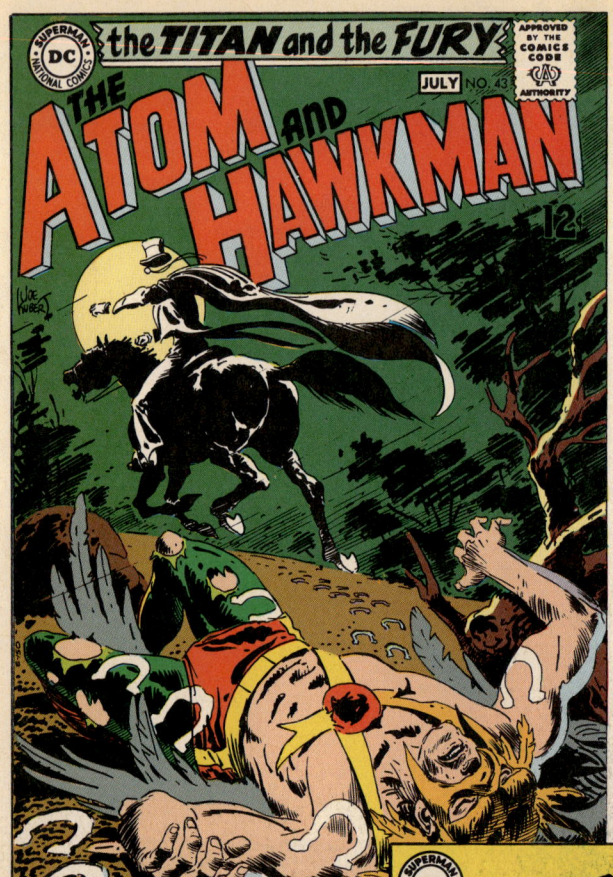

Michelangelo and Joe Kubert. No, I'm not comparing the genius of the Pietà and David with the creator of Sgt. Rock — but I'm always in awe of Kubert's talent in sculpting vivid images from the quarries of his India-inked pages with those exciting layouts, robust brush-strokes, and brilliant storytelling moments.

At age 12, Kubert skipped puberty and at once forged his individual niche among cartoonists twice his age. Later, with that same energy, he created the Joe Kubert School of Cartoon and Graphic Art, Inc., of which I am proud to be a part.

But Joe has not abandoned his craft. He's still at the board, in the quarry, carving those vivid images.

Irwin Hasen
Former DC Artist,
Creator of DONDI

Gardner F. Fox was the proverbial "scholar and a gentleman" we always hear about and all too rarely meet. He read widely, and he brought much of what he read to his work, even if he (like his contemporaries) never let a bit of scientific or historical information stand in the way of a rollicking good story. And though my contacts with him over the years were sporadic, he remained to the end what he had been when we first started corresponding in 1960: one of comicdom's true nice guys. His characters and story concepts influenced an entire generation of pros and fans — no, make that *two* generations — and they continue to influence even folks who are a wee bit uncertain about exactly what it is he's supposed to have done 'way back there in the Dark Ages (*i.e.*, pre-1980). And of course, when Gardner teamed up with a truly fine artist, as with Joe Kubert (twice!) on Hawkman, the result was a true peak in a field often notable mainly for its valleys.

Roy Thomas
Writer/Editor, Various Marvel
and DC Comics

15¢
NOV NO. 45
APPROVED BY THE COMICS CODE AUTHORITY
THE ATOM AND HAWKMAN
WORK OR DIE-- SLAVES!

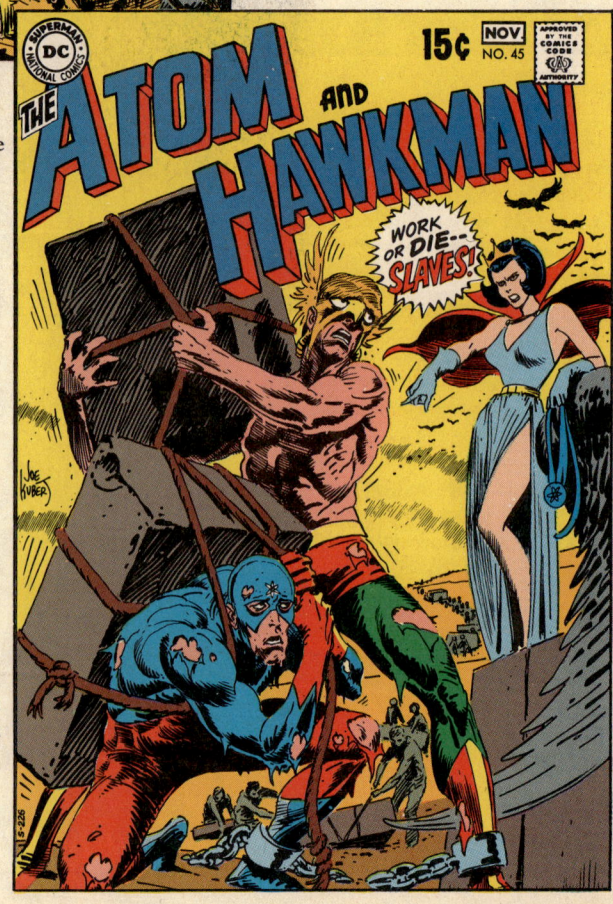